Cousin Jack's Mouth-organ

TRAVELS IN CORNISH AMERICA

A personalised US car registration plate from the
Upper Peninsula of Michigan

Cover picture: Miners descending the Empire Mine,
Grass Valley, California. c. 1905

Cousin Jack's Mouth-organ

TRAVELS IN CORNISH AMERICA

Alan M. Kent

CORNISH HILLSIDE PUBLICATIONS

Cousin Jack's Mouth-organ
Travels in Cornish America

Alan M. Kent

First published in 2004 by
Cornish Hillside Publications,
St Austell, Cornwall PL25 4DW

Typeset in Sabon by
Kestrel Data, Exeter, Devon EX1 2LD

Printed and bound by
SRP Ltd, Exeter, Devon EX2 7LW

Alan M. Kent was born in St Austell, Cornwall in 1967 and lectures in Literature for the Open University in South-West Britain. He is a prize-winning poet, novelist and author. In 1998 he received a Doctorate for his work on Cornish and Anglo-Cornish literature. He has written extensively on the literary and cultural history of Cornwall.

To Cousin Leroy Roberts – Cornishman,
American, Mormon.

CONTENTS

ACKNOWLEDGEMENTS

In playing this mouth-organ across America, there are many people I would like to thank. Foremost, I would like to thank those Cornish-Americans and others who hosted me during my travels. Secondly, I am grateful to all those pards and people whom I met along the way, and allowed me to spend some time yipping up t'em. My thanks also to Danny Merrifield and Mark Champion who with their friendship and good humour made the many miles much shorter, and to Dorothy Beckwith, Lauraine Sadleir and Les Goldman who assisted me in the preparation of the text. Here too, I would like to thank those three fine historians of Cornwall who wrote the route map: A.L. Rowse, Arthur Cecil Todd and John Rowe. Finally my thanks to Charles Thurlow of Cornish Hillside Publications.

INTRODUCTION

Beyond 56 Inch Cylinder Syndrome . . .

Like most Cornish, past and present, who have ever walked
the earth, or still stank its limits, I have developed a serious
case of '56 Inch Cylinder Syndrome'. Let me make it quite
clear: it is likely I will never quite be completely cured, but I
am trying. Years of therapy, travel and time beyond the
River Tamar have almost got me beyond this debilitating
condition. *The New Oxford University Dictionary of
Medical and Mineralogical Science* defines '56 Inch Cylinder
Syndrome' as "that singular Cornish capacity to stay
fascinated with the industrial and technological
achievements of their ancestors to the diminishment and
blindness to anything else that has defined and made them
who they are." It further adds that "it promotes an almost
bizarre statistical fascination with mining terminology and
the development of the steam engine." It is a kind of
neurotic disorder that makes us stand and stare at the
wonderful achievement of some 56 inch cylinder in a
pumping mechanism down East Pool, Levant or Wheal
Owles, but makes us neglect who we are and where we are
going in the future. Let's face it: we are obsessed with
individuals like Humphry Davy, Richard Trevithick,
William Murdoch, John Couch Adams, Henry Trengrouse
and Goldsworthy Gurney.

Indeed, there are some who still argue that '56 Inch
Cylinder Syndrome' is a necessary and essential psychological condition to define one as Cornish. As you will

realise then, '56 Inch Cylinder Syndrome' is still highly controversial and is under intense scrutiny by some interested groups. The Trevithick Society for one, fully admit that all its members suffer from the syndrome; as do some members of the Cornish Gorseth, who while differing from the majority of that select organisation – and mainly suffer from all the classic symptoms of Cornish language Fight syndrome, – do also sadly suffer from congenital forms of '56 Inch Cylinder Syndrome' in its most acute phases.

In order to try to find a long-lasting cure for this condition, not only for me, but for my nation, I decided for the past couple of summers to travel across the Atlantic Ocean, just like my forefathers and mothers, to America, in search of the Cornish. I have called the account of my travels *Cousin Jack's Mouth-organ: Travels in Cornish America.* Cousin Jack was the generic name given to Cornish miners wherever they went to work across the Earth, and as you may know, wherever there is a hole in the earth, you are sure to find a Cornishman at the bottom of it.

Incidentally, his mouth-organ isn't yet a mouth-organ proper which might play the blues but was the name people in America first used to describe the pasty, that national dish, so symbolic of the Cornish worldwide. Apparently, back then, in the time when '56 Inch Cylinder Syndrome' was not even recognised, let alone researched and understood, the pasty wasn't eaten 'mobile phone' style as now, but held horizontally by the crimped crust, and passed back and forth across the mouth, like a harmonica. The crimping picked up any metallic poison still on the miner's fingers and hands, and this was then tossed as a present to the Knockers, or in America, the Tommyknockers – the little people of the mines – who in thankfulness for their food, would let no harm come to the hard-rock miners of Cornwall while they were underground.

This book is a song though. It really is about how far pards got to roam, but it is neither a history nor a lament. Instead I hope it is a narrative song – perhaps a prose ballad – about the Cornish and their interaction with contemporary America. It is a blues, in that it shows much passing and change, and yet paradoxically, there is much too, to celebrate and rejoice. Instead of losing

2

Cornish America, which perhaps at one point we may well have done, interestingly, we have re-discovered it. In so doing, we come to understand it better. Cousin Jack culture was not just Cornish culture transposed across an ocean. It was a separate mobile entity, linked to Cornwall, but also intimately engaged with the landscape, people and society wherever it landed. My aim as a writer has never been to romance the Cornish, but to tell it like it is, so sometimes there is criticism and sometimes there are difficult questions to be answered. In all seriousness, I don't even know if there is anything as large as a 56 inch cylinder in any kind of Cornish pumping equipment. It just seemed the perfect metaphor to describe some of the issues the Cornish face in the Twenty-First Century.

Of course, my travels in Cornish America have been preceded by three notable Cornish scholars: A. L. Rowse, Arthur Cecil Todd and John Rowe. Their aim was a more academic project than mine in this instance, but it is one that owes them all much debt for they were pioneers. A. L. Rowse has now passed on, but as a 'Higher Quarter' boy too, I hope he would have some empathy with what I have written. I wrote to Rowse frequently when at University, with questions about his poetry and fiction, and now, only wished I had learnt more about his time in the U.S.A. Cecil "Toddy" Todd sadly also passed on before the completion of this book, but when he last wrote to me – just before my first trip, he 'couldn't think of a more wonderful theme – the contemporary Cornish in America'. His final comment to me before his death was 'What an epic story you will have to tell'. John Rowe, with his usual convivial humour wished me well and told me in the 'Cornish Arms', St Blazey, not to eat too many Cornish game hens. John knew that is certain to be the one question that every American asks: "You're from Cornwall. Is that anything to do with Cornish game hens?" Cornish game hens are a popular meal in America. In 1965, chicken mogul Donald John Tyson created the Cornish game hen by cross-breeding White Rock hens with Cornish hens. His intent was to create a miniature chicken, and you see them in every American supermarket. So I suppose there is a connection – somewhere out there – beyond 56 Inch Cylinder Syndrome . . .

3

One final thought: I've heard it said many a time that when cowboys 'mozeyed on down' a tumbleweed-strewn street towards an old saloon of some Wild-West town, that they walked to the rhythm of a Cornish word. *Moaz* means 'to go' or 'to proceed' in Cornish – which seems to fit. There may be no truth in it at all, but I hope there is. That way we can see how far the Cornish travelled in America – from Tangier Island in the East, to San Francsico in the West – and the Keweenaw Peninsula in the North, to Arizona in the South, taking with them not only hard-rock mining, engineering, fishing and farming, but also language, folklore and culture too.

I must have 'mozeyed on down' ten thousand miles or more to write this book, in part to record for posterity what I witnessed; in a part as a response to Robert Louis Stevenson's 1879 travelogue *Across the Plains*. Were he alive, Stevenson would detest me – and probably 'moaz on by', still sceptical of my mysterious old world race. But I'm more like Lady Hester Stanhope. This literary mouth-organ has no need to make something great of the Cornish, and so I say in the tongue of my ancestors, 'Eahas ha Sowena!' [Health and Prosperity!] to 56 Inch Cylinder Syndrome and beyond. The Cornish are great already. Don't keep it grimly to yourself.

Alan M. Kent
Lanbrebois/Probus
Kernow/Cornwall

May 2004

4

PART ONE

"At Ogden we changed cars from the Union Pacific to the Central Pacific line of railroad . . . There were no emigrants direct from Europe – save one German family and a knot of Cornish miners who kept grimly to themselves, one reading the New Testament all day long through steel spectacles, the rest discussing privately the secrets of their old-world mysterious race. Lady Hester Stanhope believed she could make something great of the Cornish; for my part, I can make nothing of them at all. A division of races, older and more original than that of Babel, keeps this close, esoteric family apart from neighbouring Englishmen. Not even a Red Indian seems more foreign in my eyes. This is one of the lessons of travel – that some of the strangest races dwell next door to you at home."

Robert Louis Stevenson, *Across the Plains*, 1879

"Those damned Cornishmen know too much."

James Fair, Superintendant of the Consolidated Virginia Mine, Nevada, 1873, cited in Arthur Cecil Todd, *The Cornish in America*, 1967

1

Oh! the eastern winds are blowing . . .

'What the 'ell do 'ee want t'live down there for?' one of my old Foxhole mates once asked me when I told him I was moving the staggering distance of five miles south to Probus. The way he asked me seemed to suggest an intolerable act of betrayal, the crossing of a border which lay somewhere between St Stephen-in-Brannel and Grampound Road, but which inevitably divided my china-clay upbringing with my somehow newly-gained sophistication. A *pee-haitch-dee* to boot too. It was a migration too far. There, I would surely lose my 'accent', drop every ounce of Cornu-English I had and never return to the homeland. I'd be forever in exile.

Fast forward six years later . . .

'What the 'ell do 'ee want to go there for?' the same mate from Foxhole asked me early in the summer when I told him I was about to try and cross Cornish America. The way he asked me seemed to suggest and intolerable act of betrayal, the crossing of a border which lay somewhere between the River Tamar and Heathrow Airport, but which inevitably delineated my Cornishness against my somehow newly-gained North Atlanticism. It was a migration too far. There, I would surely lose my 'accent', drop every ounce of Cornu-English I had and never return to the homeland. I'd be forever in exile. Vamoosed. Gone.

I suppose I moved to Probus because firstly, I'd found a house that I liked and secondly – and perhaps more importantly these days in post-Rick Stein, post-Eden Cornwall – could afford to buy. The second question was much easier to answer. Because I wanted to write a travel book about contemporary Cornish identity in America. It was as simple as that, and unlike most other Cornish writing before me, I wanted to try to make it humorous too – poke a little fun at our dour Celticity. Besides, as I explained to me' mate, the Cornish had been crossing to America for a very long time now. I was just the latest in a very long line.

I was also just the latest in a very long line at the British Airways check-in desk at Heathrow Airport's Terminal 4 on the 1st of August, 2002. Retrospectively, choosing to fly on the 1st of August was a very unwise move. It seemed like the rest of the inhabitants of these islands wanted to escape the inevitable non-event that is the United Kingdom's summer for hotter and well, more exciting climes. I thought I had arrived at the Terminal in plenty of time. After all, I had left a friend's house in Muswell Hill at the crack of dawn, and had caught the Piccadilly Line all the way underneath London down to Heathrow. I had arrived there at around eight-thirty a.m., only to be greeted by a massive queue. Another problem was that my flight to Chicago didn't actually leave until 12.30 p.m., and as the earlier flights were being dealt with first, every so often the BA staff would call for passengers to be checked in for these. Inevitably, I seemed to get sucked to the back of the queue every time. The problem was, being as ill-organised as ever, I also need to find a *Bureau de Change*, to convert my pounds into dollars, and, like the star of some Hollywood thriller, I was running out of time. Besides that, I actually quite like wandering around airports. They are a sort of dreamy between-world, that lies somewhere between sexy French perfumes and bottles of Scotch whisky available in Duty Free. Likewise they occupy a mental space somewhere between tins of dodgy short-bread and samples of vile-smelling aftershave.

Yesterday had all been so simple. The morning's in-evitable 56 inch cylinder syndrome, the unavoidable queues along the A30 at Indian Queens, the eerily 'un-hit' low railway bridge on the Goss Moor, the little St Piran's flag graffitied on the rocks of Bodmin Moor, Jamaica Inn, Lanson castle and the crossing of the Tamar into the no-man's land of west Devon and Dartmoor, and past the Druidic Grove at Lifton. Then on and on, ever further into England. To Exeter Services and beyond.

"You know what, I got here at eight-thirty and I haven't moved forward an inch yet," said an American woman in front of me.

"Me too!" I said. "We'm goin' nowhere fast!"

She didn't understand my expression but looked at me kindly. Her name was Michele Boyer. She gave me her card. She was a sculptor and lived in Los Angeles. Her luggage looked like she was carrying half a ton of marble. I looked at my own single case, and the thirty-four that she had.

"I came in from Italy last night. I've been working over there . . ."

"What do you work in?" I asked, sounding like some Tate St Ives curator.

"Mainly bronze . . ."

That explained it. Copper and tin. 56 Inch Cylinder Syndrome see. You can't escape it – not even here.

"You flying back to LA?" I asked.

"Yes – I had to come through London . . . There isn't a direct flight. Cost me an arm and leg to stay here over-night . . ."

We shuffled forward slightly.

"Where are you going?" Michelle asked politely.

"Chicago."

"You going on holiday . . . ?"

"Sort of . . . I'm writing a book . . . on the Cornish in America . . ."

"Now Cornwall's where Land's End and St Michael Mount are at. Is that right? I went there . . . years ago . . ."

"Yes – that's right . . ."

"And there are *Cornish* in the US?"

"They went there to mine . . ."

"Oh really?"

Our conversation was suddenly cut short, as the flight attendants called for all passengers on that morning's flight to Los Angeles.

"I'll look out for it . . . What's it going to me called?"

9

"Cousin Jack's Mouth-organ," I shouted at her as she headed off with a member of BA staff. It must have sounded like double-Dutch to her.

I waited for a further hour before the Chicago flight was dealt with.

"Did you pack your own bags?" the check-in desk girl asked.

"Yes," I said.

"Do you have any of the following items in your baggage?"

She showed me a post-September 11th laminated card with symbols showing oxidising substances, radioactive material, explosives, hand-guns, gases, corrosives, flammable substances, grenades, rocket launchers and nuclear weapons. I scrutinised the list very carefully before answering, "No."

"And do you think I would tell you if I was some kind of terrorist?" I said to myself.

She weighed my bag and attached the destination label. Then she pointed me in the direction of the gate. I had around ten minutes to change my pounds. I found the nearest *Bureau de Change* and hurriedly shoved notes under the window. I felt like an East-End gangster leaving the country for the Costa del Crime. When the transaction was completed I dashed through Passport Control and the Hand-luggage and Body search and made my way to the gate. Within quarter of an hour I was sat on the Boeing 747 that would take me across the Atlantic. I don't think I really ever enjoy aeroplane flights, but these days I deal with them as a kind of roller-coaster ride; some of which I enjoy, and some of which I don't. You take the rough with the smooth. Most people don't seem to enjoy take-offs and landings. Once you're up, there's little you can do. My attitude is 'if I'm going to die, I'm going to die'. There is frankly not much I can do about it. I always watch the flight attendants. If they're scared, that's when I'm allowed to be as well. Instead of worrying, I lay back and watch the films; this time *Spiderman* and *My Big Fat Greek Wedding*.

Turbulence is a different matter. That's when I go sweaty, tighten my seat-belt and grab the arm-rests or the nearest random human being. Once it is over, I look around and see who's been watching me. Then I feel stupid. The rest of the time I delved into the British Airways magazine *High Life*. It's full of the usual kind of trivia you get in aircraft magazines – advertisements for off-shore banking, yachts, watches and Geo-chron world clocks, which tell you with one glance, the current time anywhere in the world. Then there are other useful articles like ones on 'The World's Best Adventure Parks' and 'Belgrade in the Autumn'. Having said that, after seven hours in the air in the same seat in the same position, you generally find you've read them all twice, and that 'Pyschogeography' is in fact, a scintillating subject. You end up wanting to order a Geo-chron clock.

The best thing about BA flights is the little map on one of the channels of the television screen that tells you were you are. You get to fly over vast swathes of the world that you will never ever visit in a million years. I like all the places in Greenland the best: Angmogssalik, Godthaabo and Frederikshaab, though a close second is the massive Ungava Peninsula of Quebec – with places like Saglouc, Inoucdjouac and Ivugivik. I always wonder what life is like in Angmogssalik and Saglouc. Do they have MTV? Do they watch 'Eastenders'? What's hot and what's not in Saglouc? You realise how large a landmass both Greenland and Canada are.

As the aeroplane heads down across North America, I'm always waiting for Lake Michigan to appear. Then I know we're getting close. Once the lake comes into view, you wait for the plane to turn and cross the city of Chicago. Then you don't breathe again until you've landed. I like O'Hare airport in Chicago. It is just how a modern airport should look in a children's picture-book. I can't tell you how many times I have flown in and out of it, but there is now a wonderful sense of familiarity about it to me, so much so that I even recognise some of the Immigration officers at Passport Control. The airport interior is painted white and the concourses are air-conditioned, so it comes as quite a shock when you step outside into the full heat of a Chicago August. I waited for the car rental bus to pick me up with a very tanned lady who had just returned from a flight to Portugal. She was waiting for her daughter to pick her up. I helped her with her bags. They were incredibly heavy.

"Sorry, it's my rocks," she said.

I looked at her with a puzzled expression. I'd flown across three thousand miles of ocean to end up talking about rocks. There were enough rocks back home in Cornwall.

"I collected them on the beach in Portugal. They were so beautiful I had to bring them back home . . ."

"Did you have any trouble getting them through customs?" I asked.

"Well, they did ask me, but when I showed them they were just rocks, they just waved me through . . ."

I spent about an hour talking to this lady about her rocks, before the *Alamo* shuttle came to pick me up. By the end of it, I was ready to take some of the rocks and make a bolus from them. The lady's head might have been my target.

"Sorry," said the shuttle driver. "We had a bus break down today . . ."

By now, a number of other British people had joined me outside, and when the driver opened the doors it was like the January sales. Everyone piled on and sat there cradling water bottles and cokes. At least the bus was air-conditioned and we could cool down again. I waved to the lady and her rocks. Some other innocent was now helping her with her bags. I imagine her now inviting friends around for tea to see her rock collection from Portugal. I suppose they don't have rocks where she lives.

The roads around major airports always look inconceivably complex, and Chicago is no exception. You go up and under and around and down and up again before you even begin to get orientated. On top of that, O'Hare is cursed with a complex one-way system and the meanest traffic control officers you are ever likely to meet. Once your five minutes stoppage time is up, they blow a whistle to move you on. They aren't as mean to the shuttles as normal drivers, but I was glad I was being whisked away to my rental car, away from rocks and raging parking control officers. I mean, they scared me – and I was just on foot.

Car rental places are always funny. They are full of knackered people who wish they didn't have to drive somewhere new. When you think about that, it isn't a good combination. Tiredness + unfamiliarity + different side of the road = pile up. Still, I was up for it. I had to be. I had me the whole of a country to drive through. Right there and then, it seemed quite crazy what I was about to do. Completely mazed. Why didn't I just go back to the airport and catch a flight to San Francisco? When I mentioned what I was going to do to most Americans, they gave me a look which said, "You crazy fool. Haven't you heard of flying?" But then, you couldn't get a good look at Cornish America from 20,000 feet.

"Next," bawled the car rental lady.

I moved forward and presented her with all the necessary documentation.

"Sir, would you like to upgrade?"

This meant would I like a flashier car. She showed me a card, showing all the possible combinations: open top, convertibles, things with big engines, penis extensions and red ones that looked like you could spin on down the highway and easily be pulled over by the County Sheriff, just by the colour.

"No, I don't think so," I said, actually very much longing for the big red one.

She then seemed to stamp everything twenty times and then threw the keys at me.

"You're through. You'll find your vehicle in lot number 14."

I have learnt that when you hire a car, always have someone from the rental company walk around the vehicle with you. I do this, pointing out every minor scratch, splodge, chip or dent – just so no-one can accuse me of putting them there. I think I am a reasonably safe and careful driver, so I didn't want any problems at the San Francisco end. I needn't have bothered.

"It doesn't matter sir," said the attendant. "Even if you roll the car and completely trash it, you won't be charged . . ."

Well, when he put it that way, I suppose there was no point in showing him chip no. 53 on the rear fender.

I spent a few minutes orientating myself with the controls and then pulled off in my hired Chevrolet Cavalier. Like a white streak of lightning, I headed out of the *Alamo* lot, and turned onto a real piece of road. Within what seemed like seconds, I was on 294's six lanes heading south at

13

break-taking speed. Given that, you soon get to know your car. Either that, or you die. The problem is not so much driving in a new city, it is more the map-reading that you're trying to do at the same time. It's fine if there's someone travelling with you, but if you're on your own, it can be fairly frantic. I was negotiating my way through Chicago's famous toll booths to my first taste of Cornish America – Jim Wearne.

Jim is of Cornish extraction, and I'd first met him at the Cornish Gathering in Mineral Point the previous Autumn,[1] though had known and corresponded with him for some time. He was compèring the entertainment at the Opera House. Jim is one of those Americans who seems perfectly at ease on stage, and even when a crisis occurs (like a microphone stand collapsing or say a stampede of cattle through the main auditorium) is able to maintain a sense of calm and order. He has a rich, deep mid-Western voice which helps. Like me, Jim also performed at the Gathering. He is both singer and talented guitarist, and we swapped his CDs for my books. It would be wrong to describe Jim as folk singer because he is not. He is more influenced by the blues and rock than traditional folk, yet has carved himself a productive niche in Celtic America, as a purveyor of Cornish-influenced music. Let me put it this way: he sings 'Truro Agricultural Show' more like Ian Anderson of Jethro Tull than anyone wearing a white Arran sweater, drinking real ale and their finger stuck in their ear.

Jim was born in St Louis, Missouri on October 24th 1950, but looks older than his fifty-odd years. He readily admitted this to me, and I suggested that it was probably his long, spade-like beard that made people think him older. Jim lives in an apartment in the area of southern Chicago called Woodridge. He is divorced, but his ex-wife and two daughters, Cathy and Lissa live close by. Woodridge is a typical multi-ethnic subdivision of Chicago, which started as an area where the more prosperous immigrant families moved to in the mid-twentieth century, and started businesses, industries and restaurants. Now, the area is not far from some of Chicago's most important hi-tech industries on the western edge of the city – and in particular following the route of Interstate 88 across the State – Chicago's 'silicon valley'. Jim himself works in the computer industry, offering training to company employees in installing and operating new software.

I pulled into the parking lot at the back of the apartment complex where Jim lived, went around the front and pressed the buzzer.

"How you doing?" said Jim. "I'll be right down. Head 'round back . . ."

Jim appeared at the rear entrance thirty seconds later.

"Come on up," he said. "Let me give you a hand with your luggage . . ."

Jim's apartment felt fairly typical of this area of Chicago. His was on the third floor and architecturally I instantly felt I was back in the mid-West: dark, wooden panels, high ceilings and screens. It was about seven in the evening by the time I arrived at Jim's place, and the light was starting to fade. In the dusk, Jim familiarised me with his home. Opposite his kitchen was an impressive collection of books which I instantly headed towards. As well as the usual Cornish titles – were a lot of Tolkien, and books on American history and music. On the wall outside Jim's bedroom was a film poster of *Saving Grace*, the Port Isaac-set comedy, where widow Grace (played by Brenda Blethyn) decides to save her estate by growing cannabis. In the next room was Jim's musical workshop, where guitars stood on stands, or were hung on the wall. A computer workstation vied with the instruments, and on the wall a certificate of bardship from the Cornish Gorseth. His bardic name is 'Canor Gwanethtyr [Prairie Singer]'. Dominating all of this were several Ordnance Survey maps of areas of Cornwall, pinned together to make a massive single one of the whole territory.

For me, of course, in terms of British time, it was in the middle of the night, but I needed to adjust, so I suggested that we should go out and eat. Jim put on his baseball cap, which has the flag of St Piran on it, and we headed off to a family-style restaurant a few blocks away in Jim's van. I should at this point tell you about Jim's 'special' van. It is a Ford, a huge vehicle by British standards, with a very 70s' 'Starsky and Hutch' feeling interior. Outside, the vehicle is riddled with rust, but in a way, it seems to suit Jim. As he later told me, "Nobody would be seen dead in this thing, so I never have to lock it." In the back of the van are various computer manuals and training documents. They look like the kind of thing no-one would ever want to steal.

Jim 'took' a steak and I had a Caesar salad and we discussed recent events. He'd recently been in Cornwall to accept his bardship at a mini-Gorseth at Pendennis Castle, as part of the Cornish Homecoming festival. He had performed there, and we had briefly met up in Falmouth. That said, he had been busy, since he was being filmed by my friend Mick Catmul for a BBC South-West documentary about the entire homecoming event.[2] I had recommended to Mick that Jim would make an interesting person to follow. The documentary has been shown, and Jim comes across well in it. At this point though, we were still discussing what it might look like.

Between the food and beer we covered a number of subjects including Jim's music and inspiration. The first CD I have of his is the *Songs of Cornwall: Captured Alive!* (1997) collection recorded in the Washington DC area at the Potomac Celtic Festival. On this were some of the standards – 'Trelawny' and 'Little Lize', as well as those collected by recorders such as Ralph Dunstan – 'The Fox' and 'The Callington Ringers'.[3] One of the best songs is 'Old Johnny Bugger', which Jim sings with a real relish. The album *Me and Cousin Jack* (1998) is a more political affair, which demonstrates Jim's awareness of the economic situation of Cornwall. The sleeve-notes echo this: 'Efforts to re-open South Crofty have failed. It looks like it's really over. The song 'The Tin Mines of Cornwall' on this CD is about that'. This song turns out to be one of Jim's favourite pieces.

He has little time for the mystical or "new-age" end of Celtic music, and to be honest, his music would work better in a crowded pub than on a misty moor. He describes one song on this album as being 'Cornish Zydeco' while at the same time 'infusing these fine old songs with a little American flavour'. Zydeco is actually a style of music originating in Louisiana, combining Cajun and Creole. Quite rightly, he comments that his work 'might give the occasional purist the vapours', but in my culturally diffuse

16

view that wasn't such a bad thing at all. On *Howl Lowen* [*Happy Sun*] (2001) are more of Jim's original compositions, while on the track 'Delo Syvy' where Jim sings in Cornish, he amused me by writing irreverently, 'Ok, now – all you Cornish language experts – don't get all huffy if I didn't get it perfect according to the rules of Cornish to which you subscribe . . . Sorry to be defensive, but these Cornish language people can get testy.'[4] I like the way Jim put things. He was doing it his way. He didn't suffer from Cornish Language Fight Syndrome.

One of the strangest things I find about the USA is the need to carry identification with you at all times. In Illinois, that August, that seems to be even more of a priority for the authorities – perhaps in the wake of September 11th, or maybe it was just plain corporate paranoia. Either way, the waitress seemed unduly unnerved when I'd asked for a beer while we'd been talking. Apparently, not just young people, but now everyone had to show ID in order to buy alcohol. Initially, I'd put it down to my young good looks, but as we found out later at the supermarket, when Jim tried to buy some Guinness, it was a new blanket policy. There was Jim – at the ripe old age of fifty-one – having to show ID. America could be weird sometimes. It could also be inconsistent. The moment I got out of Illinois, this policy was no longer present, not, you will understand, that I tested every supermarket along the way.

I was sleeping in the living room on a spare mattress Jim happened to have. The air doesn't cool down much in the night this time of the year, and I just lay there and sweated, with the large fan oscillating between Jim's room and my own, and a smaller fan pushing cool air towards my head. Before attempting to sleep, I had a quick glance over Jim's CD collection. It was full of classic music from the 1960s and 70s – The Who, The Beatles and Jimi Hendrix. There were also a couple of albums by the Australian-Cornish singer Carrl Myriad and his group called The Ragged Band. On one album was a version of 'Pela era why moaz, moz, fettow teag? [Where are you going pretty fair maid?' translated by Edwin Chirgwin around 1698.[5] Myriad looked like Ted Nugent, but he had a wonderful voice. Sat alongside the Cornish Ted Nugent were some DVDs of the

17

Arthurian comedy *Monty Python and the Holy Grail*, and a few episodes of *The Simpsons*. I remember peering at these a lot during the night because, despite my tiredness, I didn't sleep particularly well. Coming from the frankly pathetic summer temperatures of Cornwall to this, was a shock to the system. Outside, the rest of Chicago seemed to be sleeping but I wasn't. I wondered how people did sleep in these kind of temperatures. I supposed you just became acclimatised and that was it.

Not surprisingly, I rose late. Jim had been gone hours ago. My plan that day – was to relax and get used to being in America again. There is a Chaos-theory themed Ray Bradbury story – 'A Sound of Thunder' – that I am fond of, where a group of hunters travel backwards in time to shoot dinosaurs.[6] They are warned not to step off the pathway or they might end up changing things in the future to which they return. One does step off the pathway and treads on a butterfly and kills it. In so doing, he alters the future. When the explorers return they wake up to a world that is ever so slightly different, and the spelling system has altered, dislocating them all. I always feel like that when I come to America – like I've stepped out of a Ray Bradbury story. It is not different enough to know you are in a completely foreign place, but aspects of it come and challenge you from odd angles.

I spent the morning at the supermarket where we'd bought the Guinness, amusing myself with strange and bizarre food products, noticing how magazines like *Mercenary Monthly* and *Guns, Ammo, Death Weekly* strangely sit next to *Patchworking Quilting Fortnightly* and *Christian Stories*. As well as Guns and Christianity, nothing much on the supermarket shelves seemed very good for you. A lot of it all looked very high fat and high sugar. That didn't stop anyone from buying it though. I made do with a can of Diet Coke and some fruit, and felt like a fitness fanatic. Other people piled in the Pop Tarts and Cinnamon Rolls into their carts.

In the afternoon, I amused myself by heading to what I can only call an 'out of town shopping centre'. There are lots of these kinds of facilities in America now. There is a central car parking area, around which run all kinds of stores, from, for example, *Toys R Us* to *Dunkin' Donuts*. I parked up and headed into a large *Barnes and Noble* booksellers. Everywhere George 'Dubya' Bush was looking at me. His face seemed to be on several publications which dealt with US Foreign Policy, the Republican Party's record on human rights and of course, his sparring with Saddam Hussein.

I wandered the store for around an hour, glancing at books on the Celts. Celts, by the way, in American bookstores, are always filed next to the Egyptians, Outer Mongolians and Picts, generally in the archaeological section. Cornwall never has a section devoted to it. Ireland always does. In this particular book, Cornwall was featured but almost all the information in it was wrong – it was like Cornwall, after you'd stepped on the butterfly. We apparently still speak British (They have a point I suppose!) but the map of Cornwall seemed to include most of the South-West Peninsula; but hey – I'm all for Robert Hunt's 'greater Cornwall' (I mean I'm the sort of person who thinks we should send an expeditionary force over to place a St Piran's flag on Lundy). Don't even get me onto Michael Joseph and Thomas Flamank; they seemed to confuse that rebellion with Trelawny. Still, I found more interesting reading in a *Scientific American* magazine left in the coffee bar. There was an article in it by W. Wayt Gibbs on dying or near-extinct languages. Cornwall was featured on the map but its language was said to be in a state of recovery. This inspired me to buy a couple of books: one called *Language and Nationalism in Europe*; the other *Language Wars and Linguistic Politics*, which I sat down and started to read back at Jim's place, while listening to some of his CDs.

That evening – and it was steaming hot – we headed across to Downers Grove – the home of Darryl and Carol Jones, friends of Jim since his college days. Both Jim and Darryl play together in another of Jim's musical projects – Blue Velvet Highway, an AOR band (that's 'adult orientated rock' pop-pickers), who sound (to my ears at least) like a combination of The Eagles and Kansas. Darryl and Carol have a luxurious apartment filled with antique furniture and paintings, as well as interesting Civil War memorabilia. Fortunately, Jim, Darryl, Carol and I have something of a shared musical heritage. I like much of the blues, rock and folk that came out of the 1960s and 70s, so once we'd established that, everything fitted together. Darryl works as a musician and amongst his generous collection of CDs it didn't take him long to find a Jethro Tull one, and away we went.

Obviously, Darryl had more than a passing interest in the Civil War. The flat was dotted with books on the topic, and he subscribed to a couple of magazines devoted to the conflict. We talked about the role of the Cornish and mining regiments in the conflict – both of us suggesting that more research needed to be done. One of the first companies to be formed in Wisconsin, on the call of President Lincoln, was formed at Mineral Point and known as the First Company of the Regiment of the Wisconsin Volunteer Infantry, known as the 'Miners' Guard'. According to A.L. Rowse, about a third of the company were Cornish, with a Cornishman acting as first lieutenant. Apparently, one General Allen commented, 'Dr. J. H. Vivian was surgeon of one of our regiments . . . On the whole, the Cornish were as loyal as the Americans, and made good soldiers. The businessmen of the same nationality were mostly patriotic and helped fill our ranks'.[7] The Cornish therefore fought at Bull Run and Manasses, and engaged Stuart's calvary at Thornburg, Stonewell Jackson at Turner's Pass at South Mountain, later fighting in Antietam, Fredericksburg and at Gettysburg. Darryl found all of this fascinating. Though he'd heard of the 'Miner's Guard' he didn't really know their Cornish connections. Then of course, we got on to the 96th Regiment of the Illinois Volunteer Infantry – the 'Illinois Cornish' who fought and suffered heavy casualties at the battle of Chickamauga. After the Civil War, many of the Cornish simply went back to mining and farming in the two States. Being a Jones, Darryl was also aware of his Welsh heritage and of their role in the Civil War, so we were able to share our joint 'Celticity'. The bottles of beers helped. Carol (who worked as a teacher) and I were also able to share our experiences in the classroom. It seemed schools in Chicago suffered from the same testing and target-setting as the ones back home.

Once their voices had been fully lubricated, Jim and

Darryl played a new song for the next Blue Velvet Highway album. It was a Jim Wearne composition, with Jim playing and singing lead and Darryl on bass. Both are talented musicians and the song and the steamy evening made me feel that this was the kind of America I'd dreamed of – beer, hot weather and blues. It got even better when Darryl suggested we should move onto the balcony to smoke cigars. Apparently, this was a regular event of a Friday evening. Carol lit some insect-repelling candles and we sat and sweated and smoked. Or at least, Jim and Darryl did. I just sat and sweated.

"Good luck," offered Darryl, when it came to us leaving and he heard about the journey I was about to make. "Be sure you stock up on plenty of water when you hit the desert . . ."

"Yes, have a safe journey . . ." said Carol.

"Mind those ravines, gorges, waterfalls, bears, deadly prairie dogs, police, bandits, spiders and cockroaches – and be careful in Utah," they seemed to want to say.

I'm sure Darryl and Carol meant well, but I just thought I was driving across Cornish America. The way they were speaking was as if were some kind of pioneer of old. Hell, I'd be buying up a shotgun next and surviving on racoons, rabbits and road-kill. I'd better watch out for Injuns too.

I wasn't off on the great adventure quite yet though. First off, I wanted to see Chicago again. After mining declined in both Illinois and Wisconsin, Chicago became an urban magnet for the Cornish, and many declined to move further west, and instead poured into the city. Even today, Chicago has quite a large Cornish population, perhaps equivalent to that of Detroit, although it is proving harder and harder to find them. Paradoxically, it was also from Chicago that many Cornish caught the overland trains across the country to San Francisco, and any cursory survey of studies of the Cornish in America, holds countless stories of them setting out from here. Chicago was also the southern terminus of the Hancock-Chicago railroad which carried copper down from the Keweenaw Peninsula in the Upper Peninsula of Michigan. For me, Cornwall and Chicago are intimately connected.

Cecil Todd gives a fine example of this connection by

mentioning the story of one mid-Cornwall boy, Frank Dyer, a Doctor of Divinity, born in 1875 in Golant, who was placed in service with the Rashleighs of Menabilly, but who in 1893, helped him with his fare to Chicago. From Chicago, Dyer travelled America, becoming pastor of seven churches, and eventually Ecumenical Bishop at the outbreak of the Second World War. However, after being invited to preach in London in 1926, he was finally able to visit Golant, preaching in the pulpit at the church of St Sampson.[8] I'd spent many nights of my teenage years fishing on the banks of Fowey at Golant, so Dyer's story was on my mind.

I planned to head into Chicago the next day – Saturday. I slept a little better the Friday night. It felt like I had employed every coolant system I could find, but I still woke up a little bleary-eyed in the morning. Jim agreed to drop me at the Downers Grove train station, and from there, I could catch the Metra commuter rail system into central Chicago. At Downers Grove a farmer's market was up and running in the car parking lot next to the station, and as ever, America was on early. It was only seven in the morning and everybody locally seemed to be up, out of bed and at 'em. Back home, at this time of the morning on a Saturday, most people in Probus weren't even contemplating opening their eyes yet – but that's sunny weather for you. It makes getting up early a lot more pleasant.

When I was a child, there was nothing I liked better than to go trainspotting at St Austell Station. I know that may seem like a nerdy thing to do, but there weren't computer games in the mid-1970s, and if you wanted to go beyond clay tips (which I did all the time), it was one way to go about it. That way I learnt all about the railway lines of Cornwall and even travelled to far off, exotic locations like Bristol to write down the numbers of Diesel Multiple Units and then new High Speed Trains at Temple Meads. Oh, the thrill of it all. I was reminded of this as I waited for the Metra train to take me into Chicago. I was at the end of a platform again. Unlike Britain, where railway lines are always fenced off, in America, the track just runs through the middle of most towns, and you can step across it at any point. People do as well. Even though I could see the headlight of the engine coming closer, people still just stepped across the rails with no sense of fear.

You step up into trains in America. The platform is low and you have to climb up into the carriage. Like most American trains, this one was made of gleaming metal – a silver-streak of a thing – something I'd have died to have seen back home on the down line at St Austell station. However, this Metra, to be perfectly honest, had seen better days. The carriage was painted a worn cream and the seats were a distressed brown. You then have to make a decision once you board – whether to sit up or down, since the carriages are double-deckers. I climbed up onto the second level, since I hoped for a better view of the journey into the city centre.

There is a complicated method of ticketing on Chicago's trains in order to help the ticket collector know who has just got on. The system still slightly mystifies me – but in principle, by your seat is a little coloured strip of paper. Once you sit down, the ticket collector soon spots you are there and replaces it with another coloured strip of paper. Anyway, I bought my ticket and relaxed. I was journeying through tree-lined suburban Chicago – places with pleasant-ville names like Clarendon Hills, Western Springs and Riverside. Every so often as the train twisted slightly to the left, the vast skyline of Chicago came into view. There were endless marshalling yards in sight too – once vast complexes of rail freight to be taken across American, now I suppose, replaced by trucks. Then rows and rows of derelict stock-yards, no doubt once to contain the entire beef supply of the mid-West, Now these places were all tagged by graffiti and left to rot. Despite their dereliction, there was still something spectacular and glorious about them. In a way, their despair made them all the more interesting. You'll know what I mean if you've ever walked the Great Flat Lode back home. Gradually, the marshalling yards transformed into warehouses and factories, and then once again into Chicago's city centre. Great concrete overpasses arched over the railway tracks, carrying cars downtown. Beneath, the train wheels ground and cracked as we covered multiple points outside the terminus. It became darker as we entered the subterranean light of Union Station.

Chicago's Union Station has the most comfortable benches in the world. How do I know? I sat in one for about quarter of an hour early on that Saturday morning in August, just watching people and admiring the architecture of the station. The oak benches are long, with scooped bottoms, perfect for sitting and waiting in. Whoever designed them, obviously had an idea of what makes a chair comfortable, and what shape people actually are, and although they probably originated from the nineteenth century, they were still in perfect condition. The Union, though it had been modernised in some of the underground sections, still has its grand entrance lobby. I could imagine how, at one point, much of the mid-West passed through here. Thousands of Cornish men and women had stood in this station waiting to head west. Those families remaining in Chicago had also stood here as well I sensed – Spargo, Clymo, Tremelling, Annear, Geach and Anstiss. Family names like these whistled like ghosts around the entrance lobby. Beyond these spectres, the morning was strangely quiet though, with only the cleaners mopping the tiles and a few homeless people asleep on the benches: all 'Starbucks' coffee cups filled with change and "Vietnam veteran" cardboard signs. Ironically, above them, and the mock classical columns, was a huge Stars and Stripes flag.

Outside, Chicago was just beginning to rub the sleep from its eyes. It suited my mood perfectly. Even the downtown traffic seemed sedated. The Union is located on what is known as the Near West Side, not far from Old St Patrick's Cathedral and Greektown. To head downtown, you cross the South Branch of the Chicago River. Immediately, you encounter the grey monolith that is the Sear's Tower. It was actually eerily quiet there, with concrete security blocks preventing car bombers and security already having a high-profile. I had climbed the Tower before on a previous visit; and the skydeck's views are quite incredible. On the clear July day that I went up, it felt like you could see all the way across America. Built in 1974, the Sear's Tower is one of the world's tallest buildings, but you could sense a tension there. This was Chicago's proudest achievement, its most explicit symbol of wealth and power (somehow it also stood for all those successful Cornish Chicago businesses Rowse mentions – Pascoe Incorporated, Rodda Insurance Services, Penberthy Manufacturers, Trerice and Company Instrument makers[9]), but clearly it could easily be the Al Qaeda's next target.

Crossing South Franklin Avenue, I headed into the Loop. I've always found the Loop fascinating. It is the raised railway network serving part of downtown. You've probably seen it in the movies. Trains rattle and scuttle above the rest of the traffic on green-painted, solid iron supports with rivets the size of your fist. Once you realise this, you notice that Chicago is very much a city built on a number of layers. You may be on one road, but there is often another underneath it crossing in an opposite direction. Below that is life on the green-tinged river. Add to this the Loop level, as well as the skyscrapers high above, and you will understand why this multi-layeredness defines the city. As trains pass above, they do leave a windy rush in the lower levels, and the City is on the edge of Lake Michigan, allowing the eastern off-shore breeze to blow in on the shore. However, Chicago wasn't named the "Windy City" because of this. Apparently, the name was coined by the *New York Sun* editor, Charles Dana, in reference to the city's long-winded politicians. Even now, posters around the City advertise the work of the Mayor and other rival politicians. Nothing much seemed to have changed. Another reason, I thought, connecting Chicago with Cornwall; we've a few windy politicians too.

I knew the place to visit first in Chicago was North Michigan Avenue. Known as the 'Magnificent Mile' it is where much of the city's shops and tourism are based. To reach North Michigan you cross the branch of the Chicago River that runs towards Lake Michigan and head north. The Avenue runs parallel to the shore of the Lake. On the right is *The Chicago Tribune's* Gothic-style tower, looking as if it has been transplanted from Gotham City. I know that *The Tribune* has run many stories about the Cornish over the years. John Rowe mentions how *The West Briton* would often repeat stories about mineral wealth in America first published in *The Tribune*.[10] Now, the street level is more a tourist attraction than a real newspaper office, devoted to a merchandising outlet for the newspaper and

Chicago's football and baseball teams. However, the upper levels are still the home of one of the finest newspapers in the world. I imagined the news editors, busy telephones and novice reporters learning their trade. It still looked the kind of place where on the uppermost floor, you might find the newspaper editor, wearing braces and smoking a cigar, surveying the whole of the city, and demanding a headline-grabbing story from some hapless young journalist.

The Mile is now home to any number of international stores you might find in any major European or American City, but mid-way down its pavements are still touches of old Chicago. The Chicago Water Tower and Water Works are reminders of the past, as is the spotless Fourth Presbyterian Church. I went into the latter's garden, and sat for a while next to the fountain. If there was an Eden to be found in the middle of the Mile, this was it. The fountain's waters seem to block out all the noise of the traffic. The Church lies opposite the John Hancock Center; still the world's tallest apartment block. Built in 1970, it is known in Chicago as 'Big John' and is characterised by its black steel and two radio masts painted white and red. Amusingly, trying to drum up business for its skydeck views was a young man dressed up in an outfit resembling 'Big John'. Every so often he had to pause for photographs with tourists. I imagine the first day of the job it was fun – but now it looked a bit of a drag. Beneath 'Big John' was a restaurant called *The Cheesecake Factory*, that had I the time or the money, I would have visited that day. I had been there before. I think I can honestly say it is was one of the finest eating experiences I had ever had. The restaurant spills out onto a small plaza beneath the Hancock Center, but architecturally is very wild and ornate – with orange and creme coloured flowing forms wrapping themselves around the concrete – I suppose, rather resembling a cheese-cake. In the midst of all this concrete and steel you could understand the appeal.

I didn't go into any of the stores that everyone else seemed to be dashing in and out of – 'Bloomingdales', 'Marshall Fields' or 'Tiffany & Co'. I never know what to buy in them anyway. Instead, I wandered down one of the side streets towards the Museum of Contemporary Art.

26

Near the water works, and not surprisingly, was one of the city's old fire departments. Since September 11th firemen have a new status in American society, and you could feel the gasps of admiration from passers-by at the shiny fire appliances. I wandered the Museum of Contemporary Art for a while, and then headed back down the 'Mile' towards the Chicago River. As I walked, as always, I watched. People in Chicago looked happy. This was, I think, one of the reasons I liked the city. Perhaps it was because, unlike say, New York or Los Angeles, Chicago didn't have to live up to any kind of reputation. It could just be itself. I'd noticed the same things a few years earlier when I had visited 'Buddy Guy's Blues Club'. Despite the dealers outside the door trying to ply all manner of drugs on customers, or other 'users' looking for "medication", there was still a relaxed atmosphere: a live and let live attitude that I didn't note elsewhere in America.

Back near the Wrigley Building, the skyscraper that chewing gum help build, I headed down some steps towards the office of one of the Chicago River Boat tours. I was serenaded by one of those South American Pan Pipe-style groups who appear everywhere in the world now from Truro and St Austell, to Paris and Chicago. You know the sort of thing: Pan Pipes do The Beatles, Pan Pipes do Celine Dion, Pan Pipes do Iron Maiden. No – I made the last one up, but I'm sure you get the picture. The cost of the tour was fifteen dollars, and this seemed a good deal to me. As I was alone, I managed to get the final place on the boat that was just leaving and negotiated my way to a seat near the bow. The sun was beating down by now, and I was beginning to wish I'd bought some sunscreen. I can't honestly remember everything that was pointed out to me on the first half of the boat tour (it was a blur of architecture and city history), but the two most interesting buildings were the Civic Opera House, which resembled a gigantic chair and the two distinctive Marina City carparks, which you probably know. They look like two enormous corn-cobs, and feature on records by 'emo-core' bands these days.

From the Opera House we turned around and headed back towards the Wrigley Building and the Tribune tower.

Soon, we'd be heading out onto Lake Michigan. In order to progress onto the Lake, all boats must negotiate a lock system. This is because the Lake is actually slightly higher now than the River. Therefore, though originally flowing towards the Lake, these days the River is more the receiver of water from Lake Michigan than the giver. On the city side of the lock, various boats waited to enter, many of them with tanned and rich-looking young people on them with little clothing on. Opposite the lock, lies the recently developed Navy Pier. Navy Pier was obviously a popular day-out for much of Chicago. It has an IMAX theatre, arcades, an ice rink and a huge ferris wheel.

Once out onto the Lake itself the water became more choppy, and the air was windy. I thought of all the Cornish who'd crossed this space before me, coming down from the Upper Peninsula of Michigan to Chicago. It would have been a very different view that greeted many of them, especially in 1871, when a great fire flattened some 1,688 acres of downtown. Now, I peered back at the City's skyline, which became more and more spectacular the further we went out on the lake. Clearly a lot of people on the boat were on holiday. I could tell from the accents that many of them were up from the south of the USA. Usually someone strikes up a conversation with me, but I suppose that afternoon, I was too busy taking all of it in. I remember the same feeling as I crossed on the Staten Island ferry in New York, and looked back on the Manhattan skyline.

The boat started to turn back towards the lock. On the shoreline I could see the Shedd Aquarium and the Field Museum of Natural History. I'd visited both previously; the Shedd is a multi-million dollar state-of-the-art aquarium and zoological centre, with a wonderful range of fish and other animals to see. I remembered a particularly good turtle exhibit and another extolling the decline of the world's frog population (You 'gotta' feel sorry for the frogs). The Field Museum on the other hand, gives you 'Museum Head' the moment you walk in the front door. 'Museum Head'? Well, that is my term for the feeling you get when you can no longer be bothered to examine every exhibit in the detail needed and that you are so over-whelmed by the amount of material available, that you simply can no longer cope and have to head to somewhere like the shop and buy a rubber dinosaur. I was there a whole morning and didn't cover half of the exhibitions. Like the Natural History Museum in Kensington, there was just too much to see. Their Native American centre is absolutely stunning though.

Our boat continued on, chugging up past the Adler Planetarium and Chicago Harbour, eventually returning us through the lock, and back into the Chicago River. The lock was an interesting experience for many of the ducks that populated the river. They tended not to notice that the water was either being pumped in and out, and tended to be sucked into the vortex at the opening and closing of the lock gates. Other passengers and I worried for their safety, but there they were, happy, as ducks in water, swimming around on the other side. I concluded that it was the duck equivalent of surfing.

Back at the Wrigley Building, I decided to cross the river again and head south. At Jim's place yesterday, I had called Sue Pellowe. I have known Sue for a number of years now. She runs much of the Cornish activity in Chicago, and as well as working at the Art Institute of Chicago in the Department of European Decorative Arts and Sculpture and Ancient Art, she is also a talented writer and actress. We'd met up before at O'Hare for coffee, as well as at several Cornish and Celtic gatherings in the USA and in Cornwall. She is perhaps now symbolic of the wider Cornish energy present in Chicago. Sue was born in Detroit, Michigan in 1939 and grew up in Saginaw, Port Huron on the shores of Lake Huron, and then lived in nearby Adrian. She followed in her father's footsteps by attending the interestingly-named Albion College (where the sports teams were known at 'The Brits' – "Go Brits! Go Brits!") and than attended Northwestern University and the University of Illinois. Sue worked for twelve years as an Associate Professor of Theatre at Aurora University (about forty miles from Chicago) so we always chatted about *Ordinalia* and the translation and adaptation I had been working on. What is great about her is that she always brings a real enthusiasm and humour to whatever event is going on.

Sue showed me around the Art Institute with me asking

her to point out some of her favourite paintings and asking her about how she feels about Cornwall now. Her response was complicated. She loves it deeply, but fears for it. At the same time, she is excited about its future. Her favourite artist is Ivan Albright, an American who lived not too far from Aurora. He paints pictures of images such a the famous painting of an old sailor in a yellow oilslicker holding an oar, and names it 'Heavy the Oar to Him Who Is Tired, Heavy the Coat, Heavy the Sea'. Elsewhere is another painting of an older woman, heavy with cellulite and wrinkles, which Albright names 'Into the World Came a Soul Named Ida'. Sue thinks of his technique as ultra-realism, and we both pointed out the connection between his work and those of the Newlyn School. He paints the Maine coast the way Stanhope Forbes 'does' Penwith.

As we walked around the Art Institute, Sue told me more about her own Cornish identity. Her father, William Charles Smithson Pellowe, who eventually became a Methodist minister and historian, originally came from Penryn and Flushing-based family. For some years the family lived in a former toll house on the road to Truro. The toll house was named Watergate because of the small stream that ran through the field behind. He named the cottage they lived in on Lake Huron as Watergate too. Thankfully, Sue joked, he died before the Nixon scandal conferred a new connotation. Out of this heritage, Sue has written a couple of books that I liked. Like my paternal grandmother, Sue was named after Susanna Wesley (John Wesley's mother) and she has written *A Wesley Family Book of Days* (1994) and a cookbook called *Saffron and Currants: A Cornish Heritage Cookbook* (1989).[11] The former is a an easily browseable collection of material that offers an introduction to the life and work of John and Charles Wesley, and the extended Wesley family, while the latter explains why the expensive spice that is saffron ended up as a staple of the Cornish diet, and includes (as you might expect) numerous recipes. Not only does the book sell in North America for those seeking out Cornish foodways – but it has also sold well back in Cornwall. One of the lovely things about Sue is that she works hard to serve her co-workers saffron cake whenever she can and indoctrinate them with Cornish lore and customs. She was also excited about a course she would soon be teaching in the Lay Academy of her Church: 'God Onstage'. This would take an historic view from the Greeks to the works of Schaffer, and would also include (she said with a knowing wink) the Cornish Mystery Cycles. One of these days Sue hopes to stage my adaptation of *Origo Mundi* in Chicago, if, she shouted after me as I departed, "I don't give up and move to Cornwall first . . ."

If you don't go to anything else in Chicago, then go to the Art Institute. I had been before but such is the range and quality of work on offer inside that it is worth a second look. As well as a wide range of European masters, and Americans like Albright, there is 'American Gothic' (that's the one with the old man and woman standing with a pitchfork) as well as work by Edward Hopper and Georgia O'Keeffe. Basically, you can't move for icons. My favourite part though is the design section, where they trace the history of the living room settee and the common table and chairs. There are some great pieces in there – fancy 70s and futuristic designs of what they thought the world might look like in the twenty-first century. I couldn't however, see any information regarding the chairs at Union Station though. In my view, they ought to have been featured. The Art Institute was packed that Saturday. You cudn' move in the shop for people buying reproductions of Picasso and Matisse.

After saying goodbye to Sue, I bought a few postcards and made my way outside, though I did check if they had anything on the St Ives and Newlyn Schools (They did – Sue's influence at work!). Two huge statues of lions guard the Institute and so I sat just near them, resting my legs and watching some street theatre. Once I felt able to walk again, I checked into a 'Starbucks' and had a Vanilla Creme Frappacino which kept me going on my way back to the station. From Union Station I had phoned ahead to tell Jim what time my train got back to Downers Grove. He was there to meet me. After the kind of pace I had set all day, my legs were like jelly, and Jim sensed I needed a beer. He knew of a local micro-brewery, but first off, wanted to show me the Downers Grove Methodist Church – apparently founded by the Cornish – and where Jim had attended when he was younger. The building, at the top end of the high street, was large and extensive, so different in form than those back home. Nevertheless, the starkness was still there, that as a Cornishman you come to expect. Never mind all this abstinence and tee-totalism though. And forget about your Methodys. I needed a beer.

Chicago had worked me over big time. In the early evening, the micro-brewery was relatively quiet in terms of customers, but relatively loud in terms of noise. A large jukebox was blasting out. To talk, we asked if the waitress would turn it down a little. She obliged and suddenly everyone in the bar found themselves shouting. We ordered some samples of the micro-brewery's beers and tested them, like two experts from the Campaign for Real Ale. There was much recalling of Skinners, Sharpes and Spingo, which we both argued were infinitely better than the ones in front of us. However, for now, they would do just fine. I gave Jim a present to thank him for hosting me: a copy of Jethro Tull's 1987 Grammy-winning album *Crest of a Knave*. That record had been the soundtrack of my University days, and there was one track – 'Farm on the Freeway' – that I just knew was right up Jim's street.

Talking with Jim, I sensed a real yearning for Cornwall and for a Cornish way of life, that defined many of the Cornish-Americans I was to about to meet on my travels, but which in his words was 'unachievable'. The connection to the place and his cultural sense of self were well-defined and still growing. Yes, he fancied living in some cottage in Cornwall, where his ancestors came from, but the reality of that was unsustainable. For one thing, permanent residence could not easily be guaranteed. How would he live and work? Getting back, in essence, at the start of the twenty-first century was paradoxically, perhaps more difficult than going away. Sue Pellowe had noted this as well. These issues were with me all the time as I travelled Cornish America, and Jim, at the start of the visit, helped me to define some of the frustrations. They were issues of mobility and transience. One aspect that had characterised the Cornish of the past was their flexibility in order to survive. Maybe, I pondered that mobility and flexibility were now our downfall.

Jim's position was different. He had responsibilities here in America, and though his residual Cornishness had been with him since childhood, his 'activism' in America was relatively new. All the Cornish in America knew this. They aimed to promote their Cornishness and their heritage in the best way that they could. For Jim, that was through his music. For others, it was writing, singing, organising and gathering – but it was with the same purpose. The historical invisibility of the Cornish at home in wider British history was as pervasive here in American history. The cloak of invisibility could only be changed by people like Jim being active, and myself being active in writing about people like Jim – part of my reasoning behind writing this book in the first place.

The issue was wider though. As I argued in the poem 'Curse' from my collection *Love and Seaweed*, 'Unending memory. It is the curse of my nation',[12] sometimes it seems the past prevents us from the kind of mobility of our forefathers and mothers. For a territory aspiring to progress and to self-govern, that really is a terrible burden. I hurt to sing this, but the mouth-organ needed to play it. We weren't glum at knowing this. Indeed, Jim and I were in celebratory mood as we tucked into our meal that evening at the micro-brewery. It was just a fact of understanding your Cornishness. I told Jim what I had got up to in Chicago and then we headed back to the apartment to watch television (something called 'The Man Show', a sexist squint on male life – which I am sure will soon arrive in Britain – and 'South Park) and listen to music. There was, if I remember rightly, a little consumption of Guinness as well, which may be one reason I slept a little sounder that night. The temperature had dropped too.

Morning came around quickly and that Sunday, I'd be hitting the road for Mineral Point. Jim had helped to define a lot of the issues and questions that I had about Cornish America and I was sad to be leaving him. He is an important cog in the wheel of not just Cornish, but wider Celtic America. Jim didn't give me any safety instructions. He knew me well enough and also knew that I was going to meet some incredible people and places. We'd be talking over e-mail in the coming months, and I knew I'd be seeing him again relatively soon – either this end, or back beside the Tamar. I checked I'd packed everything up and drove off into the bright Sunday morning traffic.

I was heading out west, on Interstate 88, straight through the suburbs of Naperville and Aurora. On the map, I noted that to the north was the Fermi Accelerator Laboratory (whatever that was) and following 88's corridor across the State were dozens and dozens of new high-tech industries, enclosed in sparkling and mirrored buildings, each seemingly with a fountain and artificial lake in front of them. You could feel the money and investment everywhere, and the clamour for a slice of internet pie. I hadn't been on this route before in the eastern half of the State, though had travelled the western half on my way up to a Celtic Studies conference in Milwaukee. I was thinking of that very conference as I travelled this new stretch of road. It had been a particularly eventful one – with myself, an Irishman, a Welshman and an East Indian girl beginning the night on 'So-Co' (that's 'Southern Comfort') and ending it by singing a number at three a.m. in the morning at a Blues club. I'll spare you the detail but I missed much of the first day. I was there in spirit, just not in reality.

Milwaukee is a pleasant city though, and one day I want to go back. Milwaukee has a lot of Cornish history attached to it, though it is not always very positive. It seems to be more a temporary stopping-off point for those coming in through Canada. In a fairly famous account, the west-Cornwall based Richard Wearne (perhaps a distant relation of Jim) left St Ives in 1848, headed for Canada, but upon reaching Montreal and not liking it much there, decided to travel to Wisconsin. In Milwaukee we learn how he found the lodgings expensive but managed to hire an ox-team to take him and his family to the lead-mining region in the south-west of the State.[13] Rowe also records how Milwaukee not only welcomed new Cornish emigrants but also allowed adventurers to go exploring. In 1843 an adventurer sailed from Milwaukee up to the Falls of St Mary's but found it miserable. He noted 'A country of this character will require a great deal of labour and privation as well as capital, and at least two years to determine its character as a copper region.'[14] Nevertheless, other notable

Cornishmen began their American life in Milwaukee, though were like most others, gazing westwards. At Quinnesec, the Vivian Mine was run by a Curnow from Milwaukee and one William Pengilly left the Cornish community there to become treasurer of Menominee County.[15] There aren't too many Cornish connections there now – except one: Arthur E. Angove, an elderly doctor, with a wonderfully warm personality who practices in the city, but lives nearby in New Berlin. Arthur knows all about his Cornish roots and bought several of my books over the years. He was introduced to me by Ann Trevenen Jenkin, who at that same conference had just received an award for being International Celtic Woman of the Year, because she had – amongst other things – become the Cornish Gorseth's first female Grand Bard. So perhaps Milwaukee does have something going for it, beyond beer.

Sadly, I wasn't heading to Milwaukee, but the small Illinois town of De Kalb. I don't know much about De Kalb and expect I never will. However, it must be an important place because it seems to be signposted all over northern Illinois. Wherever you look, some sign is referring how to get to it or away from it. After De Kalb I then turned north onto Interstate 39 and put my foot down for Wisconsin. Illinois round these parts is very flat. Everywhere you look there is corn being grown. Great articulated irrigation systems trundle through the fields like massive centipedes, making sure that the stalks receive just the right amount of water. This wasn't travels in Cornish America. This was travels in *Corn* America. But things were about to change.

Notes

1. *11th Gathering of Cornish Cousins, September 27-30, 2001, Mineral Point, Wisconsin*, Programme, p.15.
2. Mick Catmull (dir.) (2002) *Dewhelans / The Homecoming*, Plymouth: BBC.
3. See, for example, Ralph Dunstan (1932) *Cornish Dialect and Folk Songs*, Truro: Jordan's Bookshop.
4. For a context on this, see Philip Payton and Bernard Deacon, 'The Ideology of Language Revival' in Philip Payton (ed.) (1993) *Cornwall Since the War: The Contemporary History*

of A European Region, Redruth: Institute of Cornish Studies and Dyllansow Truran, pp.271-90.

5. For a full version of this, see Alan M. Kent and Tim Saunders (eds.) (2000) *Looking at the Mermaid: A Reader in Cornish Literature 900-1900*, London: Francis Boutle, pp.228-31.
6. See Ray Bradbury (1997 [1953]) *The Golden Apples of the Sun*, London: Pocket Books.
7. A.L. Rowse (1991 [1969]) *The Cornish in America*, Redruth: Dyllansow Truran, pp.211-2. In the USA, this book was published in the same year as *The Cousin Jacks: The Cornish in America*, published by Charles Scribner of New York.
8. A.C. Todd (1995 [1967) *The Cornish Miner in America*, Spokane, Washington: The Arthur H. Clark Co., p.143.
9. Rowse op.cit., p.237.
10. John Rowe (1974) *The Hard Rock Men: Cornish Immigrants and the North American Mining Frontier*, Liverpool: Liverpool University Press, p.210.
11. Susan Pellowe (1994) *A Wesley Family Book of Days*, Aurora, Illinois: Renard, (1989) *Saffron and Currants: A Cornish Heritage Cookbook*, Aurora, Illinois: Renard.
12. Alan M. Kent (2002) *Love and Seaweed*, St Austell: Lyonesse Press, pp.64-65.
13. Rowe, op.cit., p.51.
14. Ibid., p.72.
15. Rowse, op.cit., pp.177-8.

2

Ez Kêz . . . ?

As you cross the State line from flat Illinois into slightly
hilly Wisconsin, a sign you simply cannot miss is a large
yellow one that simply says 'Cheese ahead'. Wisconsin, all
54,314 square miles of it, in case you didn't know by now,
is very proud of its dairy industry and therefore famous for
its superlative cheese production. The sign on Interstate 90
is bigger than the 'Welcome to Wisconsin' sign and it
always amuses me that the keen cheese outlet advertisers
might anticipate that everyone heading north into the State
might suddenly feel like some cheese while they are on the
road. You could hear the conversations in cars in front of
me.

"Barney, stop the dang car right now! I've just got to have
me some Monterey Jack!"

"Me too! Edna – get me some of that there weird-
coloured spreadable cheddar . . ."

"And while we're at it, let's get us a photo underneath the
udders of that 50 foot high giant Holstein cow outside the
cheese outlet . . ."

I joke, but if you want cheese, you've got it . . .

I read the old Cornish language tongue-twister 'Ez kêz?
ez, po neg ez; ma sêz kêz, Dro kêz; po negez nê, dro peth ez'
[Is there cheese? Is there, or isn't there, if there is cheese,
bring cheese; if there isn't cheese, bring what there is] in a
reading I was giving before a packed Mineral Point Opera
House at the 11th Gathering of Cornish Cousins in 2001. I

called it 'The Cornish Cheese Poem' and it went down a storm. At the end of my spot, I got a standing ovation, and all over the weekend people kept coming up to me and secretly giving me cheese to taste. At the Cornish Village Green Fair beside the Library I quite rightly had to try every cheese going. Yes, I had to conclude, there was cheese.

The last time I was in Mineral Point for the Gathering, I barely had time to take it all in – including the cheese. If I wasn't giving a reading, I was giving a lecture (one on Cornu-English, the other on the Literature of Cornwall), and if I wasn't doing any of that, then I was meeting old friends and gaining new ones. All told, it meant that Mineral Point was a kind of bright blur of Cornish-American-ness, which this time I resolved, I wanted to take in more carefully. Mineral Point was being by-passed that summer, but I was still coming in on the old part of Highway 151 from Madison, Wisconsin's State capital. Highway 151 cuts west through rolling Galena limestone rock and dairy herds, then drops into the 'blue mound' lead-mining belt that Mineral Point is the epicentre of. A green sign greets you: 'Mineral Point, Population 2617'. Beneath, it says 'Twinned with Redruth, Cornwall, U.K.' Notice it doesn't say England. Someone here is switched on. They know their UK territorial politics do the people of Mineral Point, which in many ways you might expect – seeing as how in these parts, this town is the ultimate Cornish pilgrimage site. I can then, in all seriousness say, that I love Mineral Point. You'll soon see why.

Opposite the twinning sign, is the 'Miner's Point Eatery and Bake Shop'. It was lunchtime, and breakfast in Chicago had been a long time ago. I pulled in and eyed the attention to mineralogical and Cousin Jack detail. The 'T' of Point had cleverly been made into a pick, and outside they promised 'Miner's Steak Pie' at $3.99. Inside it was even better. Deb Blum, the assistant manager, pointed out the bill of fare. There was 'Miner's Melt' (Burger with sautéed onion, melted cheese, served on grilled sourdough) for $3.99, 'Miner's Mouthful' (Burger topped with bacon, cheddar cheese, lettuce, tomato, onion, mayo and pickle) or I could have 'Papa Pat's Pasty' (Flaky crust, fresh in-gredients – choice of beef, chicken or gourmet mushroom) for $3.59. Then, in that most American of fast-food phrases, there was the 'Pasty Combo' – which was a choice of pasty, one side and one beverage – all for $4.99. On the other side of menu were a range of ice cream treats – all with scrumptious mining-themed names: 'Landslides', 'Mudslides', 'Miner's Delight' and the wonderfully-titled 'Brownie Cave In', available in small, regular and large. In the end I settled on a 'Miner's Melt' and planned out my time at Mineral Point. Last time I had stayed with some wonderful people – Kenny and Marion Schmitz – but I knew they would be on holiday when I'd planned to pass through, so I would have to seek some alternative accommodation later on.

As I waited for my order, I peered out onto Dodge Street and contemplated all that I knew about Mineral Point's history from the first time I had visited. This area of Southwest Wisconsin is described in geographical terms as 'driftless' meaning that it was not heavily scoured by the glaciers of the last Ice Age that passed over much of the rest of the State. As a result of this, minerals at the surface of the land were not covered by glacial debris and the location of lead and zinc ores could easily be determined. This was to eventually lead to the thriving mining industry to which Mineral Point owes much of its beauty, wealth and history. Native Americans had actually been mining lead in the region for some years when the French explorer Nicholas Perrot visited the region in 1690, but it took until the 1820s for an influx of non-native miners who arrived to take advantage of the rich deposits. Most of them came from New England and States to the south, particularly Missouri. They generally only worked shallow, surface mines, with shovels, buckets and a windlass. Some of them even lived in the holes that they had dug and these were named 'badger holes', giving their name to Wisconsin, the 'Badger State', and also contributing to the State's coat of arms, which shows a cowboy and miner.

In 1836, the Wisconsin Territory's first governor, one Henry Dodge (a man whose name will be played many times by this particular mouth-organ), was inaugurated, and served his first term out of Mineral Point. It was around this time that the Cornish in large numbers, brought their advanced hard rock and deep mining skills to the area, and made their long-lasting impact. The lead industry declined in the 1860s, but zinc mining developed in the 1880s and continued into the twentieth century. After new technology slowed the demand for lead and zinc, Mineral Point's industrial focus waned and the area turned more to agriculture, with many of the Cornish buying places on the range and diversifying into supplies for the farmers.[1]

However, the 1930s saw the birth of Mineral Point's preservation movement, which developed on a larger scale in the 1960s when artists, crafts-people and preservationists began to restore more of the town's old mining buildings, – many of them built by the Cornish – and in 1971, Mineral Point was listed as Wisconsin's first historic district on the National Register of Historic Places. Any map you see of Wisconsin clearly marks Mineral Point upon it.

Deb Blum brought over my 'Miner's Melt' and I tucked in. It was delicious. It had been a long drive up from Chicago that morning and I ate the Melt in minutes. Cheese and I go well together.

After lunch, I headed down to Pendarvis – one of the most famous Cornish locations in North America. The Pendarvis State Historical Park consists of a group of Cornish miners' cottages built over 150 years ago and now restored to their supposed appearance during the lead mining area in Mineral Point. The three-story stone and log house now named *Polperro* was built during 1842-3 by an English miner named George Kislingbury. Features of the house include the exterior stone chimney and the use of logs on the upper stories. The one-story stone cottage, *Pendarvis*, was named by two important preservationists Robert Neal and Edgar Hellum after their rehabilitation of it in the mid 1930s.[2] It was built by Cornish stonemasons around 1845 for one Henry Williams and features a symmetrical front elevation with a central entrance and six-over-six windows. The walls are 18 inches thick and constructed of locally quarried Galena limestone (apologies for getting a little 56 Inch Cylinder-ish then). Just to the right of *Pendarvis* House is a two-story side-gable house constructed around 1843, also by Cornish stonemasons, the now patriotically-named *Trelawny*.

I pulled past the weeping willow trees into the parking lot for *Pendarvis*. Right next to it is the 'Merry Christmas Mine' and 'Prairie' where there are trails to lead and zinc mining remnants, a restored prairie and the miners' 'badger' holes. Later, I had a quick stank around these and was amazed at the conditions these early miners lived in. The way *Pendarvis* is now set up is that you follow a tour guide who is dressed up in authentic 'Cousin Jenny'-style costume. Ours was named Cathy Branaugh, and although she later told me she hadn't been working at *Pendarvis* for long, she had a good handle on Cornish history. She was dressed in a cream-coloured long dress, with a small kind of 'gook' on her head. The tour began in an ancillary building on the Pendarvis estate, where there was a map of Cornwall hanging on the wall. This was Cathy's starting point as she began her narrative of Cornish emigration.

It was hard to know whether I should own up at this point and tell her I was Cornish, but I had a feeling my ethnicity would come out as we wandered around the site. That afternoon, two other couples from the mid-West were with me (all baseball hats, denim shorts and tanned legs) and they were busily asking questions. The tour makes much of the concept of Mineral Point being 'where Wisconsin began'; its name being derived from the *point* at the east end of the city where *mineral* was first discovered – *mineral* being the local name for lead. In fact, you can still feel *mineral* in the water. The one and only time I took a bath in Mineral Point, it felt like I was bathing in liquid lead!

Outside we passed a workshop, which Neal and Hellum had obtained from elsewhere in the County, then entered into the first dwelling, *Polperro*. It is characterised by a limestone block lower level with white sash windows, while upstairs is formed from logs and plaster, giving an enchanting striped effect as you might expect an American cabin to be. Inside it smelt some old, but was beautifully restored. In the front room were various tools and implements used by the miners, and I made a few 56 Inch Cylinder Syndrome-style comments about the various gads, picks, shovels, cobbing hammers and rock drills on display. The Trevithick Society would have been proud of me. Upstairs were bedrooms and a compact kitchen, all very

Cornish in design. You could near smell the pasties being baked. It was close in there, as we Cornish say, on that August afternoon and hard to believe that people could have stood inside for long periods of time. In winter, I suspected, it would be a different matter.

Cathy explained that the street outside – "Shake-Rag-under-the-hill" – was so named because the women would stand outsides their cabins and shake a rag to notify the men that it was time to eat. Of course, the Merry Christmas Mine was just opposite so some did not have too far to walk back home; for others who no doubt worked further away, the signal must have worked well. Cornish arrivals in the area actually dated back much earlier than I thought, to 1819, and although there were now only three main properties along 'Shake Rag' itself, many more once existed, picked clean by local people for other buildings. I was imagining all of this as Cathy led us outside into the garden of *Polperro* and across to the Pendarvis property. You step outside onto a small brick path which winds through hostas and ferns. From here, you can glance back and see the neat stonework of *Polperro's* chimney.

We were led around the rear of the one-storey *Pendarvis* property, where a tiny human-made waterfall runs, almost like a Cornish Holy Well, and then we went inside. What is incredible about both *Pendarvis* and the *Trelawny* property next to it, is that it looks as if they have simply been plucked from St Just-in-Penwith or Redruth and placed down here. The only architectural difference is the stonework – limestone instead of granite. *Trelawny* is equally as interesting. It is a two-storey property, now fully furnished and in excellent condition.

The Neal and Hellum story is worth diverting to. It was in 1935 that Robert Neal first bought the decrepit stone house on Shake Rag Street, later to become *Pendarvis*. Neal, who had a Cornish grandmother, intended to preserve these Cornish cottages, so he enlisted the help of a partner, Edgar Hellum of Stoughton, and together, the two men took the century-old stone building from a state of collapse to complete repair and restoration, purposely furnishing them with antiques and lead mining tools.

Once *Pendarvis* had been restored, it opened in the late

1930s as a tea-room, offering Cornish specialities, including pasties, Saffron Cake, Pendarvis White Fruit Cake and Cornish Plum Preserves. The rooms are still set for Cornish high tea, and filled with mid-twentieth century recipe sheets and cards. So successful was the project that Pendarvis soon became a nationally acclaimed restaurant specialising in Cornish fayre. Over time they adapted the old dwellings to additional uses including retail and gallery space, guest cottages and the recreation of a Cornish pub, sometime between 1956 and 1964. Meanwhile the work was supported by leading figures in the town – such as the Gundry family. By 1970, the year the restaurant closed, Neil and Hellum assured the persistence of their work by arranging for the State Historical Society of Wisconsin to operate the site. Hellum was later made a bard of the Cornish Gorseth, taking the appropriate bardic name 'Pendarvis'.

When these 'Shake-Rag' properties had been seen, Cathy led us up some steps and onto the rear lawns, where at one time, teas had been served. We followed the path around to the left, past a spot where a deer and her fawn had nestled in for the night; the trampled vegetation all that now remained of her presence. That brings you out before the Rowhouse. Built in the 1840s, the Rowhouse consists of three restored Cornish miner's houses. The log cabin on the left was the first to be built, followed by the stone building on the right; then these two buildings were linked by the addition of the front and back walls to create the middle house. We went first into the lower part of the building on the right. Beneath the balcony we entered through a tiny door into what effectively, is a tiny restored and imagined Cornish kiddlywink. Alongside the walls ran wooden benches and inside is a small bar from which beer was served. Again, it felt like stepping in to one of the now few 'un-reconstructed' inns back home. In the middle property was an exhibition devoted to the work of Neal and Hellum. As well as their architectural work, there were samples of other craftsmanship they had completed and Hellum's bardic outfit.

I went for a nose in the shop and met with Sandy Molzhon, the manager. I'd met Sandy before at the Cornish

Gathering in 2001 and it was good to see her again. She took me through the shop and explained the real difficulty she had in finding St Piran's flags. I suggested a company back home that she might contact. One little amusing item they have in the shop is a carving of a Tommyknocker,[3] made by a local woodcarver named Bert Bohlin. He stands watching over the book selection, holding a pick-axe in his short, stubby arms, while a miner's candle is perched on his helmet. Sandy explained they could sell hundreds if only they could find a manufacturer of tiny Tommyknockers. You might well have come across the Stephen King novel – *The Tommyknockers*. Yes, it's based on this tradition.

Sandy then reminded me of a cold drink on the same lines. I bought a cold bottle of *Tommyknocker* 'Original Orange Creme' which went down very well. On the bottle is a Cousin Jack (complete with candle, helmet and bushy beard) about to tuck into an extra-large slice of juicy orange. The spiel on the back of the bottle ran: 'Tommy-knockers slipped into the Colorado gold camps with the immigrating Cornish miners during the 1859 gold rush. These mischievous elves guided many a fortunate miner to the Motherlode. Renew the legend – share a Tommy-knocker Orange Creme with a friend. Bottled under license from Tommyknocker Brewery, Vancol Industries Inc. Denver.' I liked the idea of 'renewing the legend' so I bought a few more bottles to take with me. I knew I'd be heading for Colorado and this was a neat way of anticipating what was to come. I gathered there were other flavours too – Root Beer, Lime, Strawberry and Almond. For a while, I chatted with Cathy Branaugh – our guide – and another helpful lady named Kristie Popp who worked at Pendarvis. We covered a lot of ground about the site's history and their future plans. Kristie recommended that if I didn't have accommodation to head up to the 'Comfort Inn'. Her husband Dennis, would put me on the Pendarvis Corporate Rate. Beauty! I left Pendarvis this time knowing it a good deal better than before and feeling like I had made some real friends there. It was a good feeling.

I took one last look back along Shake Rag. This was of course the epicentre of Cornish activity in Mineral Point. It was here that Uncle Abner Nicholls's legendary tavern lay, and from here ran stage-coaches to Galena. Rowse mentions that the one-time driver of this stage-coach was named Bob Nancollas and he brought in miners to drink and gamble from Saturday night to Monday morning.[4] Fiddles and dancing were all part of the general activity at Uncle Ab's, while a good deal of money was played and fought for on the tables. There were fights, duels and nudity. One visitor to Mineral Point – G.A. Featherstonhaugh – describes how at Uncle Ab's a man shamelessly stood before the fire, with nothing but his nether garments on. Then there were tales of the seven feet four inches tall Cornishman called 'Shaddick' who was known as the 'Scotch giant' employed at Mineral Point making lead shot, but who later reverted to a prior profession by travelling in one of the earliest circuses of the mid-West.[5] Now it was all silent but incredibly moving to be there.

I next decided to renew my acquaintances with a few of the more interesting buildings in the town. Mineral Point is a pot pourri of architectural styles ranging from American Four Square and Colonial, to Italianate and Prairie (for the latter, read modern). Add on top of that, the Cornish influence, and you have a very eclectic range of architecture. Typically the Cornish dwellings, as I had seen at Pendarvis, had stone which was carefully cut for the façade, but for the rear and sides of the building it was left rough, just as it had come from the quarry. Many of the buildings tell stories about their Cornish owners' lives. On the north side of town for instance, there is the Methodist Episcopal Church which demonstrates features from the Gothic Revival, with asymmetrical towers and pointed-arch windows. Not surprisingly the first Methodist church was organised early on – in 1834 as the Cornish arrived, by William Kendall, William Phillipps (who had served in the Black Hawk Indian War), Andrew Remfrey and James Nancarrow,[6] though this church was dedicated slightly later in 1838. I had eaten inside there during the 2001 Cornish Gathering – where I seem to remember a meal with a lot of corn and mashed potato in it. Don't laugh – it was all very tasty.

Many of the houses have Cornish family names directly attached to them. There is the William Lanyon, Jr. House (the Lanyons owned a foundry), the David Jacka House

(Jacka operated a feed and grain business, and owned a general store) and the Joseph Gundry House (Gundry moved to Mineral Point in 1845 and had fingers in lots of pies – including banking and mining, but is best known as the partner of John Gray in ownership of the Gundry and Gray Dry Goods store on the High Street, which ran between the 1850s and the late 1930s).[7] The Gundry House is built in the Italianate Style with an expansive front porch, befitting Gundry's high social status in the town. On North Chestnut Street is the Samuel Jenkins House. Jenkins came to Mineral Point in 1841 to mine lead, but was tempted to California in 1850 to mine for gold. Like numerous other Cornish, Jenkins was not particularly successful, and so returned to Mineral Point a few years later, opening a general store, and later a hardware store. He had to settle for pots and pans rather than huge nuggets.

Downtown is the Masonic Temple. The Lodge No.1 Free and Accepted Masons of Mineral Point were founded in 1841, and was the first formed in the State of Wisconsin. The building was first erected by the lodge in 1897 after fire destroyed the lodge rooms on lower High Street, and John Charles, a Cornish immigrant and architect, designed the eastern half of the building – now famed for its rusticated limestone and hip roof dormers. On the High Street you can also find the Richard Penhallegon Building (a former cigar and tobacco store) and the Vivian Building (once housing the Cornishman Dr John Vivian's medical and drug store). Midway-up is the City Hall, Opera House and Public Library, built in 1913. The Opera House now has a worn feel to it (graffiti adorns the walls backstage) but the elaborate ornamental plaster is still in good shape, if a little grubby. It has great acoustics. John F. Kennedy visited the Opera House in 1960 while campaigning for the presidency and Alan M. Kent visited the Opera House in 2001 while reading a poem about cheese. Apparently, the Opera House is due to be renovated, but I hope they keep its original feel.

At 215 High Street, built of Italianate sandstone in 1871, is the important Gundry and Gray Building. Now re-opened, the building is famous for the zinc cast statue of a dog that sits above the shop windows. He has been adopted by the community as the 'Mineral Pointer' and is now seen on everything ranging from T-shirts to tourist literature. Apparently, the canine landmark was first used as a symbol for the store following the Cornish custom of identifying stores with animal statues (a new one for me). You can now see a miniature of the Pointer on the sign that welcomes you to Redruth, back home. I like the Pointer. I think he's cute.

I could go on and on about the buildings in Mineral Point. You really need to go and have a geek for yourself. But just to give you a feel of what else there is to see, look at the Otis Hendra Building (a grocery store), the Primitive Methodist Church ('bolters' from the Episcopal), the Thomas Trerorah House, the George Huxtable House (there are still Huxtables in the town today) and the William Tregray House. At the bottom end of town, where Commerce street forks, is the Mineral Point Railroad Depot, now no longer in use, but constructed by John Toay and Philip Allen, who were two Cornish stonemasons who emigrated to Wisconsin together in 1842.

One wonders how people like Toay and Allen tolerated this first mining frontier. Stabbing, shootings and scrapes were common. A fair amount of blood had already been shed in terms of removing the earlier Indian threat from the region, but further quarrels followed. As an example, Rowe records that there was an affray between the 'two-gun packing' editor of the Mineral Point-based *Miners' Free Press*, Henry B. Walsh, and 'Charley' Breedan, one of the more prominent public figures in the mining community. Walsh had apparently called Breedan a liar and a coward in several editorials, and the feud, like many others had its origin in some of the mining claims. Breedan shot first, hitting Walsh in the shoulder, while Walsh sent a parting shot after Breedan, which missed.[8] Fortunately, there was none of this kind of behaviour going on in Mineral Point now, though I hear Friday nights can be a little rowdy.

Spatially, Mineral Point is constructed like a yoke, the main route through from Madison to Dubuque the arms of the yoke. To the north, the land of the Point dips away into the distance, and to the south, encased in the arms of yoke lies downtown and the business district. At the end of that lies 'Shake Rag' Street and the roads south to Illinois and the Mississippi. In some senses all the roads link up. If

47

you climb Shake Rag you end back up on Dodge Street; if you travel Fountain Street, you are soon back on Ridge Street. It was to Ridge Street I was heading now. As the afternoon heat began to cool, I decided to explore Mineral Point's three main cemeteries. The earliest, St Pauls, was established in 1851 and is found at Ridge Street on the western end of town. Carefully, I treaded down through the cemetery noting the names of the Cornish. There were many there. The first I came across was the name Rule, but shortly afterwards I found a Tonkin, Hamlyn and Cocking. Not far from these were Williams, Biddick, Trevillian, Trenwith and Remfrey. I worked my way down through layers of time; the earliest graves at the top, the more recent at the bottom, and especially noted the continuation of names here. Some of these were not from the nineteenth century, but much more recent. According to the historian of south-west Wisconsin, Louis Albert Copeland, the earliest man buried in a cemetery in Mineral Point was a Cornishman named Josiah Thomas, but even in Copeland's day, historians were unable to agree a date, and they and I were unable to find his grave.

I moved on to the larger Graceland Cemetery in the north. It was established slightly later in 1860 and shows how prevalent the Cornish had become in Mineral Point. One of the more spectacular monuments is devoted to Joseph Gundry, born in Porkellis, Wendron May 11, 1822 and died in Mineral Point July 17, 1899. As I explained, the Gundrys were a significant shopkeeping family in the town, and the Pointer is situated above their shop. Like its quoit namesake in West Cornwall, one of the more spectacular tombs is exquisitely inscribed with the name *Lanyon*, while near the main gate is a beautifully carved headstone with the name *Penhallegon* upon it. These family graves, in most cases, relate to the buildings mentioned above. I spent much of the late afternoon there, walking among the grave stones of people who I seemed to know: Hendra, Kitto, Nancolas, Coad, Goldsworthy, Ivey, Jewell, Quick, Vivian, Treweek, Roberts, Benson, Polkinghorn, Prideaux, Martin, Harris, Thomas, Treloar and Opie. I hoped that they had found grace in this foreign land. It looked that way. Back across the road from the 'Miner's Point Eatery' is St Mary's. This

48

cemetery is later, established in 1873, and here intertwined with Schmitz, Kauffman, Kieffer and Gevelinger were Philipps, Whiford, Cocking, May, Rundle, Goldsworthy, Tonkin, Uren and Richards. It seemed only right that they looked upon a place that sold 'Pasty Combos'. I played a blues for them on my imaginary mouth-organ.

Afternoon was becoming evening. I heeded the advice of the team at *Pendarvis* and made my way along Dodge Street out to the 'Comfort Inn'. I was greeted at the desk there by Kristie Popp's husband, Dennis, a kind and gentle man who quickly sorted me out a room and made me feel very welcome. The 'Comfort Inn' at Mineral Point is a fairly new, typically designed traveller's hotel, and comes complete with a swimming pool and hot tub, both of which I used during my stay. I had been there before. The 'Comfort Inn' had hosted the Cornish Gathering's banquet the previous autumn; one of those long drawn-out affairs where civic leaders, Governors and State Representatives make seemingly endless speeches welcoming Cornish officials like the Cornish Gorseth's then – Grand Bard, John Bolitho, and Cornwall's 'unofficial' ambassador to America, Howard Curnow, who has done so much to invigorate and inspire Cornish-Americans over the years. This was followed by a mass singing of 'Trelawny' by all of the conference delegates. Now the plush hotel was a lot quieter and seemed only to be populated by a number of construction workers who were on a permanent layover whilst the town's by-pass was being completed, and tourists heading north to the lakes of the Wisconsin Dells or the famous architectural site known as the 'House on the Rock'.

I met one of the latter in the pool later that evening. Peter was only in his early forties but already a grandfather of some years, and was taking his wife and grandson to see the 'House on the Rock'. He came from Iowa and worked for the Iowa State Agricultural Fair. It's hard to explain – but he looked old; you know, forty going on seventy. I could tell he was a farmer by his suntan. His fore-arms and head and neck were a healthy-looking bronze, while the rest of his body looked white as snow. No, let me correct that. In fact, he seemed almost blue. We swam a few lengths of the pool together and talked about how he and I had come to end up in the same pool together on this particular day. He knew all about the Cornish in Mineral Point and asked me about pasties. He'd never travelled outside of America. That interested me. I wondered how he conceived of the rest of the world from Iowa, and tried to draw that out of him. I didn't really succeed. He didn't know much about the world beyond Iowa. This vacation was the first he'd taken in two or three years and with that he'd come just one State over. I saw his wife the next morning at breakfast. She too, looked old before her time and was dressed dowdily in typical mid-western female gear – white trainers, baggy trousers and a cardigan with teddy bears on it. They were pleasant enough, but I couldn't help but fear for the very soul of America. In that single instant I understood why Marilyn Manson existed.

That evening I planned to visit the 'Cruise Bar'. I don't know how it happened, but the 'Cruise Bar' is now 'infamous' in its association with me, everyone at the Cornish Gathering in 2001, and simply anyone who is Cornish and happens to be passing through Mineral Point. It happened like this. On that trip, my Probus-born friend, Steven 'Curgie' Curgenven and myself were looking for a bar. We peered into the various bars that lined the High Street, but for some reason we ended up in the 'Cruise'. The 'Cruise' is owned by Cathy – and locally, people in Mineral Point call it 'Cathy's'. Curgie is the gregarious type (to put it mildly) and the first night there witnessed much drinking (*Amber Bock* is the boy to put you in the mood), singing and karaoke (Steppenwolf's 'Born to be 'Cornish'' anyone?).

This was followed by the second night whereupon a few more people from the Gathering showed up, and was again accompanied by a night of much drinking, singing and karaoke. Not only this but the American 'Celtic' folk band *Woad* also arrived to begin a session. *Woad* are led by the Minneapolis-based singer/guitarist and Celtic expert Danny Proud, accompanied by mandolin player Scott Soule and Frank Siegle. In their own way, *Woad* are quite special. They are perhaps what you might expect to see in an American 'Celtic'-themed group from Minneapolis; then again, they are not. Put another way: if I were writing a feature film about a typical Celtic band operating in America, I might have even called the band *Woad*. Hell, I would even cast them in the part. Then again, Danny is an exceptional linguist and very witty – able to poke fun at themselves and the Celts. I bought their album – 'One for the Woad'. On it are tracks like 'Y Gelynnen' and 'Cainc y Datgeiniad', but also the Cornish-themed 'Jowan Bon', 'Fish Tin and Copper', 'Tam Pearce' and 'Plethyn Newlyn'. I can't tell you exactly how many times we sang 'Goin' up Camborne Hill' or 'Trelawny', but they got louder and more raucous every time. What was great about it was that it was organic and eclectic. By the final night of the Gathering, the 'Cruise' had been established as the Cornish bar – well, bar none really. In short, chaos ensued. Result: I love everyone at the 'Cruise' and they seem to love us too. Probus Comrades Club and the 'Cruise' are now twinned (I don't think Redruth minds too much). Curgie and I had very, very, very bad hangovers.

When I walked back in, it was like I hadn't been away. The karaoke machine was in the same place and the same music was on the jukebox. Cathy and Bethy (why is it that everyone's name ends with a 'y'?) were still behind the bar and a display of Cornish memorabilia was up on the wall. Obviously, it was a lot quieter this time. Perhaps that was a good thing as well. I had more driving ahead of me the next day. For old times sake though, I ordered an *Amber Bock* and Cathy made me one of the Cruise's special melts. Yes – there was cheese. Lots of it.

We caught up on what everyone had been doing – where 'Hux-ay' (one of the Huxtables), 'Bill-ay' and the rest of the boys (whose names end in 'y'), who usually sat around the bar were, and remembered the previous Gathering. *The Cruise* is the kind of place you wish you had on your doorstep every weekend, and in many ways, they seemed to wish the Cornish were there more often. Then again, crossing the Atlantic of a Friday night, was a helleva long way to go for a pint of *Amber Bock* . . . When speedy time travel is invented, that'll be one of the places I'd dial up. Beam me up, Cousin Jack.

The next morning, I had another look around the town, stopping off at the famous 'Lawinger's Red Rooster Cafe' on the High Street. Here, and in Madison, the pasties are sometimes called 'teddy wedgers'. Teddy, is a corruption of tatie or potato, and perhaps they looked like a wedge, so hence the name. I'd actually fancied a bit of teddy wedger that morning, so stopped by. Besides the cafe's great name I liked the look of their 'Homemade Cornish Pasty, Figgyhobbin and Bread Pudding'. I'd been in the 'Red Rooster' before with Curgie, so I knew what to expect. There is a rectangular bar you can sit around (traditionally the kind of place in the mid-West where farmers eat and say "Yup!" to everything that should be changed in the world and 'Nope!' to everything wrong with it) while in the back and on the sides are tables proper. I sat at the bar, ordered a coke and a pasty. The woman behind the counter guessed from my accent that I was Cornish. I could feel the buzz of excitement in the kitchen.

"Hell, girls we've got a real, living breathing Cornishman in," I could almost hear the supervisor saying. "That pasty better be real good . . ."

They needn't have worried. It tasted very good, but that did not stop the women in the kitchen from coming out and checking on how it was going down. I needed that pasty that morning. I had showed up a bit late for breakfast at the 'Comfort Inn', and there wasn't a lot of choice left.

After feeling like one of the farmers at the 'Red Rooster', and having said "Yup!" and "Nope!" a lot, I strolled around the High Street a little more. Mineral Point is now famous for its artistic community and a lot of the shops were beginning to open. Although linked to the work of Robert Neal and Edgar G. Hellum at Pendarvis in their appreciation of craftwork, the movement can really be traced back to Max and Ava Fernekes, who moved here from Milwaukee in 1940 and made their living solely from their own artwork, and Harry Nohr, a now nationally known craftsman who turned bowls from wood after his retirement as postmaster in Mineral Point. There are potters, weavers, woodworkers on most of the downtown streets. One of the finest is the Brewery Pottery Studio, then there is the Sirius Sunlight Glass Studio, Smejas' Designs in Leather, High Point Arts and Against the Grain. In many ways, it was a bit like the streets of St Ives – all arty farty –

and for a 'Cornish' town in the twenty-first century, that actually seemed quite fitting – or should I say 'fitty'.

Later that morning, I was on my travels again. I'd agreed to meet up with Marion Howard, and her husband Stan. Marion, who is seventy-one, and Stan, now eighty-one, live some ten miles south of Mineral Point in the small town of Darlington. I'd first met Marion and her son in a departure lounge at Chicago's O'Hare airport several years ago. Marion is typically Cornish and a former public librarian, and she was standing next to someone who was a tall, wild-looking, long-bearded and long-haired biker, but who had a 'Kernow' T-shirt on. For ages, I peered across at them trying to work out who they were. I mean, I knew most people in the so-called 'Cornish movement'; what were the chances of me not knowing them? In the end I had to go over and introduce myself and say that I was from Kernow too.

It turned out that the biker with Marion was her son Edwin, and that he was escorting her over to Cornwall, where she was about to be barded at that year's Gorseth. I had stayed in touch with Marion and her family, and we had met up several times at various Cornish events. The last time, at Mineral Point, Ed had allowed me a ride on his Harley Davidson at the parking lot in Jail Alley, and we shared stories about music and motorcycling. Ed, who was in his late forties, now lived over in Madison and was part of a motorcycle club there. He was fiercely proud of his Cornish heritage. Thankfully he turned upside down all preconceptions of what the Cornish could and would be in America. I mean, how many Cornish do you know who own gleaming Harley-Davidsons and look like they've just stepped out of *Easy Rider*. I didn't want figgy-hobbin. I wanted a Harley.

Darlington – where Marion and Stan live – is not an explicitly Cornish town, but it is one of those places you might want to live, if you did live in the mid-West. The town has a smiling sheriff, and chainsaw-art carved cardinals – painted bright red – where trees have died. The Lafayette County Courthouse on top of the hill states that Darlington is a clean-living kind of town where you'd want your kids to grow up. It takes around twenty minutes to get there from Mineral Point. Marion greeted me on the veranda of her house on Keep Street, which is set above ferns and flowers. Outside flies the Stars and Stripes, though little St Piran's flags and Cornish icons, books and photographs are dotted throughout the house. Marion is originally a Paynter. There are lots of fragments and letters which have survived from the Paynter [or Painter] family.[9] Her family came to south-western Wisconsin in 1853 and have been there every since. There are still lots of Paynters back home. Look for them down St Ives. Stan and I realised we had met before – at the Gathering last year. He is the perfect foil for all things Cornish. Though his family, the Prisks, came over in the 1830s, Stan doesn't have as much time for his Cornish heritage as Marion, even though he is the perfect pard. We talked for an hour or so about everything from the weather there, to the Homecoming earlier in the summer.

Then we got on to the characteristics of the Cornish. Marion said something very interesting about her Cornish father – something I had actually noticed about my own father. She said that her mother, and they as children, often felt that they had done something wrong, because when he came home from work, her father rarely used to say anything. The quietness, she found, was unnerving, but after talking about it, we realised that lots of Cornish men behaved like this. Nothing was wrong – it was just a plain satisfaction in what they'd got in life.[10] It was a simplicity that somehow seemed out of reach in the twentieth century.

Marion has been working hard for the Cornish in North America for a number of years, and it was down to much of her hard work that the Gathering in Mineral Point had proceeded so smoothly the previous autumn. Her bardship for her services to the Cornish in America clearly meant a lot to her. She showed me a beautifully kept photograph album of her journey over that September for the bardic ceremony. I think Marion knows my views about the Gorseth; its performed invention and artificial mythos – but to hear her speak of the event, it was clear that the Gorseth was a very important construction of her personal Cornishness; something she and many other Cornish-

Americans were proud to be involved in. Her bardic name is *Eos an Howlsedhas* [Nightingale of the West].

Marion also sings and role-plays a character called Mary Ann, an imagining of Cousin Jenny, telling songs and stories of Cornwall to local schoolchildren and other interested groups. She had performed, like me, at the Opera House in Mineral Point, last September, so I knew her work very well. We laughed about the cheese again. For lunch, there was no cheese but Marion had prepared typical mid-Western food – ground beef in barbecue sauce in buns, alongside cucumber, potato salad and tomatoes. It was exactly what the doctor ordered and set me up for the rest of the day. In actual fact, over lunch Marion told me she was about to release a CD of her versions of songs first collected by Sabine Baring-Gould and Ralph Dunstan, to be titled *The Nightingale Sings*.

"Not bad for someone who is seventy-one," she offered.

"You'll be on MTV next . . ." I joked.

"I'm hoping to do a second volume," Marion said.

I didn't want to take up too much of Marion and Stan's time, so said my goodbyes and headed on my way down to Galena. Galena, they told me, was very pleasant. I should enjoy it there.

Seemingly in the middle of nowhere, though in all likelihood it was probably somewhere between Darlington and a town called Avon, I pulled off the main road because a signpost indicated a Bible Christian Chapel. Such are the desires of the travelling Cornishman in America! I followed a minor road for around two miles, and eventually around a bend I came across the stark form of a small, white-painted, wooden-built chapel. Next to it was a small graveyard. As some of you know, the Bible Christian movement was one of the offshoots of Methodism founded by one William O'Bryan from Gunwen, near Luxulyan. Considering my own family connection with Gunwen, this Chapel seemed somewhere I ought to stop.

O'Bryan was born in 1778 and dedicated his life to evangelism. However, after some 'glorious irregularities', Wesleyan Methodism excommunicated him and he set off aiming to preach in areas where there had not been any prior Methodist influence. Often these areas were rural and agricultural, and O'Bryan was very successful in north-east Cornwall and north-west Devon. In essence, as Thomas Shaw has shown, the 'Bryanite' movement represented a less ecclesiastical form of Methodism, and O'Bryan was also very successful in America, since he followed the emigrating families overseas.[11] To me, O'Bryan's branch of Methodism always seemed very strict. There were stories that his daughter once prayed to God not to make herself attractive to boys!

Gunwen seemed a long way away from the little building I discovered in Lafayette County. Everything fitted though. Clearly O'Bryan had followed the Cornish into south-western Wisconsin, and as agriculture became more of a priority he moved with them to the countryside. Inside, the place had the simplicity and stillness of chapels back home. It was a wonderful moment. Whatever personal doubts I had about Bible Christians, O'Bryan was certainly interesting. I liked his 'irregularities' and this little chapel in particular.

I headed on toward Galena, through the town of Hazel Green. This was where some of the earliest Cornish came to work; the place first being called *Hardscrabble*. In this so-called 'Blue Mounds' country, the Cornish and the Americans first mined by tunnelling into the mounds, but later with Cornish expertise came the sinking of shafts proper. Usually the mines around these parts were not very deep and were worked with a windlass. Many of them who found success here, later travelled on to California, but several returned to buy land and establish a Cornish farming community. Apparently by 1860 around half the farmers in Hazel Green were Cornish.[12] Despite the original mines being abandoned, many Cornishmen reworked these with new technology finding additional ore, one of the chief miners being Richard Eustice. I looked for this conglomeration of mines around Hazel Green, but the ground has long since been filled or dug-over, but during the 1860s this was one of the busiest mining areas in America. By 1870 Louis Albert Copeland estimated that the total Cornish population of the Upper Mississippi lead region was composed of around 7.000 individuals. Now most of it is devoted to dairy farming.

Numerous scholars refer to the life of the first 'Cousin Jack', Francis Clyma, who was one of the first Cornishmen to arrived in these parts in 1827.[13] He originated from the parish of Perranzabuloe, first emigrating to mine in Maryland in 1819, then travelling through Virginia and Kentucky to arrive in Missouri, from where he travelled up the Mississippi River to Galena and Dubuque, the older trading post. His wife, Frances Maynard, hailed from St Ewe and was the first Cornishwoman in the lead region. Because of the threat from the Native Americans, initially, they both had to live under the protection of Ferguson's Fort. Clyma and his wife were followed by men like Edward James of Camborne, who came directly from Cornwall through Quebec, Cincinnati and St Louis in 1830 (and who later held office under Colonel Henry Dodge, and fought alongside him at the Battle of the Bad Axe), and then by Francis Vivian in 1832, arriving first at Galena and then travelling to Mineral Point. It was men like these who began the flood of Cornish into Wisconsin and Illinois. Copeland mentions the comments made in a *History of Iowa County* about the Cornish who arrived there in 1832: 'Among those who came about this time was a colony of hale, hearty, strong-muscled and stronger-hearted Cornish pick and gad artists, composed in part of John Curthew, William Kendall and William Bennett'.[14] I liked that phrase: 'pick and gad artist'. It reaffirmed the artistry of mining.

I had read about Galena and its connection with the lead mining industry some years ago, and had long wanted to visit it. I knew it had Cornish connections. It was the main point of entry for many of them coming up the Mississippi and south-western Wisconsin's supply centre. In its mining heyday, river steamers loaded lead ore from its wharves; shipments reaching their peak between 1845-47 when they averaged about two million dollars in value annually.[15] Once Henry Dodge had suppressed the local Winnebago Indians in the late 1820s, culminating in the Black Hawk war, the way was open for miners and other visitors to travel to Galena. Rowse even notes that Herman Melville (1819-91), the author of *Moby Dick* (1851) spent a summer here in 1840.[16] Local people say he finished and proofread that novel here.

inding traces of the Cornish now would be more
ficult however. Galena is actually named after the Galena
ɪᴠer which runs to the Mississippi and is just over the State
line into Illinois. It now has a population of just over 3,000
people and was clearly a popular destination for day visitors
and touring coach parties, as well as more people staying
there for a week or fortnight's break. Jim Wearne had told
me that he had honeymooned there, and the town certainly
had a pleasant feel to it. Located on the waterfront, its wide
main shopping area is characterised by tall, red-bricked
buildings with hefty and ornate fire escapes. The general
feel of the place now is arty and creative. Boutiques and
galleries line the main thoroughfare. Galena's main fame
these days though seemed to derive from the fact that it was
the home of the Union General and later President, Ulysses
S. Grant. It was Grant of course, who took Vicksburg, in
the process dividing the Confederacy. That might be why
there didn't seem to be that many tourists from the South
wandering the streets of Galena. Grant had employed a
Cornishman by the name of Edward Kittoe, as his physician
and he went on to become the Surgeon-general and medical
director of the Army of the Tennesse (what later became
Tennessee), becoming a lieutenant-colonel. Numerous other
Cornish served under Grant including one Cyrus Pomeroy,
John Vincent and Major William Vincent. Many Vincents
continue to live on in Galena.

I mozeyed on down through the main drang, nipping into
shops now and again mainly to escape the heat. Not
surprisingly, in the bookshops there were lots of books
devoted to the Civil War. I was hopeful of finding more
titles on mining and perhaps even the travels of the Cornish
up and down the Mississippi, but I was out of luck. In fact,
the more I got to know Galena, the more it seemed very
keen on neglecting its mineralogical past and re-inventing
itself as a trendy day out. You can't blame it – there was
something very Cornish about that in a strange and twisted
way. That was okay by me as well. I needed a trendy day
out. After all, you can't '56 Inch Cylinder' all day long.

I stepped into a copy of 'Starbucks' and ordered a Vanilla
Creme Frappacino. That afternoon, I played tourist. For
some reason, perhaps the sun, I ended up in a shop that sold

sunglasses. I had a pair with me already, but the ones on sale in here were cheap and trendy. They'd look good back home walking through Pydar Street up to *Solo Records* I told myself. I tried on a few pairs, watched by the gay shop owner and his Dalmatian, eventually settling on a mountain-biking style pair with steel grey frames and black lenses.

"Ooo, they really suit you . . ." said the shop owner.

"Do you think so?"

"Definitely . . ."

"Okay – I'll take them."

"Sure . . . If I might say so, that's a very unusual accent for around here . . ."

"It's Cornish . . ."

"Corn-ish?? You mean like Corn-ish pasties."

"That's right."

"Well, I don't think I've *ever had* a Cornishman in here."

"I'm a writer. I'm writing a book about the Cornish in this part of the States. I know the Cornish were here, but I haven't found much yet."

"Oh well, you should check out the Museum. After this block, turn left and go up the steps. You'll see it . . ."

"Thanks."

"Well you have a nice day. Ooo – they do suit you . . ."

I followed the shopowner's advice and put the sunglasses on. I looked in a shop window. Yes, they did suit me. I climbed the steps and headed for the museum. It was free to get in, but again was a bit of a disappointment. There didn't seem to be anything on mining, let alone the presence of the Cornish in Galena. Still, I at least hoped that some Cornishman might have struck lucky in Galena. It seemed like the kind of place the Cornish could have prospered at least. For now though, I'd just have to be satisfied with Galena as it was – home of Ulysses S. Grant, and good place to buy sunglasses.

On the way down to Galena I had pulled past a dirt track at a place called Vinegar Hill that had a sign saying 'Historic Lead Mine'. On my way back, I went in. The sign looked ancient, as if it had been erected in the early twentieth century and hadn't been changed since. In terms of tourist amenities, I wudn' far wrong. I mean, I can't understand why some of these places haven't shut up shop years ago, but there they are still at it: trying to make an honest buck out of what little they've got. Let's put it this way, the 'Historic Lead Mine' at Vinegar Hill makes 'Poldark Mine' at Wendron look like a multi-million pound extravaganza. It makes the National Trust's Engine houses at Pool look like Disneyland. The emphasis is pretty low-tech. What you get on the surface is a very Cornish-looking set of sheds, surrounded by industrial debris – kibbles, wheelbarrows, trams and the like, dressed up with a cutesy sign that in a lamenting tone said, 'The sounds from this mine are silent, never to be heard no more. My digs on the prairie are over. There's grass around the old miner's door'. All that said, perhaps this was going to be my only real connection with Galena's mining past. Vinegar Hill is actually named after a Vinegar Hill back home in Cornwall, and it perhaps typical of one of the smaller Cornish mines that once operated here.

There was a girl aged about fifteen, chewing gum, sat in one of the sheds at the old miner's door.

"Hi," I said. "Come to see your mine . . ."

"That'll be five bucks."

She looked cheesed off at having to work there. Well, I suppose you would be, if you are fifteen and your dad says the only way to earn some money this summer is to sit in a rackety old shed taking money off tourists? She wanted to be down on the riverfront at Galena or at the Mall. In the sheds, the displays made a lot about the Irish, but there seemed to be Cornish-looking cap'ns doing most of the ordering around. Underground, it was much like going into a fogou. I can't say I really enjoyed it that much though. The sheer humidity there made me feel very claustrophobic and in need of getting through the tunnel and into some-where cool again – like my car. It did give me a real feel of what it must have been like down there to mine lead though – Hellish hot and uncomfortable.

On the drive back, I was tempted to head south to places like Lead Mine and New Diggings. The former sounded a lot like Vinegar Hill but I liked the sound of the latter place a lot. Most often across the States – from south-west Wisconsin, to the gold fields of California, it is pronounced

'Diggin's'. Somehow that seemed right. Cornish America was littered with places called New Diggin's, Old Diggin's and Not Quite so old Diggin's. In fact, a whole lot of Diggin's. Americans used it in the same way that the Cornish seemed to use 'Wheal' or 'Bal'. I came through Shullsburg, apparently the scene of quite a lot of diggin's over the years.

As Todd notes, Shullsburg is named after one Jesse Shull, an Indian trader who was part of the fur empire of Jacob Astor.[17] One of the town's earliest residents was Samuel Richards, who came from Treswithian Downs near Camborne. In 1848, he persuaded his illiterate brother George and his wife to join him in Wisconsin (Samuel's letters were deciphered by a class leader in their local Methodist Church), and the Richards prospered. They were all joined by the Copelands who consolidated profits made from Richards' mining store, by buying land and stock. Eventually it was one Louis Albert Copeland who was to write many articles on the Cornish for the local newspaper, *The Pick and the Gad*, long after he left Wisconsin for Los Angeles. Copeland, of course, was to become the first historian of the Cornish in south-western Wisconsin, who devotes the rest of his historical account to exploration of Cornish dialect (from *Art en?* to *Wessen 'ee?*) and habits (everything from their love of saffron cake and clotted cream to heavy cake and pilchards).[18] Among his more well-intended yet ultimately misguided comments are that the 'Cornish descendants are scattering, and have almost lost their identity as a race',[19] and that he felt, writing as early as 1898, that the 'typical Cornish characters are gradually disappearing, and soon the class that did so much in early days to develop the lead region, will live only in the remembrance of those who have seen them'.[20] Yet, as all the lead region towns prove, Copeland was ultimately wrong: Cornish identity has never been stronger, and that Cornish characteristics, as my travels here confirm, still survive.

Back in the middle of the nineteenth century though, the Copelands and the Richards were joined by the Tregonnings and Rules, who had much to do with the Centenary Methodist Church of Shullsburg, which though founded in 1867, still stands today, with its white-painted spire and

Cornish names inside. I stepped inside to have a look. The names instantly resounded around the building: Rowe, Trebilcock, Tangye, Shephard, Glendenning, Kittoe, Rule, Skews, Stephens, Berryman, Odgers, Tregonning, Sincock, Trewarthas, Trestrail, Tregloan, Hancock, George and Oates, and of course, the Richards and the Copelands. Methodism therefore had an indelible influence on the town. Even its streets are still named after virtues such as Mercy, Goodness, Judgment, Wisdom, Peace and Truth (just like St Ives with its Virgin and Teetotal streets). All of this Cornishness was leading somewhere. I didn't know it, but I was about to have a moment.

Signs pointed in to a mining museum. Being not yet cured of 56 Inch Cylinder Syndrome, and knowing something about the town's Cornish families, I had to stop and followed Shullsburg's One-Way system, stopping to briefly look at the Methodist Chapel. Then I picked someone to ask directions to the Mining Museum. Of all the people, I could have asked in Shullsburg, I picked Mr O' Neill. Mr O' Neill was a small man, half-shaven, around sixty years old and even though it was only half-past four in the afternoon, he was already half-cut.

"Excuse me," I said, "Can you tell me how to find the Mining Museum?"

"The Mining Museum . . ." said Mr O'Neill, but it came out more like the a-min-ing-mus-eumch. "Ah used t'work there . . . in the mine . . . then I became a guide . . ."

"Then you started drinking," I wanted to say.

"You turn left at the end of the street," he said, grabbing onto the car door to stop himself falling, "and tell them O'Neill sent ya . . . an' after that you come by here an' have a drink with me . . ."

I tried saying thank you, and he tried to make it clear that I *was* coming back for a drink. Mr O'Neill had a kind face, but he was a little the worse for wear. Then again, he had given me directions and I liked interesting characters.

"You int'rested in mines then?" slurred Mr O'Neill.

"Yeah, I have 56 Inch Cylinder Syndrome," I wanted to say, but instead said, "I'm Cornish. I'm researching the Cornish in this part of Wisconsin . . ."

"Oh – there was lots of Cornish here in Shullsburg, Wisconsin . . ."

Now I was going to have to come back to see Mr O'Neill. For the moment though, I took his advice and turned left at the end of the street. The Mining Museum was in an unusual site, at the bottom of a slope, surrounded on one side by tennis courts and on the other by a football pitch. Then, as I surveyed the landscape, it became clear that the recreational facilities had been placed on the original mining site. It was still unusual though. The museum was covered in dust. It looked like nobody had bothered to clean the place in twenty years. Or maybe the dust was just ingrained and felt to be realistic. Perhaps the dust was just one part of the totality of the museum experience. I went inside and shouted if anyone was there. No-one showed up for around fifteen minutes. I crept inside and looked at picture after picture of lead mining. Some of the pictures I had seen before in books on Mineral Point. In a cabinet were some souvenir plates I could buy. They said 'The Mining Museum, Shullsburg' and must have been a good idea once. I can tell you, I wasn't tempted. So that was it. Nobody showed up so I had a free look around.

I still wasn't sure about going back to see Mr O'Neill. The prospect of spending some time with a drunken sixty year old wudn' really that appealing. I was actually looking forward to spending time in the hot-tub at the Comfort Inn. However, Mr O'Neill had me sorted out. I had to follow the One-Way System to get back onto the main road. If I hadn't stopped outside his house, I know he would have walked into the middle of the road. I didn't want to kill him.

"Now, are you Cornish Zeltic" he asked, "like us Irish?"

He said Celtic that way, like the Glaswegian football team.

"Yes – like the Irish," I said. "And the Welsh . . ."

He wanted me to have a drink, but I declined the alcohol and he poured me an orange juice, spilling much of it on the kitchen table.

"Ah used to work with lots of Cornish men – an' my father, he worked with them too. They came down here from Mineral Point. See Shullsburg carried on mining long after Mineral Point was finished up . . . What do they call them?"

"Cousin Jacks . . ." I offered.

"Aye – Cousin Jacks . . . Lots of 'em here in Shullsburg, Wisconsin one time. Hard workers . . ."

It seemed like Mr O'Neill could never say Shullsburg, without putting Wisconsin after it. Maybe there was another Shullsburg just over in Illinois that confused people, or maybe he said it just to make doubly sure he knew where we both were. It turned out Mr O' Neill had just moved houses. One time he had owned a bar in town, and knew everyone's business. Now, he didn't know anybody's business and was clearly lonely. He didn't want me to go, and so I stayed for half-an-hour or so, trying to find out exactly where the Cornish worked and if he remembered any names or people. I couldn't get anything more out of him though. Finally, after much protesting about how I need to get back to Mineral Point (a hot-tub, sure to be packed with supermodels was waiting), I managed to make it to the car.

"Alan, you put me in your book mind, and tell the world about Shullsburg, Wisconsin . . ." he bellowed after me and staggered back inside his new home to open another can of beer.

"Don't worry!" I promised. "I will."

That then brings me to the past few paragraphs and why the small but spectacular town of Shullsburg, Wisconsin appears in my account. And also why the small, but spectacularly rat-arsed Mr O' Neill appears as well.

Shullsburg I was later to find out in an e-mail from my friend Dorothy Beckwith did have some contemporary Cornish connections.[21] In September 2002, the veteran Cornish miner, Jimmy Clemence of Four Lanes visited Shullsburg, home to his great aunt, the late Mary Emma Pool (1848–1913), wife of the Shullsburg mine owner and first Shullsburg mayor, Joseph Blackstone (1839–1902). There, he visited the 116 year old Brewster building where the Cornish descendant Marcella Cherry Russell and her husband Chick manage the Brewster Cafe. Over lunch, Jimmy met two mining soul mates – ninety-one year old Neil Copeland (not a relative of the famous scholar) of the little neighbouring village of Leadmine and seventy-six year old Fritz Saam, a resident of nearby Hazel Green. No doubt, there was a lot of 56 Inch Cylinder style chatter. If only I had known . . . I have since found out a little more about Shullsburg. A lady called Marcella Cherry Russell makes pasties on Thursdays by reservation. I shall have to reserve one next time. Deb Pirquette, Glenn Matl and Doris Hodges are all active Cornish in the town; Glen apparently a writer and excellent woodworker. Shullsburg's football team are apparently called the 'Miners'. I shall have to catch a game one day.

On the road between Shullsburg and Mineral Point were lots of hog farms. They seemed the kind of places where everything but the grunt might eventually be used, and smelt to high heaven in the late afternoon heat. I expected to find towns called Hogville and Manure Diggin's. I didn't. The smell was no problem really though. It just woke me up a bit. The road was long and straight and I had my cool Galena shades on. Shullsburg, shit and shades. How good could life be?

That evening, after I'd eaten another 'Miner's Melt' at the 'Miner's Point', I declined for the moment, the hot-tub and instead decided to head north and briefly check out Dodgeville and Linden. Both are Cornish towns, but by the time I arrived in each of them, they seemed to be rapidly bedding down for the night. I'd have to be satisfied enough on this occasion just to have visited them. Dodgeville though – which in my view is the most American sounding town ever – I discovered, was named after a man we already know well – Colonel Henry Dodge, the State's first governor, who was actually inaugurated in the town of Mineral Point in 1836. There then followed a set of 'Iowa County seat wars' lasting six years, until Dodgeville was eventually selected in 1861. It has remained the 'county seat' ever since, much to Mineral Point's annoyance. In Dodgeville the most famous Cornish mine was called Diggs's. It was first worked in 1836 and continued till 1850, eventually running down in 1870, although the mine was later revived by one Joseph Pearce, where the deepest shaft of 80 feet was once drained by a horse-operated pump.

One of the most traumatic incidents affecting Dodgeville

was the 1851 cholera outbreak, which may be put down to its poor sanitary conditions and claimed the lives of some 136 people in a town with a population around 900; paralleling an incident a few years before back home in Mevagissey. That said the overall mortality rate in the lead region was significantly lower than back home. It is Rowe's opinion that although the male miners lived longer, it was on the women whom most of the strain fell; all this in a culture where much had to be made or 'made-do'.[22] Dodgeville looked different now: the standard of living for most Americans is much higher than that to be found in early twenty-first century Cornwall. Part of this is down to Dodgeville's closer proximity to Madison; the other reason is the very Cornish-named 'Lands' End' trading company – a mail-order and internet clothing firm based in the town, who employ lots of the residents. I reflected on all of this. The 'freedom' so sought by the earliest settlers, away from such social control as gamekeepers, squires, the church (epitomised in Robert Stephen Hawker's oft-quoted satirical poem 'The Cornish Emigrant's Song[23]), and legal injustice, importantly seems to have continued unchanged. Once you understand this, you understand much about Cornish America.

In the morning, I loaded out my belongings to the car and returned my door key to Dennis, thanking him for his hospitality.

"Where are you heading next?" said Dennis.

"South," I said, "to the Quad Cities . . ."

"Well, you have a safe trip . . . and when you're next in Mineral Point, check us out again . . ."

"Sure will," I said, realising I was picking up American-isms by the truck load.

Leaving Mineral Point and the land of lead and cheese is always a sad feeling. In many ways, I wanted to stay much longer, but I had no choice. I had a helleva size country to cross and much more of Cornish America to gake at. I headed down through the High Street for one last look at the Opera House, the 'Red Rooster' and the 'Cruise'. Then I drove out past Shake Rag, and on onto Illinois. For a while, I was repeating some of the road I had travelled down to Galena but on 61, turned right to Gratiot, then turned south towards Pearl City and Lanark. This was fairly wild and windswept country. In fact, it was often desolate and haunting. It sometimes felt that the twenty-first century hadn't happened here. Rickety buildings dotted the roadside, while the farms looked battered and broken. My drive was only punctuated with occasional traffic. Otherwise, I was on my own from the State line down to the interstate. Here, I rejoined 88 and headed westwards. This was the eastern section of 'silicon highway' I had first travelled back in Chicago, only here the silicon was replaced by endless fields of soya. At this point, 88 follows the Rock River, which runs in a north-east to south-west direction across this part of the State.

It took me most of the morning to make the drive down from Wisconsin. The Quad Cities lie on the banks of the Mississippi. Their 'Quad' name is derived from the fact that the conurbation is made up of four cities. On the Illinois side are Moline and Rock Island, while in Iowa, are Davenport and Bettendorf. Technically, they might well be called the 'Quint' Cities since in actual fact, East Moline regards itself as a separate city. Economically though, the Quint or Quad Cities are the northern connecting point of traffic and commerce heading between the two States, but perhaps more famously, Rock Island itself was once the home of the US Army arsenal, located on an island in the middle of the Mississippi River. You can visit the arsenal today, although it now contains few weapons. Maybe someone realised that keeping all of the USA's intercontinental ballistic missiles on one little island in Illinois was not the most sensible thing to do. Moline and its surrounds are also the home of the enormous agri-business that is John Deere. In Moline, there is the John Deere Pavilion which demonstrates the history and development of Deere's agricultural implements. In short, this is tractor country, Boy.

Because of the way the Quad Cities have developed, each of them have their own downtown areas, although increasingly they seem to be co-operating on making the conurbation into more of a single entity. Sometimes, it is hard to know where Moline ends and Rock Island begins, or on the opposite bank, where Davenport is and where

67

Bettendorf isn't. On the whole, Moline seems more the working-class part of the Cities, whereas where Bettendorf hits the Mississippi are grand houses, owned by doctors and businessmen. These look out on some of the old-style Mississippi Paddle Steamers, most of which have now been turned into casinos. At least you could imagine the way it was a hundred years ago – very Mark Twain and *Music-man*.

I'd been to the Quad Cities a few times before. One time I'd had an invite from Joe McDowell of Augustana College to give a lecture there. Augustana is an independent University-sity sector college in Moline and Joe is one of the lecturers in the Department of English, specialising in Chaucer and Medieval English Literature. I had accepted the invitation and went there to speak on Cornish medieval drama. The students had been very receptive. Afterwards, Joe and I had eaten in the downtown area of Rock Island at a micro-brewery bar called 'The Blue Catfish'. He explained how he liked working at Augustana – it attracted students mainly from the richer suburbs of Chicago, who were looking for an attractive college destination, not too far away from home. Joe, in fact, reminded me of myself in lots of ways, and we were perhaps envious of each other's lifestyle. He admired the fact that Cornwall was so steeped in history, language and literature, and I admired the seemingly relaxed academic lifestyle he had at Augustana – a few lectures a week, the rest of the time devoted to reading and research. This time, I wasn't going to meet up with Joe since he'd be away for the summer.

Instead, I'd agreed to hook up with Nancy Laity. Nancy co-ordinates much Cornish and Celtic activity in the Quad Cities area, and she had come along to the lecture I had given at Augustana. Nancy is in her mid-fifties and enthusiastic about all things Cornish, even though she has never visited the territory. You have to remember that because of the exchange rate, it is very expensive for the average American person to visit Britain. Her Cornishness then is not so much based on bog-standard Cornish Diaspora 'revivalism' but more on the genuine songs and stories that her Cornish grandfather told her when she was a child. Nancy knew most of the other Cornish activists in the mid-West and also had affiliations to the local Welsh group. In fact they often worked together to promote the Brythonic side of American Celtic heritage.

We met up at the 'Blackthorn' in Moline, near the John Deere Pavilion and the massive 'The Mark' amphitheatre, a new indoor multi-use venue staging everything from ice hockey to concerts by *Yes* and *Chicago*. The 'Blackthorn' is a Celtic-themed restaurant offering standard sea-food, salads and steak on a menu with 'ancient' and 'magical' spin. Inside it is decorated with the flags of Celtic nations. A large St Piran's flag is in there. It was presented to the 'Blackthorn' by Howard Curnow, around the same time that I was last in the Quad Cities, lecturing at Augustana. This time, posters were dotted around advertising that summer's Celtic Games. This was seemingly quite a large event – broadly based on the Highland Games – but featuring music, food and workshops. Interestingly, not only Scotland and Ireland were on the poster, but also Cornwall, Wales, Brittany and the Isle of Man. Goodness, they were an aware bunch here in the Quad Cities!

Much of this could be put down to the work of people like Nancy who had successfully raised the profile of the smaller Celtic nations. Being a Laity of course, Nancy was connected to my good friend Paul Laity, the lawyer and Judge, who sadly had died in 2001, but whose life I had recently celebrated in a poem. Paul, Tim Saunders and I had been at work compiling a reader in Cornish law – something Paul had always dreamed of doing, and Nancy was keen to know what progress had been made. I also gave her a copy of the collection of poems which features 'Lines for Laity'.[23] Nancy is a descendant of one Richard Laity who was born in 1852 in St Hilary, although her earliest known ancestor is John Liaty who was born in 1673 in the same parish. In essence, the Cornish presence in this part of the USA can be put down to travellers such as Richard in the old mining areas in south-western Wisconsin and in places like Galena. When the mines became unprofitable, many of the Cornish families moved down-river to the next major port or moved into the interiors of Illinois and Iowa to farm. Nancy knew there were a lot more people out there with Cornish heritage. The problem was how to begin tracking them down. The best place to raise awareness was in the local media and that was her present strategy. Nancy and I enjoyed lunch together, chatting over time spent in Mineral Point at the 2001 Gathering and she learning about my travels.

Nancy has such enthusiasm for things Cornish that it is hard not to feel her energy. Her difficulty is that she wonders whether she is doing things right. Was this, she wondered, what the rest of the Cornish-American organisations were doing? I told her not to worry, to do what she wanted to do, and not be made to work in a particular mould. The Cornish were always independent, I told her, and she should take heart from that. I then understood some of the pressure that the modern Cornish of America felt. There seemed to be a way of working that had been established by links to the Cornish Gorseth, to magazines like *Cornish World*, which although laced with good intention, did not always reflect the emergent identity of Cornish America in the twenty-first century. All of that seemed very distant and unhelpful to Nancy's current needs. I was contemplating all this later on, as I wondered around my favourite Mall in the Quad Cities – South Park. No, it is not named after the animated television show, but is in the south of the Quad Cities. There is a North Park too – not surprisingly to be found in the north of Bettendorf. South Park though, was quiet that morning, but I didn't mind that. After the frenetic driving activity of the last few days, it was rather pleasant just to wander around the seemingly popcorn-scented shops and relax. I headed for the usual book and record shops and soaked up mid-Western culture for a couple of hours. Around the back of the South Park Mall, and near to the Quad Cities airport, was another 'Comfort Inn'. I decided to stay there for the night, since the experience of staying at the one in Mineral Point had been so comfortable. They had a pool too. After checking in and unpacking, I headed down to the pool and lazed in it and the whirlpool. It sounds like I was living some charmed existence with all this luxury. In fact, in the USA, such facilities come as bog standard, and the bill was a lot less than you might pay in even the most average of guest houses in Newquay. That was America for you – darn good value.

I found the same good value at a nearby Chinese Restaurant. For around $8 you ask for the all-you-can-eat buffet. You walk out having tried everything available and feeling absolutely stuffed. No wonder a few weightier-looking customers were walking in, as I walked out. Back at the 'Comfort Inn' I opened my fortune cookie and read the small slip of silky paper inside.

'Follow your dreams,' it said, 'and they will come true'.

Ah, yes, master.

The next morning I was heading west, where apparently dreams did come true: where the Cornish headed for greater pasties, greater diggin's and, no doubt, greater prosperity.

Notes

1. The standard reference work is George Fielder (1997 [1962]) *Mineral Point: A History*, Madison: The State Historical Society of Wisconsin. See also Louis Albert Copeland (2001 [1898]) *Cornish in Southwest Wisconsin*, Mineral Point: Southwest Wisconsin Cornish Society; Lawrence A. Roe (1991) *A History of Wisconsin Mining*, Madison: Roeco.
2. For the full history of this renovation, see Mark H. Knipping and Korinne K. Oberle (1990) *On the Shake Rag: Mineral Point's Pendarvis House, 1935–1970*, Mineral Point: The State Historical Society of Wisconsin and The Memorial Pendarvis Trust.
3. For explanation of the tradition of Tommyknockers, see Robert Hunt (ed.) (1865) *Popular Romances of the West of England: The Drolls, Tradtions, and Superstitions of Old Cornwall (First and Second Series)*, London: John Camden Hotten, pp.90-91 and pp.346-51.
4. A.L. Rowse (1991 [1969]) *The Cornish in America*, Redruth: Dyllansow Truran, p.205.
5. Ibid., pp.204-5.
6. John Rowe, *The Hard Rock Men: Cornish Immigrants and the North American Mining Frontier*, Liverpool: Liverpool University Press, p.57; Rowse, ibid., p.207.
7. The Gundrys are dealt with by Rowe in detail. Ibid., p.45.
8. Ibid., p.41.
9. See A.C. Todd (1995 [1967]) *The Cornish Miner in America*, Spokane, Washington: The Arthur H. Clark Co., pp.48-9.
10. See Alan M. Kent (2002) *Love and Seaweed*, St Austell: Lyonesse Press, p.41.

11. Thomas Shaw (1965) *The Bible Christians*, London: Epworth Press.
12. Rowse, op.cit., p.199.
13. Ibid., p.201; Rowe, op.cit., p.42.
14. Copeland, op.cit., p.308.
15. Rowe, op.cit., p.53.
16. Rowse, op.cit., p.197.
17. Todd, op.cit., p.29.
18. Copeland, op.cit., p.324-8.
19. Ibid., p.330.
20. Ibid., p.334.
21. Correspondence with the author, 4th October (2002).
22. Rowe, op.cit., pp.55-6.
23. See Alan M. Kent (ed.) (2000) *Voices from West Barbary: An Anthology of Anglo-Cornish Poetry 1549–1928*, London: Francis Boutle, pp.107-8.

3

Plough and Seed Artists . . .

Imagine a bad dream. In that dream, you have to travel the length of the A30 between Carland Cross and Hayle five million times on a Saturday morning in August. That is what it is like to drive across Iowa – only worse.

Before I crossed the Mississippi I didn't really know much about Iowa. The three things I did know is that they grow a lot of corn, that the capital city is called Des Moines (who sounds like he runs a haulage firm up Whitemoor) and that the rock group *Slipknot* come from there. In case you haven't heard of *Slipknot*, they are nine men in strange and bizarre S&M masks wearing orange boiler suits, who sing rap-metal. They go down very well at Ponsanooth Women's Institute so I believe. No, I'm not so sure they do. In driving through Iowa though, I understand why you might want to put on a pig's head mask and 'mosh' around the Reading Festival Stage, since Iowa's flatness and agriculture really is enough to drive a man mad.

After I crossed the Mississippi, I knew a lot more about the 'Hawkeye' State. For one thing, there is much more corn in Iowa than one person can ever contemplate. For another, Iowa is big – really big. And one last thing, I didn't find a single trace of the Cornish – not anywhere. This was travels in non-Cornish America, but I had to cross the non-Cornish to find the Cornish if you see what I mean. Hopefully, whenever the sensible and practical ancient Cornish ancestors passed through here, they took one look at the flatness and the corn and said, 'Dun't like the look o'that boy! Let's 'eave us on . . .' I was 'eaving on too. I knew this section of my journey across wouldn't hold much music for the mouth-organ. I was looking ahead to Colorado and Utah – places where I knew the Cornish had stamped their mark, spread their seed, whacked their winzes and built their buddles.

What I have just said is not entirely true. The Cornish did 'land' in Iowa and they had much to do with breaking of new Prairie ground. They weren't so much working their buddle, but more spreading their seed, since their movement westwards across the Mississippi, was in the main, accompanied by a change in profession. Once the lead-region began to run dry, the pick and gad artists became farmers: plough and seed artists if you like. Places like Dubuque began to temporarily decline, while Galena and the lead region noticed the push westwards by some miners. Iowa was organised as a territory in 1838, just as the Cornish were arriving *en masse*, yet it is in characters such as the Wendron-based Treloar family that we see the real colonisation of the State. As Rowse shows, Temby Treloar was already helping to open up Iowa, and he was followed by his brother James, who signed up for 240 acres to begin with. Whenever he wanted to expand, James borrowed money from his Uncle Sy Crase back in Wisconsin, and eventually he owned some 640 acres.[1] Other Cornish people were moving across from Eastern Wisconsin, Michigan and Illinois to farm in Iowa. One such example was James Henry Trewin (1858–1927) who moved on from Illinois to work an Iowa farm with his brother, eventually studying law and setting up a practice. Emlin G. Penrose (1844–1930) originated from Ohio but moved to Iowa in 1860 to teach and became a State Senator.[2] It was such Cornishmen who were the real pioneers during this phase – and it was perhaps Cornish independence and strong character which allowed them to push westwards where others feared to tread. One of the Cornish groups pushing through Iowa were the Moyles who were later to become one of the leading Mormon families, while the most famous were the Jameses. Samuel James left Wisconsin for the distant West as early as 1850, and spent much of the winter in Iowa, making preparation for the trek ahead. By May the group made some thirteen miles a day, but were set upon by Pawnee Indians who surrounded them and demanded a fee to pass through their territory. In Nebraska they joined other pioneers heading for California, and felt much safer, eventually arriving at Puget Sound a year later.[3] Charles Strongman who emigrated from Perranzabuloe to Mineral Point in 1841, but then travelled across the country, described the trail through Iowa to Council Bluffs as being "over the worst kind of roads."[4]

'Ee wudn' far wrong that Charles Strongman. Not much seemed to have changed in over a century and a half.

From the Quad Cities to Iowa City, there were lots of trucks out on the road. It seemed like every single truck had to pass through this section of the Mid-west. For miles, I seemed to be the only car moving. Then all this became a little more understandable as I passed one of the seven wonders of Iowa – "The World's Largest Truck Stop". Hell, I had to pull in there – just to say I'd visited it, and show the folks home the pictures. In some ways "The World's Largest Truck Stop" didn't have much going for it. It was basically a parking lot for articulated lorries in the middle of some fields – only that you could buy as much truck merchandise as you wanted, or eat as large a steak as you wanted, or buy postcards with trucks on them. I went in. I had to.

Sometimes I love sleaze as much as the Conservative Party. It was filled with men and women who looked ready for a fight. At that moment, I really wanted a large moustache, a cut-off lumber shirt and a baseball cap with a picture of a truck on it. A tattoo would have been helpful too – preferably with a truck on it. I wanted to like *country and western* and sing truckdriving blues. I could hear conversations – that strangely enough did not revolve around eighteenth-century French art nor the works of Stravinsky – but trucks, pure and simple. Or maybe that should be 'Truuuuucks – purrre an' simple'.

Now, if I was a truck driver, after a hard day's slog across Indiana and Illinois, and then into Iowa, about the very last thing I'd want to do is pull into the world's largest truck stop. I'd want to get out of the cab and go about as far away from the truck as humanly possible. Anywhere but the

75

truck. That didn't seem to be an option for most of the truckers here. Mind you, they were in the middle of Iowa. Trucks, I concluded are very interesting compared to ears of corn.

The only other attraction on Interstate 80 was the Herbert Hoover National Historical Site. To most people, it was no Disneyland. I saw the faces of children in the backseats of cars heading west ("Are we nearly there yet?"). The Iowa Tourism Department Children's Entertainment Pack had not worked. I could see them wanting to colour in corn pictures in psychedelic colours. They wanted to be anywhere but Cedar County, Iowa. All that said, I did have a new appreciation of truck culture as I headed toward Iowa City. You realise that without the trucking industry, much of America would collapse. So Iowa, truck magnet of Mid-West, I salute you.

Iowa City had a boring name, but it looked an interesting town. It was home to the University of Iowa. I didn't stop though. I might have been unable to continue if the University had an Institute of Corn Studies. I would have died of boredom. A darn Institute of Truck Studies might have been more of a temptation though. North lay Cedar Rapids. I liked the sound of Cedar Rapids for some reason. It sounded so quintessentially America, a bit like Dodgeville back in Wisconsin. Lots of truck companies had their headquarters there too, so it was bound to be good. I kept on Interstate 80 though. Several phases of the moon seemed to pass. Several eternities occurred. The universe may have imploded, reformed and exploded again. Thousands of pasties were consumed the world over. It was not noticed on Interstate 80 in Iowa. I passed a load of places where I could not imagine living – Newton, Grinnell, Williamsburg and Colfax. History didn't seem to have happened here. Only corn. It grew in the night and attacked you.

By mid-morning I arrived in beautiful Des Moines (You don't actually pronounce each 's'), and because of construction work on the freeway, had to take a detour around the city's northern limits. In his telephone book studies during the 1960s, Rowse was able to note down several well-established Cornish famiies in Iowa – the Trewtheweys, Warricks, Penrose, Pascoe, Trezise and Chenoweth, who were meeting the newer families – such as the Trevillyans, Minears, Penders, Glanvilles, as well as Trevethan, Pedarvis, Penberthy, Petherick, Curnow and Grenfell,[5] yet here and now, it seemed impossible to know where to begin to meet these families or make sense of Cornish Iowa. It all seemed pleasant enough, though I had a strange sensation that everyone in northern Iowa seemed to be headed there for the huge malls. Then again, I was beginning to doubt there was even a 'Wal-Mart' in northern Iowa. There was Pocahontas County near the town of Fort Dodge, so I was thinking of George Smith, the village of Indian Queens, and fish and chips at the 'Port and Starboard' all at once. Perhaps there was a small Cornish connection in Iowa! Pocahontas – the famous Indian Queen, now enshrined as a 'babe' forever by Walt Disney studios, arrived in Plymouth in 1616 and travelled to London, and although the 'Queen's Head' inn in mid-Cornwall (at the present site of Indian Queens) was re-named later the 'Indian Queen', it seems that this change was due to the fashionability of the name, rather than Pocahontas traipsing across the Goss Moor and stopping at Fraddon to imbibe a pint.

Still, it was nice to think she might have come to Cornwall. It was certainly nicer than looking at all the road-kill that littered Interstate 80 when I turned back onto it again. Racoons, like badgers seem never to have learnt the Green Cross Code. They do, however, seem to make it to the hard-shoulder, and collapse on their backs with all four legs pointing skywards, praying, rigamortis-laden to the god of trucks for no more sacrifices, or, on second thoughts, perhaps it was better to go that way than enter the corn. The racoons (the live ones anyway) might have agreed with me that the Interstate across eastern Iowa should be called the straightest road in the world. That would give something else for Iowa to market to tourists. Come to Eastern Iowa. We have the straightest road in the world. Get on. No – we really do. Come take a look at it. Come take a drive on it. Fall asleep on it.

No amount of music seemed to be doing the trick either. I wound down the window. It smelt like Iowa. I wound up the window. It smelt like Iowa. I was seeing Green Giants called Penrose and Pascoe stalking me in my rear-view mirror. Just as everything was turning corn-on-the cob yellow and I was about to go mad, the town of Council Bluffs came into view. Ah – Council Bluffs! For a moment, it got hilly. The shock to the system was alarming. You could see further than the next barn, farm and windmill. The scenery was definitely changing. How good could the world be? It was noon, and that morning I had crossed Iowa. Get thee behind me Iowa – thou accursed corn-growing State of unforgiving flatness.

I was excited about Nebraska. Nebraska seemed the kind of place for an adventure. I reckoned on meeting cowboys in Nebraska and branding a few heifers before teatime. Anyway, I crossed the Missouri River and pulled into Omaha for lunch. Mmm . . . Nebraska. My kind of State. You even put the emphasis on the second syllable. I celebrated with a strawberry shake and fries. In fact, I went further than that. I even drove to an area of the city called Cornish Heights, where once upon a time familes such of the name Couch, Rouse, Courtney, Nance, Toy, Trebilcock, Pasco, Jolley, Tremaine and Carew vied together. Now Cornish Heights would perhaps more aptly be named *Cornish Lows*. It wasn't the kind of place you'd want to spend any time in, and besides that, there didn't seem to be any Cousin Jacks left. The mouth-organ played a chilling blues and bemoaned them all to come back. Instead all I heard were loud blastbeats and all I saw were run-down properties.

Once I came back down from Cornish Heights, my opinion of Iowa changed. In actual fact, if I am honest, it changed more or less the moment I crossed the State line into Nebraska. I'd thought Iowa was rather faceless, a little monochromatic, full of corn, and weird. At least with Iowa, I remember sections of it – features along the way, strange little towns and places that I'd never see again, but which are locked in my memory. In Nebraska, I don't remember a single thing about the crossing. It seemed like I was just a driving machine.

I tell a lie. I do remember one thing. The reason I remember it is because I'd stopped driving. I pulled into a rest area, next to a battered but loaded Dodge. I must have been wearing a badge saying, "I am not American. Please feel free to talk to me, no matter how weird a sub-genre of the human race that you are."

"Howdy," came a voice from the backseat of the Dodge.

"Hello," I returned and saw a blonde mother in her late forties. It was half-past one and she was drinking down a bottle of Budweiser. There were four bottles on the floor of the backseat and one of her boys was picking these up and taking them over to the bin. There were several more cold ones ready to go in a cooler.

"Where y'headed?"

"Um . . . Colorado . . . Goin' across the country to San Francisco. Where are you going?"

"Back to Wyoming . . ."

"Where did you start from?"

"The South . . . Mississippi . . ."

"You moving back for a reason?"

"Sure am," said the woman, "It's too damn hot down there . . . and then there's darn BUGS . . . They have bugs down there the size of eagles . . ."

"Oh really?" I must have said. I was thinking of B movies at the time. "Haven't they had mosquitos too? I heard about malaria on the news . . ."

"Thas' right! I was down there for seven years. Had enough though. My ma and pa are helping us shift back up north . . ."

At this point Ma and Pa had returned from the restrooms and acknowledged me. I think the mother saw me looking at the Budweiser. In the Nebraskan heat, they looked tempting.

"You want one?" she said, pulling out a bottle from the ice-crammed cooler.

"No – I'm okay. I'd better not – as I'm driving . . ."

"I find it helps," she cackled, "when you're heading across Nebraska . . ."

She had a point. I thought of Cornish Heights.

I was beginning to regret turning down her offer as I headed back onto the on-ramp and rejoined the Interstate.

It was odd. All that conversation and yet not one comment about my accent. Perhaps she was too drunk to even notice. Perhaps by now I was beginning to sound American. I knew I sometimes came back from America with bits of American English exuding from my gob. Either way, the thought of that cold beer was a bit like *Ice Cold in Alex*. I was suddenly transformed into Alec Guinness in the desert. I was imagining heaving my Chevy up some sand dune in the middle of Nebraska – except Nebraska doesn't really have any sand. It just has dust.

I remember something else too. The nightmare is coming back. On the map, which I consulted, oh, perhaps only two hundred times, to see the progress I was making, Nebraska looks like Boba Fett's ship – Slave 1 – in *Star Wars*. You might expect Han Solo in carbonite to pop out the Colorado end of it. Interstate 80 runs right through it – like a go-faster stripe gone mazed. In Iowa, at least you have corn. I mean, corn is nice, corn is friendly. You can eat it. Nebraska just has dusty fields. If you see a horse, it is a major event. You feel like getting out and taking pictures. A few cows and you really feel like this is a holiday. The town of Lincoln turned out to be less than presidential and Grand Island was really a small rock. I drove on and the flatness, the unrelenting prairieness of it all came back. I thought I'd ditched it ages ago, but it came right back like a boomerang and hit me hard in the head. At least there were no mines, and even better than that, no mining museum. The only benefit was that I was temporarily cured of 56 inch cylinder syndrome.

Nebraska hasn't got a tourist authority. It can't. Here are the highlights: the Concordie Teachers' College, the State Museum of Prairie Power (we're talking windmills here), the Dawson County Historical Museum and the Fort McPherson National Cemetery. Hell, there was more to do back home in St Austell – and that *is* saying something. I can't tell you how I was longing to be back in Iowa. It was so bad I was even longing to be back in St Austell.

I made a mistake that evening. A really bad mistake. A big cock-up. Having survived the bad dream that was Iowa and the hellish nightmare that was Nebraska, I should have stopped at Ogallala. Ogallala had all the signs of being a fine place for a curious Cornishman to stop. It had a funny Native American name to begin with – that always helped – and the gas station I had pulled into was promising with loads of bizarre things to buy. You know, everything from weird condom kits to bags of red sweets called Swedish Fish. There were also a fine selection of motels covering every price range and sexual orientation. I'm kidding about the latter, but there was at least a range of quality and price. In fact, Ogallala could have been one of my finest memories of this stint, but instead of listening to my heart, I listened to my brain. My brain informed me that I was about to enter Mountain time zone. That meant I would gain an extra hour of travelling that evening, and so I headed out onto Interstate 76, which would take me into Colorado. Yippee, I went, as I crossed the State line between Nebraska and Colorado. Here was another State that I hadn't travelled through before. All seemed fine to begin with. The scenery in north-eastern Colorado, at first seemed very much like that I'd witnessed in Nebraska. No corn, just lots of prairie, which was occasionally fenced off to stop horses from wandering.

Then things changed. The temperature dropped and the landscape became more and more barren. I mean barren barren. I mean beyond United Downs barren. Nothing seemed to move or grow out there, except for clumps of grass, and they didn't seem to move much either. The traffic dwindled too, which I couldn't quite understand because I imagined there was a fair amount of traffic needing to move between Denver and Nebraska. No problem, I thought, consulting the map. Surely I will find somewhere to stay at Sterling. On the map, Sterling looked, well a 'sterling' sort of place. I mean it looked like a real town. It was bound to have a 'Wal-Mart' and a 'Kentucky Fried Chicken', like they had at Ogallala.

I was beginning to miss Ogallala. There, life was good. I looked at the map again. Then I realised. There really wasn't anything between this road and Wyoming to the north and Kansas to the east. I mean no-one seemed to live there at all. For miles and miles and miles. I think I gulped a largish gulp at that point.

Sterling came up. Sterling passed me by. Sterling had one gas station but no accommodation.

"See Cornish boy, you should have stopped in Ogallala," Sterling said to me with a sneer.

I drove on. I'd been driving for an hour and a half since

Ogallala, and the road was becoming more and more deserted. Despite the time difference, night was beginning to fall. I sucked down a bottle of water and prepared myself. Maybe I would have to hanker down and press on to Denver. I didn't want to though. I was already tired and pissed off at myself for being so stupid. Little scary dust devils (like small tornadoes) formed in the shrubland on the opposite side of the road. Tumbleweeds crossed in front of the car. At any moment I expected a coyote to emerge from the side of the road and stare me out like one that had done so in Georgia the previous Autumn.

I drove on some more – and then some more. The road was getting endless and I was getting fidgety in my seat. My right ankle ached where it had been pressed against the accelerator pedal all day. I wanted to be anywhere but here – preferably with a shower. No problem I told myself. Think of all the Cornish crossing America. Think of the Jameses and the Moyles and Charles Strongman. They were strong Cornish men. They didn't have fancy air-conditioning or bottles of 'Gatorade'. Eventually, near the town of Fort Morgan, I spied a sign for a 'Days Inn'. Whatever it cost, it would do (Why is it we Cornish always have to make do?). The light was fading fast. Whoever first designed the location of this 'Days Inn', didn't have much of a clue though. It was located on the highest, windiest bluff known to humanity (or at least around the town of Fort Morgan), and looked like it was the kind of place that would take only the most desperate of travellers. I went inside to the reception area and tried to check in. It was full of people who had made a bad decision at Ogallala.

"Next person who should have stopped at Ogallala please," the Manager seemed to saying.

Actually he wasn't, but he could offer me a room for the night, and for that I was very grateful. On a road trip such as this one, sometimes you are just glad to step out of your vehicle and this was one of those occasions. Despite the wind whipping around the complex, I grabbed my over-night bag and suitcase in one go, and man-handled them into the motel room. It was certainly not the greatest room in the world, but right then, it looked like absolute luxury. I dumped everything into a pile of road-tripness and headed

82

for the shower, turning on the television as I stripped off my Nebraskan-sweated shorts. I was glad to be away from plough and seed artists. More stuff on Saddam Hussein. He seemed like the eternal American bogeyman. Hell, I was even wishing for a bit of 56 Inch Cylinder Syndrome to come back.

I flipped the television over to VH1 and watched a biography of AC/DC, scoffing my remaining 'Hostess' cherry pie listening to 'Whole Lotta Rosie' and air-guitared across the king-sized bed. Ah, the depravity of it all.

Notes

1. A.L. Rowse (1991 [1969] *The Cornish in America*, Redruth: Dyllansow Truran, p.155.
2. Ibid., p.156.
3. A.C. Todd (1995 [1967]) *The Cornish Miner in America*, Spokane, Washington: The Arthur H. Clark Co., pp.209-11.
4. Ibid., p.61.
5. Rowse, op.cit., p.144.

4

Towards the wickedest towns in the West . . .

The morning brought no let up in the wind. More tumble-weeds crossed the car park. I was on early because I wanted this stretch of Interstate 76 to end. Of course, the morning drive was more pleasant. I headed down past Roggen, Keenesburg and Prospect Valley (no Cornish left there, so far as I could tell), and at Brighton, turned right towards the town of Boulder. The Rockies had come into sight – massive, broad forms of white and grey, rising across the Plains in front of me. Between them lay the passes and gulches which would take me into the west, and where the Cornish had sat mining away to their hearts' content.

In American terms, the Rockies were explored by Europeans relatively late and it was only in 1859 that the first prospectors arrived there in what then known as the "Kansas Territory of the Rockies". I was heading there, though they didn't seem to belong to poor old Kansas anymore. A couple of minor roads took me across Interstate 25 which headed north to Wyoming, and I knew I would soon be in reach of the foothills. Before I made the climb though, I pulled in for some more gas.

This was an experience. I filled the tank up and went in to pay the cashier. We had a clash of accents and my request for directions must have sounded like ancient Klingon to her. I was still in Cornish mode. I changed gear and trotted out the most received pronunciation that I could deliver. It made me sound frightfully English. At this, the cashier brightened up and explained where I needed to go. I thanked her and she shouted after me, "No problem. Groovy baby . . ." as if I was Austin Powers. Of course, I was travelling just at the time when the third Mike Meyers film had just been released. It tickled me to know she thought I was English and a bit of all right to boot. Yeah Baby . . .

I had researched Boulder and Boulder County a lot before I visited it. I knew I wouldn't be able to visit all the mining towns above the town, but I reckoned on visiting at least a few that morning. They were on the northern end of the swathe of Cornish mining activity in the Rockies that lay on the expanse to the west of Boulder and Denver. The first town that I visited was Jamestown. It lay to the north-west, thirteen miles from Boulder and had prospered through several booms, the mines there named the Golden Age, the John Jay and the Buena. They were all respectable producers. But it was the promoters who put Jamestown, Colorado on the map since, like many other wicked towns of Colorado's mining days, it became packed with three miles of tents, dance halls, saloons, prostitutes and gambling parlours; it was also the hometown of a boy who later became a famous actor – Douglas Fairbanks, Sr. There is very little left now.

By 1867 town lots could be sold there for a barrel of beer, and I read of one apparently contented Jamestown resident and miner who wrote a letter to the *Rocky Mountain News* the same year: "We have no mails and but very few females . . . Our supply of reading matter has dwindled down to one number of the Colorado Transcript and a copy of the Governor's message . . . We have not sod-corn enough to 'exhilarate' us. We have not even a double barrel short gun with which to shoot jay birds who come provokingly near out front door – our only one. Our chimney smokes horribly. Our gal has gone to Montana, and we are happy."[1]Fair enough, if that's what cranks your lever, but it wouldn't last.

Jamestown was just like Gold Hill, another old mining area I checked out. Gold was discovered here in 1859 and thousands swarmed these hills to work the placer deposits. The Horsfal Mine produced some $300,000 worth of gold in only its first two years. In 1872 another vein of ore was discovered and this gave the town its second boom. Famously, the Wentworth Hotel of Gold Hill (now known as the Gold Hill Inn) became the favourite drinking abode of the Denver newspaper magnet and poet – Eugene Field – who celebrated the town in his doggerel:

Oh, them times on Red Hoss Mountain in the Rockies far
    away –
There's no sich place nor times like them as I kin find today!
What, though the camp hez busted? I seem to see it still
A-lyin', like it love it, on that big 'nd warty hill:
And I feel a sort of yearn' 'nd a chokin' in my throat
When I think of Red Hoss Mountain 'nd of Casey's tabble
    dote![2]

A Poet Laureate he is not, but I felt this piece captures the energy of the mining camps.

I took Sunshine Road up from Boulder and viewed these two locations as well as many other old mining settlements on the foothills of the Rockies – among them Sunshine itself (a tellurium ore mine named after the first child born in the town, one Susie Sunshine Turner), Summerville (a gold camp famed for its treacherous winters), Salina (a gold mining town, known for its toll-charge to enter [a bit like the Devon end of the Tamar Bridge then], and for the Black Swan Mill [probably devoted to gold], worked by the Cornish), Wallstreet (founded by Charles W. Caryl, an eastern mining promoter, with seven classes of workers, ranging from $2 a day labourers to $25 a day generals [the Cornish at this end of the pay scale]) and Crisman (a silver mine, once having the 'richest specimens of any mine in the country'). All of them showed little signs of what they once were.

From Crisman, I followed Boulder Creek Road across to Tungsten and Nederland, originally a silver mining area, but eventually noted for their tungsten deposits. In 1915, Nederland was booming with tungsten production, and miners came from all over to work. Many did not find riches though and became down-and-out quickly, having to wait for meals that were '40 percent an edible product and

50 percent grease' according to a reporter who failed to account for the remaining 10 percent.[3] I could have visited any number of other mines that lay above Boulder, and any number with the same stories of 'boom', 'bust' – if they were lucky a second 'boom', and then a quick transition into a 'ghost town'.

Some survived now as tourist destinations; others no longer exist – nature reclaiming these once industrious and wicked regions. What was clear though was how intensively Colorado was mined, and how in all my travels so far, it was Colorado which clearly had the stamp of *claim after claim* written all over it. It was very different than the organised mining areas of south-western Wisconsin. Here, mining was as endemic as every hill and every mountain. It was hard to pin the Cornish down, but you knew they had been here. When it seemed pointless to continue my trails in the foothills since each new 'ghost town' seemed to recall an earlier one, I took Boulder Creek Road back down into the city of Boulder. From here, I could peer out, back over the Plains of Colorado and Nebraska that I had already travelled.

The flatness of the land had troubled me, and I was glad to be in more undulating territory. The city of Boulder looked very promising too since its urban sprawl was negated by wide streets intertwined with lots of trees and flora. Boulder reminded me of two places back in Britain. First off, it is a bit like Glastonbury in the sense that it embraces several layers of alternative culture. Secondly, it is similar to Totnes in its moneyed values and lifestyle, which reminds me of a story I must relay to you in order to set the scene in Boulder. I was once on a course at Dartington Hall, near Totnes, and a friend of mine complained of a migraine. I drove him down into Totnes in order for him to buy something to relieve his headache. He came back very distressed.

"That was a complete waste of time," he said, "I could get my bumps felt; I could have incense waved beneath my nasal passages; I could have a crystal passed over my brow; I could have undergone a course of Tai Chi, but could I find a chemist to buy some Anadin? Could I hell?"

If you have ever wandered around the hippie-middle-class

'grooviness', that is Totnes or Glastonbury then you will have some idea of what kind of a place Boulder is. In Boulder I'd actually hoped to have met up with Monica Emerich, a Ph.D candidate in the School of Journalism at the University of Colorado at Boulder, where she is researching Celtic spirituality on internet. Monica had visited Cornwall earlier in the summer on a fellowship, and I had shown her many of the more famous standing stones and holy wells, as well as other places in Cornwall connected with Celtic spirituality. We had debated some of the issues raised in *Celtic Geographies* and in my chapter 'Celtic Nirvanas: Constructions of Celtic in Contemporary British Youth Culture'. She recommended that if I was journeying across the United States, then I should call in on Boulder. I would find a lot of 'Celtic Nirvanas' there. Unfortunately Monica was out of town while I was passing through on this occasion, but she'd given me more than enough pointers for me to have a fun time exploring the city. In short, and to use a contemporary neologism, Boulder was 'wicked'.

Pearl Street is a pedestrianised area in the west of the city and houses many boutiques, galleries and alternative stores. The strands of alternative and anarchic culture are easy to spot. Many young people walk around bare-footed and many males have long hair and dreadlocks. Piercings and tattoos form another layer of this rebellion, with a fixation on Celtic and Native American spirituality. Several shops blended these – so that dreamcatchers and Indian poetry are sat next to knotwork and Celtic crosses. Crystals, dragons, incense sticks and candles jostle between them. For the main part, it was the typical, and perhaps naïve American take on all things Celtic. The focus, in general, was on Ireland, although there were one or two references to Cornwall – all the more ironic, seeing as how Boulder had originally been a mining town, and point of departure for places like Jamestown and Gold Hill, which many of the Cornish and passed through and worked in.

The eclecticism of Pearl Street was fun though. In many ways, it was just the kind of place I liked to look around, and was a complete contrast to some of the more standardised shopping experiences I had witnessed in the USA. I gave some of my, by now weighty, change to a group called *Your name is Chuckwagon*, who stood singing an acoustic version of the Tom Petty standard *Last Dance for Mary Jane*. If I didn't want to listen to the many buskers, I could try some Bikram Yoga, check out 'Tanstogo' – Boulder's finest tanning salon, enter 'Got Skate?' or 'Skin Trip', or check out 'Rocky Mountain Joe's Cafe' and 'Ras Kassa's Ethiopian Restaurant'. There was also the 'Tonic Oxygen Bar' for 'elixirs' and 'Smartinis' – where one was offered 'a joyful journey to wholesome bliss'. 'Tulaqi', Colorado's leading music venue, offered the August visitor such amazing groups as Porterhouse and Swivel Hips Smith, the Drive by Truckers and the ska-punk of the Voodoo Glow Skulls. I think you get the picture.

On 13th Street, just off Pearl, I found Conor O'Neill's 'Traditional Irish Pub' and decided to go in for a Guinness. It was, as you may imagine, about as traditional, as the Americans say, as my butt. Conor O'Neill's was the ultimate exercise in the invention of tradition, right from the carved triscals and knotwork on the bar, to the mock fittings and pictures of Samuel Beckett and James Joyce, and the supposed uniform of Michael Collins. You could buy an Irish Breakfast for $8.95, whatever that was, and there was live entertainment seven nights week. Despite my reservations, they served a nicely chilled pint of Guinness. As I glanced through a copy of the *Colorado Daily*, I wondered whether I should start a similar chain of Cornish-themed pubs in America. My model would be the Crown Inn at St Ewe, and I suppose we'd have photographs of people like Henry Jenner and Robert Morton Nance on the walls. I gave it a few minutes thought, but then had a sharp intake of breath and concluded that I would spare the world of such an abomination. We have enough invented Cornish rubbish already without 'Trevithick's Traditional Cornish Pub' opening up in Los Angeles.

Boulder, once filled with Cornish (in part due to the development of the nearby Caribou Mine, which I didn't have time to visit), seemed to be an epi-centre for organic and wholefood in this part of America. Down the other end of Pearl Street, I discovered a mall that contained a huge organic and wholefood supermarket packed with customers and expensive products. One could sense that this was not only part of the University ethos of the town, but a wider reaction against the McDonald-isation of eating. Here, the middle-class residents of Boulder were fighting back. It was quite bizarre to see, in a way, after having come from the mid-West, where vegans and vegetarians were rare. Similarly, the whole organic and wholefood phenomenon, which in Britain seemed to be a new way for the larger supermarkets to re-package certain goods and jack up the prices, seemed to be happening here too – but not in the rest of America. Boulder, indeed, was an interesting case study. It was raging against the food industry left and right. Leaflets advised me to beware of some fortified foods; there was material about sources of folate; books on Bio-Terrorism, Genetic Modification and Designer foods. As well as 'meat is murder', Boulder was big on Shakespeare too. The 2002 summer season was running *Macbeth*, *A Midsummer Night's Dream* and *Richard III*. The latter was being promoted with the following words: "Darth Vader can hang up his helmet and go home. There's a new leather-clad bad boy in town." To me this sounded more Village People than King Richard, but that was Boulder for you. Wicked.

There weren't many motels in Boulder. Most of them were close to the University of Colorado, and I soon gleaned that Boulder was an expensive place to stay. The first motel wanted $90 a night, and it didn't look like it was about to offer me a $90 dollar experience. A second I tried was very similar. You have to remember that I had been paying almost half that price back in the mid-West. Had I thought about it, I might have run with the second of these places, but being Cornish, and tight to boot, I had to look for a better deal. I entered the Formica extravaganza that was the 'Lazy L Motel'. I had almost been following around two other guys who looked like they were mountain bikers, and like me were in search of the 'economy' end of the market. The man behind the desk at the 'Lazy L Motel' quoted them a price of $70 and they accepted. It seemed I would do the same.

Within minutes of being shown my room, I was to regret my decision. The place was a dive. It was, as the Cornish say, 'hanging'. I ended up staying in the area of the motel that was obviously partly used for student accommodation and which seemed to support various other waifs and strays passing through. Ah well, I told myself, it was my bed and I'd have to lie in it. Which I couldn't, because the bed was located in an un-air-conditioned back room, that smelt of sick. My bright idea was to drag the mattress into the other room, where at least I would be cooled by the noisy air-conditioning system. Moving the mattress was difficult, and I found it hard on my own to negotiate the angle of the door. Eventually though, the mattress flopped to the floor and I flopped on top of it. In all honesty, I was counting the hours until morning so I could be on my way. I barely slept because of the heat and the air-conditioner's spluttering and gasping. It looked like it had been last looked at when the 'Lazy L Motel' was built. When dawn burst through the curtains, I struggled to move the mattress into the back room, but at least I made it look like I had slept there. At around 5.30 a.m. I returned the key to reception. I'd just got out the door when the two mountain-bikers also dropped their key off. All three of us had bags under our eyes. We didn't need to say anything. None of us would be recommending the 'Lazy L Motel' in Colorado's Guide to Bed and Breakfast. For all we knew, we might have slept in a Homeless Shelter. I felt rebellious that morning and so ate at 'McDonalds'. Shove that in your wholefood, organic town with bad motels I seemed to be thinking. They just served me up a Mc-Something and I was happy enough to have hot food inside me.

Boulder, this time of the morning, seemed, in the words of Channel 4's *South Park*, a 'quiet little mountain town'. There was little traffic as I drove south toward Denver on Route 36. For time reasons, I decided not to stop at Denver, and instead ploughed straight on into the Rockies. Denver, according to all the local tourist literature, apparently has a very English appearance to it, and is filled with lakes and parks, and houses of red brick, but I had some serious wickedness to find. The main route through the mountains is Interstate 70, the old Route 6, and it winds the driver steadily up out of Denver, past, to the south, the grave of Buffalo Bill, and to the north, the town of Golden. Within a few miles the malls and breaker's yards start to disappear and you find yourself fully in 'Mountain' country. It was the strangest sensation climbing up the Rockies. Because of the design of Interstate 70, at points, I felt like I was taking off in an airliner. Other times, it felt like I was no longer in the USA, but in southern Germany crossing over into Switzerland. The road was long and steep, heading up to 8,000 feet, with unexpected dips and turns that sent one thundering down into canyons and gorges, where the road needed to be supported on immense concrete bridges. Sometimes it would flick back and forth across rivers; other times wind around placid lakes. I imagined gulches filled with placer deposits; swarms of Cousin Jacks.

This was the true landscape of the Colorado Cornish, in Gilpin County. Compared to Wisconsin, the Upper Peninsula of Michigan and California, the Cornish actually arrived quite late here, but soon the Rockies were crawling with Cousin Jacks and Jennies. The first silver boom occurred from 1877 onwards, but this was accompanied by an additional interest in lead, especially around the appropriately named town of Leadville. When silver production declined, the new emphasis from 1891 onwards was in gold around the area known as Cripple Creek, which lasted well into the first quarter of the twentieth century. In a way, Gilpin County is almost a self-governing little kingdom, as well as being a transplantation of Camborne and Redruth, with the mining settlements all running into each other, and some of the mining towns I had visited above Boulder bisecting the runs of mineral at the northern end. The success of mining in Colorado, however, can perhaps be put down to two significant factors: first off, there was a new impulse and interest in improving mining technology; secondly, the process of furnacing, milling and processing ores had become more efficient thanks to a few Cornish geniuses who just happened to be passing through.

As Todd notes, mining in Gilpin County first started at Russel Gulch, named after a man from Georgia, who with his Cherokee wife, first found gold there in 1859, and then to Black Hawk, which was first known as Gregory Diggings after John H. Gregory, who also hailed from Georgia.[4] As it developed, Black Hawk became one of the most significant Cornish gold mines, though it faced a problem typical of the mines in the area. As the mines became deeper, the gold ore was impregnated with sulphides, which in the milling process refused to amalgamate with mercury and too much gold was then lost in the tailings. It was Professor N.P. Hill who entered into a contract with the Cornish firm of Vivian, who owned Copper Works at Swansea, South Wales, which allowed Black Hawk to improve its return.

Hill's contemporary, and later associate was one Richard Pearce, the so-called "saviour of western mining", who was born in 1837 at Barripper, near Camborne.[5] If anyone has claim to be the next most important Cornishman involved in mining after Richard Trevithick, it is Richard B. Pearce, though at the front end of the twenty-first century very few people have even heard of his name. Pearce had a 'nose for a vein' and was the son of Donald Pearce, a captain at Dolcoath. From an early age, he took an interest in mining processing. He studied at the Royal Institution of Cornwall and the Royal School of Mines in London. His first success was the invention of a new kind of a smelter for refractory ores in Swansea, but in 1871 Pearce was invited to Clear Creek by that mine's management. On his way, he met Hill and learned about his ideas; the two of them eventually coming to work together at Black Hawk. Pearce continued to work for mines in Colorado and elsewhere in America, continually improving the efficiency of separating processes and furnaces, as well as discovering uranium and radium in America. It is his contribution to this less 'dramatic' face of mining (separating gold from associate metals) that perhaps explains why Pearce's name is not a household one. He later became President of the Royal Institution of Cornwall, dying in 1927. His importance in the development of mining in Colorado was singularly important however. His house in Denver, at 1720 Sherman Street, is one of that city's most historic mansions. I was thinking of Pearce and beginning to regret not visiting his house.

Central City is 34 miles west of Denver. I arrived there still comparatively early in the morning and sought out the town's museum. Inside the exhibition, I found out that flakes of gold in local rivers were found there as early as 1858, but after Gregory's discovery during the snows of early 1859, swarms of people descended on the area and for a while – much like the area around St Day – it became the richest square mile on earth – with hills quickly becoming pockmarked with diggings. Within a few years Central City was the most important town in Colorado, eclipsing even Denver and many Cornish families arrived there. Central City is still a respectable town and there, I noticed that the Cornish are presented in a particular light. They were (and still are) seen as somewhat opportunistic, as a people hoping to build a nest egg to make life easier when they returned home and are still viewed as somewhat clannish – as soon as there was a job opening, a Cornish worker would say he knew someone who could fill the position. There was much praise though for Cornish skill in timbering and stonemasonry. Many of Central City's central buildings were crafted by Cornishmen, though it was impossible in my brief time there to tell which ones. At Christmas, apparently, they were famous for marching up the gulch at night carrying pine branches twisted into circles with candles set in them. This was a beautiful image which reminded me of some of the torchlight processions I have seen both in Truro, and at Mousehole on Tom Bawcock's Eve, when the town celebrates the end of the famine by fisherman Tom bringing in the seven sorts of fish, eventually cooked in the Star-gazy pie.

The Cornish in Colorado have been studied by various figures over time. One of the most famous accounts is by Professor Lynn I. Perrigo who gathered material in the late 1930s about the Cornish in Central City. Perrigo wrote an unpublished Ph.D thesis and then an article, *The Cornish Miners of Early Gilpin County*,[6] and was fascinated by their Cornu-English speech patterns. There was also a now lost history of Gilpin County written by Judge W.C. Matthews, who was born in Cornwall, worked in the mines of Nevadaville, and died at Denver in 1925.[7] It must have been a very interesting account since Matthews had knowledge of the 'Old' Country and the 'New'. Todd records how Caroline Bancroft in her *Historic Central City* and *Gulch of Gold* books argues that the Cornish brought "a sparkle and fun entirely lacking before" and that the Cornish were "generous, humorous, spirited, imaginative, superstitious and clannish" but "extremely reserved and not easy to know".[8] Around the town there were plenty of pictures of Cornish miners engaged in drilling contests, and though unlike Mineral Point, pasties were not explicitly available, they were still felt to be part of the town's heritage. The whole of the Central City area is much characterised not only by its Opera House (very much like Mineral Point), nor its Methodist churches and chapels, and its Miners and Mechanics Institutes, but also by its dry-stone walling, which strangely makes part of the landscape have the feel of the fields dipping down to Zennor in West Cornwall.

Georgetown, which I was to encounter later, also has runs of dry-stone walling, running across boulder-strewn fields and gulches, but was initially much less respectable than Central City – it had a rowdy reputation and a reign of terror committed by one Mike Royce, who once raided the house of a Cornishman named Arthur and wrecked the property.[9] I was thinking of one C. P. Holton who hailed from Probus, and his friend, Alfred Hill, hoping that they wouldn't suffer the same fate. This Probus-based visitor was also thinking how Holton and Hill were the only Cousin Jacks who enlisted in the service of the Union in Colorado Territory during the Civil War.[10]

I got to Idaho Springs by around 10.30am, and the sun was just climbing enough to put shadow over the road when it ducked into the canyons. Here the mountains turned red, showing the copper and iron deposits in them, and I could only gaze up over U-shaped valley sides that held endless conifer forests. In short, the scenery was breath-taking. There were a number of times when I had to stop the car to take it all in. Occasionally, up on some of the ridges I could see the remains of older mine workings, and as I progressed west, these became intertwined into the ski slopes, where swathes of grass broke through the lines of trees – the established pistes of the region. Fashionable and expensive ski lodges, built in a Swiss style, followed the Interstate.

There is not too much left of the Cornish in Idaho Springs. Once it was a kind of base camp where travelling miners rested before knocking on the boarding houses of Central City owned by Cousin Jennies like Selina Bickford and Edith Brent.[11] Rowe argues that Gilpin County had at least seven hundred Cornish residents of which at least three hundred were 'single' men, living in bachelor quarters.[12] Principally, its fame for the travelling Cornishman is now derived from the fact that it is the home of one of the most respected mining historians of America – T.A. Rickard. Rickard was the author of the 1932 book, *A History of America Mining*, which all the three major Cornish historians of America (Rowse, Rowe and Todd) draw upon. Rickard came from a Porthtowan-based Cornish family of mining engineers; his grandfather was probably the first accredited miner in California. Rickard served his apprenticeship in practical mining in Colorado, first at Idaho Springs, but then moving on to Leadville, working at the famous La Plata smelter. Rickard was serious-minded, and had no time for the follies and wickedness of that town – to his mind the 'romance' of mining was simply in the work itself. Rickard travelled widely and gained much experience and respect wherever he went. He was appointed State Geologist in 1895, but always fought hard to expose the truth of mining matters. For instance, he was famously to say that "Mines are short-lived. They yield a harvest that is gathered once only. Nine mines out of ten are sold for more than their worth; more money is made by selling than by buying them. Much of the so-called business of mining is based on a scant knowledge of its operations and a profound recognition of the essential foolishness of human nature."[13] In 1902 Rickard was made editor of the *Engineering and Mining Journal* in New York. He is, in my view at least, one of the most important Cornishmen in American history.

I made my first stop near Argo, where I visited the National Mining Museum. I didn't really know if this was *the* National Mining Museum or not. It seemed to me that virtually any State that had something to do with mining, made a claim to have the National museum. In terms of mining museums, it was rather bog-standard, but did acknowledge the input of the Cornish hard-rock miners and devoted one of its displays to the Cousin Jacks. One thing the museum did was to whet my appetite to get to Leadville. Its wickedness was made legendary in the displays. At least this museum was regularly dusted. A lot of the equipment and tools were behind glass cases, which I suspect made things rather easier. It also had lots of photographs of some of the foothill mines I had visited above Boulder. Boulder, too, had changed a good deal. I wondered what the miners of old would think of its now prevalent hippie-crunchy vibe.

Like elsewhere in America, I was picking up on a lot of the conflict between the Cornish and the Irish. Todd mentions the story of a saloon on Ute Creek, where John Levering, a Cousin Jack was shot three times through the heart, after a quarrel with an Irishman,[14] and in the museum there were plenty of stories reported about how Irish miners got drunk and vented their anger on Cornishmen. Much of this of course, was to do with the politics of labour in the mines themselves. The Cousin Jacks refused to sell their labour cheaply, because technically they were much more skilled than the Irish. However, there was also religious contention and division, fuelled by feuds over accommodation, diseases ('rocks on the chest', 'miner's con' and phthisis), strikes, dangerous working conditions and disasters. In Colorado, the Cornish-Irish fighting only came to an end in the 1890s, when the two Celtic mining races' monopoly was threatened with the recruitment of cheap labour from Central Europe and Italy. Despite strikes and passionate speeches against this move by Cousin Jacks and the Irish, the change was inevitable. However, the upshot was that the Cornish simply moved into the role of employer and manager rather than worker, while the Irish sought new horizons.

Above the museum lay Clear Creek County, famed I suppose, for its clear creeks. Route 5 up there was the highest road in the whole of the USA. Interstate 70 was high enough for me at this moment though, particularly when it came to driving through Georgetown (with its dry-stone walling), Silver Plume and the Loveland Pass. You know that anything with Plume or Pass on the end of it in America has a long drop to the bottom. From there you enter the Eisenhower Memorial Tunnel and pass through the town of Dillon. Dillon lies below the turn off for Copper Mountain and Leadville. It's high up here. The Fremont Pass is 11,318 feet high, whereas Mount Lincoln is some 14, 286 feet above sea level. Copper Mountain is a massive domed-shaped hill that glows red in the morning light, and by the look of it, was substantially open-cast mined during the latter part of the twentieth-century. As I rounded it, I could still see the remains of earth-moving equipment, but the mine itself seemed to have shut up shop.

It took me another half an hour of driving before I rolled into Leadville. The town feels like it is at the top of the world, situated at the head of the upper valley of the Arkansas River, at over ten-thousand feet. In stories back home, Leadville seemed to be one of those legendary places that the Cornish were associated with. It was jam-packed with Cornish between 1880 and 1890. Paradoxically, it was known as one of the wickedest cities in the world, and yet in its day was also one of the most progressive, innovative and richest mining towns of the Old West. It was a bright summer day as I entered the town, but I could imagine that in winter, its hillside location, would mean grim weather. I could see that just like Greensplat, how it might become one of the starkest places on the planet, and how clearly, its best days were long distant. In actual fact though, it was not lead that made Leadville, but silver. Silver and lead occur in associated minerals and were often worked together, but it was silver that had the most value per ton.

Silver was first discovered there in 1875, and until the collapse of the world silver market in 1893, Leadville 'led' the world as a glamorous and glittering silver town. In its heyday, Leadville was the Las Vegas of that era. In 1883 at the peak of its fame, the town had ninety-seven saloons, twenty-three restaurants, countless gambling halls and brothels, as well as many other dens of iniquity. Newspapers of the era carried stories of cat-fights between women and the notorious venues such as the Bon Ton, the Odeon, the National and the Bella Union, as well as Pap Wyman's Saloon – a notorious underworld spot. You could still see miners walking into the town after pay-day, peering up at the waving prostitutes, cleavages displayed to tempt the Cousin Jacks. Apparently, lawlessness reigned supreme and if you were out late at night, it was best to keep a cocked pistol in one hand. It was all very much like St Blazey on Saturday Nights after the Football club closed. Leadville hadn't changed much in my view. It still looked pretty rough and ready, even now at the beginning of the twentieth century. Many stores in the town were boarded up, and there barely seemed a place to even get a cup of coffee. Once upon time though, there were lots of Cornish in Leadville however. Todd notes many in the Leadville directory of 1800: Anthony Barrett was the proprietor of Carbonate House (Leadville had first been known as "Carbonate Camp"), while Mrs. A. Barrett was a dressmaker. There were also businesses run by William and Albert Chellew, Frank Mitchell, Philip Oates, John Odgers, Alfred Pierce, Alfred Pomeroy, David Snell, George Trevillian and F. Treworjy.[15] One of the most successful Cousin Jacks was Edward Eddy who bought several leases in the rich carbonate silver-lead ores locally,[16] though like others, had to survive very harsh winters, as well as pollution from the mining works. However, as Rowse notes, perhaps the most famous Cornishmen in Leadville was Charles Algernon Sidney Vivian, who died there in 1880.[17] Vivian was one of the founders of the Benevolent and Protective Order of Elks and a famous Entertainer. The son of a Cornish clergyman, Vivian was born in Exeter in 1846 and as a young man became famous for his songs, skits and character sketches. Somewhat chubby and childlike, Vivian blew most of his money on fripperies or wasted it on friends. When he travelled to America he found great success in California and played the mining towns of the west. Always the dandy, in San Francisco the stores soon picked up his idiosyncratic way of dressing, offering fashionable imitation Vivian hats, collars and ties. Vivian travelled all across America, reciting stories by people like Bret Harte (who I would encounter again in California) and bringing the house down with his favourite song "Ten Thousand Miles Away", its lines reverberating emotionally with the Cornish audiences. He was married back home, but divorced his first wife and married one Imogen Holbrook in 1876 at Oakland. It was Imogen, who, after seeing an elk swimming in the Missouri river, suggested that the original "Jolly Corks" dining club should change its name to the Elks. Since then of course, the Elks have gone on to be one of the largest charitable organisations in America. Vivian had produced "Oliver Twist" in Leadville, but in the severe winter of 1880, aged only thirty-three, he caught pneumonia and died.

Vivian was perhaps the most famous Cornishman in Leadville, but there were other important Cousin Jacks there as well. From 1887 onwards the manager of the Le Plata Smelter at Leadville was one Philip Argall. Although born in Ireland in 1854, Argall was actually of Cornish stock and on his apprenticeship in Cornwall, the young Argall patented a handbrake for the horse-whim while also winning a prize for the best plan and section of any mining district from the Royal Cornwall Polytechnic Society in 1878. After working in Swansea, he also travelled to New Zealand, France and Mexico, before settling in Colorado for a time during Leadville's prosperous years. Eventually, he retired to Denver, forming a consultative partnership with two of his five sons.[18]

No-one however, is more famous in Leadville than one of its prime movers, the splendidly named Horace Austin Warner Tabor. Tabor was a stonemason, who became king of this bonanza town, but later, like many of the early mining pioneers, died in poverty. He ran a set of supply stores for miners and prospected for gold for nineteen years – making a fortune, but after a love scandal, and poor investments, he lost all his millions of dollars. Tabor built many structures in the town which still survive though. You can still see the Tabor Grand Hotel and the Opera House, where entertainers such as Oscar Wilde lectured. Once the price of silver collapsed though, people left and no-one else seemed to arrive anymore. The civic leaders tried one last ditch desperate attempt to attract people to the town. In 1896, Leadville built a spectacular ice palace of real ice costing some $40,000, but that March a rare warm chinook wind blew in and the palace melted away – together with the town's star status. Now the once stylish buildings are littered with cheap neon signs, and around the grand centre now lurk all the other trappings of any other small American town. It was a salutary experience walking Leadville's deserted streets that morning. Even my turkey sandwich, in a local diner, tasted faded and unloved. Like the Cornish who had been there before me, I decided it was time to move on.

Leadville stood at the eastern end of the White River National Forest, but I could follow Route 24 north and end up in Vail, which was located about half-way through my journey from Boulder to the Utah State line. I saw more unloved mining towns on that Route, but I didn't stop at any of them. To be perfectly honest, the image of them had become rather painful; they exuded such loss and depression. I tanked on and tried tuning into a rock radio station to lift my spirits. South-west of here lay Aspen – the designer ski resort, populated in winter by the rich and famous – but it wasn't a route I particularly wanted to take. Aspen itself, was also a silver mining area on the wide plateau at the base of Red Mountain, where, according to Todd, several Cousin Jacks from Penzance made the perilous journey from Leadville.[19] Further down in the State was the San Juan National Forest. I never made it there, but it interested me because the Cornish poet Alfred Castner King remembered the mountains there in one of his poems:

Uneven crags and cliffs of various form;
Abysmal depths and dire profundities;
Chasms so deep and awful that the eye
Of soaring eagle dare not gaze below
Lest, dizzied, he should lost his aerial poise,
And headlong falling reach the gulf below.[20]

Such John Harris-like 'dire profundities', not to mention the scared eagles were clearly influenced by his experiences on the road in America. King was thirty years old and the son of Cornish immigrants from Michigan. He had come to Colorado, like the rest of his race, to mine for silver. In 1900 though, a box of dynamite had exploded in his face and as well as the resultant blindness, he grew a beard to hide his disfigurement, yet from this tragedy he is one of the few writers who have captured the experience of this moment of Cornish-American history. His two volumes of poems – *Mountain Idylls* and *The Passing of the Storm* – are dedicated "to a rapidly disappearing class, the pioneer prospectors, whose bravery, intelligence and industry blazed the trails in the western wilderness for advancing civilisation and made possible the development of the Great West":

Some blest of wealth, some cursed by poverty;
Some in positions neutral to them both;
Some wore a gaunt and ill-conditioned look
Which told its tale of lack of nourishment.[21]

I was beginning to fear I looked this way as I entered Glenwood Canyon, so stopped off for some refreshment in a roadside cafe, buying a burrito and a can of coke. When I felt I had completely prevented the onset of 'ill-condition' I drove on again. On this side of the Rockies the Interstate follows the Colorado River, which is nowhere near the size it is in Arizona, but is still impressive. For a while I raced a long train carrying freight along the Colorado. In the end, its six engines beat me, and I let the chain of tagged good's containers pass me by. I'm not sure where it was en-route from or headed towards – but Grand Junction at the western end of Colorado, sounded a good bet. There were still remnants of mining in these Canyons. I was reminded of something I had read in A.C. Todd, how Cornishmen like one Samuel Polglase from Wheal Vor, near Helston, first studied at a business college in Indiana, and then from Chicago, managed mines here in Colorado.[22] Chicago, where I had been a week ago, seemed a universe away – and yet there was Polglase looking after his interests across a continent in the days before e-mails and faxes. It was hard to believe it was possible to do that.

Polglase was probably a Republican like most of the early Cornish in North America. I was trying to make sense of this connection as I drove through the western half of Colorado. Although, it was now no longer possible to draw a connection between that political party and the con-temporary Cornish, various people along the way had offered their reasoning for the link. It was one of the core issues I asked them about. I concluded so far that it might have something to do with the fact that the Cornish were Methodist and Protestant; therefore Republican, whilst the Catholics were usually Democrat. The Cornish of the lead region were very much with the Union opposing slavery in the Civil War, and several volunteer units, were made up of Cornishmen. Abraham Lincoln received a heavy share of votes in southwest Wisconsin and was, of course, a

Republican himself. Therefore, there was a historical connection.

Then again, it could be put down to the fact that the Cornish are quite conservative in a way. Various Cornish-Americans had told me along the way that the Democrat Franklin D. Roosevelt (president between 1933 and 1945) was not very popular in their households or extended families. California and especially Northern California was a Republican stronghold. The so-called 'New Deal' was not well received by the descendants of the '49ers. There were other possibilities however: during the nineteenth century, the party of Lincoln was closely identified with the transcontinental railroad and the development of the American West. Perhaps it was not that the Cornish were Republicans, but that they were Westerners, and the West was predominantly Republican. One has to remember that in nineteenth-century terms, the north-west included places like Minnesota. Interestingly, I was later to learn that places like New Almaden were represented in the State Legislature by a descendant of the mining camp – a fourth generation Republican. This brings into question another related factor: Management versus Labour. Len Rowe, a Cornishman from Eveleth, Minnesota, told me on e-mail how the Cornish were some of the earliest arrivals in America, and were often captains and superintendents – management. Later arrivals were more likely to align themselves with the unions, Democrats and Socialists. Another Cornish-American, recently deceased, made the statement: "In my obituary, which I have written, I have said that I lived and died as a Republican, just like my father and his father before me."

The scenery was starting to change now as I contemplated the complex politicality of the Cornish in America. I ploughed on through Garfield County. The road had dropped down across vast areas of near desert. It had got warmer and I was sweating hard. I pulled into a 'Days Inn' for the night and watched the latest in 'docu-soap tv' shows – *The Anna Nicole Show*. You must know her – she is the large, tall buxom blonde (in my view rather grotesque) who married an elderly millionaire – only to claim his fortune when he died. Billed as the place where 'pop culture and

103

cleavage converge', Smith and a gaggle of her eccentric lackeys such as her sixteen-year old son Daniel, purple-haired personal assistant Kim, fashion advisor Bobby Trendy and Sugar Pie the dog are followed by the cameras around Los Angeles. Nicole sounds as if she is perpetually high on drugs, while the lackeys cater for her every whim. I watched a couple of episodes and thought back on Leadville – the place where the Cornish and cleavage converged. That night I cranked up the air-conditioning. Clearly, I'd had my touch of wickedness and was all hot and bothered. It was time to repent, and cool down. There were signs saying 'Utah' ahead.

Notes

1. Sandra Dallas and Kendal Atchison (1985) *Colorado Ghost Towns and Mining Camps*, Oklahoma, University of Oklahoma Press, p.109.
2. Ibid., p.93.
3. Ibid., p.139.
4. A.C. Todd (1995 [1967]) *The Cornish Miner in America*, Spokane, Washington: The Arthur H. Clark Co., p.153.
5. Ibid., p. 153; A.L. Rowse (1991 [1969] *The Cornish in America*, Redruth: Dyllansow Truran, pp.324-30; John Rowe (1974) *The Hard Rock Men: Cornish Immigrants and the North American Mining Frontier*, Liverpool: Liverpool University Press, p.205-6.
6. Lynn I. Perrigo (1937) 'The Cornish Miners of Early Gilpin County' in *Colorado Magazine*, Vol. XIV, pp.93-3.
7. Rowse, op.cit., p.344.
8. Todd, op.cit., p.154.
9. Ibid., p.177.
10. Mentioned in Rowe, op.cit., p.196.
11. Todd, op.cit., p.156.
12. Rowe, op.cit., p.196.
13. Cited in Rowse, op.cit., p.336. See also 'T.A. Rickard – a Profile' in A. J. Wilson (1979) *The Pick and the Pen: An outline of the history of mining journalism*, London: Mining Journal Books Limited, pp.130-47.
14. Todd, op,cit., p.162.
15. Ibid., p.179.
16. Ibid., p.178.
17. Rowse, op.cit., pp.331-4.

18. See ibid. pp.337-9.
19. Todd, op.cit., p.155.
20. Ibid., p.151.
21. Ibid.
22. Ibid., p.132.

5

Viva Las Vegas . . .

The next morning, just as I was leaving Colorado, around the railway town of Grand Junction, I began to pick up on a very worrying phenomenon. There seemed to be signs, stickers and posters everywhere indicating that I should take warning that I was about to enter the State of Utah. It was a bit like coming into Camborne from Redruth. Presumably much of this had to do with the fact that Utah is famous for the Mormon church. Utah, despite its breathtaking scenery seemed the kind of State where they would ban Ozzy Osbourne, Black Sabbath, Judas Priest and any other kind of heavy metal mining. I don't really know too much about the Mormon church – so if you are a Mormon, please accept this warning and close this book now. What I do know is picked up probably from a mixture of folklore, legend and plain old gossip (Just like other religions then!).

Basically, the story of the Mormons runs like this: they believe that the true and proper story of God and Jesus Christ was revealed to one Joseph Smith over the course of several years, beginning when he was a fourteen year-old farm hand living in New York State. One day Joseph Smith went into the woods to pray, because he was confused as to which branch of the Christian church to join. In the wood he had a vision of God and Jesus, and they told him to wait for further guidance. Three years later an angel called Moroni appeared and told Joseph that in a hill nearby he would discover a set of gold plates, inscribed with the history of an early, lost civilisation in America, found by three of the lost tribes of Israel (the Cornish incidentally are considered by some to be another lost tribe of Israel in case you didn't know). Apparently the whole history had been recorded by one man called Mormon, and buried by his son, Moroni, who was the last of his race, known as Nephrites, to survive a series of battles with the Native American Indians who were also Israelites.

Joseph Smith, with divine help, translated these inscriptions into English before very conveniently handing the plates back to the angel, thus removing any evidence of their existence. The book he translated into English is known as *The Book of Mormon: Another Testament of Jesus Christ*, and it explains how Jesus came to America after his resurrection. Amazed? Confused? You will be. Joseph Smith is said to have had twenty-seven wives, and he and the other early leaders of the church taught that because their god had taken many wives, it was all right for them to have lots of wives as well. So polygamy was in for the Mormons, and so, for a while in the early days of the church, people of colour were dismissed as being cursed by God. For all kinds of reasons the Mormons were persecuted and forced to head westwards. They first founded Nauvoo (Hebrew for 'beautiful location') on the banks of the Mississippi in Illinois, but then in the mid-1820s a group of 148 pioneers travelled to the valley of the Great Salt Lake (Deseret) in the Utah desert, then part of Mexican territory. Despite federal manifestos against polygamy, the Mormons and Salt Lake City flourished, the people showing great business flair – so much so that the Mormon Church is the largest shareholder in *The Los Angeles Times*, owns the Beneficial Life Insurance Company and, as everyone knows, partly runs the 'Marriott' Hotel chain. So that's Utah for you in three words. Moroni. Polygamy. Weird.

That's not to say there weren't any Cornish amongst the Mormons. One of the most famous of the original Mormons was James Moyle, who was born in Cornwall in 1835. Todd eloquently tells his story.[1] A skilled mason, he left home to work on the breakwater in Plymouth Sound, and back in the city he was converted by a Mormon missionary. James embarked on a treacherous voyage from

Liverpool to St Louis in 1854, with more than a third of the passengers onboard killed by cholera. However, on reaching Salt Lake City, the walls of the Temple were beginning to be built and he quickly began work, dressing the granite blocks for its construction. His father and family meanwhile, funded by James Moyle, made the epic walk from Iowa City through the horrendous heat of the summer of 1856 across 1000 miles of prairie and mountains to join him there 'in Zion', though the journey nearly killed his father.

Congress however, was still refusing to recognise the State of Deseret and dispatched some 15,000 federal troops to sort out the Mormon problem. James Moyle enrolled as a sergeant in the Nauvoo legion militia in 1857 and blocked the entrance to Echo Canyon, afraid of further persecution and massacre. After a stand off, federal troops were eventually allowed to pass through the Salt Lake City, and the Mormons prospered. James later became one of the most important building contractors in the city. During the crisis of 1857-8, Moyle's father, John, also made a name for himself by carving out of the granite mountain at Mountainville (now called Alpine) a cave, which he then castellated to protect his family from the Federal Troops, as well as from attacks from Native Americans. Perhaps Moyle had taken inspiration from the various castles back home in Cornwall. Nearby lies a small 'Cornish-style' chapel that John also constructed. According to Rowse, the castle was like a kind of 'peel tower';[2] John choosing Mountainville to live in because it reminded him so much of Cornwall.

The other famous Cornish connection to the Mormon church is with Charles William Penrose. He was born in London in 1832, his father from Redruth and his mother from Stratton. Aged eighteen, Penrose became interested in the teachings of the Mormons and initially became a preacher and propagandist; at the same time writing numerous Mormon hymns. All the time he had wanted to travel across to America and finally in 1861, he and his family crossed in an old sailing vessel. Penrose was a man full of, in Rowse's words,' co-operative idealism'[3] and eventually it was he and others who pushed through the territorial legislature. Their efforts rewarded in 1896 when Utah became a State. Penrose was a prolific writer and speaker on the Latter-Day Saints or Mormons, and he became a respected patriarch. Rowe notes that once the Mormon Commonwealth had been admitted to full Statehood, that is when really large-scale and successful mining operations got under way.[4]

Utah is mainly composed of desert and rock, and for most of the Cornish miners heading west towards California's gold, it initially held little attraction. They were clearly much more interested in Mammon than Mormon. Besides that, the first Californian 'argonauts' in search of gold, tended to take the more northerly route along the Platte and South Pass, than the more southerly route through Utah, New Mexico and Arizona. However, back home, there was still some degree of interest in the bizarre world of Mormon polygomy which must have tempted some Cousin Jacks to take a look. The initial prospectors to the area were actually the troops of the Third Californian Infantry, led by General Connor, who when unoccupied with military proceedings, found silver and lead in Bingham Canyon, discovering the Old River Jordan claim, believed to be the first recorded in Utah. Initially, the Mormons were not keen on mining happening in Deseret anyway. They wanted to keep it an agrarian 'non-Gentile' paradise, and were afraid of being swamped by miners, but they quickly realised that rather than allow others to come and mine their resources, they should also set up their own operations. Before this realisation though, one of the most famous early mines was Emma Mine, opened up in 1868. By 1870, much to the Mormon's annoyance, the area swarmed with miners, and as Rowse notes, one of the mine's directors was Brydges Willyams of Carnanton, a Member of Parliament in Cornwall who already had large mining shares.[5] He travelled to Utah to inspect the mine. Unfortunately the ore at Emma suddenly petered out in the early 1870s and many investors lost a considerable amount of money.

Park City, to the east of Salt Lake City, was also home to many Cornish and mines were worked 'Cornish style' There, the very wet Ontario Mine had an apparently temperamental Cornish pump. Enormous in size, it was a legendary feature of the local landscape, but has long since been demolished. For all of you 56 Inch Cylinder types out there, apparently it was manufactured in San Francisco, the flywheel weighing some 70 tones and was 30 feet in diameter; the pump rod was made of Oregon pine and was 1060 feet long.[6] The Cornish stayed at Bingham and Park City until the mid-1920s; some of the them staying in the Salt Lake City area, but many of them moving to other opportunities across the country. After the closure of Emma Mine, many of the Cousin Jacks then transferred their energy to the nearby Bingham Pit, close to what is now known as the Deseret Peak Wilderness Area. Originally part of the Shining Mountains, a century or more of dynamiting has transformed this into the world's largest copper mine, owned by the Kennecott Copper Company. Resembling some of the larger china clay pits of mid-Cornwall, the oval shaped quarry has now engulfed the Canyon which gave it its name, and looks set to continue to expand. Billions of dollars worth of copper have been removed from its depths since the late nineteenth century. Filled with the kind of desolation so well-known in mid-Cornwall, there is a strange irony in this: it seems like the Mormon's initial fears have been realised.

Despite all my earlier cynicism, as I travelled through the State, I actually felt I had a special connection with Utah. On my mother's side of the family, my Great great uncle Leroy (who, at one stage in his journeying, had passed through Mineral Point) made his way down to Utah to mine, I believe, at Bingham Pit. A cousin of mine, who is far more into genealogical research than I will ever, ever, ever be, has mapped the comings and going of the Roberts side of my family and organised a family reunion about ten years ago at Gunwen Chapel near Luxulyan, where many of our family were christened. Leroy Roberts, himself a man in his seventies and a Mormon, his great great nephew (or something like that) was over then to see the old country. If I had been slightly more organised in my travels maybe I could have popped in to see how the Roberts family was doing this side of the Atlantic, but to be honest, when I got to Interstate 15, I had a choice of enormous and universe-changing proportions.

I could head north to Salt Lake City, world capital of genealogical research and the Mormon Church or I could head south to the den of iniquity and wretched hive of scum and villainy that was Las Vegas. These were the choices: Gambling versus Bingham Pit. Slot machines versus Deseret. Sex, drugs, rock n' roll versus Park City. Neon overload versus the stomping ground of Penrose's hymns ("School thy feelings: there is power, In the cool collected mind; Passion shatters reason's tower, Makes the clearest vision blind . . .") Did I flip a coin? Did I hell? Hey, I'm a Foxhole boy . . . I put my pedal to the metal and headed south. Bingham, Park City and Deseret would have to wait until another trip. I'd come close to them. Besides, what could you tell me about open-cast quarrying? I'd lived with it for most of my life.

Coming off Interstate 70, just facing you are the Mineral Mountains and out on Route 21 is Old Frisco Mining Town. The romance of the name made me take a detour. I couldn't resist. I drove out there to look around, hoping to find some trace of the Cornish. Anything would've done: a pasty bag blowing by the tumbleweeds, a lone pick wrapped in McDonalds' trash . . . To be honest, there wasn't much left of anything really, aside from the souvenir shack and the old but enthusiastic woman who told me I had staggered upon 'the most amazing testament to the miners of the old west'.

"What about Emma Mine?" I asked.

"What about Bingham?" I protested.

"What about Park City?" I pleaded.

"What about dear old Leroy – from Luxulyan?" I whispered.

"I don't know nothun' 'bout them places," she said, but pointed to where I should go.

Basically, there were a lot of sheds. I mean I know that an Englishman's home is his castle, and that a Cornishman's home is his shed, but even so, it was all a bit underwhelming. Unlike Colorado, there didn't really seem much left t'all. The mouth-organ was strangely quiet here. I bought a postcard and drove back onto Interstate 15, wishing for a moment I had headed north to Deseret.

When you are on the road as long as I had been that August, a lot of the scenery merges into one. You can take as many notes as you want, take as many photographs as

111

possible, but even then the memory fails. No – it isn't old age either. It's simply running through so much beautiful scenery that individual pockets of it become distorted, so you can't remember what you saw where and when. What you saw just an hour ago can feel like it was something you saw three days ago, or maybe weeks ago. I had that feeling going through the Escalente Valley area of Iron County. Yes – there was mining. I could see whims in the foothills.

The other memory I have of this stretch was looking up into Washington County and seeing smoke rising from the tallest peak. Initially, I thought it was a volcano of some kind, such was the quantity of smoke rising off it. Volcanoes? In Utah? Then the penny dropped. This was the smoke of some fairly serious forest fires, which had plagued this part of the US all summer. I couldn't tell exactly how many acres of forest were burning as the range was still far off, but it was enough to lessen the sun considerably. Up there somewhere was the Old Silver Reef Mining town. It would have been good to have stopped there too, but I'd had my fill of ruined sheds and was a man on a mission by now. I had to get to Vegas.

It was getting on for dusk as I thundered down the bottom end of Interstate 15. My head was filled with old ZZ Top tunes and my ears were popping from coming down off the mountains. I wound down the window to feel the desert heat. I knew it was approaching a hundred outside, and I needed to restock my supply of water. I pulled over at a lonely gas station and bought all I needed. I was getting tired of the drive. The map, as so often in America, deceived me in terms of its scale. I only had that bottom inch and a quarter until I got to Las Vegas, but the traffic was moving more slowly. Maybe it was because on the other side of the road there seemed to be more state troopers than usual. Perhaps they were picking up break-away polygamist Mormons under the influence, heading back home from the gambling centre of the West.

Eventually though, Vegas rose out of the desert in the way that you always imagine. Casinos now littered the sides of the road instead of Joshua Trees. The further downtown I got, the madder the driving. Why was everyone is such a hurry for the crap tables? I must have passed three accidents before I saw my exit. I perked up and turned off at Cheyenne Avenue. That sounded very Western. Hey, I was driving down Cheyenne Avenue in the middle of Vegas! Whoopee! In Las Vegas, I'd actually arranged to stay with an old friend of mine – Kristen Maul. Kristen had been an American teacher-in-training who had completed six months under my guidance (or perhaps incompetence) when I was Head of English and Drama at Sir James Smith's School in Camelford. She'd been an exceptional student with a good relationship with the pupils. I'd said that I'd look her up if ever I was passing through Vegas. Kristen was now married to a guy called James Woodall, who worked as a personal fitness instructor and they'd just had a baby – James Woodall the third, who they'd nicknamed Trey (the third – like the Cornish 'try').

Like most professional people in Vegas they lived in a brand-new gated community about ten miles out from the 'Strip'. Their house was wonderfully designed and mansion-like in its dimensions. I gazed in awe at their standard of living. Kristen and I were able to carry on a dialogue about her memories of Cornwall, and how much she'd learnt about teaching at Camelford. I'd taken her to a few of the touristy places back home, but her overwhelming memory was of the damp and the mist which of course, pervades north Cornwall and Camelford in particular. We spent a lot of time chatting about members of staff and former pupils. Kristen had loved Tintagel, Boscastle and Bodmin Moor, even though we agreed, they were about as different to Vegas as you could probably find.

What is amazing in Vegas is the heat. It's a heat I find easier to stand than that in other parts of the US though. It's a dry, arid heat, with low humidity. That means it's much more comfortable for the Cornish than say, the climes of the mid-West or Florida. In fact, in order to counter against humidity James told me there were strict conditions in place in Vegas about how many plants and what kind of plants you could have in your yard. He told me that since he'd been living there – he'd noticed more humidity, so the authorities were cracking down. Keep your garden like a desert they seemed to be saying. I was imagining the signs:

"Minimise your lawn!" "Plant more cactuses!" and "Use more succulents!"

All of my preconceptions about Las Vegas were blown away. Somehow I'd always conceived of it as a kind of American Blackpool – slightly seedy and slightly run-down, full of sad people gambling their lives away. That was soon knocked out of me. My first taste of Las Vegas's sophistication was a trip down the 'Strip' more or less from 'Million Dollar', 'Vegas World' and the 'Jackpot' casinos in the north to 'Mandalay Bay', 'Klondyke' and 'Luxor' in the south. Let's clear one thing up. When I say casino, it is not some dodgy room above an Amusement Arcade in Penzance, oh no. These are multi-million pound entertainment complexes. We're talking light years beyond the slot machine here.

The first casino we entered was one of the grandest – the 'Bellagio'. Outside the building were multiple traffic lanes for the arriving guests (we'd actually parked round the back in the cheaper 'day' visitor area) to be greeted by top-hatted concierges, with cut-off, sleeveless dress jackets (a nice touch I thought, in 100° heat!). The place oozed money. Inside the mock classical air-conditioned lounges and marble thoroughfares were displays of balloon art and rotating seasonal flower displays. Palms poked from every corner. There were fountains everywhere. We trundled around the gaming floors and heard the whip and buzz of the slot machines. Elsewhere, flashy dealers made smart moves with cards. Now if only they played euchre . . . What would my opening gambit be? Perhaps, a suit, a cigar, and a pint of Skinners. Now, woz on?

Across from the 'Bellagio' is the Eiffel Tower. No, I'm not kidding. And no, it hadn't been moved here in an act of Breton Nationalist terrorism either. It is an impressive scale model of the real thing, which is still quite a structure in itself – all part of the 'Paris' Las Vegas Complex. There too, is a mini-Arc de Triomphe, and I suppose, because I did not enter that one, any manner of French-themed gaming. Somehow, for the Americans, France still represents the height of culture. To the left was the famous 'Bally's'; then along the road, 'Aladdin'. Down the road, a bleddy great mock pyramid belonging to the 'Luxor', complete with exterior hieroglyphics and a Sphinx. Las Vegas liked to hold the whole of the world's money in its hot sweaty little hand. And good luck to it. It was, after all, a lot of fun. So if the first phase of my look at Vegas was daytime orientation, it was viewed best to make our next attack in the night. So we headed downtown, which was when, in fact, everyone else decided to make their attack too. 'New York, New York' was lit up like that city's skyline (the hotel is a model of the most famous buildings in New York. No twin towers by the way.), while we followed a taxi offering free transport to 'Striptease' – a 'Gentleman's Club'. I almost asked James to follow that cab, but instead we turned into the back lot. Neon signs wove their magic everywhere: 'Welcome to the City of Entertainment'; purples, yellows and greens beckoning me – with all of my ten dollars of gambling money . . . proper Cornish, see, tighter than a duck's ass. We parked up in the hottest car park I have ever been in, and James and Kristen locked their car. Believe it or not, Trey was with us in his buggy, though he was sound asleep. He seemed decidedly un-impressed with the Strip, even though, like me, this was his first visit.

Meanwhile, in the searing Nevada heat, I was searching for Arthur. I had quested many miles "my friends" to reach him and my journey would soon be complete. I was ready to kneel before my ancient Celtic lord. I was so certain I would find him, I could see choughs in the sky (well, actually the landing lights of 747s – but in this kind of heat, they'd do). I had 'Nyns yu marow myghtern Arthur! [You are not dead King Arthur!]' on my chapped lips. In case you don't know, for the Cornish, King Arthur is the ultimate Celtic resistance against the Anglo-Saxons. He is the ultimate Cornish champion, born, of course, at Tintagel, and probably having a residence at Castle-an-Dinas on the Goss Moor, in mid-Cornwall. None of this French embellishment for us. And none of this Arthur – 'the English king' in a St George Cross. In fact none of this English Heritage rubbish at Tintagel either. I won't go on. I might end up being like one of the Stannary Parliament. If you want to find out more about my take on King Arthur, then read *Inside Merlin's Cave: A Cornish Arthurian Reader*, but if you're like me, then the only film about King Arthur that captures anything of the legend, is John Boorman's *Excalibur*, and probably, if you're like me (rather sad in my quest for Cornish-related films) you might have also seen Sean Connery and Richard Gere in *First Knight* – a mid 1990s' weepy capturing the love triangle between Arthur, Lancelot and Guinevere. The most amazing thing about that film though is not the plot but its incredible vision of Camelot, which in this author's view, made the Arthur's 'English' seat more like a huge sponge fairy cake, with blue icing on the tower rooftops than any believable castle. If you have some idea what I am talking about, then you will known what 'Excalibur's' Casino looks like. It looks like a huge sponge fairy cake, set down in the Nevada desert, only the towers have red and gold icing as well. *Excaliburs* is basically 'L'-shaped with the casino locked in the middle between two tower blocks given a 'medieval-style' make-over. During the daytime, in the central tower above the main walkway into the building is a clock, but at night this revolves, and instead sits a very lost looking Merlin with a laser wand. I heard him talk to me.

"Pard," he said, "how in the hell did I end up here?"

There was more inside. Murals adorned the walls like some crazy Mists of Avalon. Here's what you've got: someone took a bit of Pre-Raphaelite Arthurianism and 'Vegas-ised' it a little, so near the cloakroom, there's Arthur stramming along in his boat, with Excalibur jumping out at it. Meanwhile there's poor Merlin again, looking stressed at Arthur's incompetence to pluck the sword from the lake. Still he could chill out under the many little tree-like groves and fountains that lay between the roulette tables. It was all very St Nectan's Kieve in my view, and in its own way, rather tasteful. In fact, I went home wanting a tree-like grove in my own living room. Fur certain, twudn' no Dozmary Pool and thas' a fact.

There was, however, a lot on offer for the average Cornishman seeking his King. I could go along to the Tournament of Kings – 'a time when honour and glory were chivalrous goals'. There I could enjoy dinner while watching some jousting. The show features jousting, invading armies, dragons, fire-wizards and dinner – all for a total of $41.95

116

plus tax. It sounded a bit like a Ronnie James Dio concert – right up my street. Alternatively I could 'Catch a Rising Star' in the theatre (a sort of Dark Age *Pop Idol*) or go and witness the six-pack, groomed male revue known as 'Thunder from Down Under', – basically a striptease featuring knights of old – but these didn't tempt me as much as 'The Court Jester's Stage' or 'Fantasy Faire Midway'. The latter sounded particularly interesting – particularly if it turned out to be the female equivalent of 'Thunder from Down Under'.

There was also the 'Round Table' buffet to be sampled (basically, a lot of pies and shrimp). I could find that on the Medieval Village Level. Tonight though, I would have to settle for the tacky dragons and medieval paraphernalia on offer in the children's fayre beneath the casino. It was a bit like the Cornish Gorseth for sure. Here, they taught young children how to gamble, with activities that I thought went out with the Ark, or at least the old Fairs that used to come round our village. Still, they did have some good plastic swords and armour. I could almost hear the Bards swearing allegiance to Arthur and the shout of 'Es Cres?'. After being overwhelmed by the ultimate tackiness of the souvenirs, James and Kristen took a photograph of me sitting between the front paws of a big purple dragon. It was like Tintagel on acid. I checked out their website later on. The whole site has that sort of 'medievaly'/'Celticy' writing (it could be straight out of the Cornish Language Board to be perfectly honest!) and lots of people dressed up in knightly and damsel garb, like a Renaissance Fayre on the internet. Jesus, I thought, this is just like it is back home the first Saturday in September.

I reached in my pocket and pulled out ten dollars and held it up against one of the mock electric torches. The face of the aide to General Washington and co-author of the Federalist Papers, Alexander Hamilton, looked me sternly in the eye. Cue: soaring music and a halo of light. I had found my grail and was about to shoot my load. For me, this is how gambling goes. I play ten bucks, no more no less. I begin to win some money, and pop it into my little cute plastic 'Excalibur's' bucket. The quarters pop into the tray of the machine. So then I think, here's what I'll do, I'll just gamble the amount I have won, so I get to keep my original stake. That way, I'll have fun and I won't lose any more. Then I start to lose. Well, I'll just put two bucks in. I lose. I'll put another buck in and see what happens. Repeat. Repeat. Repeat, so I win, then lose that lot. So now I just put three bucks in, and so on. The reel flashes its last sword, suit of armour and dragon at me, and my little plastic bucket was empty. It was time to head home. James and I stayed up late watching *Star Wars: Episode IV, A New Hope* on his mega-huge movie theatre system with surround sound. We drank beer and ate pizza and all seemed good with the world. I'd lost, but hey, I'd lost a lot less than most people in Vegas that day.

On Sunday morning, like many Americans (and surprisingly many Cornish-Americans I encountered during my travels), Kristan, James and Trey went to church. Being a twenty-first century lapsed Methodist and feeling somewhat pagan for saying I didn't want to go), I stayed in bed. I was actually on an inflatable mattress in James' work-out room. The mattress was amazingly comfortable, and for the first time in several weeks, I managed to catch up on some sleep. On the road like this, one of the strangest feelings is how everything seems so distant, and these thoughts were going through my lapses into wakefulness. For one thing, the life you have back in Cornwall seems a million years away – almost as if you had completely stepped outside of yourself.

I was still contemplating this as I poured a Strawberry and Banana yoghurt onto some milk and cereal, and assumed the position of that great American pass-time known as channel-surfing. *Star Trek: The Next Generation* was on, and so I watched that for a while, recalling that yesterday, we had eaten lunch in 'Quark's Restaurant', a Star Trek-themed venue and museum inside the Las Vegas 'Hilton'. It was all good fun with Star Trek-themed burgers and salads being served to you by the Ferengi and the Borg. The 'Hilton' ran some good events as well. *The Who* had recently passed through (culminating in the cocaine-influenced death of the bass-player John Entwhistle) and *Yes* were on their way. As we had passed other concerts and shows advertised around the City, I had instantly thought of my good friend and sometime co-writer Tim

Saunders and his daughter – Gwenno. Now Gwenno, as well as being a speaker of Cornish and Welsh, is also an exceptionally talented Irish dancer, and had spent a considerable amount of time, while still a teenager, performing in Michael Flatley's *Lord of the Dance*. I wondered how she had found Vegas. It was her big break. She had given up a lot of her education and 'normal' youth for that, but after her time in the show, she landed a part as a lap-dancer in the Welsh-language Soap Opera – *Poebl y Cwm*, ending up being voted Wales' Number One bachelorette. She has recently launched her own pop career, releasing as I write a latter-day Madonna-esque single titled 'Mor Haid' – the first real Cornish language pop single. To use a very Vegas expression, it rocks. In my view, Gwenno is about as big an advert for the Cornish language as you can get.

That afternoon, we headed over to James' parents' house. If Kristen and James's house was manorial, then his parents' place was palatial. James's father, James Woodall the first, I suppose, was a Vietnam veteran pilot. Being the first I'd met in America, I was rather keen to talk to him about the war and his experiences. I was dredging up from the far depths of my mind relevant material on flying learnt from my days in the Air Training Corps 1225 St Austell Squadron. Somehow it didn't really match his experiences of flying Phantoms, and then later F.10 Eagles. His daughter was out in Afghanistan chasing Taliban, piloting some kind of gunship. It all made me feel very humble and rather ineffectual, on some mad crusade around Cornish America. Still we did the 'Cornish' thing – which means explaining who the Cornish are and why we like to think of ourselves as different. Over lunch, James Woodall the first, now flying for Southwest Airlines, explained how when people came to Vegas on flights, they were, in Cornish terms, 'full of it', drinking, screaming and partying hard. On the way home he said, the flights were a lot quieter, the passengers either lamenting their losses or regretting leaving Las Vegas. Perhaps a bit of Hunter S. Thompson's fear and loathing too.

Meantime, I had been called out to the pool. I'm never really confident with pools. I mean, in the one day of sunshine we have every summer in Cornwall, who do I know with a pool? The nearest thing I had when I was growing up was Carpalla Pit and that was most often filled with mica and stolen cars. This though, looked like something out of a David Hockney painting. There was not a cloud in the sky and the thermometer on the wall inched around to 117°. The pool sounded very good indeed. I lathered up on waterproof suntan lotion and dived in. I can tell you that I soon became super confident with pools, and moved deftly between the main pool and the bubbling spa. James the Second's mother brought me out a Margarita and a straw hat to cover my head. This was the life I told myself. Who could be bothered about the Cornish in America, when you could gamble, watch *Star Wars* on a home theatre and lounge around in a pool in Nevada? As bubbles of water hit me all over, and I took another sip of the Margarita, I wondered if A.L. Rowse had ever dealt with these feelings. It was an 'if they could see me back home now' moment.

I was to see a very different side of Las Vegas the next day. Kristen took me down to the facility where she now works. She is a counsellor and teacher for children in crisis at a unit attached to a large Las Vegas Police Department in the southern part of the city. There, children who have been abandoned, abused or attacked can gain refuge and an education while their individual or family problems are sorted out by the Police and Social Services. It was a very modern and friendly building with a good sized auditorium, doubling as an assembly and library. In the Infants' room I was amazed to see a range of top-notch lap-top Apple Macs being used, while in the Senior's form room were a range of animals including large snakes, spiders and iguanas, which the children cared for. Kristen, the rest of the teaching staff and I bemoaned funding, curriculum changes and some of the pressures on teachers, but at least, I told them, they were all tanned – and that must help! Somehow I doubted there was this level of infrastructure ready for kids back home in Cornwall, but then Cornwall was no Las Vegas. Vegas is America's fastest growing city. Every day another 1,000 people arrive in the city, and with that comes all the broken pieces that Kristen and her team have to pick up. It was a good feeling for me to see how she had developed professionally. She seemed to think I'd had some hand in making her a good practitioner, so we celebrated with a trip to 'Starbucks'.

Kristen had been keen for me to meet her father, who, in originating from Colorado, not only had a good knowledge of some of the mines and the Cornish there, but also had visited many of the quarries and mines in his line of work as an investments manager for various companies. When we headed over there for dinner, he was full of so many good stories, that I wished I'd taken a tape recorder along with me. I told him about my trails across the State, and he knew the mining region around Boulder very well. He remembered the legends of Cousin Jacks in the Rockies and knew of them as hard men, who were well-respected. When he was a young man, he recalled he and a partner, trying to buy up some of the old mining claims around Central City, and develop the property – probably into skiing hostels and lodges, but the deal fell through and it never happened. I wondered if these belonged to Cornishmen. We agreed that if he'd still kept copies of the old claims, we'd perhaps be able to tell from the names and dates – but it was one that would have to remain a tantalising mystery. I told him that I'd found Utah very beautiful, and he told me a yarn about the time he been flying up from Arizona to Montana (to see some mine workings there) and, for a prank, the pilot took them under some of Utah's rock arches.

"That must have been scary," I said.

"No," he said. "Not as scary as some of the mines up in Montana I had to go down . . ."

He paused for a while, then said, "There were Cornish up there too weren't there?"

"Yes," I said. "A lot around Butte . . ."

For a place that felt like the mouth-organ would have nothing to play, Los Vegas actually carried a lot of Cornwall and Cousin Jack in it. It wasn't in the old mine workings – but was elsewhere, in the memories of Kristen's father, in Kristen's own experience and learning with Cornish children, and in the myth, however tacky, however naff, of Excalibur's Casino. Tintagel on acid. Yes, Tintagel on acid was what it was.

It was hard saying goodbye to Kristen, James and Trey.

They're the kind of people who you know you'd hang out with if they lived closer. Besides, James was the kind of personal trainer I liked. He made me feel fit. He also told me I didn't look thirty-five, so that Tuesday morning things were already off to a good start. It didn't last for long. I pulled out of James Harbin Avenue (named like other roads in this subdivision after a dead police-officer) for the last time, wondering how on earth this poor cop had been killed and looked back on the Woodall family waving after me. They were free of the mad Cornishman at last. Who was I going to talk to about *Star Wars* now? I needed gas so Kristen had advised me to pull into a station about three miles down Cheyenne Avenue which had a huge stars and stripes flag waving.

"You can't miss it," she said.

She wudn' wrong. The flag dwarfed the station. It looked like it had been planted there by some passing patriotic Bolster giant, and might have even dwarfed the 'Luxor' pyramid Casino in sheer terms of scale. People in these parts sure do feel proud to be American. Beneath it was a typical subdivision gas station, and I was about to have an American moment. I knew I was going to be driving through the desert that day, and although I love deserts, they also scare me. I continually worried about what the hell I would do if the car broke down. I couldn't 'zactly ring up Hawkins Motors for a tow. For desert driving you needed to carry water, food and fill up on gas.

Petrol pumps in Britain are pretty damn regular in my view. You pick the pump handle up and off you go – expensive as hell – but off you go. In America, petrol pumps come in all kinds of varieties – types you press a button, types you pull up the suspension arm of the nozzle, types where you have to create a suction over the tank to make the thing work, types where you have to pledge allegiance to whatever gas company it is and turn around three times (I made the last one up, but it felt like that sometimes). Besides that, then there's all the varieties of unleaded petrol. Sorting out what is regular unleaded can be difficult. There's extra-zappy unleaded, then slightly super unleaded, then regular – but even then, that's called something else.

What was going to make my morning though was the

payment method. Unlike Britain, where drive-offs are fairly uncommon (unless apparently you work at any of the services along the M4 motorway), a good many gas stations insist on you paying before you pump. Most tell you that on signs on the pumps – clear as mud. Well, not this place. Instead I spent five minutes trying to extract any small amount of gas from the first pump I tried, then moved my car to a second pump. I tried waving to the cashier, but she just waved back. What on earth was I doing wrong? In the end, I did my best Hugh Grant impersonation and asked in what seemed to me like my most formal English, "Why isn't Pump 4 working?"

Unfortunately the combination of my unnatural voice and the Vegas cashier helped me no further. I went outside and tried pumping again. Then it dawned on me – I probably would have to pay cash first. I scanned the court. Did it look the kind of place where dudes in do-rags would spin off with a tank-full? Well, not really I concluded, but still everyone else locally seemed to know what to do. In any case, I was one of the few customers in gas stations generally who paid with cash. Everyone else seemed to be using credit or debit cards. Suddenly cash seemed very last century, but I handed my twenty bucks over the counter and pointed to where my car was. This time the pump worked. Only then did my morning get better. There was that lovely feeling of watching the so slow-turning dials as the fuel chugged into my gas-tank. Then the same question: Why aren't people back home in Cornwall rioting over the price of fuel? Just to celebrate, I purchased that road-food *par excellence*, the 'Hostess' Cherry Pie and a Diet Coke. Rick Stein – look at me now.

"I'm sorry honey," said the Cashier. "We just didn't know what you were about."

"Don't worry about it," I replied.

"Where you from anyway?"

"Britain," I said, "A place called Cornwall – in the west.."

"You a long way from home then . . ."

At least she didn't give me the Austin Powers thing.

I looked at the fuel gauge. It pinged as it went over the edge of the completely filled mark. To my right I had a

Cherry Pie and a Diet Coke. To my rear were enough bottles of water to supply the French Foreign Legion, and assorted snacks in case the desert and I met head on. It was only seven in the morning and already the sun felt high in the sky, brewing the kind of heat that in Cornwall would have people convinced they'd not seen a summer like it for many a year.

"'Ebm seen nothun' like ut maid," I could hear old boys saying.

Notes

1. A.C. Todd (1995 [1967]) *The Cornish Miner in America*, Spokane, Washington: The Arthur H. Clark Co., p.233-5.
2. A.L. Rowse (1991 [1969] *The Cornish in America*, Redruth: Dyllansow Truran, p.302.
3. Ibid., p.309.
4. John Rowe (1974) *The Hard Rock Men: Cornish Immigrants and the North American Mining Frontier*, Liverpool: Liverpool University Press, p.203.
5. Rowse, op.cit., p.314.
6. Ibid., p.316.

6

'Ee was in some State boy . . .

I joined Route 95 heading northwest out of Vegas, passing yet more gated communities, car dealerships and neighbour-hood casinos. Ahead of me lay most of the 'silver State' of Nevada and a lot of wild and inhospitable desert. On the map, Nevada looks like a rectangle with an isosceles trian-gle placed beneath it. The State's geometry only becomes scat out of place in the bottom right hand corner where Lake Mead and the Black Mountains meet Arizona. I was seeing more of what Nevada looked like, since when I'd arrived, I'd been driving in the dusk. Route 95 snaked though the Spring Mountains to the south and the Spotted and Sheep Ranges to the north. Occasionally Joshua trees popped their heads out of the scrub and made me think of U2 and their 1987 album of the same name.

I was headed for Cornish country up in the middle and north of the State close to the Californian border. Just north of Vegas were a lot of restricted areas to the left and right of the road – the former a prison (hence the warning signs not to pick up any hitch-hikers), the latter a 'Military Restricted Area' which put me in mind all at once, of Hanger 18, Roswell and the X-Files. For a population of some 1,206,152 people, Nevada looked plain deserted. Most of them must live in either Vegas, Carson City or Reno. It definitely had that kind of Stithians eerieness about it.

Some of the eerieness may come from the fact that

Nevada is regarded by many as one of the hardest places to mine on the earth. The area was originally California's first colony and most of the Cornish and other nationalities who entered it, were following the natural direction of the Comstock Lode in from California. Indeed, for many of the Cornish in the 1850s, Comstock was actually synonymous with Nevada. The first discoveries of gold and silver were made in Carson Valley in 1849 and gradually, the mining areas of Carson City, Virginia City, Gold Hill, Silver City and Stage Coach were opened up in the area that lies north-east of the trendy snowboarding resort of Lake Tahoe, just back from the present State line with California. The mines in Nevada were characterised in general by horrendous working conditions: a miner could often be working in high temperatures below ground, with scalding hot water, and then climb to the surface to be faced by snow and ice in long winters. Mining camps also faced supply difficulties, landslides and avalanches, flash floods and the mines themselves were beset by a number of horrific accidents. From the boom and bust economies of these towns, the Cornish then moved in a westerly direction to places such as Battle Mountain and Eureka, and also south-west, back over the eventual State-line to Death Valley, and towards Pioche in Lincoln County, then back at the start of the twentieth century, to the towns of Tonopah and Goldfield.

I trundled on – past Indian Springs Air Force Base. As I slowed down, the guard watched me wondering why in the hell some idiot with Illinois licence plates was out here driving through Nevada. Must have taken a wrong turning up in Iowa or something, I could hear him thinking. Little did he know about the secret mission I was on. Indian Springs Air Force Base wasn't too far away from Lincoln County and Pioche – or at least, it looked that way on the map. In reality, it probably would have meant an immense struggle over the Pahrangat Range and the Delmar Mountains, taking me almost back into Utah again, but I would have dearly liked to have seen Pioche. As a Cornish mining town, it was active in the early 1870s, and had something of a reputation as being the toughest camp in the whole of Nevada. Apparently, rival mine-owners there hired gunmen to fight for the control of mining claims, and were said to have brought them back at the rate of a score a day![1] In the Cornish newspapers back home there were always scandalous reports of what life was like there. One writer, in the *Cornish Telegraph*, explained how water had to be brought eight miles by wagon, and sold at six cents per gallon. Of the twelve hundred people who lived there, half of them had been in the State prison, while the graveyard at Pioche had forty-one graves, only two of which were filled by death from natural causes.[2] Another writing in *The West Briton*, explained how "gambling, theatres, balls, saloons, and, not the least, houses of ill-fame, drain the working man dry . . . and many Cornishmen are here to-day who are bumming around the saloons for a drink, and are half-starved."[3] Such correspondence was bound to put off the Cornish back then, but now it somehow attracted me to it.

At Amargosa Valley a sign pointed to Death Valley. I have to say it too, looked fairly inviting. I'd always wanted to go there. There are signs you read as you enter which inform you of how many people have died there in the past few years. I imagined all the earlier Spanish and Mexican explorers who had somehow accidentally ended up in Death Valley filled with its foreboding petrified forests, vicious alkali basins, cacti, snakes and strange Gila monsters. They must have thought they had somehow stumbled into Hell itself. Today it is marked by places with hellish names like Dante's View, the Devil's Golf Course, Furnace Creek, Stovepipe Wells and Funeral Mountains. Todd records how in making a short-cut from Wisconsin to California, one William Lewis Manly led a party through Death Valley in 1849 and must certainly have found Cornish miners there, for he recalled the miners they met would not accept paper money and only preferred silver dollars or English sovereigns, something apparently very characteristic of the Cousin Jacks.[4] Sadly, thirteen of Manly's party eventually died in the Valley.

The most famous Cornish connection to Death Valley, however, are the exploits of one Vernon Tregaskis. Todd notes that Tregaskis had initially made his way down through the Comstock Lode, from Portland to Tonopah, but in 1906 became a prospector in the Valley looking for silver.[5] Unable to wash in the brackish and alkaline waters of the Valley, he and his clothing became infested with lice, though when he remembered that red ants eat lice, he stripped himself naked and threw his clothes into an ant nest. Then he remembered that despite the daytime heat, it becomes very cold in the evening at an altitude of 7,000 feet. It remains unclear whether Tregaskis's prospecting was successful, but we can assume he put his ant- and lice-ridden clothes back on in the evening. Tregaskis's enterprises almost tempted me to turn left.

Instead, I headed north to the township of Beatty. Beatty looked pretty beat-up, kind of like St Dennis in mid-October. I was quite an event in the Beatty tourism office. They hadn't had a Cornishman pass through before, and so threw leaflets at me showing loads of mining trails that I could hike; perhaps these were the original treks of Manly and Tregaskis. What made me laugh most about Beatty was that it promoted itself as the 'Gateway to Death Valley'. When I crossed the railroad in the middle of the town, it was like crossing the river Styx. Somehow it seemed very appropriate.

That's one thing I like about America, is that no town is ever too small to have some relevance. I must have passed hundreds on my travels: 'Welcome to Pleasant Dale, Nebraska: Biggest Corn Producer in Lancaster County', 'Moron, Iowa: Home to the River Beavers Baseball Team' or 'White River, South Dakota: Dakota's finest river'. None of these really exist. I just made them up – but go, see what I mean. Then, in the blink of an eye comes the 'We're missing you already' sign, usually scrawled on the locality's water tower. I want more Cornish towns and villages to have such signs. I know what my childhood village Foxhole, would be: 'Foxhole: More mica than you can handle' and Probus would be: 'Probus: We're fine now we're bypassed'. Invent your own. Hours of fun.

In the end, I decided Death Valley was not for me and continued northwards. It was about 9.30 a.m. by the time I'd made it through the Amargosa Desert onto the Sarcobatus salt flats. The heat was making the road a mirage in front of me, rather like the way it had made asbestos look like silver for poor old Vernon Tregaskis.

Vultures, or what looked to be vultures were circling. A sign was coming up on the right hand side. I passed it, then stopped immediately, backed up the car and re-read it again: 'The Shady Lady Brothel, 2 miles'. Brothels advertising? This was like *Denny's* hamburgers.

I put the car into Drive and sped on. This I had to see. Sure enough, two miles on was the Shady Lady Brothel. You know how comparatively early in the morning it was. There must have been fifty trucks and cars parked outside the place. The brothel itself was a one-story kind of shack, there bold as brass on route 96 north. Then I remembered. In some counties in Nevada, prostitution was legalised. Well, the ladies inside were making good advantage of morning wood, I concluded. I supposed there wasn't much else to do on Sarcobatus salt flats.

Besides I thought to myself, what brought the brothels here to begin with – miners, and who were those miners – well, many of them were Cousin Jacks: setting the agenda of sexual commerce in this end of the State from times back in Pioche. This was great – I was meeting the rotten, seedy underbelly of Cornish America; the kind of stuff you just didn't seem to get much of in A.L. Rowse. I was to revisit the theme of prostitution on my later arrival in Grass Valley, but for now, this made my morning. There was more to come too. About five miles along, just before Scotty's Junction was another brothel: 'The Bobtail'. It was enough to make a Cornishman reach for several bottles of water. It too, was packed for morning business. As I drove past, I remembered Les Douch's words when I was once sat researching Cornish Methodism in the Courtney Library at the Royal Institution of Cornwall. He said to me gravely, "You dun't look like a Methodist . . ." I protested and informed him how I'd been brought up a Methodist – all proper like. I wondered if the girls way back when, minded if any of the Cousin Jacks were Methodist. Either way, it didn't look like there were too many Methodists left at Scotty's Junction.

The radio died in the desert. All I could find was an obligatory Country and Western station and another Christian broadcast; intermingled with more words of advice from Dr Laura. Haven't I told you about Dr Laura?

129

This show provided me with hours of entertainment on the road. Listeners phone up Dr Laura mainly from the States of Nevada and Utah (though today bizarrely, the station informed me, that today people in Boston for some reason, could also phone in), asking advice on such matters of enormous consequence as to whether it is appropriate for a woman to wear a pant suit at a wedding, whether she should marry Chuck – this is her fifth try, or what one should do if they knew an underage girlfriend was sleeping with an older man. The Christian advice to the latter from Dr Laura was to tell her parents – no matter what the consequences. But what if I lose her friendship, the caller asked. Dr Laura was adamant – that didn't matter. Somehow I was longing for the now retired Chris Blount and the alternative medicine practitioner – Jan de Vries ("Can 'ee spell 'un again Jan??") back on BBC Radio Cornwall. Rebelliously I whacked on a Def Leppard CD and pretended I was on VH1. I crossed Stonewall Flat and peered up to a mountain that I reckon was named Gold Point. The map showed a track heading up there and certainly some Cornishman stanked up there once, but today, I didn't have time to stand in his footsteps. You see, today I had a date with Big Bob Plock and his Goldfield Rock Shop.

Every time I think of Goldfield I want to trot out a James Bond-style Goldfinger anthem and after saying *Goldfield* in the Shirley Bassey-style, insert the appropriate wah wah wah. *Goldfield* (wah, wah wah) was no Goldfinger though. Instead it was the ultimate Nevada boom town gone bad (try saying that tongue-twister after several pints of Skinners). It was the final destination of the Cornish heading south from the Comstock Lode, and to be perfectly frank, was now the arse-end of the whole of Nevada. According to the one authority on the place, Mr. Stanley W. Paher, 'In 1908 magnificent Goldfield was Nevada's largest city and boasted the modern Goldfield Hotel, the finest between the Rockies and the Pacific coast. Other buildings down the street served a population of more than 20,000 restless souls'.[6] The restless souls concept sounded quite cool to me. I liked the idea of the Cornish being restless souls. It seemed to fit our wanderlust.

In a lot of old mining towns all over the world, the marker of the place's history is usually a lone (not to mention, poetic) mining wagon. All over America, people pointed out mining wagons to me as if they were wonders left by the gods. You probably know the ones scattered over Redruth. There's one right outside Tesco which says, 'This is what we used to do. Now we come to Tesco to shop with money we ebm' got'. In fact, Goldfield reminded me a lot of Redruth. For one thing, there's the famous 'Welcome to Redruth' sign, where some wag had sprayed on 'You're' before the welcome bit. Here it seemed appropriate too. 'You're welcome to Goldfield . . . there's bugger all left, and what's left ain't worth taking'. It was my first mining wagon in Nevada, and so I stopped the car and took a photograph of it. Clearly it had been placed there by some civic committee, celebrating Goldfield's historic past. Then when I noticed the several other hundred laying about the town, it seemed somewhat less impressive, and maybe had just been accidentally left there. All around the town were ruined shacks, sheds, emporiums, shops and churches nestling between the mountains and the sagebrush.

Every mining town has a story of how the 'rush' started and Goldfield was no different. They usually begin with the words 'It all began . . .' Ahem . . . It all began in 1902 when a couple of young Nevadans Billy March and Harry Stimler headed south from Tonopah and camped at the base of the Malapai Mesa (you'll have to take my word for it). Working one day in a tremendous storm of alkali dust, they discovered gold in the surface dust and named their claim the Sandstorm. A tent camp formed up while the media of the day promoted the newly named Goldfield as "the greatest gold camp ever known". By 1904, the population had reached 8000 and the stables, saloons and general stores were soon opening their doors to more. The search was on for quality hard-rock miners and the Cornish (opportunists to the end) moved in. Holidays, like elsewhere over western America, were marked by drilling contests which tested the strength and stamina of the miners.

As Paher notes, for around five years Goldfield grew exponentially, but by 1907 tensions developed between the mine owners and the unions, and the financial slump of

131

the same year meant that several men were laid off. Flash floods in 1913 and then a fire in 1923 put paid to many dwellings in the town.[7] Now around 150 people live there, and they all look like they want to leave.

"Yes – when you go through Goldfield, check out the Rock Shop . . ." James Woodall had said to me back in Vegas. After orientating myself in the town, and gazing out over several still operating hoists, I found the Rock Shop. It wasn't easy to miss to be honest. It lay on the first right-hand bend from Vegas in Goldfield and proudly promised 'Rocks, Relics, Gold, Gems, Bottles, Minerals'. It sounded almost too fascinating.

I was greeted by the owner, Big Bob Plock. Yes, Bob was big. He was around seven foot tall and with his straggly beard and hair, looked like a bear. He'd also injured his left foot and it was held in one of those cradle devices so that he couldn't flex his ankle. It looked like a scary mining injury – the kind they describe on the plaques down the 'Poldark Mine'. I didn't ask. I pulled up outside the shop and clambered out into the heat. Before I'd put on my sunglasses, Bob was up and at me, his two Dalmatians sniffing around; probably the scent of Vegas was still on me.

"Howdy!" he said.

"A'right," I said. Bob looked like he might understand a Cornish greeting.

"Whatcha int'rested in?"

"Um . . . mining. The Cornish . . ."

"The Cornish. Yep – lots of them here once, like the Irish . . ."

"Any left?" I said, as if we were some Native American tribe.

"Not really, not anymore."

All the time I was gazing at the collection of minerals, rocks and quartzes dumped around the front of Big Bob's shack. When I was younger, it seemed to me that a high proportion of elderly Cornishmen that I knew seemed to have more than a passing interest in collecting mineral specimens (They seemed to have the allied disease to my own: *Bits of Cornish Crystals in Cabinets Disorder*). Whether it was just because they found them around and about Hensbarrow, I do not know, but certainly it seemed the practice, like Euchre, wrasslin', or fighting amongst one another, was one of our most culturally characteristic activities. But honestly, this place made the collection in the Camborne School of Mines look like a schoolboy hobby. 'Twas some show. Much of it, of course, was just 'eaved in on top of each other, and you had to wrestle your way to the piece you liked. I suppose that was a piece of imitation mining. Museums these days would call it 'an interactive experience'. Elsewhere in the store were lumps of gold, foils of gold, fool's gold, fossils, rock carvings, Indian dream-catchers and books, all of them covered in dust.

I asked Bob if he had a public restroom. He didn't, but he let me use his own personal toilet in the back. Here too, was his bedroom and computer. While I cooed with relief (it had been a long drive up from Vegas), Bob told me how he was standing to be Sheriff, and how I shouldn't worry because the toilet already leaked. That was good, I thought. Goldfield needed someone like Big Bob to be Sheriff.

"Do you know much about the Vikings?" he said to me squinting in the noon light.

"A bit," I said, not knowing what was coming next.

Clearly, I must have looked like I knew something about the Vikings. Perhaps it was the double-headed axe I was carrying, and my long blonde hair and beard. Well, I was from Europe – and well, the Cornish did form an alliance with them to fight the Anglo-Saxons at Hingston Down near Callington in 838.

"They made it to Nevada," he said, "I've got all the evidence . . ."

At this point, Big Bob showed me Diagram 1, followed by Diagram 2, followed by Diagrams 3 to 433 to prove his theory to me. It sounded crazy but looked good – a bit like the Mormons and the lost tribes of Israel. I couldn't concentrate though. For one thing, I was wondering whether to buy one of the old recycled railway pins adorned with little Cousin Jacks mining for gold, or whether I should go for something more genuine, like one of the old rusted carbide lamps out front. Then Bob floored me.

"I'm part Cornish. Cornish came through here of course

133

back from Pioche. And the Welsh. I'm part Welsh too . . .
Have it all written down here somewhere . . ."

No wonder the bugger had so much junk and so many
sheds. Clearly, he was Cornish. It didn't take any genealogical research. You tell by his stance too. I know it's weird,
but there's a Cornish way of walking – a kind of national
gait, which I can never explain. I just have to look at my
great uncle and father. Sometimes I even catch myself doing
it. Despite his ankle injury, Big Bob still had it.

"Forgotten all o' that before you showed up . . . You
want a soda?"

"Sure."

Bob placed a dollar into a Coke dispenser and a cold one
rolled out for me.

"Thanks."

His Dalmatians panted while I slurped the cold, dark
liquid.

"Are people still mining out there?" I asked pointing out
on the horizon.

"Course they are," said Bob, as if I'd asked a stupid
question. "And in Cornwall too?"

"No – the last tin mine closed a couple of years ago. They
still mine china clay though – open cast quarrying . . ."

"Shame," said Bob. "A real shame . . . Listen, where you
headed next?"

In all honesty I didn't really know.

Over the next few days I had to get to San Francisco.

"How long does it take to get to San Francisco?" I asked.

"Jeez . . . I couldn't tell ya . . . A lot o' folks come through
here, but they go all sorts of ways . . ."

"I was thinking o' going to Virginia City, then cutting
back down again. Virginia City was a Cornish town wasn't
it?"

"I wudn' do that meself. I'd go through Yosemite. Pretty
country over there. Take 265 through Silverpeak."

I still had a mind to see Virginia City though, and this
might be my only chance.

Big Bob and I swapped e-mail addresses and I pulled out
of his lot, heading past the old closed Goldfield Hotel,
which apparently had not seen a paying guest since 1946.
There was still a grandeur in the place though, still a

passion present, but hey, we Cornish d'knaw about that sort of thing.

I pushed on through the desert and found the turning to Silverpeak. This meant that I would miss the once important Cornish town of Tonopah, but if it was at all like Goldfield, I knew what was to be expected. Instead of Tonopah, I had elected for more desert. All kinds of open-cast quarries could be seen out there. Some were looking for limstone deposits; others for iron. As I drove on though, the route through Silverpeak became more and more isolated. That kind of isolation and that kind of heat is unnerving. You are wondering what you would do if the car broke down here. No civilisation for one hundred miles that way. No civilisation for one hundred miles the other way. The sky was completely blue. The closest thing to me seemed to be the aeroplanes flying at 20,000 feet above. I empathised a lot with Vernon Tregaskis.

The town of Coaldale, however, appeared to me around lunchtime, and I pulled into 'McDonalds' for something to eat. I didn't have much of a choice in all honesty. Aside from McDonalds was another mining museum and up in the Monte Cristo Range a few shafts and mine workings. They looked interesting, and I half-wished I had the energy to walk up and have a look at them, but instead I plumped for some fast food. McDonalds at Coaldale did feel wonderful though. It was air-conditioned just at the right kind of temperature a man needs after making it through the desert. When I spoke to the Britney Spears-lookalike behind the counter, she asked about my accent, and I told her I was Cornish. Her look told me what she was thinking: 'What in the hell are you doing on holiday out here in Coaldale?' She was sixteen and probably the daughter of a coal-mining family. You could tell she was itching to escape from Coaldale. I looked outside and saw desert, more desert, junk, ruins and mines. I sympathised with her. It looked a long way to go to find a disco. It looked like they might benefit from a European Union Heritage lottery bid if you know what I mean. Then again, World Heritage status wasn't just around the corner.

After contributing ten-fold to the world's waste problem, I headed out of 'Micky Dees' and started out again, turning north on 95 through the Excelsior Mountains and past Hawthorne. Out there in the wide space of Nevada, north east of me, were the Cornish mining camps of Battle Mountain and Eureka, but they would be impossible for me to visit within my time schedule. They were actually not too distant from the mines around Salt Lake City. One story I liked that A.C. Todd records is how in Eureka in the year 1888, below Prospect Peak and the Diamond Mountains, a young Cornishwoman, Miss Lavinia Johns just happened to come across one William Spargo from Stithians, and without further ado married him.[8] I suppose it was a case of like finding like in an inhospitable region of the earth, and reminding each other of home. Initially, they wandered the south-western mining frontier, then returned to Helston to open a restaurant. However, Spargo was more of a Cousin Jack than Lavinia thought, and he was soon back in the wickedness of Leadville, where she and their family later joined him. Eureka itself, according to Rowe, had a Cornish population six hundred strong in 1881, when it was nearing the end of its fourteen-year bonanza period, during which it had produced forty millions dollars worth of silver and about half that value of gold.[9] Battle Mountain meanwhile, was a typical mining community located in the Shoeshine Range, operating at peak in 1870 when only a few Cornish miners had their wives with them.[10]

As I drove north, I found lots of other mining towns along the way – like Mina and Luning in Mineral County, but I didn't stop. I wanted to get to Virginia City as soon as possible. The landscape temporarily changed as I came off the desert, and became more luscious and green, but as I climbed the mountains again, it became drab and hot. The road up there is still fairly barren since it is virtually locked in by hills and canyons. These days, like many other places I had encountered on my travels, Virginia City is presented as a historic mining town *par excellence* and is now home to America's largest National Historical District, complete with saloons, museums, quaint shops and restaurant. It is also now home to some famous Camel Races, but in my view, if you are wanting a town with 'authentic' Western atmosphere, then this is perhaps the one to spend time in. In a way, if you have ever looked at pictures of some of the old

Cornish mining towns in America (and believe me, I've probably looked at several hundred), then Virginia City really hasn't changed that much. I mean, of course it has expanded, and now has a 'strip' and every other fast-food franchise you can find in every other American town, but in reality, its city centre, is much as the average Cornish man or woman might have found it in the early 1870s.

The first finds of gold in the Carson Valley area were apparently made in 1849 by a Mormon group from Salt Lake City, led by an elder named Thomas Orr. In the group was a Cornishman called William Prouse, who while washing himself in the canyon's waters, noticed flecks of gold in the gravel.[11] Ten years later more gold and silver were discovered at the meeting points of Gold Canyon and Six Mile Canyon, by two Irish miners named Pat McLaughlin and Peter O' Reilly. This was on the slopes of Mount Davidson and it was along this five-mile stretch that the twin towns of Virginia City and Gold Hill grew up. Another miner, by the name of James Finney nicknamed "Old Virginny" from his birthplace is reported to have named the town during a drunken celebration. He dropped a bottle of whisky on the ground and christened the newly-founded tent and dugout town on the slopes of Mount Davidson "Old Virginny Town in honour of himself". The first problem all the miners faced there was the sticky blue-grey mud that clung to picks and shovels. You can still see that colour everywhere in the landscape and soil of the town, and it soon became trapped on the underside of my Chevrolet.

What is perhaps so important about Virginia City and Gold Hill is that their heyday coincided with the onset of the final decline of tin-mining back home in Cornwall, and so they poured in from the Old Country. The biggest bonanza came in 1873, when the Consolidated Virginia and Consolidated California mines yielded millions of dollars of metals, and made Virginia City the most important town between Denver and San Francisco. Like Colorado, and to a certain extent, Utah, much of the yield may be put down to the mechanical and technical progress made with mining equipment; although at the same time, many mines were overvalued, and corruption seemed to have a lasting influence on how the Cornish viewed Virginia City and its surrounds. According to Rowse, the temptation, however, to come and work in the mines of Nevada was great for the average Cornishman. By 1869, Camborne men working in Nevada were supposedly sending home large sums year after year, compared to Cornish earnings.[12]

Much of the early development of the town matches that occurring simultaneously in Cornish California with the place, on the one hand, developing its churches, libraries, opera and theatre; on the other its squalor, depravity and extravagance. Even now, walking the streets of Virginia City, you can see that history of duality. It was a boisterous town with something going on virtually twenty-four hours a day above and below ground. There were visiting celebrities, opium dens, newspapers, fraternal organisations, a thriving red-light district and the first Miner's Union in America (featuring one F. Polkinghorn, who was elected to the finance committee in 1871, but few other Cornish – since their pay was rarely an issue). Today, many mansions such as *The Castle*, *The Mackay* and *The Savage* stand as monuments to the once opulent life of the Comstock. I didn't have time to look at them all, but *The Castle* is an incredible property. St Mary's-in-the-Mountains is still a spectacular church. As I walked though 'C' Street, the main business street of the City, I peered at the 1860's and 1870's buildings, erected when the Cornish first stanked down here.

Not far away is North 'B' Street, on which is Piper's Opera House. I went in for a look around, and discovered that it is about to be restored. Not only is it now viewed as one of 'America's Treasures', and a sign at its front told me it was about to receive 'earthquake retort of the ground floor and front façade'. Also available are narrated trolley tours which I didn't go on, but overheard, mentioning the Cornish miners in passing. In shops I could buy the heavily promoted 'Good Old Songs' – piano music recorded from Virginia City, sample jellies and jams in 'Country Cupboard', or visit 'The Original Bucket of Blood Saloon' – perhaps, I figured, named after the one at Phillack, near Hayle. Nearby were tours available to the Ponderosa Ranch – home of television's *Bonanza*, 'Teddy Blue's Bunkhouse

Old West Re-enacting and Western Movies' (that sounded fun), and the 'Julia C. Bulette Red Light Museum'. All of it was tempting, but in the end, my stomach ruled an end to the wandering and I went into the Wagonwheel Restaurant. There I made enquiries about what remained at Gold Hill, but the waitress informed me that there was nothing much left there now. Boot Hill cemetery was worth a look, but I probably didn't have the time that day to go there. I suspect I would have found many Cornish, their lives cut short by mining accidents. For some reason, historically, accidents in the mines of Nevada seemed more commonplace than everywhere else in Cornish America, though it was not easy to work out why this was the case. Todd mentions a statistic of one accident every day of the year, of which one in five was fatal.[14] The notorious Yellow Jacket mine was the scene of many a disaster.[15] There, work had to be stopped in 1879 because the temperature underground reached 134° Fahrenheit.[16] In another accident at Consolidated Virginia, one John Trembath was riding in the tub down the shaft when the rope ripped out a piece of timber. The timber fell 150 feet and passed like a spear though his liver.[17] There are countless other examples to be found in the pages of Rowse, Todd and Rowe.

There is a heritage of Cornish entertainment in Virginia City. Apparently, so popular were wrasslin' matches that when a famous Irish patriot once came to lecture at the Piper's Opera House he spoke to empty seats. The Cornish there also boxed amongst themselves, although more famously with the Irish – pandemonium broke out one day after a contest between the Cornish champion, a young Camborne man named Jimmy Trevillian, and Patsy Hogan, after Trevillian was accused of placing a piece of iron in his glove.[18]

One of the travellers to nearby Carson City was the boxing legend Bob Fitzimmons. Many Cornish from Virginia City must have travelled there to see him fight. Fitzimmons, originally a blacksmith by trade, was born in Helston in 1862 (hence the reason he is now so celebrated in *The Blue Anchor* public house there), but grew up in New Zealand where his parents had emigrated. Fitzsimmons arrived in San Francisco in 1890 and quickly

139

became a pugilistic sensation. On reaching Carson City in 1897, Fitzsimmons knocked out Jim Corbett on St Patrick's Day, thereby winning the heavyweight championship of the world. He retained the title for two years until he was beaten by James Jeffries. Bob won more fights however, and travelled on the lucrative circuit all over Cornish America. He carried on fighting until 1914, when he was aged fifty-two.

Wells Drury, a Virginia City journalist at the time of the peak of its prosperity in 1874, records much of what life was like there for the Cornish. Not only does he comment on their characteristics of independence, thrift, geniality, excitability and contempt for familiar dangers,[19] but also recorded their Cornu-English speech. A Cornishwoman he mentions, expresses her lack of sympathy for someone else: "What's it to we, us don't care for she!".[20] Drury also tells the story of a production of Shakespeare's *Hamlet*, where the famous actor Edwin Booth, demanded a 'practicable' grave for the last act. Apparently, "a section was sawed out of the stage-floor, a couple of Cornish miners did valiant pick-work, and that night the gravediggers shovelled some interesting specimens of ore on to the stage",[21] and according to Todd, the actors hit their shins on bedrock.[22]

Another performer mentioned by Drury was the Lanner-born Richard Jose, who left a career as a blacksmith in Reno for the stage. Jose became one of the most famous ballad-singers in the world, and was very popular over Cornish America. Jose's life was an amazing story: his father died in 1878, leaving his mother to care for him and three other siblings. She sent him, aged only nine years old, on a journey from Redruth to Virginia City, to an uncle out there. On the crossing he sang to the other passengers, but when he arrived in Virginia City, his uncle was no longer there. He began to sing in places like Carson City entertaining the miners, but the Women's Temperance League felt the boy was being exploited, so had him removed to Reno by the local sheriff. It was there he met a relative, Bill Luke, a blacksmith. He then joined a minstrel troupe, and after years of struggle found a place on Broadway singing at Carnegie Hall. Contracts and tours followed in America, and other destinations in South Africa and South America.

He died in 1941, then a respected Public figure. Bizarrely however, as Jose continued in his professional career, he became more and more convinced of a Spanish descent; perhaps because of his fame amongst the Hispanic communities of California – eventually becoming the exotically named Juan Ricardo José. That said, maybe he was also thinking of the age-old ethnic 'darkness' of the Cornish, rumoured to have its origins in the Spanish raids committed on Paul, Mousehole, Newlyn and Penzance in 1595.

Drury also reveals how the Miner's Library in Virginia City was well-stocked with books.[23] This may seem slightly strange when one considers some of the illiterate Cornish miners of earlier times. However, what we should realise is that the miners of Virginia City were a generation on, and they had grown more educated and sophisticated. This was reflected in the more genteel atmosphere of the town, which was different from what I'd found in either Mineral Point or Leadville. The last thing I did in Virginia City was to enter the City's Museum. I was back on familiar 56 Inch Cylinder territory again. There, I found a working model of a Cornish pump and the remaining beam of another once installed in the Kossuth Mine, a few miles away at Silver City. It seemed fitting for me to stroll around these exhibits before the museum closed.

That evening, I found a cheap, unbranded motel on the route back down to Wabuska. The room was small and poky, and despite being in the non-smoking section of the motel, still smelt of cigarettes. That evening, as with all on this trip, in hurriedly scribbled diary form, I wrote up my experiences and noted down other things I wanted to remember. One of them is a comment on American bathrooms; that is to say how well-designed they are. In Britain, we have that ludicrous design flaw in all bathrooms I know, where the bathtub edge meets the tiles on the wall. The solution is for us to fill it with some kind of silicon based product, or put a strip of plastic across. You'll know the problem – that kind of sealant never works as well as it should and inevitably it leaks. In America (home of good design) you buy a pre-formed unit, so the side reaches up to head height and there is no break between where the wall ends and the bath begins. I know it's small, but you notice these kind of things when you have hours in motel and hotel rooms in America. This I told myself, was the kind of thing that made it tempting to live and work in America. With such knowledge, you understood why men and women from Ponsanooth or Praze-an-Beeble ditched their lives there and caught the first boat across.

In the morning, the motel thankfully handed out coffee, blueberry muffins and bananas, which set me up for the journey back down through the western side of the State. Reno was tempting, as was Carson City itself, but both, I imagined, were somewhat like Vegas. Tahoe also sounded good, not least because it has been mythologized in Britain as the ultimate snow-boarding resort, and because a Republican-supporting female bus driver who I have travelled with in Chicago, on several occasions, told me it was the ultimate holiday destination – especially for someone my age. I resolved to return there one day with loads of money, a snowboard and a vacationing attitude. For now though, this modern Cousin Jack had plenty of miles down-State to cover. You go back down past the Yerington Indian Reservation – their ancestors probably fought my ancestors – and then go past Walker Lake, one of the few stretches of water you are likely to encounter in Nevada. By eleven a.m. I was back in Tonopah Cornish country again, about to enter the final State of this journey, as well as the final destination of thousands of Cornish over the years – California.

I turned back west, onto Route 359 and went past the Excelsior Mountains and into the forests of Toiyabe. Boundary Peak – the highest in Nevada at 13, 140 feet – was in the distance, towards the south. It was in all honesty, quite a scary route. It climbed steeply and was without any barriers on the sides of the road. Trucks passed me by, hammering on at 70 miles per hour. I was slightly slower, looking carefully down the drops on each side – the kind of scenery you've seen in the Roadrunner cartoons. Rocks were piled precariously on top of other rocks. My hands and feet became more than a little sweaty. I gripped the steering wheel a bit tighter. Gradually, the scenery changed and became more grassy and wooded. I was leaving Nevada behind. Of course, then I had to go down the mountains of the Excelsior Range. The trucks now seemed to go even faster. I, meanwhile, took it steady, and gazed at the distance I had to go. I couldn't even see any mountains in front of me, and that was slightly worrying in the sense that I had anticipated seeing the tallest Yosemite peaks from here. Clearly, I had a long way to travel before touching the National Park.

Soon I reached the California border. I knew what to expect. When I had driven on Interstate 40, to the south, I knew that I might have to stop and be asked some questions about what I was carrying in the car upon my entry to the Golden State. It was a bit like the questions they'd asked me back at Heathrow airport when you fly: "Do you have any of the following items on you? Did you pack your own bag? Has anyone given you anything to carry?" That's when the person at the check-in desk points to a sign with explosives, weapons and other things that look dangerous. I respond to all the questions – somehow still feeling guilty. Perhaps the check-in staff just examine people who look guilty. I suddenly felt myself looking like a member of Kernewek Jihad.

At the California border, they ask you questions about fruit. No kidding. Fruit. I jest, but there is a serious side to it. The fruit-growing authorities of the State want to make sure that any easterners aren't carrying any diseases or pests into California. I gingerly pulled into the checking bay. This place was isolated as well. I mean, I felt like I was the only driver who'd been through there this morning. She saw my Illinois plates and said to herself, 'I've got a right one here'. I was obviously an easterner with the potential to maim the entire orange groves of California.

"Good morning," I said.

She ran through the so-help-me-God style list of things that I wasn't meant to bring out. It came out as one sentence and included seeds, plants, soil and animals. I told the lady I didn't have any dangerous fruit with me. Neither did I have any exploding oranges or nerve-gas exuding bananas. I didn't have any critters with me either – aside from the several thousand bugs and flies that had hit my windscreen in the desert and were now juicily ensconced on the car's wiper blades . . .

143

"You have a nice day," she said to me.

"Thank you," I said.

"And you be careful with your fruit," I thought I heard her shout after me.

All this for fruit.

I stopped and shouted back, "Which way to Yosemite?"

"You can't miss it . . ." she shouted to me.

She wudn' wrong either.

Before I tell you all about the Cornishman in Yosemite though, I want you to imagine the scene. It is 1973 and I am in Foxhole Primary School. It is before the invention of video recorders and players, and my class are sat watching a grainy colour film, playing at the wrong speed. Miss Metters, my teacher, is trying to broaden her horizons for we are clay kids who, in the normal manner of things, should end up working on the hose at Blackpool Pit. It is one of several hundred we seemed to watch at Primary School and I can remember them now – clear as mud, as they say. You have to imagine the happy-go-lucky American announcer, with lots of funny little jokes about bears and deer, and pictures of clean-cut rangers encouraging people not to light fires, and pictures of very large mountains. One of them I remember was about Yosemite, and aside from rangers, bears and big mountains, I don't recall much else, but it must have had an influence on me though, to bring me here a quarter of a century later.

Nothing, not even films like that, can truthfully prepare you for somewhere like the Yosemite National Park. I had wanted to go there, not only to relive my horrible flared trousered and woollen purple tanktop schooldays, but also because some of the first trails through Yosemite had been made by Cornish miners heading west. I wanted to see what they had accomplished and what they had to get through. The other interesting thing about Yosemite is that it is made of granite, and there is no-one on earth who knows granite better than the Cornish, so I suppose I felt like looking at a few lumps of the grey-stuff to remind me of home. Before entering Yosemite, just past the prehistoric-looking Mono Lake, the road starts to climb and climb and climb and climb and climb. I think it is probably the highest road I have ever been on. It was also the scariest. More scary than

144

Colorado. More scary than Utah (and that included the Mormons). And more scary than Nevada. I had to swallow several times to account for the popping in my ears, as I gained altitude. After the climb the road moved into glacial meadows that looked like I had just stepped into the landscape of Disney's *Bambi*. Ahead was a queue of traffic awaiting entry into the Park proper, next to a Ranger Station.

I pulled up to the hut and a female ranger poked her head out. She wore the same uniform I used to see in the films at school. I paid my twenty dollars entrance fee and she gave me a ton of leaflets, maps and information about the Park. To be perfectly honest, the twenty dollars entrance fee was slightly unexpected, and in my view, was slightly unfair. Huge RV vehicles with seemingly entire families from Arkansas inside them got charged the same price as little old me. However, this was hardly the time to turn around and say I didn't want to drive through the so-called 'incomparable valley'. Somehow I couldn't imagine my Cornish forefathers and mothers doing that – so I didn't either.

Instead, I pulled over to a rest area and read the leaflet. Apparently bears were a real problem in the Park. They are attracted to human food, even if it just looks like human food. Many bears had lifted soap in the last few seasons thinking it was food. The bears didn't worry me too much. Besides they probably smelt very charming after all the soap they'd nicked. I was more worried about the mountain lions. Here is the Park Ranger's advice about what to if you encounter a mountain lion: 'Do not run or crouch down. Pick up children. Wave, shout, throw stones! If attacked, fight back.' No – I won't fight back. I'll just let the lion gorge my innards. Squirrels too apparently 'can inflict serious injury'. From then on I was very wary of squirrels.

I was entering some serious 'wilderness designation'. I don't know quite how to begin to describe Yosemite, but basically, amazing scenery follows amazing scenery. You think that the last waterfall, rounded dome or towering cliff was the most spectacular piece of natural scenery you've ever come across, and then you instantly come across another. I wanted to stop the car get out and write poems about it all. Either that or start painting water-colours. The glacier-carved canyon contains massive monoliths of granite which rise above open meadows sprinkled with wildflowers, and mixed-conifer forests of ponderosa pine, cedars and Douglas firs. There are lakes which could be seas and the harder portions of rock left intact after the glaciation process look like sleeping dinosaurs. Among these are the famous *El Capitan* and the *Cathedral* Rocks. You feel very small. To help you feel tiny are groves of giant Sequoia trees – the oldest, the Mariposa Grove's Grizzly Giant, is some 2,700 years old. Such is the scale and the vastness, that you wonder how on earth the original Native Americans of the Valley survived, and how the Europeans managed to make their way across it.

How they built a road through was also a source of fascination for me, considering that much of the Park, and the road that I was travelling, are actually closed during the winter months. This route – known as Tioga Road – was constructed as a mining road in 1882-83 by the Great Consolidated Silver Company, and remained pretty much in its original configuration until 1961 when it was realigned and modernised. I spent the rest of the afternoon dealing with Yosemite. I say 'dealing' because you barely know where to begin. In the Valley Visitor Centre I briefly tried to gain an overview of the Park and decide what I wanted to see, but even that foxed me. I'd have needed literally a couple of weeks to see everything, and even then I doubted whether I would really have covered much ground. It seemed the kind of environment where I'd need to spend an entire vacation, not just a piece of it.

The afternoon was rolling on into evening and I needed to find accommodation. I'd been advised however, that the accommodation in Yosemite itself was rather expensive and that I would be financially better off to drive on into the Sierra Nevada foothills before I stopped for the night. I wasn't, for example, about to stay in the famous Ahwahnee Hotel, the Park's first grand hotel, which originally opened in 1927 and has counted numerous presidents, Queen Elizabeth and Prince Philip, Lucille Ball, Judy Garland and Shirley Temple as its guests. No – I was more in line for a cheap-as-chips 'Motel 8'.

At the eastern end of Yosemite, you begin to notice just how high up you are. The road begins to spiral back and forth down spurs, and what looks like more typical Californian scenery comes into view. This was not before I had stopped at a couple of Historical Markers – both outlining early mining activity high up in the Yosemite end of Stanislaus Forest. Sadly there weren't any more details than that – the marker didn't say anything about the nationality of the miners. The spiralling road made me feel like I was being secretly filmed for a car advertisement for Chevrolet. At one point, I had an option to take what literally looked like a helter-skelter-style shorter route, that absolutely and totally forbid anything like trucks, caravans, RVs or any kind of towed vehicle, but to my eyes, it looked so dangerous that I stayed on the spiral route down to the Valley floor. It was getting dark now. Ahead loomed the towns of Buck Meadows and Groveland. I'd find something there. Sure enough, there was a Comfort Inn in Groveland, which would do me. I pulled into the lot and checked in.

"How-d'-y'-like-Y'semite?' said the girl at the desk in one mouth movement.

"It blew me away," I said in several mouth movements.

"Have-y'-travelled-far-t'day Dr. Kent?"

"From Virginny City," I said feeling proudly Cornish, and pronouncing Virginia like they did back home. It made me sound western and a bit of a twit to boot. She looked a me oddly. Then again, I was Cornish and odd. I knew this. See, most people might have kicked back with a beer or two that evening and watched a ball game or some football. Not me. Oh no. I was suffering bad from 56 Inch Cylinder syndrome that night and sat down to read up on the 'Forty Niners'. Readers, that's how sad and pathetic I am.

When I woke up the next morning, I barely knew where I was. The room looked the same as the one I'd stayed in at Mineral Point. Was I still in Mineral Point? Maybe I was. Maybe I hadn't toured across Cornish America. No, as my brain came to, I knew I'd made it through Nevada into California, but where the hell was I? I wasn't that far from Virginny City and I knew I was somewhere between there and San Francisco. It turned out that I'd actually

147

accidentally stumbled upon southern California Gold country. How did I work this out? It eventually became clear by the number of Gold-themed leaflets about local attractions that I picked up in the Comfort Inn foyer and which I read over breakfast. I didn't know it, but that day, I was about to become a gold mining expert. I was going to see the elephant. Apparently, in this part of the world, the phrase "going to see the elephant" came to mean the kind of excitement the miners felt at the possibility of finding gold in 'them thar hills'. The phrase supposedly originated from a story about a farmer who had heard of elephants but had never seen one. When a circus came to a nearby town, he loaded his wagon and set out to see these near-mythical creatures. On meeting the circus parade, led by an elephant, his horses became terrified. They bucked and overturned his wagon. "I don't give a dang," said the farmer – apparently in a very Cornu-American accent – "for I have seen the elephant."

The original gold-seekers, the 'Forty-Niners' were also called the Argonauts, and although 1849 is viewed now as the year the Gold Rush of California began, some arrived as early as 1848, while others as late as 1853. So the leaflets told me, in the spring of 1848 there were less than 15,000 people in California, not counting the Native Americans, but by 1852, this had swelled to almost 225,000. Most of the miners came from other parts of America; some 100,000 via overland routes through places like Yosemite, while others braved voyages around the Horn or endured two voyages and a trek across the Isthmus of Panama. The Chinese had a late start in all of this but quickly made up for lost time. In 1850, there were only 600 Chinese in California. By 1852, their numbers had grown to 25,000. I was to discover this latter statistic on Highway 49 as in the morning I looked around a town, not far from Groveland, called Chinese Camp. The Camp sits in the middle of grass and tarweed fields, marked with occasional oak trees. It is immeasurably beautiful. There is debate on where the Chinese who settled here came from and why they arrived here. They could well have been employed by Cornish prospectors or they might have been part of several Chinese crews who deserted their ships in San Francisco, but by the

148

early 1850s there were around 5,000 Chinese mining in this area alone.

Trouble arose in 1856 though, when one day a large stone from one of the diggings rolled into another group's diggings. A fight developed, but when it ended the arguing parties sent word to their respective tongs for help – the *Sam Yap* and the *Yan Wo*. Each tong felt it had lost respect and the only thing to do was to go to war. Weapons and barricades were made, with the American and Cornish miners hired to instruct the Chinese in how to use muskets. On October 25th, 1856, the 1,200 members of the *Sam Yap* tong met the 900 members of *Yan Wo*. They obviously went for it hammer and well . . . tong. When the smoke cleared, only four people were dead, although several dozen were injured. About 250 of the Chinese were taken prisoner by the American authorities for causing such disorder. When the battle was over, there was nothing to do but go back to working in the mines.

It was hard to imagine this kind of wild event as I walked around the now tranquil town. Having said that, I could just imagine some of the Cornish finding the famous Chinese Camp battle highly amusing. In the local store, I bought a postcard of the Miners' Ten Commandments, which I suppose tried to give some genuine degree of order in the early days of free-for-all wild mining camps (It clearly worked well in Chinese Camp). The following was apparently enacted into Federal law in 1853:

1. Thou shalt have no other claim than one.
2. Thou shalt not make any false claim or jump one. If thou do thou must go prospecting and shall hire thy body out to make thy board and save thy bacon.
3. Thou shalt not go prospecting before thy claim gives out. Neither shall thee take thy gold to the gambling table in vain.
4. Thou shalt remember the Sabbath. Six days thou mayest dig, for in six days labour thou canst work enough to wear out thy body in two years.
5. Thou shalt not think more of thy gold than how thou shall enjoy it.
6. Thou shalt not kill thy body by working in the rain. Neither shall thou destroy thyself by getting "tight" nor "high seas over" while drinking down thy purse.

7. Thou shalt not grow discouraged, nor think of going home before thou hast made thy pile.
8. Thou shalt not steal a pick, a shovel or a pan from thy fellow miners, nor borrow a claim, nor pan out gold from others riffle box. They will hang thee, or brand thee like a horse thief with the letter R upon thy cheek.
9. Thou shalt not tell any false tales about "good diggings" in the mountains, lest your neighbours return with naught but a rifle and present thee with its contents thereof and thou shall fall down and die.
10. Thou shalt not commit unsuitable matrimony nor neglect thy first love. If thy heart be free thou shall "pop the question" like a man, lest another more manly than thou art should step in before thee, and then your lot be that of a poor, despised, comfortless bachelor.

There was, I concluded, something inherently Cornish about all of this, though I wondered how many of those original argonauts followed these commandments to the letter. That morning, alongside these rules, I learnt a lot about the varieties of gold mining in the Mother Lode. Many of the original argonauts naïvely expected to pick up nuggets off the ground and were quickly disillusioned when they realised the amount of hard labour required to get a day's wages. Gold mined in the Sierra Nevada foothills came from two main kind of deposits, Lode and Placer. Lode deposits contain native gold, mostly in hard-rock quartz veins, that ascended in mineralised solution from deep in the earth, just like back home. This was the kind of metal the Cornish were experts in mining. Placer deposits contained gold that had originally been in Lodes, but which through the erosion of water had been 'placed' else-where. Panning was the earliest method of retrieving Placer deposits, and served as the basis for other more advanced methods such as Rocking the Cradle, Long Toms and Sluice Boxes.

After a decent gake at Chinese Camp I decided to turn right and head up to Jamestown. Jamestown was the site of the discovery of a 75-pound nugget in 1848 and, like Las Vegas, seemed the kind of place where I might strike it rich. Apparently, for a time, miners were digging out $200 to $300 dollars a day with a pick and knife. If I had wanted, I could have gone on a Gold Prospecting Expedition from 18170 Main Street. There was also Columbia Mining and Equipment on 18169 Main Street, which looked a fairly serious endeavour. Instead, I ended up at the Railtown 1897 State Historical Park, where alongside this historic Sierra Railway property, I could go and pan for gold. It looked like I could have the 'seeking the elephant' experience without actually having to yomp through the foothills. I went in and gave it a try. I'd done something like this in the Wisconsin Dells a few years back, but this looked a bit more authentic. From the stream the Park had created, you gather earth into a pan filling about one third full. You place the pan under the water keeping it flat, then use your hand to mix it into a soupy mass while breaking up clumps of earth. Then you remove any larger rocks, while swirling your hand in a circle, mixing the dirt and water allowing other particles to float away. While shaking the pan from side to side, you then slowly tilt it until the V formed between the sides and the bottom of the pan is on the bottom. The gold (if there is any) will begin to collect in this V. I sluiced dirt around for about an hour, until my hands went white and looked like dried grapes. The toddlers next to me seemed to be having more luck than I did. Having said that, the gold they found was so microscopic that I doubted it would move the scales at all. Still the whole thing was great fun, and I felt like a real argonaut. I remembered my imitation leather bound Time-Life books back home on *The Miners* and *The Forty Niners* and there were pictures of hardened men sluicing for hours a day. At least now, I had sluiced. Big Bob Plock would have been proud of me.

My hands had now warmed up, and I decided to venture back into Jamestown for lunch. It was one o'clock and the town was bathed in beautiful afternoon sunlight. This was probably one of the reasons that Hollywood liked 'Jimtown'. It has appeared in movies such as *High Noon* and *Butch Cassidy and the Sundance Kid*. To me, it looked like the set for a Western, and there were moments where I wanted to tie up my horse, swagger into a saloon, order a whisky and play a hand of poker. All this, and I can't ride; there weren't any saloons; I hate whisky and I can't play poker. At least I could pretend I was having a shoot-out with Lee Van Cleef as I jaywalked across the Main Street. Then the Community Methodist Church looked down from me on high, and I became all serious again. In a restaurant I ordered a Goldminer's Burger and fries and reflected on some of the original pioneers out there.

There was John C. Fremont (1813–1890) whose name cropped up everywhere in Northern California. Almost every major town, had a road or avenue named after him. Fremont made a lot of money out of gold-bearing land in the Sierra foothills and with this wealth behind him, he became one of California's most influential people – standing as the first (but unsuccessful) U.S. presidential candidate of the Republican Party in 1856. The Cornish must have liked him. But then, his mining enterprises were badly run and he lost much of his wealth, and his political opposition to Abraham Lincoln cost him his military command, his political influence and his public prestige. He died penniless in New York, but that has not stopped the West celebrating him. Then I read about the legend of Joaquin Murieta – the Robin Hood of the Southern Mines. Originating from Sonora in Mexico, Murieta arrived in Saw Mill Flat in 1850. Supposedly, it was in the town of Murphys that the handsome young man swore vengeance against Americans who persecuted Mexican miners. According to legend, a group of Yankees had tied him to a tree, beat him, ravished his wife and murdered his brother. Apparently a Frenchman made Murieta a bullet-proof vest, but he was eventually hunted down and shot to death in southern Mariposa County by a lawman named Harry Love, who cut off the bandit's head, put it in a bottle of alcohol, and used it as proof to claim a reward. It was a great story and I was pleased to learn that the Mother Lode had its own romantic hero. I drank down my Miller Lite and thought of poor Joaquin.

I settled the check and set out on the road again; this time back along Route 108 past Knight's Ferry. This place, so an historical marker informed me, was originally the site of a ferry which took miners across the Stanislaus River, but was eventually replaced by one of California's few remaining covered bridges. I wound down the window and noticed a change in the air. It was beginning to smell like the

152

California I knew: sweet and tangy. I hit Oakdale and then turned right onto 120 into Manteca. The road became straight and I was suddenly flanked by hundreds of orange and citrus groves. I checked to see I didn't have any explosive fruit with me. After all, I was heading for a city very much associated with 'Peace' and 'Love'.

Notes

1. John Rowe (1974) *The Hard Rock Men: Cornish Immigrants and the North American Mining Frontier*, Liverpool: Liverpool University Press, p.180.
2. Ibid.
3. Ibid.
4. A.C. Todd (1995 [1967]) *The Cornish Miner in America*, Spokane, Washington: The Arthur H. Clark Co., p.110.
5. Ibid., p.112.
6. Stanley W. Paher (1977) *Goldfield: Boom Town of Nevada*, Las Vegas: Nevada Publications, p.1.
7. Ibid., pp.14-15.
8. Todd, op.cit., p.180.
9. Rowe, op.cit., p.191.
10. Ibid., p.190.
11. This story is recounted in A.L. Rowse (1991 [1969] *The Cornish in America*, Redruth: Dyllansow Truran, pp.287-8.
12. Ibid., p.166.
13. Todd, op.cit., p.188.
14. Ibid., p.183.
15. Ibid., p.192.
16. Ibid., p.196.
17. Ibid., p.201.
18. Ibid., p.195. See also Rowse, op,cit., p.293.
19. Ibid., p.296.
20. Ibid., p.292.
21. Ibid., p.295.
22. Todd, op.cit., p.191.
23. Rowse, op.cit., p.295.

7

If you're going to San Francisco, be sure to wear a mining helmet . . .

Check out the grumbling letters pages of *The Cornish Guardian* or *The West Briton* newspapers for a few weeks, and you're sure to find somebody whining about windfarms in Cornwall – either those built already, those being built, or those just in the planning process. I must admit I've had my moments too. In my long poem *Out of the Ordinalia*, I complained about a Japanese company developing a windfarm on St Breock Downs.[1] My point was that St Breock Downs was an ancient place (there's two standing stones there, one beautifully called the *Mên Gurta*) and that a windfarm was just plain unsuitable there. Maybe I'm just as bad as the rest. Maybe I'm just as 'Nimby' as the next person.

I was contemplating all of this as I passed through Tracy on Interstate 580 in the middle of California. Here, people don't seem to have the same doubts or anxieties about windfarms. In front of me, on what are known as the Golden Hills (due to the parched yellow-looking grass that grows there), were literally thousands and thousands of wind turbines, all turning in a kind of futuristic ballet, greeting all of us heading for San Francisco. Certainly, this was no Delabole or Carland Cross. The sun was starting to set and the whole effect made me feel mesmerised by their turning motion. They keep turning and I kept watching.

Driving into the setting sun in America is never easy.

154

Although it is often beautiful, the problem is that you can't see any of the road-signs properly as they are often in shadow, or else you are blinded by the sun's low rays. This was the other problem that faced me as I headed into the Bay Area. I had a good idea of where my friends Gage and Ilka lived, but this necessitated me making a horse-shoe shaped drive around Hayward and Fremont into San Jose and then up into Sunnyvale. When I passed through Livermore, I knew I really needed to take the 680 south – but we Cornish sometimes really do have clotted cream for brains. I ended up missing the exit. I put this either down to me being cut up by some seriously bad Californian driving or by not being able to correctly see the signs due to the setting of the sun. Anyway, a quick check of the map told me it wouldn't matter too much. I'd just head down through Castro Valley and go through Hayward and Fremont. I took the exit for Mission Boulevard, and more by luck and instinct than by skill and judgement, found myself on the right road heading south. It was, in American terms, a 'strip', filled with car dealerships and various kinds of fast food franchises. I continued on, though by its nature, the route was rather stop-start, so I lost time. By the time I'd rounded San Jose, it was dark.

Eventually I got back on 680 and rounded the bottom of the horseshoe. The exit for Sunnyvale came up and I pulled onto the ramp and then into a garage. Here, I was sure to find a telephone so that I could phone Gage and tell him about my arrival. I filled up the car with gas and got some change. The cashier pointed across the street to where I might find a telephone. I didn't know it but I was about to have another little American moment, just like the gas station in Vegas. In reality, I suppose, there will come a time when all the public telephones of this world will be hopelessly outmoded. We will all have our own mobile communication devices – in Cornwall we have our 'mobiles'; in America we have our 'cell-phones'. I have a 'mobile'; the only problem being that it does not work in the USA. Again, I suppose if I had been better organised I might have signed up with some deal that would allow me access while over there, but being, like most Cornish, a bit 'close' when it comes to money, I decided not to.

At least telephone boxes in Britain are fairly standard. You know what to expect. The smell of urine and a crushed Coke can on the shelf; a few scratched numbers on the metal surround, some local taxi company's number. In London, a selection of cards offering the services of Miss Whiplash. At least, they are lit and made for 'normal'-sized people. I have found that invariably public telephones in the USA are placed in the most least helpful places. Secondly, they are never lit and thirdly, they are designed for people about half the height of a normal human being. Fine, if you are a little person, but in the dimly lit streets of Sunnyvale at around 8 p.m. at night, I must have pressed in Gage's number several times before getting it right. Then there are all the varieties of calling methods available: 10 10 10 10 600 or something like that. Machines ate my money all over America, without me sometimes even getting through to the operator.

Was I stressed at this moment? Slightly – after the machine ate most of my quarters. Then I realised it wasn't working properly. I drove until I found a second telephone. This one wasn't working at all. I drove on to another one, outside a Liquor Store and eventually got through to Gage. Where was I? Frustrated at the end of a phone. I gave him directions. Luckily, it turned out I was just a couple of blocks away.

Gage McKinney and his wife Ilka Weber live in a standard-sized, to me, typical Californian bungalow. I say typical because it had a similar layout to many houses I'd been to before in Los Angeles. The house was open-plan with beautiful wooden floors. To welcome me, alongside the Stars and Stripes, the flag of the State of Californian and the Union Jack, Gage also had a St Piran's Cross flying. Gage had good collection of books, many of them on literature and poetry, but also a considerable Cornish collection – probably one of the finest this side of the Mississippi. I had been corresponding with Gage for a couple of years by now, and we had managed to meet up at the Cornish Gathering in Mineral Point, as well as at the Dewhelans/Homecoming event in Falmouth. It was good to see him. Ilka was not at home since she worked as a Flight Attendant for United Airlines and was en-route back from a trip to China.

I was however, introduced to Gage's green-feathered parrot – who amusingly he had named Quiller after his favourite Cornish writer – Arthur Quiller Couch. Quiller has full run of the house, and scuttles and flies around the rooms with full territorial authority. Quiller had an amusing personality. Apparently, he doesn't take to everyone, but seemed fairly comfortable with me as Gage positioned him onto my forefinger. Ironically, only a few weeks earlier, I had been showing some Breton friends around Fowey, passing the 'Q' Memorial near the Bodinnick Ferry and of course, Quiller Couch's house. Now I sat with his namesake on my finger enjoying a piece of banana. Aside from the occasional loud squawk, Quiller proved to be no more demanding than any other kind of pet, and was to provide me with much entertainment over the next few days. There was a lot to talk about. Gage and I caught up with what we had been writing and researching, and all other matters Cornish and non-Cornish. Quiller chipped in with the occasional caw of approval or disapproval. Gage told me to help myself to anything I needed, and that since he would be off to work in the morning, there would not be anyone around until Ilka's arrival. Yet again, I adjusted to my new sleeping environs and read for a while. Finally, I gave into my tiredness and sleep came over me.

Ilka was just getting in off her flight from Canton to San Francisco. A taxi dropped her from the airport back to the house. I was already up, though feeling a little groggy from the long drive over from Yosemite and Nevada. I sat nursing a bowl of multi-coloured *Cheerios* and a banana for breakfast. She advised me that if I was to climb the mountain at New Almaden, it would be better to do it in the morning, rather than in the afternoon, as in this part of California, that's when the temperatures really started to soar. It was already 9.30 a.m. so I needed to get my skates on. The Cornish settlement at New Almaden was around a half to three-quarters of an hour drive away. Last night Gage had handed me a more detailed map of the area than my Rand MacNally Road Atlas offered, so I set off from Sunnydale into the San Francisco traffic.

Kitty Monahan, the President of the New Almaden

Quicksilver Mine County Park Association, was due to meet me at New Almaden, though she apologised for not being able to show me around the museum proper, since this being a Thursday, the Park Warden was working elsewhere. The museum usually only opened on Friday, Saturday and Sunday. It didn't matter. I'd seen enough mining museums on my travels to last a lifetime, and besides, I knew there were several more coming up in Grass Valley. But I'm getting ahead of myself . . . On the telephone, Kitty had advised me to take the Almaden Expressway all the way down to Almaden, then follow the road to New Almaden. I'm never one for following advice like that when I'm travelling. Besides this meant taking Interstate 280 once again, and after the previous evening, I'd had my fill of Interstates. I pulled off earlier taking me down through Cupertino and Campbell, then joined the Almaden Expressway a little further down. I drove through wide boulevards and avenues oozing money and wealth, and where the trimming of palm trees seemed to be in season. I had to keep dodging piles of newly cut fronds left in the road. Everyone else seemed to cope with it well enough. It was just me who seemed to have to keep swerving them.

At this point, I have to say I was tempted to veer off my Cornish quest, and maybe head down the coast to Monterey. Monterey seemed the kind of chilled-out coastal resort that made Newquay look like a surf shack, but I held my course. Then there was Salinas, which wasn't too far away either. That was John Steinbeck country, and after keeping a clear distance between myself and his writings for about ten years, in the six months prior to this trip, I'd consumed more or less everything he'd written, but clearly re-living *East of Eden* or *The Grapes of Wrath* was going to have to wait. I was more *Travels with Charley* – except I didn't have a poodle.

Incidentally, while I'm at it, Almaden simply means 'The Mine' in Spanish. The mines were named New Almaden after the world famous Almaden mines in Spain. What was more difficult for me to get my mouth around was how to say Almaden. The emphasis locally is to virtually ignore the first and second syllables and to put the stress on the DEN.

Being Cornish of course, it is my natural inclination to put greater emphasis on the second syllable. I drove on in the car, repeating it over and over again like some kind of nerd. Eventually I got it – but there had to be a kind of Spanish vigour in the way I pronounced it. Honest man, I felt like Zorro.

In front of me I could see the hills rising to become what looked like mountains. That scared me slightly. I wasn't 'zactly best equipped to be climbing the Everest-looking structures veering upwards. In particular, my sandals barely looked the sort of gear for a *Lord-of-the-Rings* style trek up a mountain. I began to worry. I passed several malls on the way down, noting what would be possible solace for me on the way back. There was a 'Starbucks' and a 'Barnes and Noble' bookshop – which I needed to check out anyway. On this trip, I became a bit of a 56 Inch Cylinder specialist, seeking out any kind of mining book going. Well, as you've seen, you never knew when you'd find a bit of Cornish . . .

The traffic slowed for a cross-roads. There seemed nothing particular special about this cross-roads. I must have stopped and started on about ten of them which intersected with the Almaden Expressway on the way down. Only this one was *different*. In a sea of roads and words like Los Gatos, Saratoga and Santa Barbara, this one stood out like a sore thumb. There it was bold as brass – right above my head: Chynoweth Avenue. I looked left and right to see if everyone else had spotted this. There, a piece of Cornish language, slap bang here in southern San Jose. Of course, to everyone else, it was just Chynoweth Avenue – it was where you turned into if you needed to shop at 'Safeway'. For me though, it was like some mystical symbol, leading me on to the misty mountains of New Almaden. I thought to myself, I'm probably the only person on this road to know what that words means and why it's here. In case you don't know – Chynoweth is Cornish for 'new house'. Then I heard a parp of a horn behind me. The lights had turned green, and the driver at my tailgate couldn't understand why I wasn't moving. I could feel the glare at my Illinois plate.

"Damn hick out here from the mid-West," I felt him saying.

Eventually I moved off with other drivers gazing at me

like I was insane. Maybe at that moment I was. I'd had moments like this before in the States: at Grants in New Mexico, at Mineral Point, at others, but when it comes, you still can't quite believe it – like some bit of the old place transplanted across, and still there, still relevant in many people's daily lives. Hell, it wasn't mining museums I was writing this book about, it was about moments like this.

Plunging further southwards, the Almaden Expressway just came to a halt. In essence it was one long commuter track, and the road for New Almaden bent around the mountain, past organic food outlets and even richer looking properties. If there were any Cornish still left in these parts, they seemed to be doing rather well for themselves. The road transformed into a path between two mountains and the vegetation became more lush. I was looking for a two storey red-bricked building named the *Casa Grande*, which housed the New Almaden Mining Museum. It soon came into view and I pulled into the car park. I stepped up onto the decking and a door opened.

"You Gage's friend from Cornwall?" came a voice.

"Yes," I answered.

"Well, come on in . . ."

It was Kitty Monahan. Kitty was a retired schoolteacher with enough time on her hands now to co-ordinate the local historical society. I'd asked if there was any kind of library in the building that I could look through and she pointed me in the direction of a back-room, while at the same time handing me leaflets about New Almaden. I have always found American people very accommodating when it came to helping anyone researching history or literature and Kitty was no exception. The library had some great books, which had I time, I would like to have sat down and read. Among these were a 1954 volume edited by A.L. Rowse – *A Cornish Waif's Story*, as well as Margery Dorian's *The Three Boys of New Almaden and other stories of Early California* and JoAnn Chartier and Chris Enss' *With Great Hope: Women of the California Gold Rush*. According to Rowse, if we had got access to the museum, there I might have found some Cornish candlesticks, organ stops from the Methodist church, parts of a Cornish wheelbarrow, lengths of tramway the Cornish introduced, and the working beam

160

from a Cornish pump,[2] but for now, I would simply have to make do in imagining these items.

Kitty and I talked about the history of New Almaden. We went back a long way. It seems that around 10 million years ago, hydrothermal activity caused by tectonic plate movements caused some of the serpentine rock to change, at the same time depositing the red ore of mercury, known as *cinnabar* (Whoops, I'd better stop . . . I felt a bit of 56 Inch Cylinder Syndrome coming on there . . .). Anyway, the local Ohlone Indians called the ore "mohetka" while the word cinnabar comes from the Persian word 'Zinjifrab' meaning 'Dragon's Blood'. This seemed to suit because there was a vivid reddish tone to the landscape.

New Almaden's mining history really kicked off in 1845 though when a Mexican cavalry officer by the name of Andres Castillero was taken by the Ohlone to see the source of the red ore. He filed a claim and was granted the right to mine the area by the Mexican government, only things didn't turn out well for Castillero. When the war between the US and Mexico occurred he never came back. Rowse comments that 'by the treaty of Guadalupe-Hedalgo, America got California and the whole of the Southwest for $15,000,000—within seven years New Almaden had produced as much'.[3] It was the firm of Barron Forbes Company who then acquired some of Castillero's shares and began to develop the 'Hacienda de Beneficio' reduction works. By 1854 there were thirteen furnaces in operation. The workers built houses on the ridge above, which would later come to be known as Spanishtown. After this time lots of legal wrangling ensued, as to whether Barron Forbes Company had properly established the Castillero claim, the upshot of which was that in 1864 they relinquished ownership to the Quicksilver Mining Company, under the leadership of one Samuel Butterworth. Butterworth was philanthropical in nature and built a store and schoolhouse for the miners' families high on the ridge. There were now around 1,800 people living there, but this population was swelled in the 1860s by the Cornish, who established 'Cornishtown' on Mine Hill (at least, this was the name on old maps – it later became known as 'Englishtown'). This little township was distinguishable by its neat white, wooden houses with white picket fences, and as Gage McKinney has shown, in his history of New Almaden, titled *A High and Holy Place*, a Methodist Episcopal Church.[4]

By 1871 Butterworth had resigned and was replaced by one James B. Randol. Randol, so it seems, had a vision of what New Almaden could become and so he initiated the construction of a new shaft, named after him, which would become the richest of the mines, produced $10 million in quicksilver, while the Beuna Vista shaft was developed with massive granite block foundations to hold a large pump engine. The Quicksilver Mining Company continued to work the area throughout the late nineteenth century, but by 1912, all mining operations had ceased and both Cornishtown and Spanishtown became deserted.[5] The Hacienda furnace yard was stripped, and although some piecemeal operations continued up until 1976 (when environmental awareness of mercury's toxicity at last began to be realised), in reality, the great age of the Quicksilver Mine of New Almaden was over.

Rowse has noted many famous Cornish at New Almaden,[6] and I was thinking of them that morning. One of the most important Cornishmen during the 1880s was Captain James Harry who found a large body of ore which became known as the 'Harry ore-body'. He had worked in the mines of Cornwall since the age of ten, and in 1869 he had moved to California, first settling in Nevada County and then moving to New Almaden in 1872. He had experiences of working as timberman, pumpman and as shaft-boss, so the progression to Captain was logical. In addition to introducing the Cornish skip for raising and lowering men, he also married one Elizabeth Carlyon, had six children and was a class leader and trustee of the Methodist Church the Cornish built. A 'Harry Road' perpetuates his memory. Another important Cornishman at New Almaden was a man named Berryman who moved from Marquette to Grass Valley, and then on to New Almaden, where he was killed in a mining accident. One Arthur Berryman – a probable relative of the former – also ended up working at New Almaden for twelve years, after first travelling to South America. In 1887 he gave up mining altogether though, and went into that very American industry of an insurance and real-estate partnership. Then there was Captain Richard B. Harper, born in Redruth, who also worked at New Almaden during the 1870s, being one of the first to build a quicksilver furnace there. Later he spent time in Mexico purchasing a quick-silver mine for an American company, but came back to retire at New Almaden. According to Todd, there were perhaps 30 or more Cousin Jacks with their families between 1860 and 1870 for the census of 1860 enumerates 44 miners described as "English", but by 1870 this had increased to 70.[7]

But enough of history. We Cornish are sometimes obsessed by it, and sometimes that isn't good. I told Kitty I really should be making tracks for the climb to Cornish Camp. I thanked her for her help and then drove a mile up the valley. After a quick look at the Catholic church of St Anthony and a memorial placed by the irrepressible *E Clampus Vitus* mining historical association (56 Inch Cylinder-lovers to the end!) to a water wheel, I parked the car at the Hacienda entrance to the park, and gathered everything I needed for the climb. Ilka had lent me a backpack, which was much more useful than my standard and, I suppose, characteristic satchel. Just as I locked the car doors, from down the hill came a mountain biker. He was sweating-hot and bronzed in the way that only Californians are. I talked to him for a while. His name was Bob and he was retired. He made most Cornishmen I knew who had retired look like potato couches, and rode the Almaden Quicksilver Park every couple of days, between looking after his innumerable grandchildren. It was people like superfit Bob who made me want to forget Cornwall and move to California for the rest of my life. He'd probably get home, make a smoothie and chill in his pool for the rest of the day. Tomorrow, he'd cycle the coast road to Monterey.

"How far is it to Church Hill?" I asked.

"Oh – not too far. Maybe a couple of miles. Take you about an hour to get up there . . ."

"Say, you English?"

"No. Cornish."

"Cornish?"

"Yes – the Cornish don't think of themselves as English . . ."

"Oh really?"

"There were a lot of Cornish who came here to mine and live . . ."

"Oh right – yes, now you mention that – I did know that."

"I'm writing a book about them . . ."

"Neat."

I noticed Bob and I had similar sunglasses on. I didn't realise the pair I'd bought back in Galena were mountain-biking specs. I looked at his skin and wished for that bronzed look. I knew I had it up to my knees but after that everything seemed milk-bottle white. I looked like the farmer I'd met in the pool in Mineral Point – and that simply would not do. Bob and I said our farewells and I began the trek up the mountain, stripping off, trying to get a good Californian tan.

Right from the word *go*, I realised the map of Santa Clara County of the Regional Parks and Recreations Areas was a most deceptive piece of cartography. In fact, it could have been straight out of the Mappa Mundi. On the map the route up to the Cornish camp looked perfectly straight. In reality, it curved and veered hazardously across Mine Hill. Any sense of scale on the map, did not match the reality experienced. The sun was high in the sky by now and it was a beautiful August day. I was followed by butterflies and scrub jays as I made the lower part of the climb. At one point a skunk tumbled out of the Chaparral and down a slope, pausing in front of me to have a gake at who I was. I expect I'd completed no more than 1% of the total climb when I sat down for a breather and my first sip of water. I looked down. Already my sandals and feet were covered in dust and I could feel the sweat dripping from my face. Oh boy, this was going to be fun.

I tried to think of other climbs I'd completed. There was St Stephen-in-Brannel Beacon back home. I could virtually run up that. Then there was Brown Willy and Rough Tor. They took a while but weren't exactly strenuous. Ben Nevis was a bit more challenging. This was clearly going to be more in the Ben Nevis category simply because of the heat.

The southern facing slopes were enormously hot; I could feel the sun burning the back of my neck and calves. I was gruffing and grunting like a boar pig and sweating like a poultice. I was stinkin' like a fitcher too. But I plodded onwards and upwards.

As I was about to turn off onto the Mine Hill track proper, a walker passed me and we exchanged greetings. Clearly he was more of a man than I was, because he was carrying not only a weighted backpack, but also weights around his wrists. He looked the kind of guy who did that for fun. You see such Royal-Marine types running around Plymouth with bags of sugar in their rucksacks. The road got steeper and rose higher into the mountain. As you climbed it did become cooler, but this was offset by the fact that the track became more vertical. I can't tell you how many times I stopped for water. A lot. Usually, I headed for some shade from the Blue Oak trees that lined the path. Christ, I thought, it was a long way for anyone to go to the shops.

To my left, across on Haldago Ridge was the sulphur flume chimney of the mine, and was a significant landmark for the local community. Back in the Museum offices, local children had made models of it. The flume wasn't rounded or tapered shaped like most standard Cornish ones, but square-shaped in cross-section. I kept looking at it, to see how much further up the mountain I had climbed. The problem was that it didn't seem to be getting any smaller. I re-checked the map again. No – I was on the right path. I was just plain knackered on my way to a knacked bal.

'Take only photographs, leave only footprints', my guide leaflet said.

I felt like adding, 'Bring extra oxygen'.

All the time I was remembering the drive through Yosemite. I remembered looking at all these mad fools who'd stepped outside of their cars and were bounding across grassland towards some distant mountain. Fools, I had said to myself. Why are they out there doing that? Now I was asking myself the same question. It was a Wednesday morning in August and why was I climbing an obscure mountain in the County of Santa Clara? Well, if the Cornish hadn't been defeated in getting up here over a century ago, then I sure in hell wasn't going to be now. After all, I was Cornish. My ancestors had probably lugged parts of some 56 inch beam enjun up here. I reckon I could handle some sandwiches and bottles of water.

There is always that moment of satisfaction in a climb, where you get to where you want to be. It doesn't come when you arrive there; it actually comes just before, when whatever it is you've been aiming towards becomes tangible, becomes touchable, do-able, real. It means that the agony of hauling yourself up some great height is about to pay dividends. Better than that, you know you can make it. I had this moment. Just before me stood a couple of ruined cabins, then some kind of workshop. To my right were another couple of structures, which had been recently repaired to stop further collapse. Not far away was the hill where the Methodist Episcopal Church had stood. All around were the ghosts of the Company Store, the Mine Office, the School House, Centennial Hall and Helping Hand Hall. I could hear Cornish voices, Cap'ns, preachers, maids and boys.

Now, all that remained were these ruined structures hiding in Dove Lupine, Fiddleneck, Larkspur and Golden Poppies; these wildflowers intermingling with California Purple Needle Grass. Beneath them I knew was an intricate system of shafts. I wondered around the ridge where Cornishtown had been, then sat down beside some pieces of mining debris to eat my sandwiches. It could have been Goongumpas Moors outside St Day. Instead, I was at an elevation of some seventeen hundred feet, looking northwards up the San Francisco peninsula, and out across to the Pacific Ocean. I spent half-an-hour or so at the summit, exploring the ground and wandering what it must have been like to have lived here. Cornish America was all around me.

Going down, as you can probably imagine, was infinitely more pleasurable. I got that burn in the back of my legs where the muscles were really working hard. The sun was full in my face and for a moment or more, all seemed right with the world. I knew my legs would hurt tonight though. Nothing mattered much now though. I'd done it. I'd made it up to Cornish Camp – been there, had a gake around and been where Annie Andrew Taylor had strolled. She must

166

have been up and down this track a time or two. Annie Andrew Taylor is one of my heroes. I'd heard about her lifestory a few years ago, but on this trip I actually managed to get hold of her autobiography.[8] Annie Andrew Taylor was interviewed by her grand niece Janice Paull in San Jose in 1955, when she was aged ninety years old. She'd been born in St Austell on the 17th April 1865 and had travelled from Cornwall, first to Pennsylvania, then on to Chicago, across the Plains to arrive in San Francisco in 1876, where her father, after time working in Montana, came to work at New Almaden. Annie lived in the Cornish town I'd just visited and married a man she refers to only as Taylor, who was a miner, as well as a talented concertina player. Her life-story then revolved around following the movements of Taylor, as he moved across the western USA to wherever there was work. Most times he went on ahead of her, so she had to save money (normally by cooking and cleaning for other miners) before she could afford the travel to join him. Many times they moved away from New Almaden, but it was always their base, and they often returned.

My favourite part of her autobiography is when she and Taylor start dating. Her father, John Job Andrew, a man from Mount Charles in St Austell, doesn't approve of their courtship. Annie writes, "[Taylor] went outside and I stood in the door and he said, "Blow out the candle." I said, "No," as Father could see me from where he was sitting. With that he said to come outside and I said, "No." He blew out the candle and asked me a question, "If I take you, will you go with me?" I said, "Time will tell for itself." He said, "All right," and went home."[9] I love those words, "If I take you, will you go with me?" They are so gentle and kind, so politely Cornish in their own way. The ghosts of Annie and Taylor followed me down the mountain.

The car was steaming hot inside. I opened up all the windows and poured a warm diet coke into my mouth. It was a bit like drinking a cup tay, more than a cold soda. Unlike most Californians, I didn't have any kind of screen to place in the front windscreen area to keep the car cool. I whacked on the air-conditioning at full blast and for a while at least, just cooled down and tilted my seat back. I wondered how those Cornish who came here dealt with the extremes of temperature. This wasn't like Vegas, but coming from Mount Charles, you'd surely have felt it.

New Almaden had been a wonderful experience. It had been hard reflecting on those buildings at Cornish Camp, imagining all the activity, the Methodist Church, the rough and tumble of life on top of the mountain. Though now much of it had gone, and the rest left in ruins, there was a certain aura surrounding it. Indeed, in Gage's words, it was a high and holy place. Had the Cornish emigrating overseas ever got further and higher? Right now, it was hard to think of anywhere that matched it. Later Gage and Ilka were to tell me about the wild boar that roamed the mountain, and then there were the mountain lions. I gulped. Then they told me about the tarantulas and rattle-snakes up there. I was just grateful for them telling me that *after* I'd made the climb. If I'd known there was that kind of wildlife, well, I might not have gone up there at all. I crossed Chynoweth Avenue again, this time not causing traffic meltdown, and headed into a 'Barnes and Noble' to cool down further. Inside this particular branch was a 'Starbucks' franchise. Right away I ordered a Vanilla Creme Frappacino and collapsed. I felt like everyone was looking at me. My feet were lagged in dust and between the toes were horrible sweaty brown bits. I tucked my feet in under the table and watched other beautiful people breeze in and out.

I spent a good while in the 'Barnes and Noble' shop, buying some guide-books and a couple of volumes of plays by Timberlake Wertenbaker, who incidentally, in her play *Our Country's Good*, writes about the female Cornish convict and highwaywoman Mary Bryant from Fowey, who was transported to New South Wales. It was, admittedly, an odd combination, and looking at my feet, I think the cashier felt I'd just rushed in from prospecting somewhere in San Jose. On the way out I glanced at an amusing book of George Bush-isms. The press that summer were filled with debate over his projected attack on Iraq, and one could sense the unremitting anniversary of September 11th just around the corner. 'Barnes and Noble' had a proliferation of books exploring all aspects of the date, and all its agony. It was a reminder of the day I myself had been flying across to America, and the aeroplane had to turn back to London.

Inside the shop I had glanced at one expensive coffee-table book showing some of the photographs that had been assembled of that day. A year on, and the images still shocked. I could still sense the hurt across America every where I travelled.

Back home at Gage and Ilka's I sat outside and read my new Gold Rush guidebook in the later part of the afternoon. After we ate a tasty walnut, orange and spinach salad, Gage, Ilka and I sat down to watch *Eastenders* – one of my favourite shows back home. I believe BBC America is more up-to-date, but on this channel, the episodes were from several years back, so it was amusing to see what crisis affected particular characters back then. It was hard to resist the temptation of up-dating Gage and Ilka on all the characters' lives and movements, but the retrospective episode was fun to see. American television is interesting though. One of the most popular British shows is still *Are You Being Served?* It didn't seem to matter that it was filmed between 1972 and 1985. Americans the country over, seemed to love Mr. Humphries' 'I'm free' and Mrs. Slocombe's 'pussy'. Meanwhile, I had enjoyed re-watching a couple of episodes of *Cheers*, which had been on British television while I had been a student at University. It was, clearly, a strange media world that we lived in.

I was up early in the morning for I was heading to San Francisco. I had the Mamas and the Papas going through my head. A bit of Led Zeppelin too. But then, I always had a bit of Led Zeppelin going through . . . The Caltrain that took me up the peninsula and into San Francisco itself reminded me of the one that I'd taken into Chicago a few weeks earlier – only this one was cleaner and more modern. It was the same double-decker affair, with the similarly complex ticketing arrangements – or at least arrangements for the guard to know whose ticket had and hadn't been checked. You bought your ticket at an automated machine on the platform. If you got it on the train then this would incur a three dollar surcharge. I was to see that in operation later that day, when on the return train, a woman got on at Mountain View to go one stop to Sunnyvale. The guard pounced and she was aghast at paying the surcharge – only apparently introduced within the past few days.

I was travelling in with the commuters. Most people had laptops and occasionally there were the polite tannoy notices asking people to be considerate when using their mobile phones. I thought about some of the train journeys I'd made up to London to see my publisher, and how that would never happen on trains in Britain. It was all incredibly sedate and polite, unlike trains back home. I watched a lot of people on this trip. Americans are always well-dressed. They seems to know what clothing to wear to suit their body shape – especially in places like California. I looked at my own sandals, still grubby from yesterday's climb up the mountain at New Almaden. I'd read somewhere (probably in British Airways' *High Life* magazine) that women judged men on the kind of footwear they had. I hope they weren't looking too closely. I might be a hobo; even worse – a Cornish hobo.

There were lots of reasons why I wanted to go to into San Francisco. First, there was all that Summer of Love. I was born that year, in 1967, so it seemed especially relevant. I mean I don't think there was too much of that going down on Hensbarrow Downs back home, but I sort of liked the concept anyway. I mean at this point, I was all up for going up to Haight Ashbury and seeing what it was all about. Talking of which, in the various newspapers I read while I was travelling, it seems that the Grateful Dead had reformed and were presently touring the country, without of course, their leader Jerry Garcia, who had died a few years back. I mean I realise their significance, but ask me to name one of their songs, and I'd be stumped. That's not very good for someone who normally prides himself on his knowledge of rock history.

Another reason for going to San Francisco was Alcatraz. I don't really know why but the island prison has always had a kind of macabre fascination for me. Perhaps it was the number of occasions in my youth where I watched Clint Eastwood in *Escape from Alcatraz*. Other films were weighing on my mind too – there was *The Birdman of Alcatraz*, then there was *Bullitt* with Steve McQueen, then *The Rock* with Nicholas Cage and Sean Connery. All of these were intermingling with *The Streets of San Francisco* and car chases up and down the city's hills.

Then there was the whole Cornish connection. As well as those passing through, journeying to the gold fields, many Cornish people had lived and worked in San Francisco. One of the most famous in my view was the journalist and poet W. Herbert Thomas (1866–1951). Born in St Day, Thomas worked as a reporter in the city before becoming a staffer on *The Cornishman*, and then editor of *The West Briton*. I've always felt Thomas an underrated Anglo-Cornish poet, so that was the reason I included him in *Voices from West Barbary*.[10] Thomas also edited the highly influential collection *Poems of Cornwall*, which he seemed to hope would remind homesick emigrants of the 'rocky land of strangers'.[11] I suppose I wanted to walk in his footsteps around the city, even though it had changed enormously from his day. For me then, San Francisco was about to offer the perfect eclectic mix of rock n' roll, classic film, jailbreaks, Anglo-Cornish poetry and earthquakes. What more could the travelling Cornishman ask for?

The Caltrain more or less followed 101 up the peninsula. This early in the morning (it was a little after 7 a.m.), the mist still clung to the mountains in the west, and the Bay itself looked gloomy. A lot of investment seemed to have been put into the Caltrain operation. All the stations were modern – yet designed in the style of old Western stations, with a kind lettering and style that I can only describe as "Sante Fe", as if we are meant to believe we are still in the Wild West, yet while peering at our shiny laptops. Colourwise – the predominant theme is maroon and green. The stations were busy, but not overbusy. As we trundled northwards, Palo Alto soon came into sight. This was the station for Stanford University. Next was the San Mato bridge across the middle of the Bay followed by San Francisco International Airport. South San Francisco is fairly industrialised, though one senses the realignment with more of the Silicon Valley and 'dot.com' industries further south.

As we moved closer into downtown San Francisco, besides great tagging on trackside buildings, we passed massive homeless communities, where countless tramps awakened from nights under cardboard. The closer we came to Fourth and King – which was the terminus, the more extensive these camps for the homeless became. Perhaps it was because of Union Station in Chicago, but I was somewhat *underwhelmed* at San Francisco Central Station. It was a modern building with only about seven tracks coming in. Somehow I'd expected it to be larger and bigger, but all told it wasn't that much bigger than Penzance. Then again, Chicago was a different deal altogether. Trains ran there from all reaches of the plains and the mid-West. Here, they seemed only to come up the Peninsula and from places like Los Angeles. Of course, the other reason for the station's smallness, was the fact that San Francisco had its extensive BART (Bay Area Rapid Transport) system which took care of many of the commuters from places like Oakland and Berkeley.

As in most large cities, a lot of homeless people were congregated around the station, many trying to sell *Big Issue*-style magazines and other products. One intrigued me. He was selling bookmarks for 25 cents. I bought one, used it to mark my copy of Ian McEwan's *Enduring Love* and looked for my bus connection to Fisherman's Wharf. Eventually the right one came and I boarded, finding a seat near the rear. In fact, bus is the wrong word. San Francisco people call them Trolleys, since they are powered by over-head cables. While I was waiting for the Trolley I observed the amount of new building going on around the station. One in particular caught my eye. It used a kind of cladding brickwork – so that instead of laying bricks one by one on the upper layers, the cladding was made in sections which imitated bricks. The only problem was it didn't look like particularly well-laid bricks. In fact, they were at quite a jaunty angle. This, I told myself, did not bode well in a city famed for its earthquakes. I only hoped someone would notice before the building was finished. As it was more or less the first building you saw as you stepped off the train, it might be as well for them to get it right – or else other tourists might wish to leave as quickly as they arrive.

This was not the case down on Fisherman's Wharf. Like a kind of tourist Newlyn, by 8.30 a.m. the place was already buzzing with visitors. It seemed like Pier 39 was the place to go, so I headed there first. Alcatraz was looming out of the sea-mist like some apocalyptic St Michael's Mount. Vendors vied for trade as far as the eye could see, promising amazing trips out into the Bay. What I needed was a trip that would get me onto Alcatraz, but this wasn't to be. The biggest company – the Blue and Gold fleet – who ran the boat trips out to Alcatraz were booked up for a week in advance. It seemed all the major tour operators in America had pre-booked all the places, so instead I elected for the Golden Gate cruise which obviously went under the famous bridge, but also circumnavigated Alcatraz. What amused me greatly as I later wandered the Wharf, was how many dodgy geezer-style salesmen were offering trips out to Alcatraz for just a few more dollars. Such tickets had obviously fallen off the back of a lorry somewhere between Piers 39 and 45.

Our boat chugged out into the Bay. I was imagining what the Cornish must have first felt as they arrived in this harbour, up from Central America a lot of them. I was thinking of the *Royal Cornwall Gazette* of 1849 quoting the London *Times*, in which respectable gentlemen announced that 'a seafaring man is ready to go equal shares in purchasing a schooner to sail (to San Francisco) on speculation', and of the Mineral Point-based Oscar Paddock and Henry Butler, who in order to travel to San Francisco built a Newlyn fishing-vessel style boat, to sail down the Mississippi. They were fine until they reached New Orleans, but then ignored customs advice and were seized by the Spanish. Eventually, they made it up the Nicaragua River, selling the boat for a thousand dollars. Only then, did they secure their passage to San Francisco. But what effort, to arrive here, where I was now sailing. Apparently, in the years from 1852 to 1860, a total of 871 passengers sailed from British ports to San Francisco, many of whom were Cornish, but this does not even begin to account for the huge numbers, already in America who went across the plains or who found other routes.[14]

San Francisco was the most convenient entry to the alluvial gold bearing area along the rivers running into the Sacramento, to which thousands of men came. According to Rowse, 5000 men were there digging in 1849; five years later there were 100,000.[15] Soon the idyllic days of individual prospecting were over, and it was San Francisco that mining became more organised, under the control of capitalists from that city. Business people also saw the possibilities of profiteering from the new furore. It was shipping, equipment and outfitting firms that prospered in the city, many run by the Cornish; but on the other hand, many arriving Cornish were ripped off by such enterprises as well. San Francisco also became the port which allowed the Cornish to travel up the coast and into the territories of Oregon and Washington. From here, they took boats to Puget Sound and the Yukon, and also into British Columbia. Later, boats took them to similar dreams in Australia, so in many ways, San Francisco had been both port of arrival and port of departure for generations of the Cornish. Although initially San Francisco was as rough and notorious as some of the interior mining camps, it quickly became more respectable. Probably the Methodists had a good deal of influence on San Francisco's Committee of Vigilance, which sought to redeem the city.[16]

An important event in the linkage between Nevada City and Grass Valley, and San Francisco, was the completion of the Central Pacific Railroad from Oakland to Cisco along the southern border of Nevada County. Its purpose was silver transportation, but it had the additional benefit of making San Francisco only a day away from the Northern mining region. Some of course, would disembark probably around these very same Piers, many of them originally built from lumber cut by Cornishmen in the Californian and Oregon forests; others would carry on toward the north-east, travelling the forty mile stretch of water inland, past Grizzly Bay, to the port of Stockton, where they'd disembark for the gold fields.

It was cold out on the water, so I was forced to enter the covered part of the deck. At least in here, I could hear the commentary better. The boat headed past the colonies of seals and sea lions which populate the entrance to the harbour then set on a course past the Palace of Fine Arts on San Francisco's northern shore. From the Bay you could clearly see the hills of City as well as landmarks like the 48-storey Transamerica Pyramid towering above the central business district and, slightly nearer, the Coit Tower on Telegraph Hill.

One of the early Cornish in San Francisco was William

174

Trenouth, a bricklayer, who ignored the temptations of the diggings. Instead, he went to San Francisco in 1850 to work while the city was rapidly expanding, but once having made some money he took to ranching, fruit-growing and farming in Santa Clara county.[17] There was also the botanist William Lugg, from Egloshayle, who in 1849 passed through San Francisco, not making his way for the gold camps, but instead, the forests of the redwood and douglas fir.[18] Todd comments that in all probability, during this phase of Cornish history that one could talk to a miner by a harbour wall, who had never been to London, but could quite easily describe the streets and taverns of San Francisco,[19] and it was true that as Rowse notes, in effect, the places I had already visited like Virginia City and Gold Hill, though several hundred miles away, were almost operated as suburbs of San Francisco, as were Nevada City and Grass Valley.[20]

I contemplated this while looking at the upper supports of the Golden Gate Bridge. They were still shrouded in fog. I knew that many Gold Rush schooners (in all likelihood, several with Cornish onboard) had been foiled by the fog and were shipwrecked here. Looking back on the vastness of the city, it now seemed hard to believe that with the discovery of gold near Sacramento in 1848, that San Francisco was transformed within two years from a tiny settlement of 500 people to a major metropolis of some 25,000 residents. It quickly became the West Coast's major seaport and financial centre. Our boat passed under the Bridge. In that sense, the Art Deco orange of the Golden Gate seemed particularly appropriate. At Lime Point, the boat turned around and headed back towards Alcatraz.

Alcatraz, it turns out, was discovered by a Spanish explorer in 1775, the 22-acre island named *Isla de los Alcatraces* (Island of the Pelicans) reputedly for the colony of pelicans found roosting there. The US military then recognised the importance of the island's strategic position and by 1854, the Army had established a fortress as part of the harbour's defence. It was then converted into a military prison during the Civil War. Then in 1934 it was turned into a federal penitentiary housing such U.S. "public enemies" as Al "Scarface" Capone and "Machine Gun"

Kelly. Apparently, during the 29 years that Alcatraz was a maximum security prison, there were no successful escapes, but at least four convicts disappeared, and have not been accounted for. The prison was closed in 1963, but in 1969 a group of Native Americans occupied the island for 19 months claiming it as "Indian Land." I saw their graffiti on the island's buildings.

I have to say, as a Cornish nationalist, I have a lot of empathy with the struggle of the Native Americans. I think all small nations would too. The irony, of course, is that the Cornish themselves have much to answer for, not only of their exploitation of Native American resources, but also in their use of Indian labour within mines all across the country. But our history doesn't tell us that . . . It was a sobering thought. Whether other people were thinking this, or just captivated by the island prison I couldn't say. The boat was strangely quiet though. We chugged eastwards then towards the dual span of the Bay Bridge. The top span of the Bay Bridge collapsed after 1989's earthquake, which made me feel slightly concerned about using it at any point in the near future. The island of Yerba Buena (this was San Francisco's original name) forms a support in the middle of the Bay while the other half of the bridge heads over to Oakland. I checked carefully for cracks in the supports.

Back on dry land, I decided to go shopping. Along Fisherman's Wharf are huge boiling pots serving up the Bay's famous Dungeness crab, alongside the equally famous sourdough bread. To the west, and near Ghirardilli Square, was the converted Cannery, now housing speciality shops and boutiques, but once the canning plant for the wharf. I was reminded of Steinbeck's novel *Cannery Row*. On the opposite side of the road were souvenir shops selling everything from Alcatraz pyjamas to scale models of tramcars, the Golden Gate bridge and seals. I wandered into an NFL store and the beefy shop assistant pounced.

"How can I help you today sir?"

I mumbled a "Just looking thanks . . ." to his perkiness, and gazed at all the merchandise. He was caught off guard by my weird accent and didn't trouble me any further. It's always been something of a worry to me which American football team to support. My mate Curgie went naturally,

176

so it would seem, for the Pittsburgh Steelers. Well, Pennsylvania was a Cornish kind of State. I'd initially felt that I ought to support the Green Bay Packers. They were, after all Wisconsin's team, characterised these days by their fans wearing foam cheese wedges on their heads at games, and still owned by the city of Green Bay. However, I was beginning to veer towards the San Francisco 49rs. What other team was there that captured the spirit of the Gold Rush? In any sense, sadly it all seemed a bit speculative, because despite the game of American Football being explained to me on several occasions, I still haven't much of a clue what is going on.

After sampling a crab salad on the waterfront, I selected to take a tolley tour of the city centre. This after all, would get me a little more orientated in San Francisco itself. It was one of these hop-on, hop-off deals that allows you to take it at the pace you want. Our 'Gray Line' driver didn't speak very good English, but made a good job of making everyone feel welcome. On my side of the tolley I was joined by Clint and Patsy. They weren't really called Clint and Patsy – but they were up from Arizona, and Clint had a good 'tache going and a Harley Davidson T-shirt on, and Patsy was dressed in the 'Sante Fe'-chic style. They probably listened to LiAnn Rimes and Garth Brooks, the occasional album by Lynyrd Skynyrd. We all had to tell the driver where we were from. I didn't think he would be able to handle Cornwall. Hell, it seemed he was just getting a grip on San Francisco, so when he asked me I said, "Great Britain." To complicate matters there was an English family on the opposite side who told him they were from "England". Occasionally during the tour the driver would shout things like "And how is everyone from Ennnnnngland??", "How is Idahoooooo?", "How is Great Britainnnnnnnn?" much to everyone's amusement. He was certainly crazy. His greatest feat was to take the tolley car to the top of Telegraph Hill, and amid much pretend testing of brakes, to let the Trolley go hell-for-leather down the steep sections of the Hill. It made my crab salad move a little I can tell you.

After we'd seen Lombard street (that's the one with the really bendy one-way street in all the car advertisements), he headed through Chinatown to Grace Cathedral at the top of Nob Hill. Grace Cathedral is an imposing granite structure that apparently looks wonderful at night. By British and European standards, it is fairly modern in design, but looks like it had taken its cues from Paris's Notre Dame. Interestingly part of the Cathedral's bells were donated by a Cornishman – one Nathaniel Coulson. His story has been fully mapped by Todd and is worth diverting to.[21] He was born in Penzance in 1853, and was left an orphan when his mother died before he was a year old, and his father deserted him before he was seven. He lived for a while in workhouses in Plymouth and Bodmin before being apprenticed, aged ten, at Penquite Farm near Lostwithiel. Aged fourteen he enlisted in the Royal Navy and then emigrated to Pennsylvania, then later travelled to New Zealand to find his father, who promptly disowned him. Real change in his life however, occurred after he enrolled as a student at the University of California's dental school, and qualified five years later, building up a considerable practice in San Francisco. Once his career had been decided, he donated 500 dollars to the laying out of a public park back home in Lostwithiel, which still bears his name, and then after it was decided to build a new Grace cathedral, Coulson promptly offered to fund the north tower and a carillon of bells. The north tower was completed in 1937 and the bells were hung in 1941. On the great bourdon bell are inscribed the words: 'First Installed in Great Tower of Golden Gate International Exposition, February 18, 1939. Gift of Nathaniel Thomas Coulson. Born at Penzance, Cornwall, England, August 8 1853. Graduate of University of California, 1885'. This was all in great contrast to *www.GraceCathedral.org*, a website which I later visited. There, I attempted to find out a little more about the Cathedral's history, but instead met with articles such as 'Episcopalians Speak Out: War with Iraq?', 'The Spirituality of Sports' and 'Habit of the High-Tech Heart: Living Virtuously in the Information Age'. No doubt, Nathaniel would have approved of these.

When the tolley car stopped outside *Macys* in the middle of downtown San Francisco, I hopped off, and explored Market Street. The driver probably wondered where "Great

178

Britain" had gone. The English couple look quite startled too. I knew I wasn't going to find anything very Cornish here. Instead I plumped for the 'Virgin Megastore' and flicked through the CD rack for twenty minutes or so, looking for obscure Deep Purple bootlegs. I couldn't find anything I wanted or needed so pushed on up one of the hills towards a 'Borders' bookshop. Halfway there I succumbed to another Vanilla Creme Frappacino in a 'Starbucks'. 'Starbucks', from their humble origins in Seattle's burgeoning 'Grunge' scene have now become the 'McDonalds' of coffee, but what can you say? They sell a good product well. And their banana and nut muffins aren't bad either. A girl from England came in to the coffeehouse. She didn't need to speak. I knew she was English, in the same way I was able to tell Americans at distance in Cornwall. They ooze something which tells you who they are – before they even talked. This made me wonder if the Cornish oozed Cornishness. Sometimes I think they do. You can just tell. Right then I was contemplating how good it would be if 'Starbucks' opened more franchises in Britain. There were a few in London I'd been into – but come on, how about Truro? As Curgie would argue, that was Cornish racism – why we didn't have these worldwide franchises west of the Tamar. I blame the letters pages of the *West Briton*.

The 'Borders' bookshop I found was absolutely massive and I spent a good hour touring its various levels, then strolled back down to Market Street passing the 'Gold Dust Lounge', Est. 1988, which offered 'Ragtime to Rock & Roll, Live Music 7 nights, 8.30 'til 1.30'. Inside was a wooden statue of a man panning for gold, next to boards offering Bushmills Irish Coffee, Champagne and Margaritas. If it had been established in 1888, it might look the kind of place where any self-respecting Cornishman might enter. I was tempted to go in myself, but seeing as how it was approaching five o'clock, I needed to get back to the train station. The trains were fairly regular but I had my eye set on one that left at around twenty-five minutes to six. As I walked back to the station, I realised that my legs were beginning to ache. For two days now, I had been marching around California in search of the Cornish. I'd found them

179

and found a bit of me along the way, but it was time to kick back and take it easy. I was drooling over the memory of sitting back in the swimming pool in Vegas with a Margarita in my hand. Instead I had to make do with the Caltrain seat and a Diet Coke. Still, it had been quite a day. It takes around an hour for the Caltrain to wind down the peninsula to Sunnyvale.

Back at the ranch, Gage and Ilka were enjoying a quiet drink in the back garden and poured me a Sierra Nevada beer. It went down well. My body ached, in that good ache kind of a way. I knew I was in for it though. That night I was exhausted, and when I eventually hit the bed, it didn't take long for me to get to sleep. he sleep that I had that night turned out to be of epic proportions. I didn't necessarily realise it was going to be that long, but I suppose my body was telling me something different. Either way, when I did wake I knew it was midday. The hot sun was streaming through the blinds and Quiller was giving out some serious cawking in the living room. I elected to have a shower and begin my slow adjustment to being awake again. Gage and Ilka had recommended that I took a look around the city of Sunnyvale itself, since, in particular, there was an important Cornish connection to Grass Valley. First though, I decided to hit a mall for a couple of hours. There is no denying it, I now realise, I love wandering through American malls because they give such a wonderful insight into life there. Everything from the labels on boxes of sweets to the design of shopping trolleys fascinates me. The Sunnyvale Mall was the first one I had entered since South Park back in the Quad Cities. It was not an ostentatious Mall at all, and in fact, many of the units were closed and shut, due to the eastern end of the site having some major re-development. I went through 'J.C. Penneys' first, admiring the low-cost men's suits available, then moved on to 'Target', pausing at the latter to look at the seemingly endless range of self-improvement books available. I almost bought a book on Yoga, but then realised I would probably never use it. My legs just aren't bendy. I looked for a 'Chicken Soup for the Cornishman' but it was not available. After 'Target' I managed to stumble into 'Hallmark' which was filled with the kind of cutesy rubbish no-one ever wants to be given on their birthday, and what I can only describe as Christian-themed presents, which I decided I didn't really want to be given on any day of the year. There were other shops but I decided not to step inside. I might have been persuaded to buy a Disney musical box inside 'Musical Box World', or some Cartman-style Weightgain 5000 in 'Healthy Living'. The Mall, all told, was a bit of a disappointment. I had been warned though. Ilka had advised me to check out the one at Stanford which was much better, but I was too lazy and still too sleepy to make the drive.

Instead, I drove across the railway line to seek out what slivers of Cornishness existed in Sunnyvale. Actually they were fairly impressive and far more significant than I'd ever imagined. A few blocks away from the Sunnyvale Mall is an engineering plant founded by one Joshua Hendy. Now Hendy was a Cornishman who had set up his first factory further up the peninsula around 1856 in South San Francisco, but eventually moved his operation down here in 1906. Not only did the cream-coloured plant buildings produce many of the stamps (examples of which I was to later see) and mining equipment for Grass Valley, but during the Cold War, Hendy's Engineering manufactured many military products for nuclear submarines and firms like Lockheed. Over the last thirty years the firm moved away from heavy engineering, and in many ways pioneered the kind of information technologies and computer hard- and soft-ware, which we now associate with California's 'Silicon Valley'. The Hendy site was large and still very significant in the economy of Sunnyvale and San Jose. Many Cornish people had worked at the Hendy plant including Gage's grandfather – Ken Hughes – who had moved down from Grass Valley when the mines there started to decline. There was nothing particularly Cornish about the site in look or feel, but that perhaps, I decided, was a good thing. It was incredible to think that this Cornishman's work had in actual fact, kick-started much of the computer and 'dot.com' industries of California. Outside the plant, I stood at a set of 'memorial' mine stamps that the Hendy Foundry had cast,[22] peering across high-tech San Francisco, and back across America. It was a humbling moment. Now I knew how stamps and 56 Inch Cylinders had made a country and a culture.

Notes

1. Alan M. Kent (1995) *Out of the Ordinalia*, St Austell: Lyonesse Press, p.37.
2. A.L. Rowse (1991 [1969] *The Cornish in America*, Redruth: Dyllansow Truran, pp.12-13.
3. Ibid., p.267.
4. Gage McKinney (1997) *A High and Holy Place: A Mining Camp Church at New Almaden*, New Almaden: The New Almaden County Quicksilver Park Association.
5. For a detailed history of New Almaden, see A.C. Todd (1995 [1967]) *The Cornish Miner in America*, Spokane, Washington: The Arthur H. Clark Co., pp.79-103. For contemporary accounts, see Constance B. Perham (ed.) (n.d.) *Life in 1877 at New Almaden as Pictured in Word and Illustration by Mary Hallock Foote, February 1878*, Fresno: Valley Publishers; Francis P. Farquhar (ed.) (1966) *The New Idria Mine and The New Almaden Mine excerpted from Up and Down California in 1860–1864 by William H. Brewer*, New Almaden: New Almaden Quicksilver Mining Museum.
6. Rowse, op.cit., pp. 267-9.
7. Todd, op.cit., p.87.
8. Janice Paull and Freda Taylor Anderson (eds.) (n.d.) *Annie Andrew Taylor's Life Story*, New Almaden: New Almaden Quicksilver Mining Museum.
9. Ibid., p.3.
10. Alan M. Kent (ed.) (2000) *Voices from West Barbary: An Anthology of Anglo-Cornish Poetry 1549–1928*, London: Francis Boutle, pp.195-201.
11. W. Herbert Thomas (ed.) (1892) *Poems of Cornwall*, Penzance: F. Rodda, p.4.
12. John Rowe (1974) *The Hard Rock Men: Cornish Immigrants and the North American Mining Frontier*, Liverpool: Liverpool University Press, p.98.
13. Ibid., p.103.
14. Ibid., p.113.
15. Rowse, op.cit., p.244.
16. Rowe, op.cit., p.267.
17. Rowse, op.cit., p.265.
18. Todd, op.cit., p.15.
19. Ibid., p.9.

20. Rowse, op.cit., p.287.
21. Todd, op.cit., p.53.
22. See S.V. Griffith (1938) *Alluvial Prospecting and Mining*, London: Mining Publications Limited, pp.86, 96 and 97. These pages show numerous items of Joshua Hendy equipment. For many years Griffith's work was a course book at Camborne School of Mines. It is a 56 Inch Cylinder Syndrome read of extraordinary proportions.

8

Been brought to Grass . . .

After a meal of wonderfully tasty, locally-made Burritos (I suppose, in essence, the pasty of Mexico), we hit the road for 'Graaaaass Valleeeey'. Ilka and Gage advised that the best time to leave was later on in the evening, to avoid both the San Francisco commuter and weekend traffic. We took Interstate 680 around the bottom of the Bay, then headed north-east towards Livermore and Tracy. From thereon, we travelled Interstate 5 up to Stockton. Although Stockton is some forty miles or so inland, it is a major port, and like San Francisco, was a site of disembarkation for the numerous Cornish heading towards the Gold Rush. Stockton is still busy. As we headed through places like French Camp, you could see some sizeable vessels in the river. Stockton was once home to the Tretheway family from Cornwall, forming a partnership to operate the Stockton Iron Works.[1] They must have looked over a similar view of the river, many a time. At Stockton itself we took a break, stopping at a trucker-style gas station, all three of us rushing in to use the restroom.

After the relief of that, we browsed. In the store were the usual essential/unessential truck stop items – snow-globes of San Francisco and the Golden Gate Bridge, Elvis or Native American velvet wall hangings, key chains for the '49ers, weird vitamin pills which promised sexual prowess, various types of doughnuts and any kind of Citizen's Band radio equipment needed by mankind. That's a 10-4 there buddy.

The bizarre mixture fascinated me and Ilka and Gage had to pull me out screaming. I'd managed to buy a packet of *Oreo* cookies though – that's the ones with the Bourbon-like outside with a creamy filler.

We headed toward the State capital of California, Sacramento: Population 400,018. When Rowse passed through here in the mid-1960s, he estimated a very large number of Cornish (among them, families such as Trestrail, Treffry, Blamey, Anstiss, Endean and Keast[2]), which is perhaps not surprising given its early links to the gold rush and mining in general. It was at Sacramento in 1849 for instance, that the Jewell brothers from Wendron gathered, before they began their not too prosperous assault on the goldfields.[3] The city was founded that year and was California's first charter city. The Pony Express and the first continental railroad all began there. Sacramento is now a modern and thriving centre, dominated by sophisticated architecture and wide parklands; *Newsweek* magazine recently naming it one of the best ten cities in the United States. To look at it now, it seemed a far cry from those early Cornish 'argonauts'. As we passed through Sacramento, I saw signs north to Marysville. This town had also drawn in the Cornish, though I only knew one thing about it. Rowe mentions the story of a Marysville journalist who asked a Cornishman why a horse-shoe was nailed to a door in one of the town's main streets.[4] According to the Cornishman it was there to 'keep the devil out', since next door there was a Chinese wash-house, and the Chinese continually burned paper to keep evil spirits out. No doubt, the Cornishman was afraid they would enter his place instead. Interesting that a piece of old world superstition should be supplanted here, but then again, we Cornish are a very superstitious people still.

We then took 80 north, passing the sweet-smelling air of Orange Vale and Citrus Heights. Truck-loads of near-ripe oranges and lemons passed us by. Beyond Citrus Heights lay a little Cornish moment for me – the town of Penryn was signposted, though I have to say I know little about it, and what its exact Cornish connection was. It didn't look a lot like Penryn back home, but there it was, probably named by some old boy who couldn' forget old Cornwall. I relayed

185

the famous rhyme to Ilka and Gage: 'When Falmouth was a fuzzy down, Penryn was a working town'. There was, we remembered, the Saltash one too – 'When Plymouth was a fuzzy down, Saltash was a working town'. Both of course, had some measure of truth to them. There were a lot of Plymouths in America – I felt it best not to bring up the Saltash rhyme in those towns though. We drove on, talking about the new Combined University of Cornwall campus at Tremough in Penryn. Somehow Gage and I both doubted that Cornish and Celtic Studies would be high on the agenda of its shakers and movers.

Signs for Grass Valley and Nevada City started to appear and we turned off at Auburn. All around, the landscape changed from citrus groves into dark forest, as we began to climb the Sierra foothills. As you know, Grass Valley is twinned with Bodmin. Now Bodmin to me these days is – how having lost the Court, failed to gain a University – something of a sad Cornish town. It is probably now more famous for John Angarrack's washing machine repair shop and Cornish nationalist activities than anything else. I have great affection for it, but I suspect, like a lot of Cornish people, *I wudn' want t'live there*. I always felt the old Hospital site of the town would have made a fine University campus, but who am I to comment? I dun't knaw nothun'. Still, twinned with Bodmin it was. Now, if I recall, on any entry to Bodmin, the signs proudly demonstrate the town's twinning with Grass Valley, so I was expecting to see the same thing – like with Redruth, in Mineral Point. But no, there was nothing. Apparently the twinning signs are only put out when someone from Bodmin arrives. For a moment, I wanted to hail from Nanstallon or Berrycombe Vale . . .

I can genuinely say that I felt weary from so much travelling on arriving in Grass Valley, but at the same time a kind of frontier excitement was running through my veins. I was imagining how James Benallack or Joel Rowe first felt when they arrived here all that time ago. You have, of course, expectations of what it will be like. I thought Grass Valley was going to be something like Mineral Point, just as sedate and polite. Boy, was I mistaken. It could have been a scene out of a Hollywood Wild West movie. When we pulled into East Main Street at around half-past twelve at night, the place was jumping. It looked like Newquay on a Saturday night while *Run to the Sun* was on. Scantily-clad girls staggered drunkenly across the street, while throaty motorbikes cruised the streets. Music blared out of the Holbrooke Hotel and the Nevada Bar. People waved at me as I drove past (I expect my eyes were like dinner-plates having a good ole' gake at ut all) and I waved back.

To orientate me, Ilka drove around the block, showing me the bookshops and where they would be staying. Then she pulled up outside the Holbrooke Hotel so that I could check in. The bar's French windows were open, and people drank on the two small balconies. They watched me enter. It had to be me didn't it? It was the nightporter's first night on duty and he was a bit confused as to what to do with me.

"I explained I would be arriving late," I said trying to be helpful.

I wasn't being helpful, the nightporter seemed to suggest. Basically ,'ee didn't have a clue, Boy.

Ah well. While he found my key and the paperwork, I surveyed the Hotel. In its heyday the Holbrooke was probably one of the swishiest and swankiest hotels in the northern mining region. A plaque outside showed that it was Californian Registered Landmark No. 914: 'The present bar of the Hotel had been in continuous operation since 1852 when it was known as the Golden Gate Saloon. The wooden building had a rear extension called The Exchange Hotel and offered food and lodging by January 1853. The saloon was destroyed in the fire of 1855 and rebuilt out of fieldstone with a brick front. The Holbrooke, built in 1862, had the adjacent Golden Gate Saloon incorporated in the hotel building.'

It now looked a little world-weary, but a postcard on the reception desk showed me what it was once like. Horse-drawn coaches passed the veranda on which walked sophisticated ladies and gentleman of the day – all bustles and long moustaches (and that was just the women). On the upper balcony, paraded richer visitors who could afford such luxury. The lettering, the architecture and the doors all made it feel like I had really stepped into Wild-West history. In many ways, it reminded me of the architecture and style of Virginia City. A grand staircase led to the upper rooms and shiny mirrors reflected the patrons of the bar. I read the guide's description again: 'At the Holbrooke, touches of yesterday and today blend happily: TVs hide in armoires and claw-footed tubs enliven modern baths. It is a downtown beauty.' I was looking forward to blending happily with this downtown beauty as long as the nightporter could get a move on. He was being surprisingly 'dreckly' in his dealing with me. Eventually though, the registration was completed and my room ready for me. I waved good-night to Ilka and Gage and surveyed the Holbrooke.

"Any jobs goin' up the Empire Mine?" I wanted to say, strolling into the bar. "Just got in from the Old Country. You'n call me Cousin Kenty if y'like. Now, woz on?"

I didn't though. Instead, I unpacked and fell asleep, not before looking out over the town. I was staying in the Robert Fitzsimmons room. Yes, the Cornish boxer. Beauty. I was treading in the shoes of a Cornish champion.

I'd been reading up on my history. Grass Valley, at some 2,450 feet, is a actually a very carefully preserved historic mining town, where elegant nineteenth-century homes overlook miner's houses and mine tailings. Clearly, now though, it is a fashionable day out and place to stay in Northern California. There was much to discover I knew. The town's fame came from hosting gold mining when it hit its peak as an industry. Grass Valley was never really the place of the single uncovered large nuggets, but rathermore a centre where big machinery and equipment were moved in to take as much gold out of the ground as efficiently as possible. The headframes and inclined shafts surrounding the town once employed thousands of men. By the late 1800s, Grass Valley's population was 85% Cornish.[5]

Of course, it was Cornish technology that kept the water from seeping into the shafts. Once the Cornish pumps stopped operating, water flooded into its tunnels, and today the water is approximately 150 feet below the ground surface. Remembering all of this, my 56 inch cylinder pride swelled. The big difference between Grass Valley and the other 'Mother Lode' mining areas was that when the larger mining companies developed the area, they attracted other peripheral industries, so the town was one of the first places to have a broad economic base. The Cornish too, allowed mining to no longer be a case of hit-and-miss. They were experts in the field, and had been so for hundreds, if not thousands of years.

The Cornish were literally everywhere in Grass Valley. The census information is difficult to interpret, in that much of it alludes to the families being 'English'. For example, in 1860, Grass Valley had a population of 3,940 of whom 530 were 'English' (some 470 of these 530 were miners).[6] However, a quick check of the names reveals a very different ethnic pattern: the majority of these were Cornish. The Cornish, so it seemed, had been in Grass Valley for a long time. In the Episcopal Church, founded in 1855, there is a memorial window to one Mary Tredinnick,[7] and they continued to be active throughout the twentieth century. As Todd notes, over a hundred years later, in 1957, Richard Heather from Hayle was the Mayor of Grass Valley. The one time president of the *The Union* newspaper was Robert Ingram from St Ives and the managing director, the Penzance-born Earl Caddy.[8] And it is a continuous performance. That August, along Main Street, rested a mobile pasty shop called 'Cousin Jack Pasties', complete with a cartoon of a Cousin Jack and the splendid odour of warm pasties. Just across the way stood some historic stamps made at Joshua Hendy's foundry in Sunnyvale. Cornishness oozed from the streets here.

Like all the other mining centres I had travelled through in America, Grass Valley also has its first big strike story. You know how that always begins by now . . . It all began when one George McKnight, who had set up camp on the surface diggings in 1849, was out chasing a wandering cow in the moonlight, when he stubbed his toe on an outcropping. Now, the surface diggings weren't known then to be particularly rich, but McKnight's toe loosened a piece of rock and he noticed the glitter of shining metal in the moonlight. McKnight soon forgot about his cow and took the rock back to his camp to crush it. Within minutes, he knew it was gold-bearing quartz. News of the find brought in miners from across the country, and by the summer of that year a mill had been built near the toe-stubbed outcrop by the Gold Hill Company. In seven years, they took out gold estimated to be worth four million dollars.

189

Other mining companies soon followed: the Empire, North Star, Pennsylvania, Idaho-Maryland and Brunswick. Around 500 miles of underground tunnels were dug under Grass Valley and its northern neighbour Nevada City. Millions of dollars of gold continued to be taken out of the ground well into the 1950s. The most disastrous fate that befell Grass Valley was a huge fire in 1855, which decimated the 300-odd frame buildings that made up the original camp. It was possibly the most disastrous of all the fires which occurred in the Gold Rush Camps, and so inspired a particular kind of architecture now very characteristic of the town and area – heavy masonry walls with iron-shuttered windows, intended to prevent such fire damage ever occurring again.

I looked out of such a shuttered window onto the bright Saturday morning. It was 7.30 a.m. and there were no *Oreo* cookies left. I was hungry. Breakfast at Holbrooke was one of those curious affairs that American hotels seem to specialise in. There is no real sit-down service, much like the 'Comfort Inn' at Mineral Point. You just help yourself to cereal, muffins, bagels or bananas, find a spot in the dining area and sit down. I quite like it really. You can have as much or as little food as you like, and there's no hanging round, for the waitress or waiter to fetch things for you. I selected a wholemeal bagel, mixed fruit jelly and cream cheese, and grabbed a complimentary copy of Grass Valley's *The Union* newspaper. It turned out this was the very day I should have been reading it. Great consternation surrounded last week's Nevada County Fair, since there had only been a single Cornish pasty entry in the Cornish pasty competition.

"Good heavens above!" I spurted, almost choking on the bagel.

I joke, but this apparently was a serious business, not only requiring a re-examination of the town's whole ethnicity, but a whole critique of the judging, timing and positioning of the Nevada County Fair. The letter pages were full of observations upon this phenomenon. One lady offered the idea that while other pies could be prepared the day before, the most tasty pasties really required making in the morning, rendering them to perfection at midday – and since the pasty judging was held at half-past ten in the morning, there was no time to even make pasties properly. She seemed to have a point. Pasties were a serious business in Grass Valley. Cousin Jack's mouth-organ had met its match. Meanwhile *The Union* not only dedicated its editorial to the crisis, but also had its lead cartoonist – one R.L. Crabb – draw a half a page witty exploration of the pasty in history ('Being the grandson of a Cornish miner, I was raised on pasties!', 'It's like tradition, Man!' and 'You can even use packaged pie crusts, but be advised . . . it's a capital offence in some parts of the county.'). Other guests seemed to be looking at the same pasty page as me. I could only imagine what they were saying.

"Well, Marge . . . they sure as hell take them Pasties seriously up here . . ."

"You're dang right there Chuck. We'd better make sure we're armed with a pasty by noon . . ."

I concluded that one or perhaps both of two phenomena were occurring. Like back home, any decline in 'Cornishness' was up for discussion by the media, or concurrently, the fact that there was so much debate about the 'pasty' issue demonstrated that Cornish ethnicity was, paradoxically, alive and well in Grass Valley. There was one thing you could guarantee: that next year's Nevada County Fair would have a helleva' lot more entries in the Cornish pasty competition. From then on I paid special attention to old ladies around the town. You could sense them preparing for a show-down already. Their hands were just itching to crimp.

After breakfast, Gage picked me up to take me over to Nevada City. He was researching the effects of the Great Depression in the Grass Valley area, and I was on my seemingly endless search for Cousin-Jack literature. Both of us finding the pasty crisis amusing and interesting, we headed out on the short distance of highway 49 between Grass Valley and our destination. Highway 49, viewed as abhorrent to most local people, cutting as it did across an historic area, straddled a shopping mall, which served both of the towns.

Much like Grass Valley, Nevada City began life as a camp, then progressed to become a tent village, and finally evolved into a town of wooden buildings. It was razed to the ground several times by fire and so after the great fire of 1856, the authorities decided, like those at Grass Valley, to rebuild using masonry. Not only that, but they formed fire companies and built three fire stations, two of which are still in use. The whole of the downtown area of Nevada City is a 'National Historic Landmark'. I don't know quite what this means, but it presumably refers to all the carefully preserved buildings which now house boutiques, galleries, restaurants and museums. The place is filled with broad balconies, roof turrets, mullioned windows, gazebos and picket fences – in many ways, more the kind of architecture you'd expect to see on the banks of the northern stretches of the Mississippi, like at Galena, than here in Northern California.

Just like its twin further down the valley, Nevada City has its origins in the year 1849, when miners were panning along Deer Creek. It has had a history of names – all of which I think I like better than Nevada City. First off, it was Caldwell's Upper Store, then Deer Creek Dry Diggin's, then Coyoteville and eventually Nevada. The City was added when the neighbouring State appropriated the town's name for its own – or at least, that's what they say in Nevada City, and who am I to argue? Gage took me past Coyote Street, apparently so-named because of the local "coyote holes" – small shafts used to get at the gold buried deep in the gravels of old river beds. One story amused me greatly: the old miners of Nevada City were so eager to find gold that many was the time that they simply dug up the streets of the town. A merchant angrily demanded that the miner stop digging up the street. The miner, being a Cornishman, I suspect, stated that there was no law to prevent him from digging up the streets, and that he could do so if he wanted. The indignant merchant told him that he would make a law and put a revolver to his head. Mining in the streets ceased immediately.

I couldn't see any mining in the streets at we pulled up to the Doris Foley Library for Historical Research. I scrubbed at the ground a little, but no-one put a pistol to my head. The librarians at the Doris Foley Library – Alisa Austin and Steffanie Snyder – were both incredibly enthusiastic and helped me sort the *Hydraulic Press* from the *Daily Miner Transcript*, and then the *Nevada Democrat* from the *Foothill Weekly Tidings*. They also let me go through all their stock, comprehensively searching for poems, stories, songs and memoirs of Cousin Jacks and Jennies. In so doing, I learnt a great deal about these two towns, and the whole of the northern mining area. Gage meanwhile, ploughed through the 1930s.

We took lunch in a very Californian restaurant, which reflected much of Nevada City's bohemian atmosphere. The open-fronted kitchen had cooks with lots of facial piercings and tribal tattoos, while alt-rock group Jane's Addiction's 'Ritual de La Habituo' burst through the music speakers. In many respects, it was my kind of place. Alternative music press and anarchic literature littered the in-house bookshelves which diners were, of course, allowed to read. The great, the good and the tattooed of Nevada City seemed to dine there. On the walls were curious paintings of little dinosaurs appearing out of still life fruit bowls.

"Hi – my name is Nathan and I'll be your server today. What can I get you guys?" said our little waiter, who was tanned, around twenty-five with a chin piercing, and looked like he'd just left the Red Hot Chili Peppers.

We ordered standard fare – some turkey sandwiches and iced teas.

"You know," said Nathan, sitting down next to us, to *share*, "I'm reckoning on about two years here, learn the ropes, then open one of these down in Sacramento. What do you think? Is it a runner?"

Gage and I nodded.

"That's so Californian," said Gage. "Not only do we get the waiter's name and history, but also his life ambition . . ."

Perhaps we ought to have *shared* as well. We didn't: being Cornish, we, in the words of Robert Louis Stevenson, 'kept grimly to ourselves'. Instead, we tucked into our turkey sandwiches, and gave him a good tip, thinking in some small way that we Cornish had contributed to his ambition.

Strolling back over to the Doris Foley Library, we darted into a couple of bookshops. In one, I bought a 1971 novel by the Pulitzer Prize winner Wallace Stegner, called *Angle of Repose*.[9] It was the story of one Susan Ward, a pioneer travelling across America in the nineteenth century to places like Grass Valley, New Almaden, and Leadville; the controversial fictionalisation of the story of a Cornishwoman, Mary Hallock Foote, whose reminiscences I'd also been reading.[10] There was the usual debate over Stegner's narrative, and how accurate (or not) his telling was. Either way, both kept me stimulated for the afternoon.

As we reached the library, we somehow got onto the topic of hydraulicing. A few miles north-east of Nevada City is the Malakoff Diggins State Historical Park. The Malakoff Diggins was the scene of the biggest hydraulic mining operation in the world between 1866 and 1884. Now, for those of you who don't know, basically, hydraulic mining is the same kind of mining that has been used throughout the entire history of china clay mining operations back home in Cornwall. Basically, the mineral you are after is washed from the ground, using a high-pressure washing hose – sometimes called a monitor – after the swivelling guns on early US warships. The mineral is carried in sediment and then refined. Like back home, I got the impression real underground miners sneered upon it, as not proper mining (Indeed, it might account for the fact that while Redruth and Camborne's mining history has been signed, sealed, revised and endlessly re-negotiated, Cornish historians were only just beginning to scratch the surface of the china clay extractive industry).

The mining at Malakoff ceased in 1884 after the authorities realised the amount of pollution it was causing. Malakoff now looks very much like the landscape of mid-Cornwall, although the tourist authorities in California try to pass it off as a 'scenic wonder'. The 'Malakoff Alps' anyone? Apparently, in June 1971, the town of Malakoff used one of the old hydraulic nozzles in a Homecoming celebration, which promptly washed away part of the town's only sidewalk. I wondered what the people of Malakoff would think of somewhere like Melbur pit (where I worked for a few summers, while a student at University), which had eaten away whole villages (such as Meledor) over time. It also reminded me of the time a clayworker in my shift, named Phil, who used to drive his Robin Reliant three-wheeler down the bottom of Virginia Pit, which was also worked 'hydraulically'. Being of a generous build, Phil could never be bothered to walk down to the hose-hut. I always remember the phone-call up to the gravel pump: "Alan, you'd better come down bottom. Phil's chicken chaser is being washed away . . ." Even though, it wasn't deemed very environmentally friendly, I liked the sound of Malakoff. It made me feel right at home. Pollution. Environmental destruction. Very Cornish. Industrial Celts to the end . . .

We spent much of the rest of the afternoon in Doris Foley, only being interrupted by the grand re-opening of the Searls Historical Library across the road. The Searls Library was the headquarters of the Nevada County Historical Society, and Gage, Steffanie, Alisa and I went over for some fruity punch and some peach pie, to celebrate its re-opening. I wasn't quite sure what they were re-opening for, but I think someone had painted the walls and moved the books around a bit. Either way, it seemed a good occasion for some punch and pie. I was introduced to Brita Rozynski, the Society's current president, and she took me on a tour of the library. They, like the Doris Foley, had gathered a lot of Cornish sources (we discussed my compasses – Rowse, Todd and Rowe), and she herself, though now having a Polish name, was a Berryman, her family originating from Menmundy, in, she said, ". . . Some parish called . . . I think . . . St Stephen-in-Brannel . . ." You can imagine my response. I explained, how that was my home parish, how I went to school there, and how I still lived close by. I expect in the next hour we went through everything – from china clay, hydraulicing, farming, the parish church, the Hockings, to Menmundy itself. The mouth-organ was playing loudly here, the tune resoundingly Cornish.

Brita and I swapped e-mail addresses. She was sad that I couldn't stay any longer, and to be honest, so was I. She showed me her family's book – a beautiful piece of genealogical research, illustrated with old pictures of the Parish, some of which I had not seen before. There and then, I resolved to send her a copy of Salome Hocking's *Some Old Cornish Folk*. I knew it would probably move Brita to tears.

We'd have a lot to talk about in the future. I have to say there was nothing false or invented about this; nothing performed or false. This was just two people responding to a genuine sense of place. For a moment, it felt like I had cut a sharp swathe across the 'invention' of Cornwall from an Cornish-American perspective.

That evening we agreed to have dinner at the 'Owl Tavern'. Ilka had still been jet-lagged from her flight, so had spent the day relaxing at their friend's bed-and-breakfast (incidentally owned by a lady whose maternal line was named Penhallow). Besides, unlike Gage and I, she had no serious interest in researching the intimacies and complexities of the Cornish in North America. I have a feeling she is the sensible one. Before I met them, I decided to hang out in the Holbrooke Bar and catch up on some reading of Mary Hallock Foote while sipping a pint of Guinness. Donna, the barmaid, asked what I was doing there in Grass Valley and I explained. She talked about her memories of childhood in Grass Valley, about pasties and about how important the annual Cornish Festival now was. It was strange, since like me, she realised how embedded her Cornishness was, even though we were both brought up thousands of miles apart. She'd moved around a lot, but felt happiest back here. The Guinness was on her. I like to think I'd reminded her of something good in her childhood.

The Owl Tavern is now one of Grass Valley's classier dining joints, but a few years ago, it was much frequented by the miners from the Empire. Its stripped back brick-walls try to imitate a kind of Gold Rush theme. The conversation at dinner fell onto the controversial subject of high-grading. I'd heard rumours of it all across Cornish-America, from Mineral Point to Leadville, but here, right now, it was being debated openly. High-grading was all about stealing already mined quality gold ore,[11] and it was an occupation carried out by just about everyone involved in local mining. There were rumours of men who still wouldn't step into the 'Owl Tavern' (apparently the haunt of High-graders and traders) for many years, for fear of reprisals. Even now, it was good to keep a look out behind one's shoulder.

I was exhausted by the time I got back to my room, but that has never stopped me in America. It was approaching one in the morning, but I still decided to flip around the television channels. On one station was a film called *Vegas Vacation*, with Chevy Chase playing the lead role. In an effort to bond his family, he takes them all to Las Vegas for a holiday; whereupon his family disintegrates, he blowing lots of money, his wife falling in love with a lounge-lizard singer, his daughter becoming a dancer and his son becoming a Mafiosa. I had to watch it. The film had lots of the locations where I had been a week ago and amused me no end.

Even though it was now late – or very early in morning depending on your view of time, I still read for a while. One of the leading historians and authors of the Grass Valley area is a man called F.D. Calhoon. I'd read his book *Coolies, Kanakas and Cousin Jacks* (1986) a few years ago at the Cornish Studies Library in Redruth, but found it again in the Doris Foley Library. There's a good chapter in there about the Cornish, which I photocopied.[12] Bizarrely though, whenever I mentioned his name to librarians, historians or just the normal folk of Grass Valley or Nevada City, they kind of winced and made their apologies to me, scuttling away. Perhaps I had smelly armpits. I checked. I didn't. Gage set me straight. Apparently, F.D. Calhoon (who is now dead) had been incarcerated for the murder of his wife, not too long ago. Well, this place was still rootin' an' tootin' I thought. Perhaps she took exception to the very chapter I was reading. We shall never know and perhaps that's a good thing. Apparently, Calhoon's last testimonial was a book protesting his innocence.

The other author who I was reading at the Holbrooke was Bret Harte, who once stayed there, and is commemorated by having one of the rooms named after him. If you haven't come across him, then I'd commend Harte to you. I bought a cheap volume of his *Gold Rush* stories,[13] which though not always alluding to the Cornish or Cousin Jacks directly are full of intriguing references to Cornish lifestyles, on the western mining frontier. Typically his narratives are filled with rough miners, who speak in a combination of Cornu-English and Western drawl ('The damned little cuss!' and 'Snoopin' round yere'), pistol-packing preachers, tough women and gamblers. Here, according to one of his most famous stories, 'The Luck of Roaring Camp', the "strongest man had but three fingers on his right hand; the best shot had but one eye." In the background of the narratives lurk Cousin Jinnies, hands of euchre, Dungeree Jack, pards, long-handled Cornish shovels, brass bands and characters like Dick Bullen, who must have been a Cornishman.

Harte's personal story in itself is interesting. He was born Frances Brett Harte in Albany, New York in 1836, the son of a destitute teacher of Greek, who died in 1845, leaving a widow and four children. After he left school Harte worked in a law office and then a counting house, while his mother journeyed to San Francisco. He was twelve years old when gold was found in California, and only eighteen when he came to California (like the majority of Cornish, via the hazardous sea journey and the difficult crossing at Nicaragua) to join his mother and stepfather in Oakland. As a young man Harte wandered the mining landscape of Northern California, taking jobs as a druggist, Wells Fargo stagecoach driver, schoolteacher and even as a miner. The miners considered him something of a 'tenderfoot', but superstition said that such a tenderfoot always brought luck, so he was always welcomed wherever he went. Despite his fame now as the recorder, and indeed mythologizer, of the Gold Rush in California Harte actually kept his distance from the miners, always the fastidious dandy, wearing boiled shirts and patent leather shoes, asserting that the Sierra foothills were "hard, ugly, unwashed, vulgar, and lawless." That seemed very much like the Cornish. Harte later abandoned Northern California, for a career in publishing and in the newspaper industry back east, but even until his death in London in 1902, the mining West formed the inspiration for his writing. In essence it is Harte we owe much to, for the world's perception of the Wild West, igniting the later twentieth-century passion for the Hollywood Western.

Harte wasn't the only writer celebrating the Gold Rush. Mark Twain (1835–1910) – actually the pseudonym of one Samuel Clemens – also had a hand in the cultural geography of Northern California. Clemens' family, I am told by several authorities were Cornish, and the Cornish historian of Methodism, John Probert, remembers a Mrs. Clemens in Redruth, who claimed she was a distant relative of 'Mark Twain'. Clemens had tried prospecting in Nevada, but then moved to become editor of the *Virginia City Enterprise* newspaper, and came to meet Harte. In December 1864, Twain visited the Gillis brothers, who had hosted Harte a few years earlier. While at the Gillis camp, Twain heard an old Mississippi River pilot tell an old yarn about a frog-jumping contest. A couple of months later, Twain published the mining-themed *The Celebrated Jumping Frog of Calaveras County*, which became an overnight literary sensation. According to what I have read about Harte and Twain, it becomes clear that they celebrated the mining country in different ways. Twain seems to have learnt more of the miners' habits and trade. He once said, "I know the mines and miners interiorly as well as Bret Harte knows them exteriorly."[14] I was certainly glad of Harte and Twain on the nine hour flight back from San Francisco. The in-flight entertainment system had broken down, so their stories kept me going just fine.

As well as the Bob Fitzsimmons room ('Prize Fighter') I had commandeered, the Bret Harte room ('Author and Legend') and the Mark Twain room ('Author and Legend') in the Holbrooke, many other famous people had stayed there. I took some time to go around and have a gake at who had stayed there. Appropriately enough, right next to the Helston-born boxer was the Irishman James Corbett ('Prize Fighter'), then there was Gilbert Barry ('Actor'), Lotta Crabtree ('Singer and Dancer'), William Bourne ('Gold Baron') and Black Bart ('Californian Outlaw'). By them was also a room named after Ulysses S. Grant, but intriguingly he didn't have a note of explanation – perhaps people just knew who he was. Then came the other U.S. Presidents: Benjamin Harrison, Grover Cleveland and James Garfield. My favourite though was Lola Montez, described on her plaque as 'Femme Fatale'. Montez was actually born Eliza Gilbert in Ireland in 1818, but after a sensational theatrical career in Europe (simultaneously conducting affairs with Victor Hugo and Alexander Dumas) she moved to America to tour. However, the jaded Californians did not rate her performances, so eventually she retired at 248 Mill

Street in Grass Valley. After this, I decided that I also wanted a room named after me in the Holbrooke Hotel. I quite fancied one of the 'Author and Legend' ones. It was the *Legend* bit I liked.

"Do you remember that Cornish author by the name of Kenty in here – oh way back when in the early '00s? I remember when he downed those five bottles of Southern Comfort and went out whoring on the streets of Grass Valley?"

"Sure do! He's one helleva legend . . ."

"Came back and had another couple of bottles and fired up the Karaoke machine . . ."

One of my favourite things about the Holbrooke was not only that it felt like I was walking in a real Western saloon, but that it was the focal point of the community of Grass Valley. I feel, like at the 'Cruise' in Mineral Point, that I could step in there tomorrow and barely anyone would bat an eyelid. I had become an accepted member of the bar community. They served wonderfully cold Guinness too. On Sundays, drinking in Grass Valley begins early. By the time I had dragged myself out of bed, had a shower and felt ready for the day, it was eleven o' clock and when I stepped into the bar, a few hardened men of Grass Valley had already sat themselves down.

The bartender, Donna, asked me if I wanted another Guinness, but I declined, asking instead for a coke. While I was waiting for Gage to pick me up, she introduced me to a local author named Michel Janicot. I'd heard of Michel already and had glanced at his book *The Ladies of the Night: A Short History of Prostitution in Nevada County, California* in the Nevada City Library.[15] Considering my experiences in the State of Nevada, I thought the title had seemed interesting, so I was glad to run into Michel. He was a short, wiry guy with a long 'tache, well-read and knowledgeable about all the different ethnic groups who had populated California. To begin with we discussed the Breton origins of Jack Kerouac and, of course, *On the Road*. He'd also written extensively on the history of Nevada County. Now sixty-four years old, he'd been born in France, his mother having married an American airforce pilot. He had taught both in California and in Africa with the Peace Corps. Presently retired, he earnt money by house painting and spent his time between Grass Valley and Zihuantanejo in Mexico. Michel looked dressed for life in Grass Valley. He had a great tan, was decked out in an loud Hawaian shirt and made his own rollies, which he had to go and smoke outside.

"Stupid bastarding Californian smoking laws," he said to me. "I bet you don't have this in Cornwall . . ."

We stepped outside into the daylight while he drew down deep on the rollie.

"So you read my book?" he asked.

"I picked it up in the library . . . had a glance through . . ."

"It's a best-seller," he joked. "The only one to go into a second edition! Everyone buys it. They want to see what went on here."

All morning Michel and I talked about sexual commerce on the Comstock Lode. There was Bridget McCloskey's brothel on North Pine Street, the present home of an attorney office, "The Cottage" situated at the junction of National Alley and Spring Street, site of the 1881 killing of Fannie Colby, a local inmate, Eileen Ellias, alias Texas Tommy "the last of the great madams", the Golden Gate Rooms above Frank's Pizza, the Nevada Rooms on East Main Street, the Empire Rooms, Jo May's bawdy house, Limpy Go Fetchy and Funeral Mary "two loveable citizens of yesterday" and Miss Maybelle Foster, who was proclaimed the miners' friend.

"Oh, I think she helped the Cornish a lot," joked Michel. "You know, there is more I need to write, but I am waiting for a few people to die off before it can be published . . ."

In all honesty Limpy Go Fetchy and Funeral Mary didn't 'zactly sound like Madonna or Kylie Minogue.

"You have to think how isolated it all was," said Michel. "In the Census from the year 1860, Nevada City had 24 prostitutes, while Grass Valley had 19."

He had a point. Miss Maybelle Foster, whose face looked like the back end of the No. 21 bus to Newquay, might have looked rather ravishing after a twelve-hour shift down Empire Mine.

One story in Michel's book concerned a Cornish-sounding woman called Carrie Smith Pryor, known locally as "Spring Chicken". She lived at Truckee in the eastern end of Nevada County. Her lover, George Pryor (a Cornish name if ever there was one), got into a fight with Jack Whipley, Belle Butler's pimp, in a saloon, where Pryor was left permanently crippled and soon left town. Carrie invaded Belle Butler's boudoir in Lotta Morton's bawdy house, where Belle worked her charms. Both women rushed to each other's throats, but Belle, however, drew a pistol and hit Lotta and some bystanders. Pryor was later wounded in a Front Steet saloon, and Belle served 18 months in jail for the shooting. "Spring Chicken" got her Cornishman, but her triumph was short-lived. In 1875, she was in Virginia City, Nevada, where she was arrested for assault and battery. Placed in jail, she tried to hang herself with a handkerchief. According to the Truckee *Republican*, Carrie Pryor "had led the most dissolute, abandoned life and has been the direct and immediate cause of several homicides . . . It is only a year since she plunged a knife into a man's body and left him lying in the street, apparently dead."[16]

Such tales were pretty commonplace in Grass Valley and Nevada City. Nice to know the Cornish could shake it up a bit. Then, it was good to know someone like Michel had taken a look at this trade. While back home, we are content enough to lament the loss of 56 Inch Cylinders, how many Cornish scholars have looked at the sex industry in Cornwall? Answer: None. Apparently, the 'Market Inn', next now to the Hall for Cornwall in Truro had at one time at least some similarities to the Nevada Rooms (Note to self – must investigate further . . .). By now, Michel and I had shared several anecdotes and at least a couple of rounds of drink. I'd downed the coke quickly and moved onto Guinness. I can honestly say, it was a real pleasure talking to him. He was well-informed on mining, all the Cornish families of Grass Valley and knew the similarity between the Bretons and the Cornish.

"So, you been to Tijuana North yet?" asked Michel.
"Eh?"
"Tijuana North . . . Nevada Silly . . ."
"Eh?"

"That place up the highway . . . Nevada City . . . I call it 'silly', because it's where all the nuts go . . ."

"Yes – I was there yesterday. I know what you mean . . ."

Michel was referring to the bohemian and boutique feel of Nevada City, and how the two towns were rather like chalk and cheese. Originally Grass Valley was clearly working-class; Nevada City, the mine owner's town, more middle-class and sophisticated. At that, I had to tell Michel the Christmas stocking joke about west Cornwall.

"Why is Penwith like the bottom of a Christmas stocking? Because that's where all the nuts go to . . ."

I think Michel understood.

"That's near Land's End right?" he questioned.

"Yes – it's where all the potters, painters and pagans go . . ."

"Just like Nevada Silly eh?"

At this, Gage arrived to pick me up for a tour of the North Star Mining Museum and the Empire Mine. He was glad to see Michel too, and we chatted for a while before leaving. Michel and Gage concluded that at this end of the Holbrooke Hotel bar was probably the only place in North America were the price of gold was still known and debated. You could almost see flecks of it on top of the polished wood.

Before we arrived at the Museum, Gage showed me a few more Cornish places around Grass Valley. There was Bennett Street named after a famous Cornish family, but even more interestingly there were roads named after the Cornish and Cornwall. We circled back under the highway, and pulled down a short track into the North Star Mining Museum.[17] I could tell from outset it was going to be a bit 56 Inch Cylinder-ish and I was not to be disappointed. We parked the car under some shade, and even from there, I could see rusted piles of boilers, hydraulic monitors and rows of stamps. Our guide was named Paul and he was a real beauty. He could talk the hind legs off a donkey – or perhaps I ought to say 'dunkey' if I'm being fitty.

I thought I had sorted out how to deal with American Mining Museums and their staff by now. You had to walk in really carefully, not allude too much to the fact that you were Cornish, or you might be blinded with technological data causing brain overload. I thought I was beyond 56 Inch Cylinder Syndrome. Here, though, my cover was blown. Gage introduced me and announced that I was "*Cornish*" and interested in mining. I'd made Paul's day. See, most of the tourists who passed through the museum didn't know the difference between a Polrose (for all of you out there not as *au fait* with mining lingo as *moi* - that's the pit under a water wheel) and a Pare (that's a gang of men), but me, being me, happened to identify a few pieces of rusting iron, and Paul beamed like I was the Director of Camborne School of Mines. It didn't take much for him to point out all the Cornish miners in the picture archive, nor show me the working of some stamps they had rigged up to imitate their movement in crushing ore. I expect they're still talking about my visit now.

"Boy, do you remember when that Cornish guy was in here?"

"Sure do, Paul. He knew what a stamp foot was . . . He must have been the first visitor we've had in here for darn near forty years who knew what a stamp foot was . . ."

"We won't see the like again in our lifetime . . ."

"That's for sure."

As in all mining museums, there was a layer of dust over everything, including all the new (or newish) books for sale. You'll know the score by now – a working model of a typical Gold Rush mining scene (some kind of take on Charles Christian Nahl's famous painting 'Sunday Morning in the Mines'), complete with animated mule and dog; the mock-up of an underground shaft, complete with Cornish-hard rock miners and pasty bucket; the wire and plastic models of the underground levels; the growth and development of the carbine lamp; various kinds of tools all displayed, but no-one really having much of a clue as to what they were used for. Big Bob Plock would have liked it, I knew. I wanted to send him a postcard of it, but after viewing the massive super-efficient Pelton Wheel (patented by Lester Pelton of Camptonville, California in 1878), Paul ushered us outside.

But hold on, Paul! I need a moment. For all of you not beyond 56 Inch Cylinder Syndrome – the wheel is 30 feet in diameter, weighs 10 tons, and operated for 40 years. It steadily cranked the massive connecting rods of two 30 inch and two 18 inch pistons to power the mine's hoists and drills, delivering compressed air through 800 feet or six-inch pipe at a pressure of 90 pounds per square inch. Christ, I could be a fully fledged member of the Trevithick Society at this rate . . .

In the sunshine, we were to view the aqueduct across the River Yuna and (a drum roll, please) the Cornish pump! Well, blow me down with Trevithick's statue, I almost replied, who'd have thought it, a Cornish pump right here.

"You want to see it work?" Paul asked, a strange madness in his eye.

"Yes please," I asked.

"You got fifty cents . . . ?"

You had to put fifty cents in to see the pump lower and rise, counterbalanced by a small selection of stones.

"It doesn't need many rocks to counterbalance it," I offered.

"No," said Paul. "We rigged it with a motor, just to make it work. Looking a bit dry though . . ."

He was right. Not much water seemed to be coming out of the ground.

"Tank's probably a bit low . . . I'll fill her up later on . . ."

We were joined by a family who watched the rise and fall of the beam.

"What is that?" the mother asked.

"That there is a Cornish pump . . . and this here guy, he's from Cornwall . . ." said Paul, as if the machine and I were somehow in perfect unison.

That confused her totally. We all watched, mesmerised by the pump in action. Eventually, after about two minutes, it spluttered to a halt.

"Is it broken?" the mother asked.

"No ma'am – works by fifty cents . . ."

"Paul, we should be getting off now. We're heading up to Empire Mine now . . ." said Gage, sensing Paul's on-going wish to show me yet another piece of industrial detritus.

I got Paul's name, thanked him for the tour and told him he'd be in the book. He seemed pleased. We got back to the car and I explained my 56 Inch Cylinder Syndrome to Gage. He understood – and sympathised. It was a bit like museum-head, only worse. It was ethnic. Did I mind going to another mine though? Hell, I was Cornish. I loved going to mines. I lived for it.

There is a famous photograph of a 'core' (or shift) of miners at the Empire Gold Mine at Grass Valley. You've probably seen it in various accounts of the Cornish in North America. The year is about 1905 and the miners are about to descend the main shaft on skip wagons which are tilted on a hoist at an angle of about 27° to the horizontal, since that is the angle of the shaft. The miners' faces all look rather sombre (as they well might be, entering such a dangerous darkness). A framework of wood lifts the miners high into the air above the entrance portal to the mine, and they are sat there as if this were some twisted underground fairground ride, rollercoastering sadistically down through the shaft. The incline extends some 4,650 feet down. In all honesty, it is a remarkable photograph, as well as a piece of remarkable engineering. Many of the men on that skip incline are Cornish.

One of the highlights of my travels in Cornish America, was looking down the mouth of the Empire Mine's inclined shaft. Propped with metal and wood, with two tracks running down, it really does look like the jaws of Hell from *Ordinalia*. Right now, the State Park Department of California owns the Empire Mine site, and they have partially opened the shaft so visitors can peer down it. There are plans, I gather, to open the shaft further and take people underground, but nothing can really prepare you for the enormity of the Empire Mine. It makes South Crofty, look well, like the proverbial piss in the ocean (or what about a slash in the shaft?). It was the largest, richest and deepest hardrock gold mine in California. The mine includes 367 miles of tunnels and shafts, many of which extend under the surrounds of Grass Valley and Nevada City, and a model of which is contained in the State Park's Exhibition centre. From its beginnings in 1950 to its closure more than a century later in 1956, an estimated 5.8 million ounces of gold were extracted from underground.[18]

The mine is now set in woodland, with carefully main-tained pathways and exhibits, but it does not need much imagination to realise what it was like in its heyday. The Bourne Cottage (the owner's mansion) is beautifully preserved, as are the mine management buildings which are available for visitors to look around, complete with gold-weighing equipment and massive safes. Towards the rear of the site are wagons, trains, kibbles and drilling equipment – much of which hails from the middle of the twentieth century, rather than the nineteenth, now all brought to grass for people like me to touch and feel in bright sunlight.

Around the Park you'll see photographs of one Jasper Dailey, said to have been a typical Cornish miner circa 1880. He has a pasty pail, and is touching pipe for a bit; his pants and boots flecked with mud. I don't expect Jasper knew it, but his stance and face are now an icon. What is incredible is that whoever the photographer was, he or she somehow knew that – that Jasper might be worth capturing. Likewise around the site, were a number of photographs of mules. The animals worked underground in the nineteenth century. They were lowered down the shaft in canvas sheets, and then once down in the mine, never saw the surface again until they were dead. The mules were apparently well-respected though. Any man caught maltreating one of them would be sacked on the spot. I bought a postcard of one mule named 'Fanny' – a photograph dating from around 1895. I don't care what you say – it would suck big-time being a mule down a mine.

The Historic Park was popular. Clearly, a lot of the Californian public found this attraction, and Grass Valley and Nevada City an interesting day out. There were guides to the Park, but Gage and I felt we both knew enough about hard-rock mining to dispense with them. We talked to a female blacksmith 'in costume' inside the smithy's shop. It didn't take long before she recognised my accent as different, and asked where I was from.

"Sort of like a pilgrimage," I said, though I'm not sure she was convinced at what I was doing.

I looked at the candle-holders she was making; a copy of the one the Cornish miner, Jasper Dailey was holding. It involved a twist of steel, forming a 'holder' just large enough for a candle to sit in – sometimes called a 'sticking tommie'. The spiked end of the holder was then ideally wedged into the stope somewhere, or otherwise rammed into a wooden prop. They were well-made items, but I suspect at twenty dollars a throw, neither Jasper Dailey nor I would be buying one. I was being 'close' as they say in Grass Valley – something the Cornish have a bit of a reputation for in California.

"So where is Cornwall?" the blacksmith asked.

I explained. Clearly, Gage was unimpressed. She hadn't been in the area long. We didn't say it, but clearly she needed to bone up on her history, particularly if she was pretending to probably be a Cornish metalworker. Smiths are important to we Cornish, as anyone on the road from St Keverne to Blackheath will tell you.

The 'mouth-organ' (in its widest sense) and music were alive and well in Grass Valley though, as I was to discover that night. One of the more famous local Cornish activities is the musical tradition of the town. Music had a public premiere in 1875, when the Thomas Brothers' Silver Cornet Band presented a special Christmas Eve concert of Cornish carols, and since then, over the years, there have been a variety of choirs, all with different names, but sharing memberships, directors and an inherent Cornishness. Traditionally, the carols (or "curls") and songs – many derived from Cornish writers like Thomas Merrit, W.B, Ninnis and J. Williams – were learnt by rote, and passed down from one generation to the next. The choir was first broadcast from San Francisco's Grace Methodist Church (now lying in one of the city's rougher neighbourhoods) as early as 1927, but perhaps more famously, in 1940, the famous Cornish choirmaster and St Austell-born boy, Harold J. George, directed members of the Grass Valley Carol Choir in a live national broadcast from the 2,000-foot level of the Idaho-Maryland gold mine. This was to be repeated in successive years and recordings survive from 1946 and 1959. Although the choir disbanded in 1967, partly in the wake of the industrial collapse of the gold mines, the carols were never forgotten. Neither were the steps of the town's distinctive *The Union* newspaper building, where the choir would often gather to sing. I'd sat on those very steps earlier that Sunday, wondering what it would be like to sing here at Christmas – with the air cold and frosty, the voices floating up into the valley. I could hear the icy carols, the freezing airs of 'Sound! Sound!', 'Salutation' and 'Lo! The Eastern Sages Rise'. I could hear the wonder ringing back and forth from Cornwall to Nevada County.

We all ate at the Holbrooke that night, outside on the deck, in the balmy August evening. I felt very relaxed, and was chatting to Gage and Ilka about music in Grass Valley. One important person sitting next to me, who I haven't told you about yet is Eleanor Kenitzer. Eleanor is the sort of person I'd like to take back home on the plane with me and have for keeps. She made me feel so welcome and easy in her company that it was easy to forget she actually had a proper job as the front-desk manager of the Holbrooke. The daughter of a Baptist minister, she hailed from Rocky Mount, North Carolina, and still carried that State's beautiful accent. She was about as far removed from the Cornish in America as anyone could be, but when she moved to Grass Valley in 1988, she quickly became involved in choirs and singing around town. In 1990, Eleanor helped kick-start a reunion concert of the Cornish Carol choir and hasn't looked back since. She recruited and trained new voices, had the choir tour America and Cornwall, made new recordings on CD, and though acknowledging the tradition of the Choir, had also progressed its musical repertoire. Gage, as well as telling the story of New Almaden much better than me (I just staggered up the mountain), has written a really fantastic book on the history of the Grass Valley Choir, which I commend you to read, for it is a real account of the soul and song of a community. Here, I can only offer the basic story, but Gage sets it all out. *When Miner's Sing: The Grass Valley Carol Choir* is a comprehensive study which details the origins, the development and present state of the choir.[19] What I can tell you is that the choir is not in some state at all. It is very healthy, much of it thanks to Eleanor's commitment and forward-thinking ideals, as well as people like Gage, who understand its importance and cultural relevance to anyone from Nevada County.

I saw the Grass Valley Choir at the *Dewhelans*

Homecoming festival in Falmouth in 2002, and they were magnificent, and I was lucky enough to sing with a few of them around the piano in the Holbrooke that evening. Eleanor had e-mailed and phoned as many of the gang as possible, and since a lone Cornishman was in town, it only seemed appropriate that we should blast through a few of the classics. I tell 'ee, 'twas sounding good. We kicked off with 'Goin' up Camborne Hill', had a crack at 'Lamorna' and 'Little Lize' then moved on to 'The White Rose', 'I've been Working on the Railroad' and 'The Old Clock'. It all reminded of the version of 'Goin' up Camborne Hill' I performed at a University of California, Los Angeles Celtic Studies conference dinner, in a Korean restaurant. You can rest assured, I then near-matched my friend Benjamin Luxon in terms of wondrous performance and rapturous applause. Well, perhaps not.

The music aroused interest from lots of the other guests and barflys at the Holbrooke, and it wasn't long before they wandered in to see what was going on. There was a lovely elderly couple there from Louisiana, who were treated to *The Song of the Western Men: Trelawny* (our national anthem), followed by *Dixie* (the South's national anthem). Afterwards they told me *Trelawny* was very patriotic, which I obviously agreed with. They asked me what it was about. I tried explaining that it was written about an imaginary rebellion led by Sir Jonathan Trelawny (1650– 1721), but written in the nineteenth century by one of Cornwall's finest Anglo-Cornish poets, Robert Stephen Hawker of Morwenstow – based on a traditional refrain. They looked at me askance. I shouldn't have bothered. We just celebrated devolution, ordered some more Southern Comforts and coke and got down to some more Cajun/ Cornish/Southern mixing.

"This is just the finest thang I have seen in a good long while," said the Southern belle to me, looking every inch as if she had once been in Tennesse Williams' *Cat on a Hot Tin Roof*. Indeed, the thang was a proper job.

"The name's George, Son," George said . "You e-mail us any time about this Cornish thing . . ."

To me, he looked like Big Daddy, and maybe he was expecting me to get down to talking about some Mississippi

210

Delta 'mendacity'. Suddenly I had a vision that Lawrence Kazdan was going to come in and direct us all. Quick as a flash, I suggested we'd best get back to singing the dirty verse of 'Goin' up Camborne Hill'. Several Southern Comforts and cokes made the '*I 'ad 'er I 'ad 'er I did*' lines come out splendidly. It was like Saturday nights at Tyacks. Puzzled guests and residents wandered through. The Louisiana couple looked even more puzzled the next morning when they found me nursing a coffee, while reading Michel's book on prostitution in Nevada County.

"Nice mornin'" I offered, and got back to some sexual commerce.

They nodded and sat over the other side of the room. Tennesse Williams would be proud of me.

I'd actually risen early so that I could walk out to the cemetery before the sun became too strong. Heading up the hill to the graveyard, I survived being chased by a particularly vicious dog (I was imagining the headlines in the local *Union* newspaper: 'Cornish writer maimed by mastiff while visiting ancestors'). I don't know what it is about barking, vicious dogs; sometimes I seem to attract them. This one was less on the bark, but more on the chase and gnashing teeth however. Sometimes, I wish dog owners would just be a bit more responsible. There, I'll get off my soapbox and get back to the graveyard.

It was as dry as old boot up there. Any vegetation had turned yellow, and even the graves seemed to have been cracked and weathered by the extraordinary heat of a Californian summer, and I suppose also by the cold winters. Like in Mineral Point, a combination of nationalities filled the hill-top graves (some Swiss, Finnish and Irish), though it did not take long to spot many of the names that Shirley Ewart and Harold T. George refer to in their excellent book *Highly Respectable Families: The Cornish of Grass Valley 1854-1954* - the Georges themselves, the Henwoods, the Bennallacks, the Rowes and the Tremewans.[20] But there were others too – the overtly Cornish language names like Trevithick, Angove, Polkinghorn, Trezise and Constantine, but others too – actually the more common working-class Cornish names, which so many scholars ignore – Bennett, Harris, Pollard, Hooper, Berryman, Williams, Keast, and

211

Thomas. I stood for a while at a Roberts' grave and wondered if they were distant relatives on my mother's side. All the graveyards I'd visited in America produced an intense, quite indescribable emotion in me, and this was no exception. Long dead, I could somehow still hear their songs and language rising out of the ground. On the way back down, the dog no longer tried to maul me. He'd heard the ghosts talking.

Back in town, I took a stroll down Mill Street towards the Art-Deco feel of the Del Oro cinema. There was a shop I wanted to look around in Neal Street that I'd noticed on Sunday – 'Verlinda Vanderfords' Famous 49er'. The name itself was too good to stay out of, and the window display was fascinating, filled with old bill posters, mining tools, lumps of rock and a few cobwebs. It turned out to be what I can only describe as a Mining and Hunting shop, but with a Christian twist to it. On the one wall, weapons of mass destruction (knives, guns, bigger knives, bigger guns) to maim, kill and butcher every small and large mammal this side of Yosemite National Park; on the other, a selection of *Bibles*. On the another wall, all the equipment a discerning 49er might need – gold-washing pans, pickaxes, shovels, weights right next to booklets which said, "If you trusted Jesus as your Saviour you have just begun a wonderful new life with him. Now: Read your *Bible* every day to get to know Jesus Christ Better." Scary stuff. Now I knew why the shop was famous.

"Can I help you?" said Verlinda Vanderford.

"How much are your plastic gold pans?"

"Four dollars."

"I'll have one please," I said, not really knowing what the hell I was going to do with a plastic gold pan back home in Probus. Perhaps I'd convert it into a fruit bowl.

"Would you sign our visitor book?" said Verlinda Vanderford.

"Sure . . ."

I can't remember what I put, but it was something like 'Nice knives'. I thought that was very Christian of me.

"I'll put one of these in here for you too, Honey . . ."

She put a piece of Christian propaganda in my bag.

"Thanks," I said.

212

It reminded me of a particular overzealous Methodist minister who'd once remonstrated with me over my wearing of an apparently Satanic-themed T-shirt at Foxhole Methodist Chapel Friday Night Youth Club. I think the song on at the time was Iron Maiden's 'The Number of the Beast'. It was 1982 and I was fifteen. I think it put me off Methodism for life – that was until I wrote *Pulp Methodism*, and actually re-considered what a reforming and progressive force Methodism was. Ah well, I was a sinner, according to Verlinda Vanderford, but at least I didn't sacrifice small mammals high up in the Sierra Nevada.

During my final wanderings in Grass Valley that morning, I picked up a promotional magazine from KVMR 89.5 FM – Nevada City's 'Music of the World, Voice of the Community'. That September, they were running their 6th Annual Celtic Festival and Marketplace.[21] To my utter amazement no Cornish bands or events were planned, and yet there was much promotion of the English folk-rock band Fairport Convention, and assorted other Irish and Scottish acts like Wolfstone and Wake the Dead. There'd be jam sessions, Scottish Games, Pipe and Drum bands, Celtic Dance lessons (whatever amalgam that is), historical re-enactments and Celtic Food and libations. Mmm . . . this was different than the Celtic Festival in the Quad Cities.

Here, yet again, it seemed, not only the Cornish, but the Welsh, the Bretons and the Galicians were the poor relations. Could it be that the Cornish festival was so big anyway, that it was felt a separate Celtic Festival was needed – or was it sheer ignorance about Cornish Celticity? I tried to be positive, but it was the latter I feared, and perhaps again, our status as 'industrial Celts' left us in the cold. The festival logo was composited around flowing knotwork, and a very Scottish-looking castle lurking high in the mountains. Half of the bands playing had never even set foot in a Celtic territory and were probably woefully politically naïve. I was thinking of bands like *Dalla* back home who really deserved a crack over here. I swore to myself to e-mail the station about it when I got back home. I was also minded of my good friends *Gaelic Storm* back in Santa Monica in Los Angeles, who do know their pan-Celtic music and politics. Their lead guitarist, Steve Twigger hailed from Looe. If you don't know *Gaelic Storm*, check out the multi-million pound blockbuster James Cameron directed-film, *Titanic*. When Leonardo de Caprio and Kate Winslett are dancing in the steerage section, that's *Gaelic Storm* playing the music. This overall lack of recognition infuriated me. Despite all I'd seen, all the Cornish prowess that had gone into making America, we were still the poor relation to the Irish and the Scottish. There was a great swathe of America that I hadn't been to, who felt the Irish and Celtic as synonymous.

The small, grey cloud over me didn't last long though. I looked at the time. It, as the Cornish say, was coming up for dinner. Just up Neal Street and around the corner is *Marshall's Cornish Pasties*, baked fresh daily. I was in the mood for a bit of Cousin Jack's mouth-organ and stepped inside. The young owner, Marie Marshall greeted me, and realised my pasty prowess.

"I'm Cornish," I said.

It was as simple as that. She took a step back, as if Egon Ronay had walked in.

It was one of those ultimate Cornish moments of my time in North America – the surveying of the pasties. I'd had it in Mineral Point too. First of all, there was Marshall's Pasties logo to consider. It was fun and apparently age-old, showing a wagon pulled by two horses, with Marshall's logo on the wagon's canvas. It looked like it could contain enough pasties for the entire Gold Rush. Marshalls didn't mess around either: they proudly stated 'No preservatives or artificial additives'.

On the wall was a sign. You could hear the American documentary announcer: "What's a Pastie? Pronounced "Past-e", they are a traditional food, brought to the mining areas by the early Cornish settlers from Cornwall, England. At Marshall's Pasties, we keep our operations as close to the "old west days" as possible. Our pasties are flakey baked delicacies, rolled and crimped by hand, and filled with *fresh* vegetables, including potatoes, onions and parsley. We prepare several varieties including Chicken, Turkey, Broccoli and Cheese, Beef, Ham and Cheese, Vegetable, and even a dessert "Apple Figgy" pastie, mildly

214

spiced with cinnamon and a touch of raisins." I selected the beast I wanted (a beef one) and she put it into a bag which I instantly unravelled.

"You going to eat it now?" Marie asked.

"Yes," I answered.

I told her the joke about the Cornish driving test; the one where to pass, you have to do a three-point-turn, holding the wheel with one hand, and a pasty in the other. I mean if mobile phones are illegal, perhaps they should make pasties onboard illegal too. Having said that, the Cornish economy might not survive such legislation considering the effect it might have on time and motion.

Marie gave me her card. It was beautifully designed, though I wondered what I would do with it. Maybe it was just for me to be reminded of my ethnic eating habits – or maybe, it was for if I somehow accidentally staggered into a 'Burger King', I could phone the emergency number and dial-a-pasty.

"Quick! He's Cornish and must have a pasty injection right away . . ."

"What if he doesn't?"

"Don't even think about that, Nurse . . . The consequences could be catastrophic. A Tsunami wave might hit the River Tamar, the Cornwall Rugby squad might never win at Twickenham again . . ."

"Does it taste good?" Marie asked.

"'Andsome," I replied, spitting no end of pastry and onion at her, like you do.

And it was 'andsome too, but just a bit different than the ones back home. The flavour, pasty experts, is somehow drier, yet at the same time, a little spicier than the ones back home. I thought of Curgs here – how he'd complained of a pasty he bought in London and how it was too peppery for him. This wasn't. By the time I'd made it back up Mill Street, the pasty had gone. I'd played on Cousin Jack's mouth-organ in the middle of Grass Valley and it was a very satisfying moment. Celebrating, like some mutant Cousin Michael Jordan, I dunked the paper bag into a bin. I'd travelled a helleva' way for that pasty.

Ogie ogie ogie! Oi Oi Oi!

Ogie! Oi! Ogie! Oi! Ogie! Oi!

Ogie ogie ogie! Oi Oi Oi!

Michel happened to be walking down the other side of the street, and was heading for his usual lunchtime drink.

"Hey Al," he shouted, like as if I had lived in Grass Valley all my life. "You're making the street look shabby . . . You want a beer?"

"Be right there," I shouted.

Funny how something like that can bring you to grass – smiling.

Notes

1. A.L. Rowse (1991 [1969] *The Cornish in America*, Redruth: Dyllansow Truran, pp.264-5.
2. Ibid., p.271.
3. Ibid., p.250.
4. John Rowe (1974) *The Hard Rock Men: Cornish Immigrants and the North American Mining Frontier*, Liverpool: Liverpool University Press, p.290.
5. For a detailed history of the Cornish in Grass Valley and Nevada City, see ibid., pp.113-126; Rowse, op.cit., pp.257-63; A.C. Todd (1995 [1967]) *The Cornish Miner in America*, Spokane, Washington: The Arthur H. Clark Co., pp.54-79.
6. Rowe, op.cit., p.113.
7. Todd, op.cit., p.55.
8. Ibid.
9. Wallace Stegner (1971) *Angel of Repose*, New York: Fawcett Crest. For Grass Valley, see pp.9-66.
10. Rodman W. Paul (ed.) (1972) *A Victorian Gentlewoman in the Far West: The Reminiscences of Mary Hallock Foote*, San Marino, California: Huntington Library.
11. For a useful exploration of high-grading as a phenomenon, see Rowe, op.cit., p.200.
12. F.D. Calhoon (1986) *Coolies, Kanakas and Cousin Jacks*, Sacramento: Calcon, pp.294-316.
13. Reuben H. Margolin (ed.) (1997) *Bret Harte's Gold Rush*, Berkeley: Heyday Books.
14. Barbara Brassch (1996) *California's Gold Rush Country*, Medina, Washington: Johnston Associates International, p.68.
15. Michel Janicot (1986) *The Ladies of the Night: A Short History of Prostitution in Nevada County, California*, Nevada City: Mountain House Books.

16. Ibid., p.20.
17. For a history of North Star, see Roger Lescohier (1995) *Gold Giants of Grass Valley: History of the Empire and North Star Mines,*
18. Ibid. See also F.W. McQuiston, Jr. (1986) *Gold: The Saga of the Empire Mine, 1850-1956,* Grass Valley: Empire Mine Park Association.
19. Gage McKinney (2001) *When Miners Sang: The Grass Valley Carol Choir,* Grass Valley: Comstock Bonanza Press.
20. Shirley Ewart and Harold T. George (1998) *Highly Respectable Families: The Cornish of Grass Valley 1854-1954,* Grass Valley: Comstock Bonanza Press.
21. For an excellent analysis of the Celtic-American music scene, see Martin Melhuish (1998) *Celtic Tides: Traditional Music in a New Age,* Kingston, Ontario: Quarry Music Books.

PART TWO

"They are like hogs in every sense of the word . . . I am disgusted with the want of public spirit in the place. A crowd of whisky soaked Beer Bellys are the blue-eyed set of the Cornish."

Henry A. Hobart, on the Cornish at the Cliff Mine,
Keweenaw, c.1863

"Remind me to tell you
bout the old silver miner
name of hard rock Pete,
had his house built on a slope,
They say one of his legs
lived in Calico."

Deep Purple, 'Somebody Stole My Guitar'
from the album *Purpendicular*, 1996

9

Back on the Tourist core: From Tinner Hill to Capital Hill . . .

It was July. A whole year had passed. A lot had happened: I'd got a new job lecturing in literature with the Open University. I'd edited some newly-found poems of Jack Clemo. I'd signed with a Literary Agency in London. I'd trained my cat Budleigh to fetch balls of rolled-up kitchen foil. I'd done a reading and lecturing tour of Germany. I'd been to Brittany. I'd finally bought a new lawnmower. I'd been elected Assistant Secretary of Probus Comrades Club. I'd read a load of books on Methodism. I'd been writing madly. I still hadn't learnt to play the mouth-organ . . . It seemed a helleva long time since I'd had that final beer with Michel at the Holbrooke. Too long.

Actually, I was in counselling down Camborne. Didn't I mention that? I'd signed up with '56 Inch Cylinder's Anonymous'. The sessions were very helpful over the course of the year, for survival, of course. There were about fifteen of us in the group – all with various degrees of the syndrome. I knew mine was well-advanced, but some of the guys in there – well, they'd had a lifetime of it – one chap (formerly of 'Holmans') had been back six times. Another ex-employee of the 'Imerys' china clay company was rocking back and forth – his eyes crazy, as if he really needed to service a gravel pump right there and then. I remember the first session: the brave acknowledgement that you were one of them. The group welcomed me. It was all,

'My name's Al and I'm suffering from 56 inch cylinder syndrome'. Cheers and claps from the circle. There – the first of twelve steps completed: the admission. The fifth session initially went well too. Outside, it was hot and I was itching to go down Botallack and have a stank around, but instead I resisted it. My turn came.

"I didn't look at a piece of mining debris yesterday . . ."

Cheers and clapping.

"I went surfing instead."

More cheers and clapping.

It was okay in counselling. It was outside of the circle where the syndrome hits you the most. After the fifth session, I found I really needed to get my fix. I needed industrial debris. I had to have some rusty mining kit. A bit of a kibble . . . or a rock drill . . . anything. I tried to abate the hunger with a pasty. Even though I was back playing the mouth-organ, there was no discernible affect at all. I was shaking all the way down Trelowarren Street. I had the D.T.s. I needed that rush . . . and it wasn't going to come from looking through a dusty publication from D. Bradford Barton. I was thinking of heading to the next parish past Land's End again . . . There I would surely be able to satiate my evil desires.

My saviours came in the shape of my Probus Comrades' Club drinking buddies – Champi and Dan – two proud Cornishmen. Mark 'Champi' Champion is aged forty-eight but looks eighteen. Age hasn't touched him. He's into football, fish and women – in that order. Champi had a wish to go to America firstly just to experience the place, but secondly, and perhaps more importantly, to find one of his ancestors buried in some small desert cemetery, in Globe, Arizona. Many is the time he'd showed me a faded picture of Jacky Champion's grave next to a weird-looking tree. Everything in it looked dusty and red, but it was as cool a destination as any to try and locate. Danny Merrifield meanwhile, was hitting a milestone birthday (one that he'd prefer me not to write about) and so rather than suffer the obligatory drinking event followed by the obligatory hangover event, he'd elected to travel with me too. Even better, his wife Jo had agreed to pay for his ticket. Dan was Curgie's brother-in-law. So this time – there were three of us – three Cornish musketeers ready to take on the new world. Somehow we'd looked a fair bit different than Raleigh, Grenville and Carew . . .

Champi had decided that this being an event, he would get some tour T-shirts printed up – so there we were strolling around Terminal 4, Heathrow at 7 a.m. with a picture of Carn Galver Mine on our chests, emblazoned with the legend 'CORNISH ERECTIONS STAY UP LONGER'. Champi had a point. As the Carn Brea Mining Society (of which I am a member) can tell you, Carn Galver had probably been there for about one hundred and fifty years. Still he was getting the result he wanted, as various leggy air hostesses all gave cute and embarrassed smiles at us. In actual fact, they were probably more embarrassed for us. After a couple of pints of Guinesss (which is rather strange at 8 a.m.), we met Shane Ritchie stepping out of the British Airways executive suite. For those of you not in the know – he plays the happy-go-lucky Queen Vic bar manager Alfie in BBC's *Eastenders*.

"Wos tha' say then Cornish boys?" said Alfie.

Champi pointed at this shirt.

Dan shook his hand.

Alfie walked away smiling.

"Nice one boys," he said – or something like that.

At the security check, we met another celebrity. At least we thought it was another celebrity, because neither of us asked her. It was the actress who plays Mrs Bucket (that's Bouquet) in *Keeping Up Appearances*. After the Alfie encounter, Champi seemed keen to play the same card again, but I suspect she regarded us as three scruffy Onslows. She wudn' far wrong. The date was August 2nd; a year and a day since my last trip began. Once installed in our particular section of steerage, we still seemed to be attracting attention as the complimentary drinks were served before the meal.

"These are hearty Cornishmen," said the sauve steward. "Give them two cans . . . They'll handle it . . ."

He probably thought we were right knobbers, but no matter. We were heading to America and were colour and clothing co-ordinated.

I had bought a Barry Unsworth novel called *Losing*

Nelson – all about a scholar trying disprove the character assassination of Lord Nelson that has come to dominate Nelson scholarship of late. Momentarily I'd thought of the famous victory at Trafalgar – the announcement being made from the balcony inside the Union Hotel in Chapel Street in Penzance, but got distracted by the start of the latest film on the in-flight entertainment system. As usual, I re-read the *High Life* magazine over and over again. Next to useful articles like 'The Joy of Being in the Buff' and 'India's New Sophisticates', was one on surfing in Newquay: 'Waved Off: This Month, the Cornish coast will be inundated with blue-juice addicts'. I was thinking how this actually corresponded with the A30 over Goss Moor being inundated with muppets from the 'sarf-east' and broken-down camper vans. The article was full of language that no-one in Cornwall uses, like 'nose-rider' and 'shaper' that left me needing a dictionary, even though I consider myself pretty fluent in surf-ese. Laughably under the 'How to get there section' it said 'British Airways flies to Newquay from London Gatwick'. Well, that summer the Cornish newspapers had been full of how British Airways had decided to pull out of this route because it was not financially viable. Members of Parliament like North Cornwall's Paul Tyler seemed to be moaning about it everywhere. A bit of last minute selling perhaps on BA's behalf. It was all rather ironic though, and perhaps more than endemic of Cornwall's economic position at the start of the twenty-first century, despite projects like Objective One.

It took an eternity to get through Passport Control at Dulles International Airport, Washington (It said Washington, but for that, actually read Virginia, since the airport is about twenty-five miles east of the city). Since last summer the United States of course, America and Britain (but not so-called 'old Europe') had gone to war with Iraq. The US was on high alert, with sniffer dogs everywhere, and there was a feeling that I'd made a crucial error in trying to visit the place. We were at the back of a massive line that seemed to have started with some Islamic African country's flight arrival, and the distinguished and very different-looking ladies from Africa (compared to everyone else in the USA at least) were having all manner of questions asked of them.

224

I was imagining the conversation going on at Security Control.

"Well, boss, what we going to do about all these tourists coming into Dulles this afternoon?"

"Boy, just make sure those damned tourists know this is the United States, and we have the right to keep them waiting just as long as possible. Keep 'em waiting and any goddamn extremists will collapse in the heat . . . And if there are any French in there, keep them waiting longer than anyone else. While you're at it – get me some of them French – I mean Freedom – fries . . ."

Meanwhile, a girl from Germany (who had visited Cornwall) got the t-shirt joke. Everytime we saw her in the snaking queue, simultaneously we all said, "It's a building!"

Another guy from England seemed to think we were on a stag outing.

"If I was on a stag outing," noted Dan, "I'd be butt-naked and on a train to Edinburgh by now."

The German girl again: "It's a building!"

We survived this and the heat, but my heart started to beat a little faster, when at the final hurdle, one of the Customs staff seemed to take issue with our t-shirts. He looked about sixteen, even though he wasn't, and it appeared that he might do his darndest not to let the Cornish into America that day.

"Does that say 'erection'? Now you know that's a rude word ain't it?"

Champi was in with a retort, like he was 'eaving in a penalty against my old team – the clay goats, Foxhole F.C. Quick as a flash he said, "We're Cornish. Our forefathers helped founded your country. We came here with our mining expertise."

Champi sounded like a true orator. The erection distraction was complete.

"So what is your purpose in visiting America?"

"We're visiting the graves of our forefathers to pay our deepest respect to them . . ."

It sounded convincing. I knew we'd bound to be looking at a few graves in Cornish America. He took one last lingering look at our passports and let us through.

"Nice one Champ!" commented Dan. "It's a building!"

One collective thought was on our minds: we've dun 'un. We'm in America.

At the 'Alamo' car hire point, we picked up our mean and lean road machine. Last time the Chevy had suited me well enough, but three of us meant we needed some comfort to cruise the highways of Cornish America. I'm not great on cars overall. I mean I don't spend hours drooling over them, or comparing engine sizes. I took Dan's recommendation.

"Have that," he said with glowing admiration of the white, palatial ve-hic-le in front of us, shimmering like some Arthurian steed. "The Mitsubishi Gallant . . ."

Cue mystical music and Awen-style beams of light from heaven.

"Why that one?" I asked.

"It's the business, Boy . . ."

He was right. The car was excellent and remained reliable for the whole trip.

I always feel car hire is trying to rip you off. I don't know why I feel this way. Perhaps it's the way they breakdown the bill, or maybe it's the way they give you an upgrade you didn't ask for. Being Cornish, I had to check it over a couple of times. The airport tax of $75 bothered me.

"Where d'y' recommend staying for a night?" I mentioned to the guy at 'Alamo', after he'd explained the bill to me again.

"Try somewhere around Tysons Corner or Falls Church . . ."

We couldn't even find Tysons Corner, or rather, we could see where it was, but there seemed no way of getting off the freeway to get to it. At first I thought it was just my incompetence, but apparently the freeways around Washington (I was later to learn) are notorious for it. I had to drive around Falls Church for some time before coming to the Stratford Motor Lodge, 300 West Broad Street. It was getting late by now, and even though this was an old style lodge, it would have to do. The place would have looked ancient in the 1960s, and although not as bad as the place I had stayed in the previous summer in Boulder, it was probably next up on shoddiness. We were up on the second floor too, and having negotiated a two room deal, it was decided that as I'd done the driving from Cornwall to

London, and would be doing so over here, that we'd all be best served by giving me a separate room, and obtain some serious sleep.

I flopped down on the bed and put on the local television channel. I'd been intrigued because in driving into Falls Church, my Cornish-America radar had been on, and I had noticed an area of town named Tinner Hill. There had to be a Cornish connection, I had said to myself. I was wrong. There was no Cornish connection at all, so the television documentary told me, but the story was interesting nevertheless. It all began back in 1890 when the Town Council of Falls Church voted to give away most of the African-American owned land in the town from Tinner Hill to Arlington Boulevard back to Fairfax County. This virtually cut the size of the town by 20%. Then in January 1915 the Falls Church Town Council went even farther by adopting an ordinance establishing residential segregation. The Town Council formed a Committee on Segregation to create a map of the segregated areas of town. African-American families already living in the parts of the town designated for whites could stay but no new African-Americans could move into these segregated areas. They could be found guilty of a misdemeanor and be fined from $5 a day the first week of the violation and then $2 a day after that.

In January 1915 Dr. Edwin Bancroft Henderson and one Joseph Tinner organized the Colored Citizens' Protective League. The group wrote letters to the Falls Church mayor and city council and hired an attorney to try to block the ordinance saying that it violated their 14th Amendment rights of equal protection under the law. As a result the town council reversed its position and did not enforce the segregation ordinance. The Falls Church and Vicinity Branch also helped to organize other branches in Arlington, Fauquier, Prince William, and Loundon counties in Northern Virginia as it tried to reach out into other rural areas where the Ku Klux Klan and racial bigotry were the strongest. Over the next 50 years, Tinner and Henderson organized civil rights activities that set a precedent for the rural South. Our Tinner then was no tinner, but more a miner of human rights.

There was now a Tinner Hill Foundation which is a

non-profit corporation organized to provide awareness of the contributions of African-Americans and other cultures in particular in the development of Falls Church, but also to Fairfax County, the United States and African descendents in the diaspora, by disseminating information and providing community services. I was very impressed with all of this, and it somehow seemed profoundly relevant given both the fact that we were about to see the spot in Washington where Martin Luther King Junior gave his famous 'I have a dream . . .' speech, but also in the light of the fact that such exploitation and civil rights also have affected the Cornish. I mean our language has only just been given official status by UK government.

That evening, we visited that most American of chain restaurants 'Applebees' enjoying something called Mesquite Sauce, which is put onto steak and various other dishes. So much did Champi enjoy this concoction, that he was to spend several hours in several supermarkets seeking out the said sauce so that he might enjoy it back home. We ended the evening in a bar called 'Ireland's Four Provinces' talking to local people about the journey we were about to make, and listening to some terrible Irish folksinger who appeared to use every cliché in the Irish folksinger vocabulary. Still it was Saturday night and everyone seemed to be lapping it up, staring at their collective Guinnesses and wondering why they bought this horrible, sour tasting black stuff to begin with. It always fascinates me that many American people seem to think that such a trek was mad, and that they would never contemplate it themselves. It again surprises me how many Americans have barely travelled out of their own State, let alone elsewhere in the world.

When Dan and Champi said that we'd all get up early in the morning and head into Washington before every other tourist arrived, I didn't realise quite how early they had meant. In what seemed like the middle of the night, there was a knock on the motel room door. I'd been sleeping well. It had been virtually forty-eight hours without sleep, so I was out for the count. At 4 a.m. a bleary-eyed me opened the door to a bright and bushy-tailed Dan and Champi, both shaved, showered and ready for the off. There were like two dogs ready to be let out of their traps. Clearly the several pints of Bass they had downed at the 'doi doi de doi de doi' bar had made no discernable impact.

"Be with 'ee in a minute," I gurgled and set about awakening myself. This usually involves banging into something in the room, stubbing my toe so that I swear a lot, and managing to find a comfortable temperature in the shower. This was life on the road in America. How I'd missed it! About ten minutes later, I had 'eaved all my things into my case, and we headed off on Interstate 66, through the area in eastern Washington called Arlington, and into central Washington DC. In so doing we were crossing the Potomac River from Virginia into the District of Columbia itself.

For the record, on the map, Washington is constructed as a tilted square, which apparently juts into parts of present Virginia and Maryland: an odd community as we were soon to discover. At 5 a.m. in the morning, what you are most likely to see in central Washington are prostitutes and heavily-armed police. This makes for an interesting mix, since as we cruised down Constitution Avenue and turned right into the Ellipse before the White House, we were greeted by the skimpiest of thongs and the heaviest of breasts followed by the skimpiest hint of a welcome and the heaviest of weapons. I suppose in retrospect, three mad Cornishmen marching around Washington on a site-seeing tour at this hour must have looked pretty peculiar. No wonder then, that as we stopped for a while outside of Capital Hill, we were monitored closely by the authorities.

"A'right?" said Champi to one of the officers, who briefly nodded back, not understanding him at all.

To hell with it. While the prostitutes were doing their thing on New York Avenue, we were going to do Washington that morning.

Getting to the front of the White House is fairly complicated, not least in the fact that you seemingly are not allowed to park within a five mile distance of the building itself. We elected to park around the back, not far from where the most amazing of the thongs gyrated herself at passing drivers. I must admit it was tempting to go and have another look, but instead we circled the President's shed. In these times, it was clear to see the additional security that had been mounted. Lots of fender-crushing concrete roadblocks, and newly-constructed security areas which architects had tried, at least, to blend in with existing buildings. Later, we saw the underside of every car being searched with mirrors on the end of long sticks. I suppose it was all necessary.

I don't really know why we were heading towards the White House. I suppose it is iconoclastic in the same way that the Eifel Tower or the Empire State Building is. All I could think about though was that sequence in *Independence Day* when the aliens blast it to pieces. Interestingly all the pictures of the White House make it out to be much bigger than it actually is – and in the postcards, you can see more of it. That is because someone needs to trim back the trees and bushes growing in the front lawn. My father would be in there like a shot. He hates trees. That's growing up in Cornwall for you. They say there's not enough wood in Cornwall to make a coffin. They're right: some of it was used to build boats, some was used to make charcoal for blowinghouses smelting tin; the rest went underground. There is now a veritable subterranean forest propping up shafts and adits from Caradon to St Just.

I'd always imagined the White House railings to be somehow different than they actually were. In fact, they followed the curve of the gardens. I'd expected them to be straight. Too many news reporters maybe – standing closer perhaps? On the floor, was the worn look of too much tourism – some litter, cigarette butts and bubblegum ground into the sidewalk. How many thousands had their photograph taken here? And now me, doing exactly the same thing. The one consolation was that we had it to ourselves. The morning was very still and humid. I wondered if Mr Bush was awake yet. Most likely he wasn't even there but out in Texas somewhere, taking a break from running the world.

We walked around and down the Ellipse, across to Constitution Gardens. A few vagrants were asleep on the benches. This scared me slightly. I'd heard that Washington was quite a violent city. Dan and Champi had been full of tales of several shootings in the Washington vicinity just from last night's television, so we were on full alert – a bit like America itself. It seemed like if there was any place someone might pull a gun on us, it might happen in Washington. We survived though, only being hissed at by a couple of mean ducks. It was still early. The sun was just rising in the east, and lit up the Lincoln Memorial beautifully. We climbed the steps up to where the huge statue of Abraham Lincoln sat, gazing back down towards the rectangular pool, in which the huge Washington Monument is reflected. I only noticed the reddish stone floor plaque recording the spot where Martin Luther King Junior made his speech on the way back down. This recorded the March on Washington for jobs and freedom, August 28th 1963. King was only thirty-four years old when he made perhaps is what is the most memorable of speeches in modern times. Some 200,000 people stood before him, but sadly less than five years later King was assassinated in Memphis. It seemed only too apt that Lincoln gazed over this spot – himself knowing the vagaries of political events all too well. Tinner and King had done a proper job.

The only movement this time of the morning were the various friendly squirrels which darted over the steps of the Memorial, and below the men in the four makeshift huts of 'The Last Firebase' the 24-7, 365 day vigil dedicated to all those Prisoners of War who haven't made it home. There, we chatted to some of the guys running the 'Missing in Action' campaigns, and found us praised for British support of the American position on Iraq.

"Your Tony Blair is right there with us . . ." one of them said.

"You English have been great . . ."

We had to explain that we were Cornish, and the Cornish didn't mind being labelled British, but never English. They didn't get it, but we said it anyway.

It wasn't the time to argue my anti-war stance, nor to go into a detailed discussion of Celtic geo-politics, so I just browsed the badges and insignia, my mind full of the memorable scenes that were imagined here in *Forrest Gump*. That, *The Deerhunter*, *Platoon* and *Full Metal Jacket* jumbled into one. These filmatic interpretations were still flitting around my head when we headed over to the Vietnam Veterans' Memorial, erected in 1982: '*In honor of the men and women of the Armed Forces of the United*

States who served in the Vietnam War. The names of those who gave their lives and of those who remain missing are inscribed in the order they were taken from us'. I must tell you – the angled monument is a beautifully crafted memorial. Apparently the designer, Maya Ying Lin conceived her design to be harmonious with the site, so this is partly why it gently slopes down into the ground. To further achieve this harmony she also chose polished black granite for the walls, which means that its mirror-like surface reflects the surrounding trees, lawns and people looking at the monument for the 58, 209 names.

The National Park Service gives you all the facts: the walls are 246.75 feet long and there are 140 pilings, with the average depth to bedrock being 35 feet. Apparently the names begin at the vertex of the walls below the date of the first casualty and continue to the end of the east wall. They resume on the tip of the west wall, ending at the vertex above the date of the last death. Each name is preceded by one of two symbols: a diamond or a cross. The diamond denotes that the individual's death was confirmed. Some 1,150 persons with a cross denote that they were either missing or prisoners at the end of the war and remain unaccounted for. If a person returns alive (as some have done) then a circle (the symbol of life) will be inscribed around the cross. In the event an individual's remains are returned or are otherwise accounted for, the diamond will be superimposed over the cross.

The whole effect of the memorial was very moving for me. I walked its length. Virtually the equivalent of the entire population of Cornwall had been killed during the conflict. Near the entrance to the Memorial are rain-protected index booklets. A quick scan through the Tre, Pol and Pen names in the index of the dead showed me how many men and women of Cornish extraction died in the conflict. In just these prefixes I noted around one hundred, not accounting for all the other Cornish families who suffered loss. It brought the whole thing home very powerfully. It's perhaps not even something that's much thought of at home. Some of those who fought might only have been second or third generation Cornish-Americans. Hanoi was a long way from Helston. Occasionally, at the bottom of the pilings you could spot a Stars and Stripes flag or a votive candle burning. There and then, I really wished I had brought a small St Piran's cross to place before some of the Cornish names. Instead, I took a photograph of myself and the Constitutional Gardens reflected in the granite. It was what Maya Ying Lin had imagined.

On the southern side of the Reflecting Pool is another memorial dedicated to those American men and women who fought in the Korean War. Many people forget about this conflict now, but lasting from 1950 to 1953, it began when the Communist government of North Korea launched an attack into South Korea. Some fifty years later, and North Korea remains as much of an enemy to America as Iraq, with constant fears over its nuclear capability and weapons of mass destruction. Again, although I did not look through the listings here, many Cornish-Americans fought in that conflict, as did many Cornish. One of them was Lieutenant Phillip Curtis from Saltash, who while serving with the "Glorious" Gloucesters, was killed in action at the Battle of the Imjin River the night of the 22nd April 1951. His bravery, after bring wounded by a grenade won him a posthumous Victoria Cross. His story is told in the Regimental Museum of the Duke of Cornwall's Light Infantry at Bodmin.[1]

Here, a group of nineteen stainless-steel statues depict a squad on patrol, while strips of granite and scrubby juniper bushes are used to try and depict the harshness of the North Korean terrain. The statues were designed by one Frank Gaylord. What I liked about these statues was their realism. The windblown ponchos really did seem to recall the harsh weather the members of the U.S. forces faced. Opposite these statues is an etched granite mural based on actual photographs from the conflict, while at the end of the patrol group is a Pool of Remembrance, the theme being 'Freedom is Not Free', a slogan echoed on many bumper sticker in the U.S. that summer, in the light of 9/11 and the Second Gulf War. To experience the stillness of these memorials in the early morning light is not something I will easily forget. The whole thing was very humbling.

Going back up 17th Street, we were aiming on finding some breakfast, but only found the home of the Daughters of the American Revolution. The DAR is something like the Women's Institute of America – but to join you have to be 1) female, and 2) prove that your ancestors fought on the right side in the Revolutionary Wars. Up until fairly recently of course, it was best that you were white too, but it was nice to see that at last, the leading Daughters were running an exhibition on African-American daughters of the American revolution too. One suspects, the political pressure on them got too great. Again, my mind turned on Tinner Hill.

In 'McDonalds' – the only place open – we took in a fast-food breakfast. By now, Champi was beginning to realise that asking for 'tay' was very much a non-event, although he had been sensible enough to buy a last-minute packet of Earl Grey back at Heathrow, and kept asking for hot water. Even so, the food was good after the dawn patrol around the city's monuments. As I sat there munching through my hash browns, I began to realise that much of the open space in Washington seemed to be ready for some new dedication or memorial. Already, down at the eastern end of the Reflecting Pool, the authorities were building a massive new memorial to those who served in the Second World War. There seemed space for more memorials – almost like the place was waiting for the dead to be counted.

This was the case with the US Marine Corps Iwo Jima Memorial near to the Arlington National Cemetery, back on the eastern side of the Potomac. The Iwo Jima Memorial must be one of the most recognisable statues in the world. Based on a an inspiring Pulitzer Prize-winning photograph taken by Joe Rosenthal, it is a 78 foot high bronze sculpture of five Marines and a Navy hospital corpsman. They are raising a Stars and Stripes flag on the top of an extinct volcano during of the Second World War. The volcanic island of Iwo Jima lies 660 miles south of Tokyo and one of its outstanding geographical features is Mount Suribachi, that forms the narrow southern tip of the island and rises 550 feet to dominate the area. By February 1945, U.S. troops had recaptured most of the territory taken by the Japanese in 1941 and 1942; still uncaptured was Iwo Jima, which became a primary objective in American plans to bring the Pacific campaign to a successful conclusion.

Erection of the memorial was begun in September 1954. It was officially dedicated by President Dwight D. Eisenhower on November 10, 1954, the 179th anniversary of the U.S. Marine Corps. The Swedish granite base in itself is around 12 feet high, and all the Marines' conflicts since 1775 are recorded on it in gold lettering. The second Gulf War of 2003 is already on there. What's frightening is how much room is left for future conflicts. In so many ways I was hopeful that all that blank space would not ever need to be filled in.

We probably could have spent a week in Washington. The Smithsonian Institute and Museum, I have been told by several people, can take a week to do fully. Instead we had to settle for a morning, but considering what we had seen, we were fairly pleased with ourselves. Washington DC – tick. Possibly Washington DC had seen its swiftest visit from a Cornish delegation in a number of years. We hopped back into our Gallant and decided instead, that all other sites of interest would have to be viewed in this way. I headed down 17th again and we went past the John Paul Jones Statue (a bit of a non-event) and turned south around the Tidal Basin to see the more impressive Thomas Jefferson Memorial. From there we stopped a while, and looked out over the Potomac. Dan was hoping to see a few bald eagles. I think we saw some ospreys, a few pigeons and some mosquitoes. Meanwhile the Potomac flowed on. The Potomac is a massive river by British standards; probably fairly average by American standards, but from there we could see the morning flights coming in low to land at Washington National Airport.

The Potomac interested me, because if there was one place in Cornish-America that held a real mythos for me, that was Tangier Island. Now Tangier Island is actually at the head of the Potomac River, where it flows into Chesapeake Bay. Tangier somehow was right up there with the mythical start of the European discovery of America – right up there with St Brendan and the Irish, the Norsemen and Vinland, Prince Madoc and the Welsh Indians – even though its discovery came slightly later. I'll attempt to explain why. In effect Tangier is a tiny stretch of sandbar to be found just south of the Virginia – Maryland State line.

The land area (composed of three islands in effect) is about five miles long and about half a mile wide and it has a population of about seven hundred people. According to several sources I have read (including James G. Daley's undated *History of Tangier Island, Virginia* and Rick Parks' 1997 book *Tangier Island: A Moving Account of Tangier's History and Culture*[2]) apparently the island was discovered by one Captain John Smith around 1608, when he was looking for fresh water. According to legend, the island was settled more than three hundred years ago by six or so fishermen and their families from Cornwall. Lots of the guidebooks refer to the 'old brogue or accent' of the people on the island, and the 'special melody of their speech' – supposedly derived from the fact that their Cornishness has survived over centuries. I have been told other stories that the initial fishermen actually came from the Isles of Scilly, and that they set up a community there on Tangier, because it reminded them so much of the Isles.

Main Ridge is now the largest community on the island, but the earliest community was based around Canton. This the place where the early Cornish or Scillonian fishermen and women settled. We do know that Joshua Thomas (a very Cornish-sounding individual) once ran the first store on the island at Oyster Creek Ridge. Some traditions also state that the island was first founded by one John Crockett and his eight sons in 1686. He does not sound very Cornish, yet the evidence is sketchy. There are still a few Crocketts in the 2003 Cornwall and Isles of Scilly telephone directory. What is known is that the 1800 census of the Island showed that seventy-nine people lived there and most of them were descendants of this Crockett family one way or another.

The Revolutionary War had a major impact on Tangier. By March of 1813, the British had begun to try to take control of Chesapeake Bay and began to build defences there. The first British attack from Tangier came on May 30th 1814. We also know that in 1805, following the growth of Methodism, a preacher by the name of Lorenzo Drew convinced Joshua Thomas and others to develop a Methodist community on the island. This was fully established in 1835 when the first Methodist church was built. I'd loved to have gone there, but it was too far to the south for this journey. First, we would have had to have driven through Baltimore, and headed down into the Atlantic peninsula of Virginia, where we could catch the ferry out to the island from Crisfield. An alternative route might have been to go via Richmond and cross the Chesapeake Bay Bridge, then head north. This time I would have to be happy enough with the tantalising possibilities of Cornishness surviving on Tangier. Perhaps one of these days though, I will get across and see how genuine that old 'brogue' is.

The old 'brogue' was carrying on within the Gallant though.

"We'd better make 'iss," said Dan, "if we'm goin' t'reach Pottstown. I d'reckon 'tis a good four hour drive."

At this point Dan was navigating and for some reason the Interstate system in Washington was defeating us both. There were some hurried and heated discussions, with much passing back and forth of the Rand McNally roadmap. Now that we'd got off it, getting back on it again was now causing us difficulties. Part of the problem, as I am sure any European will tell you, who has driven in America, is the complex way of labelling road systems. Put another way, I am sure it is not complicated if you live in Washington, or are American, but labelling the same piece of road with the same number when one leads to a dead end by the Potomac, and the other leads to the Interstate seems to me t'be completely mazed. Ah well . . . eventually we got out of north-eastern Washington following the tail-end of Interstate 270 through Bethesda, through Rockville and Gaithersburg. At the latter location we stopped at a 'Flying J' for a re-fuel. Dan bought some beef jerky and Champi phoned home. There was a sudden but quiet realisation that we'd survived the guns and thongs of Washington.

The eventual aim was to hit the Cornish slate-mining country of eastern Pennsylvania, but we were to stay with my friend Albert Jenkin in Pottstown, actually in the south, nearer to Philadelphia. We turned onto Interstate 81 and crossed in a north easterly direction. I know understand why it was called Pennsylvania. It had more trees than I think I had ever contemplated and was humid as hell. The air conditioning was on to the max, and I could begin to see

Champi and Dan quietly and politely sweating. I put on the crotch air fan to full tilt.

To the north were the Tuscarora Mountains, and funnily enough to the south, were the South Mountains They obviously weren't too creative with names in the south of Pennsylvania – but we let them off. By the middle of the afternoon, we'd been through Cleversburg (which amusingly we felt, was home to Shippensburg University of Pennsylvania) and made it to Walnut Bottom, which sounded like something you didn't want. Only one problem lay ahead: Harrisburg. The interstate at Harrisburg looked like a bowl of spaghetti having a fight with the chef – the chef being the Susquehanna River, which had its origins in the north of the state, and then flowed like the Potomac into Chesapeake Bay. The Susquehanna is a slow, meandering monster of a river, which looks as if it is going to burst its banks at any point. Sometimes, it felt like you were less travelling above it, but more inside it, watching the fish and debris go downstream, and finding that you, in your 2003 Gallant were following on with it, heading out to Chesapeake and I daresay, coming to rest upside-down on the shallows of Tangier Island.

Harrisburg itself looked a fairly high-tech city, full of the kind of new American architecture you find on the roads running north-west out of Chicago – all mirrors, fountains and red sandstone; the kind of place you might imagine 'Sex and the City' being shot in – or rather 'Sex and Harrisburg'. Still Dan the Man kept saying, "Trust me on this one", "This exit" and "Sorted" and somehow we got across the Susquehanna in one piece. As we crossed I was 'pitying the fools' (to quote the *A-Team's* Mr T) who at some point back in time, were crossing it the other way. We got on Highway 422 east passing through places like Lebanon and Reading. At Reading we stopped at 'Wal-Mart' and made the first of many shopping excursions to this highly selective retailer. Champi and Dan had already been shocked by the gas prices. When they saw how cheap clothes were, it was like they'd found shopping nirvana.

I could hear the shopping assistants.

"Ah those poor Cornish . . . They are so deprived . . . not being able to buy t-shirts for a couple of dollars . . ."

By early evening we were running into the outskirts of Pottstown. I was glad the driving was soon going to be over. I had Albert's last frantic but wholly accurate e-mail to me on my lap: "Arriving at Pottstown on PA100, you will see on your right Pottsgrove Manor, the home of ironmaster John Potts, founder of the iron works and the town. The house is now a museum. Turn right onto King Street, and follow it until you see a Cornish flag in front of No. 638. I'll have the kettle on for tea. Oll an gwella, Albert." He was true to his word. When we rolled up in front of Carwinnion Cottage, the flag was unfurled and it felt like a kettle inside might well and truly be on. Champi might get his longed-for cup of tea. I knocked on the door. Outstepped Albert Jenkin looking like the finest Cousin Jack you could ever hope to meet.

"Want a cup taa?" he said. "What's that T-shirt say?"

"It's a building!" we replied. "Want one do 'ee?"

Notes

1. See citation in the Historical Archives of the Duke of Cornwall's Light Infantry Museum Bodmin.
2. James G. Daley (n.d.) *History of Tangier Island, Virginia*, Tangier Island: Jim's Gift Shop; Rick Parks (1997) *Tangier Island: A Moving Account of Tangier's History, Culture and Present Day Life*, Parsons: McClain.

10

*You knew the difference between the Scots
and the Cornish because you could
understand the Scots . . .*

Dan had been packing an awful lot of Cornish fudge in his
crammed-to-bursting suitcase before we left, which caused
Champi and myself endless amusement. It now became clear
what all the fudge was for. While Champi was sizing up
Albert with a 'suits-you-sir' complimentary tour T-shirt –
which I am not sure he will wear walking through downtown Pottstown (he might get pulled over by the police for
an obscenity charge) – Dan handed over the fudge: cream
fudge from one Cornishman to another. It was a sweet
moment. Meanwhile, I'd lined up Albert a copy of one of
the *Racca* dance and music books because I knew Albert
really wanted to develop the Cornish dance scene in Pennsylvania. As he poured the steaming tea into bone china
cups, Albert looked bemused, and somewhat amazed at the
proliferation of presents heading his way.

"You boys done me proud," he said, his voice carrying
the traces of the old country, yet I further noticed more
Western tones than his present Pennsylvanian residence.
You can barely see Albert's lips move though, since he
has a splendid well-cultivated handle-bar moustache,
which during conversation moves up and down, and which
from time-to-time he must smooth gently back into
place with his thumb and forefinger. It makes him look
highly distinguished and rather mythical, matching his

Gandalf-esque white hair and beard. Like my Auntie Riss back in Foxhole, he also suffers from psoriasis, so every so often he would have scratch his skin. It was not, I imagined, an easy condition to have in the stinging heat and humidity of Pennsylvania. Fortunately, the afternoon's sweat began to disappear as a thunderstorm crackled outside and rain bucketed down. It was a welcome relief for all of us.

Like so many Cornish-Americans I now knew, I'd first met Albert at the Gathering in Mineral Point. His wit and mannerisms had amused me greatly, for he seemed to have a very dry, wicked, and peculiarly Cornish sense of humour. We'd renewed our friendship at the *Homecoming* event in Falmouth, but this was an opportunity to see *his* Cornish America. As Dan and Champi delved into more tea and fudge, Albert showed me his house. It was an older-style cottage property with a large cellar, which he now used as a workshop. The living room was a shrine to the Celts and Cornwall. He began on the living-room wall, showing me a large *National Geographic* map of the Celtic Europe from May 1977.

"This one's very sought after by scholars now you know," said Albert. "I'm told it's outstanding . . ."

He was right. I'd heard it was good. It was clearly a proud possession, as were the small 'Lilliput Lane'-style models of Cornish tin mines made by David Winter designs, and the collection of Celtic and Cornish books. Pleasingly, there were a few of mine alongside those of Rowse *et al.* On the tables were copies of *Cornish World / Bys Kernowyon* and *Scryfa*, which he had picked up at a recent Cornish Gathering in Bowmanville, Toronto; next to the front door, a hand-written, framed copy of a typically perverse but clever piece of verse by Arthur Quiller Couch:

> I laye a-wakyne, and lo! the dawn was breakynge
> And rarely piped a lark for the promyse of the daye,
>> Uppe and sette yr lance in reste!
>> Uppe and foreward on the Queste!
> Leave this issue to be guessed
> At the endynge of the waye.

As I laye a-wakynge, 'twas soe she seemed to saye,
    Whatte and if all be feygnyng?
    There are better thyngs than gaynynge,
    rycher prizes than attaynynge.
And 'twas truth she seemd to saye.

Whyles the dawne was breakyng, I rode upon my waye.

For a moment it felt like the Fowey boy was following me over Cornish America – what with Gage's parrot, and now this. I re-read the verse several times while I was there, and Albert and I talked much on Q's qualities as a writer. All of these items fascinated me. They were Albert's markers of what made him who he was.

"If you don't mind me asking . . . how old are you Albert?"

"'Course not. I'm the same age as the dog," he said cunningly, "and the dog's been told to keep quiet . . ."

Traveller 'the wonder dog' (a Queensland Blue Heeler or Australian Cattle dog with a lot of dingo in the mix) was following us about the house, probably on a continual quest for food. He looked at me. He wasn't telling.

"Yes, yes m'andsome . . . I'm coming," Albert said, tickling Traveller on his neck.

We'd also quickly picked up the fact that Albert was a widower. His wife Evelyn had been taken ill with a stroke in 1993, and died in 1999. There were photographs of her around the house. She was a beautiful woman and I sensed Albert still missed her incredibly.

"We stored things in the microwave," Albert said, "because Evelyn was too short to reach it, to ever cook anything inside."

He had a point. The microwave seemed to be mounted in an Everest-style position on the kitchen cabinets.

All was so comfortable and welcoming, but I barely slept at Albert's place the first night. We were in one room in the upper half of the house, packed in a little bit like sardines in a tin can. Don't get me wrong. I was very grateful for Albert hosting us; the problem was more to do with Dan. Dan's one of those people who seems to be able to sleep instantaneously, so while my thoughts were still ranging around Washington DC, and the prospect of a day up in the Slate Belt, Dan was already in Never-Never Land, snoring like a kindly troll. He was snoring so much that the vibrations had a kind of seismic effect on my bed. Champi was trying all sorts to divert Dan's snoring. He tried clapping his hands, then rocking Dan gently – but all that seemed to do was increase the vibration to 10 on the Richter scale. It was going to be a long night.

In the end I elected to join Albert's dog Traveller out on the landing, dragging my sheet and pillow behind me and laying down on the floor there. Very probably, Traveller had never seen this phenomenon before, where a human nestled in next to him, but at least that way I got some sleep. That was until around 6 a.m. when I was awoken by the sound of Highland bagpipes. Had I somehow been transported to Glencoe? No. I was still at Carwinnion cottage. There was no sound of the kindly troll either. A voice shouted up the stairs.

"I didn't have any Cornish bagpipes! I thought this might do the trick. I play that CD when my grandson stays; he rushes out of bed to turn the music off. Works every time!"

In a rather spiffing blue chequered shirt and grey trousers, Albert was hard at work in the kitchen. We gradually roused ourselves and showered; coming to rest in the dining room's already sticky heat, at close to seven in the morning. After a hearty breakfast of spicy sausages, scrambled egg and toast, we bundled into Albert's roomy van for the trip up to Pen Argyl. Things got off to a good start. On Pottstown's spacious streets we passed the First Methodist Church and followed a black Dodge *Ram* north east. The Dodge *Ram* truck is a huge, black beast of a vehicle that looks like the Devil himself might be at the wheel. This one was a limited edition; on the back was a small sticker with a pickaxe and shovel, named 'Prospector'. How apt.

To travel to the Slate mining belt, we drove northeast on the lolling and twisting Route 100, passing through places like New Berlinville, Bally and Old Zionville, eventually heading into the conurbation of Allentown and Bethlehem, just on the Pennsylvania-New Jersey State line. At this point, we realised how close we were to New York City. There was a a brief flicker in me wishing to re-visit

243

Manhattan, but it soon passed in favour of the scenery around us – which consisted of pleasant woodland groves interspersed with lakes, and even at this early hour, plenty of men out in small fishing boats. Albert was an excellent guide, pointing out places of interest, between telling us his own experiences of Cornish-America. Now, unlike Britain, where it seems retirement happens when you are forty-five, many Americans work longer into their more senior years, and Albert was no exception. He presently worked at 'Borders' bookstore, which might account for the spectacular *Lord of the Rings* film souvenirs he had accumulated around his house, and for his up-to-date knowledge of American cultural events.

As we drove along, I also learnt that he sometimes went under the name of *Hwethlor Pen-An-Vre*, which anyone from the Cornish Language Board will tell you means 'the storyteller from the top of the hill' – and this was something he liked to do locally, and at Cornish Festivals and Gatherings, regaling his audience with yarns. I have to say Albert was an excellent storyteller. Unlike a lot I've heard, he really had pace and verve, and knew how to hold an audience in the palm of his hand. The moustache helped I think.

But without even telling a narrative, Albert's story in itself was interesting enough. Although born in Massachusetts, he ended up as a young man in Nevada. His first job out of high school in 1951 was working for the Nevada Northern Railway, helping to construct track. This was being laid in Steptoe Valley, and would eventually carry thousands of tonnes of copper out of that area. The following year, he went to the University of Utah, where he enrolled in the Naval Midshipman programme, but dropped out of that in 1954. Around the same time he met Evelyn, and they went to live in San Francisco, California, although between 1954 and 1955 Albert was working at sea as a Merchant Sailor, so they didn't get to see a lot of each other. By 1956 though, he was enrolled in San Francisco State University reading for a diploma in international relations, and then from 1960 to 1976 he worked for the Pacific Far East, the infamous steamship line. In the late 1970s when during the recession it became clear he needed to re-train,

Albert went back to school and took a degree in Civil Engineering Technology at Cogswell College, San Francisco, then served ten years with the Bechtel Group, supervising and trouble-shooting at construction sites, a post than took him all around California and eventually to Pennsylvania, where he was sent to help build a power plant. For several years then, he worked partly as an architectural consultant for a Minneapolis-based company and did some teaching for Construction Associations in Philadelphia. After Evelyn died, he found himself twiddling his thumbs, so signed up with the local bookstore. As always, it was interesting to hear just how pards had roamed, and Albert had roamed a lot.

"In 2006 the Nevada Northern Railway celebrates its centenary. I hope to be going out there for that," Albert said with some pride. "I expect I'll be one of the oldest there . . ."

He had grown up in White Pine County, Nevada. During the early twentieth century, over 25,000 people lived there supporting the copper industry with a number of large Cornish families.

"It was a place the size of Connecticut," said Albert.

As well as the Jenkins, there were Rosevears, Merretts and Rowes, but when the mine closed, the population dropped right back to 5,000, and the Cornish became scattered again.

Albert's father – Albert George Jenkin – was born in 1905 in Lowertown, Helston at An Vower Mill (one of Albert's prize possessions back home was a photograph of the Mill). He came to work in Ohio in 1926 with a relative – one Uncle John Wonnacott (from North Cornwall), who was travelling with his wife Ena. It was Ena who introduced Albert's father to his mother Nellie Davis (who on her birth certificate is described ethnically as 'Danish-Red Indian' and 'declined to state'). It was Nellie, Albert explained, who had once commented that, "You knew the difference between the Scots and the Cornish because you could understand the Scots . . ." For me this was a beauty comment, which proved a theory I'd had for a while, that the trans-national Cornish didn't really need any further definition of their identity – they were already different enough. Albert's father later went on to study at Ohio's Bowling Green State University, and then eventually trained for the ministry in Boston. He died in 1937. During the Second World War, the American government moved people of Japanese ancestry to so-called relocation camps further inland. Albert's mother went to work at one of these camps in central Utah; and that was where she re-married, and she went with him to Nevada, taking Albert along too.

Albert first went back to Cornwall in 1969 (his and Evelyn's second honeymoon), and later showed me a well-loved scrapbook recording the trip. He tells a good yarn about him reaching his father's birthplace back at Helston, and finding his father's half-brother Ronnie. Apparently, as Ronnie was showing Albert around, he shouted in to a local man by the name of Hedley Pascoe, "Tell Hedley – t'put his boots on . . . an' come out 'ere . . ."

Hedley Pascoe staggered into the morning sunlight.

"Take a good look at this chap. You 'ent never seen 'un before," said Ronnie Jenkin. "Make sure you take a good look mind . . ."

Hedley Pascoe gazed at Albert, studying his facial features.

"I've seen yer face before. There's something about those eyes . . . Hang on! You'm George's boy!!"

Apparently Hedley Pascoe had been Albert's father's friend all those years ago. George Jenkin had left in 1927, and when Hedley looked at Albert, he saw *his* father. Some forty-two years had passed. Apparently later on, a local lady was to comment, "I seen un on the road the other day. I don't knaw who he were, but I knawed he was a Jenkin . . ."

I can think of no more perfect a story of Cornish emigration than this. Celtic memory is long and unrelenting. Albert summed up the whole narrative with, "The apple dun't fall far from the tree."

Pen Argyl, which is heard to pronounce if you are from anywhere in the south-west of Britain, because you instantly want to say 'Pen Argyle' as in Plymouth Argyle football team, when the emphasis is actually on the 'gill' part of the word, is a very Cornish piece of America. Eight out of ten people are of Cornish descendancy; the rest Italian and

246

Welsh, and although the Welsh obviously named the nearby community of Bangor, the Cornish were very strong there, as we were to find out. Pen Argyl runs in a linear fashion along the bottom of the Blue mountains. To the right were many old slate quarries, and piles of mining debris. Its sister town of Bangor is more of a town proper. That's where we headed first – past the 'Wa Ching' laundry, all too easy for Champi to make a joke about 'Wash – ing', which still had us laughing as we ran down the hill into downtown Bangor. At the lights we turned right and pulled in front of old Borough Hall, which houses the Slate Belt Heritage Centre.

Inside, and upstairs in the Heritage centre are rooms dedicated to the different ethnic groups which developed the slate Belt: the Italians, the Welsh and of course, the Cornish. There waiting for us were two members of Penkernewek – The Pennsylvanian Cornish Association – of which Albert was president. They were Carolyn – aged sixty seven – and Harry Bray, who was seventy-one years old. Now obviously, much of the Cornish population of Pen Argyl and Bangor had come from the slate-mining region of North Cornwall, centred around Delabole, but also from villages such as Tintagel and Boscastle. Harry's family was no exception. His grandfather had come out to work the slate of Pen Argyl from Tintagel. Carolyn was also Cornish and had a famous relative, as I would later discover.

The Cornish room was beautifully laid out with lots of memorabilia and Carolyn and Harry delighted in showing it to us. I dun't think I've ever seen such a loving couple, nor such a loved collection of exhibits. I gave them a book for their Cornish library and took photographs of the pasty pails and the old Cornish range. There was mock saffron cake, pasties being made, as well as somewhat anachronistically *Tommyknocker* creme soda bottles, and an old Furniss biscuit tin.

"Although Bangor was more Welsh than Pen Argyl, of the first sixteen mayors, thirteen of them were Cornishmen," Harry wanted me to note.

Harry went on to show us some of the machinery that the top-workers used to split slate. There were plenty of old photographs of the slate mines on the wall, which someone needed to collate and put into a book. Old plans of the two towns showed how extensive quarrying operations were, and what methods were used to bring the slate up from the floors of the quarries.

"They haven't changed much at all," said Carolyn. "You'll see what I mean this afternoon."

One thing I liked in the museum was that the local high school baseball, football and athletic teams were all called the 'Slaters', and they had some old shirts and penants hung up in another room. I found an interesting anonymous poem called 'The Old Quarry' first published in the 'State Centennial Programme of October 1st -3rd, 1936', enclosed in the *Bangor Daily News*. I hurriedly scrawled it down into my journal, and it is perhaps worth repeating here (a 'holobobber' incidentally, is a young boy who kept the slate wet):

Dumps, dumps, quarry dumps,
What signs of better days
    these piles of slate will tell!
Big piles, little piles, holes too deep to fill.
With all the cars and rubbish piles
    round our lovely hills.

Shanties, shanties, old time shanties,
What memories of former years
    these worn out houses bring!
Big men, little men and holobobber, too
Made all the blocks from solid rocks
    by cutting them in two.

Derricks, derricks, sturdy derricks,
What mighty strength and power
    your cables large display!
Big strands, little strands, huge cords of steel
With engines puffing behind the wall
    of Bangor's common weal.

Whistles, whistles, piercing whistles,
Made sleepers jump out of their beds
    to climb the slaty bank.
Big pails, littles pails, pasties not a few!

248

While roads and far off lanes
    were filled with toilers, hard and true.

Revive, revive, once more revive,
Return to us with all the noise
    that filled our sleeping vale:
Steam drill, hand drill, blasting loud and long.
Bring prosperity to our town, to fill our town,
    to fill our homes with song.

Was there ever a more positive ode to mining than this? I couldn't think of one, and it tickled me that it had survived. Intriguingly I felt there was something else in there; maybe in the final verse, where the lines reminded me of Padstow's May Day Song: 'Unite and Unite', replaced here with 'Revive, revive'. Either way it sounded like it had been written by someone from North Cornwall.

Near to this poem, on a table in the Cornish room was a folder dedicated to the Hayle-born Rick Rescorla. Here it was clear that Rescorla had rightly assumed a new role as a Cornish-American hero and icon for the twenty-first century. In case you don't know, Rescorla was in change of security for Morgan Stanley Dean Writer. On September 11th, he successfully helped 2,700 of its employees out of the World Trade Centre's South Tower. Then, perhaps thinking of the soldiers who had died in his arms in Vietnam, where he also served, and of his wife, Susan, he went back and climbed the tower stairs looking for stragglers. He never came back. Perhaps the best book on Rescorla is James B. Stewart's *Heart of a Soldier*, and there were a few excerpts of it in the folder.[1] The whole story was so amazing and incredible that I was very glad there was now a memorial to Rick in Hayle. Bravery like that only comes along once in a while. He is perhaps the most famous Cornishman of the modern era.

After we'd signed the visitor book downstairs, we had a brief look at the museum of the local fire brigade, in which was encased a very old fire engine, which I can only describe to you as looking like something which ought to have been featured in a *Keystone Kops* film (the series of which were actually filmed in Pennsylvania and New Jersey). I could imagine many comedic fire-men hanging on for dear life, and the machine turning sharpish around one of Bangor's street corners. It was Cornish, Welsh and Italian money which had paid for that, and I was glad it was so well preserved. Carolyn left to go and pick up the pasties for us, while Harry joined us in Albert's van.

Harry was another great guide.

He was reminding me of that show on BBC2 called the *Kumars at No. 47* all about the British-Indian family, and the father who keeps telling his children that various famous and historic people are Indian when they clearly aren't. In this case, Harry went up the street pointing at various buildings and imagined people.

"Cornish!"

Pause.

"Cornish!"

Pause.

"Cornish!" he kept saying.

The climax of this was the Pen Argyl cemetary, where he pointed out a heart-shaped grave amongst other Harris, Jago and Angove ones.

"Jayne Mansfield: Cornish!" went Harry. "Carolyn is related to her . . ."

We looked closely at the grave. It gave her dates: April 19th 1933 to June 29th 1967. She was only thirty-four when she died, and still the object of many a man's fantasy. Her origins are complex, but lie with the Cowling and Lobb families from Delabole and Port Gaverne respectively. Sometime during the late nineteenth century a slate-worker named Robert Cowling, his wife Mary (a Lobb) and his family emigrated to America, and decided to make Pen Argyl their home. One of their daughters – Eliza Jane Cowling married Henry Jeffrey there, and they had a daughter by the name of Bessie. Bessie then married a Pen Argyl slater named Herbert Palmer and it was Jayne Mansfield who was their daughter.

Shortly afterwards Herbert Palmer died, and the whole family moved to Texas; her mother marrying one Harry L. Peers. As Jayne grew older it was clear that she was outstandingly beautiful, and with some initial success under her belt, became resolved to make it in Hollywood schmoozing producers with her captivating figure. She did not appear in many high-quality films, but rather like today's Elizabeth Hurley, she captivated the press with her figure and pink outfits. After her Hollywood dream faded she did several nude shoots for *Playboy*, and ended up in a travelling burlesque show, culminating in a striptease. She died in a car crash while travelling from Biloxi to New Orleans. Her body was returned to Pen Argyl, the Cornish community to which her family had travelled, and in which other members of her family still live; people like Carolyn Bray. 'We live to love you more each day' ran the legend on the marble, beneath two flower pots holding plastic pink flowers. Apparently the marble was originally pale pink in colour, but it over time it has faded.

I recalled a photograph I had seen of her with Madonna-like cone breasts and leopard-skin bikini. Jayne Mansfield was the original Barbie doll. I was suddenly brought back to reality when Harry enquired, "Would you like a look at Delabole?"

"Na – I dun't think we want t'be bothered to go all that way now," said Champi joking.

"I mean Delabole here . . ."

"Of couse," so Albert took a right from out of the grave-yard and headed down towards the hamlet of Delabole, Pennsylvania. In my four years at Sir James Smith's School in Camelford, I'd taught a lot of kids from Delabole. It was perhaps one of those places where, as a young person, you longed to get away from, but perhaps once away, realised how special it was. In a lot of ways Delabole back home was much like my old childhood village of Foxhole: grey, foggy and right next to a massive hole in the ground. You could see how the Delabole here was preferable. It didn' stop the slate quarry workers from Cornwall naming it after the old village though. We pulled alongside a slight dip, where once a railroad had ran, and in the trees to the south, a former quarry. Now it was quite quiet though.

"Just over there, in that house was where I was born," said Harry.

"Have you been back – I mean to North Cornwall – Harry?" I asked.

251

"Aw – yeash – several times now. It ain't much like here is it?"

There was only one answer: No, this was a kind of Eden – except for the slate. Everywhere you went were little tailings of slate running down the hillside, the green only just beginning to cover them, all these years later after they were first worked.

Over the course of our travels, Dan was to not only gain an unhealthy fixation with fudge, but also a somewhat strange interest in the smell of skunk. I'm not talking cannabis here, rather more the small, black and white American mammal, which upon being threatened, exudes a wholly sour and disturbing scent. I've grown used to it in my travels across North America, and I have to say, when back travelling by car in Britain, I do sometimes miss it. Skunk kind of acts as a nasal decongestant. It clears the senses of anything else.

"Skunk!" shouted Dan loudly as we rounded a bend.

Everyone smelt the air.

We all confirmed Dan's speedy diagnosis at a particular virulet piece of skunk odour.

"You'll be wearing that back in Grampound Road," joked Champi, – "Odour d'skunk, the new fragrance *pour le homme . . .*"

The stank around Delabole, the graveyard and the old Borough hall had left us hungry. Our lunch stop was 'The House that Pasties Built'. This, literally, was the community hall, which had been paid for by pasty sales, and this site, coupled with the bandstand at Weona Park had been the site of the 10th Gathering of Cornish Cousins in 1999. Round the side of the bandstand was a commemorative plaque to that occasion. All neatly prepared for us on some benches was our crib: 'Hand-Made Mr. Pastie Beef Turnover (U.S. Inspected and Passed by Department of Agriculture Est. 9764)'. "Pass the pass tee!" said the little man on the wrapper, who looked a little bit like Albert. They had an email address: mrpastie@ee.net. I e-mailed them when I got back to Cornwall, to tell them how good their pasties were.

We had Carolyn to thank for this lot. She'd been busy helping a neighbour, but soon returned to eat with us. As we ate, Albert commented, "My Grandfather Davis said he only used to stop eating when his stomach touched the table, full or not . . ."

I was fairly full from the first pasty, but I wun' going to let the peach-filled dessert one go to waste. So I had that too. Y'hear a lot about sweet pasties, but y'dun't see them very often, so this was something special. All this was washed down with home-made lemonade. It was the perfect lunch. As the food settled, I looked around and about. There were tailings everywhere, and I laughed to myself at the name of the park. It had been named from a competition in 1923 organised by one Corrine Broad (who must have been Cornish). Weona had been suggested since it was short for 'We own a Park'. Corny as hell, but somehow very Cornish too.

In the afternoon we went to Dally's Slate Quarry. Dally is an old Cornish name in these parts. For me it was like pulling into Cornwall. I had a bit of 56 Inch Cylinder Syndrome craving and looked over some of the pulleys and cables strewn down in the old sheds. Then we peered over into the quarry. Now you may know Delabole slate quarry. It's more or less round, in descending layers much like Dante's imagining of hell. Delabole's slate, I believe, is set spirally in the ground. Here though the quarry is incredible. Because of the local geology, the beds of slate virtually lie symmetrical and so the quarry and its walls are all square and perpendicular – as if the ground itself were man-made instead of being natural. You simply cut straight down through the band. At the bottom we could see men working, cutting chunks of rectangular slate away from the walls, and hooking chains around them. On known signals an operator set the pulley cables to go, and up they came like pre-made menhirs, cut so smoothly you could almost lay them as a kitchen floor.

The first people I got talking to were two of the meanest-looking gentlemen you could possibly imagine. Tattooed, tanned, bearded, and beer-bellied, Ray Reed and Johnny Branhan, landed chunks of slate at the quarry. They had the weariness and wiseness of doing the job for umpteen years – probably since leaving school – and I imagine, knew very little else other than the ways and wiles of slate.

"You Cornish?" said Ray, looking at me like James Hetfield out of Metallica. "They said some Cornish people were comin' t'look 'round today . . ."

I confirmed my ethnicity.

"Well, your people found a lot of this out here . . . Y'all should be proud of that. Hell, I wouldn't have a job if it weren't fur them comin' out here. Know what I'm saying?"

I knew very well what he was saying.

Johnny piped in. "Hey – you wanna' ride the hook down . . . ?"

At that moment, I began to realise what he meant. To get down into the quarry, the men either had to climb down an exhaustive set of ladders, or otherwise ride the hook. This was somewhat akin – in my view – to sheer madness. Apparently, although shall we say, 'discouraged' by modern mining inspectors and every Health and Safety organisation in North America, it was still 'on-going' practice. You just stood on the hook, wrapped some chain around you and down you went, on one of the steel cables slung across the quarry, like a Cornish bungee jump. In some ways, I'd love to have done it. Just as many crazy things still go on in the china clay works around St Austell. In many other ways I was sweating like a bull and wishing the Slate Belt's ground might swallow me up right there and then.

"You're alright . . . Even this one," said Johnny smiling knowingly, and pointing to Ray, "won't do it these days . . ."

We wandered over to the mill, following the path of the dump trucks which carried the four metre long lengths of slate brought up from the quarry 'on the hook'. The mill was a hive of busy cutting activity. Although most of the men there knew how to split slate by hand, most of the cutting was now done by industrial diamond-edged saws, all computerised and water-cooled. There was a lot of 56 Inch Cylinder Syndrome-style conversation going on, which I tried to keep up with, but with the noise of the trucks and the saws, I'm not quite sure how much of it I understood or got right. I'll try though. Apparently in 1900, there were some 4,000 people alone employed in the Pennsylvanian Slate Belt. Now, one of the workers reckoned on there being only 35 people in total.

"We blame it on the cheap foreign stuff," he said.

I had to tell him the ironic story about slate arriving in Delabole from South America – because, apparently, it was cheaper. The same thing happened in Pennsylvania.

I did pick up some information. There are many varieties of slate to be found in the Americas. The naïve me just thought slate was slate. They have names like Bird's Eye, Maple, Oak, Chewing Gum and Delaware. A 'ribbon' shows where the layers are and where to cut a good section. Cutters are always on the look out for ribbons. You can split a piece of slate twice, but you must cut it on the third. We were shown good and bad sections. I'm not sure I could tell which was which. They all looked like nice, pleasant bits of slate to me, which I'd love to have transported back to Cornwall. We made do with some beermat size pieces that I planned on using with the first can of *Tinners* that I opened when home back in Probus.

Outside I saw a white pick-up pull up, the driver of which seemed to know what he was doing. The driver got out of his pick-up and stood in silhouette in the mill's doorway, then mozeyed across to us. Gradually, as the man-with-no-name came closer, I saw that he was smoking a pipe, wore a white T-shirt, crumpled quarry jeans and a pair of industrial boots. He had the kind of presence amongst the mill-workers that seemed to indicate he knew everyone – and everyone's grandpoppy.

"Howdy Fred . . ." Carolyn Bray said respectfully. "These are the fellas from Cornwall . . ."

This was Fred Doney – seventy-five years old and fit as a fiddle. Fred was the former owner of the quarry and talked it like he walked it. His family had originally come over from Delabole so it was clear he knew a little bit about slate. Fred sucked on his pipe, and said to me, "So where d'y' want t'begin?"

It was a helleva question that I was utterly unprepared for. Suffice to say, no stone was left unturned about slate production in Pen Argyl. I was beginning to think I knew more about it than Carolyn, Harry and Albert by the time I'd interviewed him. Like Albert though, he had an eye for a good story.

"Let me tell y' this one . . ." he said, pointing over to Ray

255

and Johnny. "Y'see the hook there. Well, riding the hook down is kinda' frowned upon. One day, my father Albert rode the hook down inta the quarry, and up top was a mines inspector. The inspector was there looking at his watch, waiting for my pa t'come up. When he came, no sooner did his boots touch the floor than the inspector said, "I'm going to report you to the president of this company. Now where is the president?" Quick as a flash, my father replied, "I *am* the president. Now report me to him . . . !"

"Y'see Alan," Fred said to me, "When y'open up a slate mine, you'd better know what yer doing. If y'put a half a million dollars in, if you're wrong, you end up with a huge hole in the ground . . ."

Now Fred's great-grandfather was a man by the name of Thomas Jewell, and when he arrived in Pen Argyl, aged just seventeen years old, that is what he faced. Luckily the quarry here had survived a good time and looked to carry on mining for a few years yet. This was a cue for another great story.

"Now when mining first started out here, no banks would lend any man money. There was a fella by the name of Dickie Johnson – I don't think he was Cornish. I think he was from London. He was aged twenty-three, not much older than my great-grandfather, and he wanted to open a quarry, so he went to the bank for a loan. They were having none of it. They didn't want to lend this slater any money, so sure enough, he took a pick and shovel, struggled hard, real hard, and took off fifteen feet by himself. Then he found slate. Then the bank said they'd loan him money, but do you know what he did – that Johnson – he got his own back. That boy opened up his own bank. He loaned money to anyone who wanted to mine round here . . . Put the other sons of bitches out of business."

Fred had been working at the quarry since he was ten years old. He knew slate like the back of his hand. Perhaps that was the reason he commanded such respect. He began by helping out in the crane room and in the blacksmith's shop, then he quit school ("I was tired of it.") and did the landing of the blocks. At the quarry he could smoke ten cigarettes a day, but never got caught by his father because he could always quickly hide the butts under the slate.

"We use the tried and tested methods here," said Fred. "Nothing modern . . . There's no better way of getting the slate up . . ."

In all honesty, I could have stayed yapping to Fred all afternoon, but time was getting on, and we needed to be heading off to another place Albert was keen to show us. The weather was beginning to deteriorate too. By the time we had pulled out of the quarry, there was thunder and lightning up on the Blue Mountains where we were headed. Rain came hammering down and water was streaming down the hills of Pen Argyl. As we climbed and you looked back down over the town, it suddenly reminded me of another Cornish town in America – Grass Valley. Similarly, the mines lay to the right of the main road through. Perhaps deep down there was something connecting all these places together – something elemental that the Cornish who came out here were looking for.

There was a surprise up on the mountains. Near to Pen Argyl is a centre of megalithic revival. Megalithic revival? Well, okay then, a stone circle – or rather stone circles x fifteen. It is at a place named Columcille. Rather like St Merryn's own Archdruid of Cornwall, Ed Prynn, who has erected the Seven Sisters, as well as contemporary inter-pretations of other famous Cornish ancient stones and sites in his bungalow's garden, here, a gentleman called Bill Cohea has made a wonderful megalithic and Dark-Age park. At the gate to park, you are told to 'Come as you are! (Isn't that a song by Nirvana?) Respect the land. Go in Peace.' A noticeboard informs you of courses available in 'sacred place-making'. Even though the rain was still falling heavily, all of us had a wander through the Park, which I have to say is a marvellous creation. We found such things as the Infinity Gate Entrance, which encourages one to 'Come dance in Another kind of Time', the Menhirs and Guardians ('Peace to the four directions'), the Stone of Centering and Grounding (how very Californian somehow), the Druid Stone of Wisdom and the Stone of Remembrance – 'listening to our ancestor's wisdom'. I could go on. There were loads more, all of which were lovingly placed around a trail. I headed off to the Sacred Men's Site reading a poem dedicated to Myth and Mystery on the tour guide:

257

Stones are guides and connect
to the source of Creation in the
beginning timeless spirit
of consciousness.
    Joining stars to stars;
    age to age.

Come dance with the stones.
    Touch them.
    Hear their songs.
Prepare to enter realms unknown.

Okay. Okay. I was there. I was entering realms unknown. I was dying to hear what someone like Fred Doney would think about this though – a man who'd spent his lifetime ripping the timeless spirit out of the earth. I suppose that's one of the contradictions of being Cornish, of being an industrial Celt. We can feel all this 'age to age' stuff but we can rake up the earth with the best of them. I suppose I, and many others, won't ever resolve that. Indeed, to me, that dilemma is what makes us who were are. Apparently at the Cornish Gathering, the Cornish Gorseth had a ceremony here. It must have looked good, almost as good at the original one at Boscawen Ûn back in 1928. All the time I was there, though, I was thinking of Ed back in St Merryn. I believe him, like Rick Rescorla, to be one of the finest Cornishmen of the modern era. Practical to the end, Ed's like me in that he knows what it means to be a kind of 'Druidic Methodist'. Two things sum him up for me. On the outside of his bungalow, you'll find hundreds of slate plaques put up there with the names of famous Cornishmen and women, or people who have helped Cornwall. It's a kind of alternative college of bards. One day, I noticed a space missing.

"Who's missing?" I asked.

"Well Alan (he always calls me Alan) that was for Peter de Savary (the famous property developer) . . . but after what he did t'Land's End and Penzance Dock . . . I had t'take 'un off an' put 'un up in the attic . . ."

Ed has been on advisory missions to other megalithic revival sites and always attracts the ladies. One day Ed

258

was fighting off the affections of a very attractive young woman.

"Ed, you're the living re-incarnation of Merlin . . . Please will you impregnate me . . ." she apparently said.

It was Ed the Methodist and practical Druid who answered.

"Now my 'andsome. T'me you'd be best off, goin' home after we've finished this stone circle, and gettin' a proper job . . ."

All this was kicking around my head, as I explored. It tickled me then to find in the shop there, a book by Rob Roy (not the kilt-clad one!) called *Stone Circles: A Modern Builder's Guide to the Megalithic Revival*,[2] which featured both Bill Cohea and Columcille, as well as Ed and the Seven Sisters. It also referred to the stones at Glen Innes, in New South Wales, Australia, which had been featured once on the cover of *Cornish World / Bys Kernowyon*. All at once, everything seemed to link up; past and present merged – as a child I was back up on Hensbarrow Downs next to the Longstone. I hope I don't sound too cynical. I love all this stuff really. More power to the megalithic revival. I even have a couple of bits of granite in my own garden that sort of look like Columcille or the Seven Sisters (Note on return to Cornwall: must try Ed's cattle-trough hot-tub down in his fogou – especially with Pen Argyl-style Barbies). So we came as we were – soaked to the skin. We respected the land – unlike other Cornish who were digging it up the world over. We went in peace. We were quiet for five minutes at least.

Ten miles south of Pen Argyl was another small Cornish community named Chapman's Quarry. The Quarry has long since been closed, but gave its name to the town. Now, tall trees are embedded in the workings, but a two mile drive around its edge, showed us how important this quarry had once been. In the centre of town was a United Methodist Church. According to Albert the place had been almost solidly Cornish until fairly recently. It was still tipping down outside and there wasn't much of chance to wander around, so we pushed on towards the southeast. It was only after Allentown that the rain decided to stop. In the sunshine, Dan and Champi noticed a few cornfields.

They weren't nearly as common here as where we were headed in the mid-west, but some were labelled up with different 'testing varieties'.

"When do they harvest it?" asked Dan.

"Well," said Albert, "The corn should be high as your eye by the fourth of July. Depends. It's been a bit wet this summer. Ideally, you want a longer dry spell . . . but fairly soon . . . say early September . . ."

Driving back home, I noticed that there was a nearby town to Pottstown called the 'King of Prussia'. Of course, my mind was looking for a connection to the well-known 'free-trader' John Carter, the famous Cornish smuggler of Prussia Cove. I didn't even need to ask. Albert had the same thought many years ago upon his first arrival to the area. Apparently, this town, which took its name from the public house, was actually named after the real King Frederick. Carter himself, clearly following events in the Seven Years' War, admired Frederick, and styled himself after the Prussian King. This all fitted, considering just how many German and Prussia names there were locally. It was no smuggling then, in eastern Pennsylvania.

In the evening we went to an unusual American Brewpub down in central Pottstown which went by the name of 'Ortliebs'. According to Albert this place used to host some of the finest big bands of America. You could see what he meant. The restaurant seemed to be the site of the large dancefloor and exhibit hall, and where the great vats of beer were brewing was probably once the stage. You could imagine young men and women 'bopping' (if that's the right word) to 'Take the A Train'. Now the rafters were littered with neon beer logos and American football paraphernalia, just like the tacky Chicago Rock pubs back home.

It was here however, that a classic little Cornu-American moment occurred, and which I must relay to you. There's a sequence in *Robin Hood: Prince of Thieves*, where a blinded retainer named Duncan hears the voice of Azeem (played by Morgan Freeman)- Robin's Islamic fellow escapee from the dungeons of Jerusalem, and when the servant hears Azeem he thinks he might be Cornish. Well, when the barman at the Pottstown Brewpub served Dan, so strange and bizarre was his accent (remember Dan dun't even speak the Cornish language), that he thought Dan was Puerto Rican. Not that being Puerto Rican is a bad thing you understand, it just amused Champi and myself no end. That was it: Dan was the Puerto Rican Cornishman – Ricardo Tregaskis. At this Dan nearly spluttered his brewpub glass of beer all over his steak (with mesquite sauce of course). It all reminded me of my encounter back in Virginia City with the heritage of Juan Ricardo José – or rather Richard Jose of Lanner.

We laughed about it for days afterward. We couldn't help it. On countless occasions over the next few weeks, everyone was asked coyly, "Do you think he looks Puerto Rican?" I reckoned Dan had a bit of that ethnic darkness in him. I was back with naturalist and racist W. H. Hudson looking at Cornish orang-utans down Land's End.

"No I dun't . . ." Dan muttered.

"You're just in denial Dan . . ." assured Champi.

The Puerto Rican jokes were still coming thick and fast the next morning.

I felt a little more alert since I spent this night downstairs on Albert's settee. There was no seismic activity in the living room, so I was feeling a bit more awake and up for another look at Cornish America. Today we were going to an iron forge started by a Cornish family, and somewhere else I had always wanted to visit – Gettysburg. Going down to Gettysburg I learned something else about Albert. He and Evelyn had once been very active in the 'Society for Creative Anachronism'. To a certain extent this didn't surprise me. The 'Society for Creative Anachronism' is a big deal in the USA, holding Renaissance Fayres at various locations throughout the summer (in fact, we were to pass one in Phoenix later in the trip). In effect, such Fayres gave the opportunity for grown-ups to dress-up and imagine themselves to be mainly European characters from past ages. There was a good deal of research needed in developing the character you were interested in, and in effect, at the Fayre you role-played that character for various members of the public. It might seem a bit 'geeky' for most people from Britain, but given how many e-mail questions I've had about various issues of costuming, language, literature and the Celts in general, it was certainly no small endeavour. Needless to say, Albert had his own character: one Uren

Pen-an-Vre who he imagined to be fourteenth-century minor gentry, and went to study architecture in Paris. I knew Albert could perform this well. Suddenly, in my own little piece of creative anachronism, I was looking at John Trevisa (1342–1402) – the St Mellion or St Enodoc (depending on which scholarship you believe)-born Glasney College scholar and perhaps the greatest of Middle English prose translator of Latin texts into English, and one of the so-called saviours of the English language. Suddenly, John Trevisa transformed himself back to Albert Jenkin again.

"Look at that signpost." said Albert.

We looked.

"Can you stop the van?" I asked.

Albert pulled up the van sharpish, and we all went out to have our picture taken under a sign pointing to somewhere called 'Cornwall'.

Next to it was another sign saying 'Enter Here' – so we did, running the half a mile down to a place called Miners Village, which did not really look much like Cornwall, though the houses did have a kind of Cornish solidity and purposefulness. Made of locally-hewn block – perhaps in a style you might see in somewhere like Bugle or St Dennis – they were edged with red brick, and several had verandas. Just across the road from a red hydrant was a chainsaw-carving of a miner, standing proudly in his helmet, with both hands on the handle of a spade. Further up the hill was Gold Street, now sandwiched between gazebos and garden sheds. All in all, Miners Village seemed quite a respectable place – now made somewhat disrespectable by us showing up.

The road gradually followed around to the right a little way, and there on the corner, was Miners Village Mennonite Church. Somewhere along the way, a few Cornish had probably joined the Mennonites. 'O Worship the Lord in the beauty of holiness' the Church's sign said, quoting Psalm 96.9. Several of the Mennonite community must have been connected to the so-called Cornwall Banks iron mines. These open-cast quarries were now flooded but were the oldest continually operated iron mines in the North American continent. A sign informed the visitor that the 'quarries had been mined for more than two centuries and that it was still the greatest iron ore deposit east of Lake Superior'. Ferns and trees now made it difficult to view the lakes, but the whole place looked still and tranquil. Obviously, it was this iron that had founded Cornwall and Miners Village.

This whole area is actually a landmark of the Pennsylvanian iron industry as we were to learn, since we stopped for a morning tour of Cornwall Forge and Iron Furnace. This operated continually from 1742 to 1883 and is typical of the charcoal, cold-blast iron furnances that dotted the Pennsylvanian landscape in the eighteenth and nineteenth centuries. Just about the first person we ran into was the curator, Fred Conrad. Aged forty-four, he loved the fact that some Cornish people had showed up, and initially took great delight in showing us two postcards on his office wall – one of Land's End and another of Mên-an-tol.

"What the hell is that thing anyway?" asked Fred. "Sure looks like an oddly shaped piece of stone to me . . ."

I explained.

"Do they still do that now?" he asked, eyebrows rising, after I'd given him the list of its curing properties.

"Of course," I said, tongue, very much in cheek.

We learnt that the first ironmaster of Cornwall Furnace was one Peter Grubb, who hailed from Cornwall. The Grubb family had established themselves along the Delaware coast, where John Grubb, Peter's father, had a tannery. Later he moved to Marcus Hook in Chester County, Pennsylvania, and here, in 1700 was where Peter was born, the youngest of nine children. He converted to Quakerism in order to marry Quakeress Martha Wall in 1732. Then after the birth of his first son, Curtis, in 1733, they moved to Lancaster County, seeking a good location for iron ore outcroppings. He found it at Cornwall Banks. By 1739 his enterprises were well under way. He had accumulated over a thousand acres of land, where mining operations were in progress, and an indenture was made for the construction of a charcoal furnace to be called Cornwall (in memory of the place where his family had come from). The Cornwall furnace was in operation by 1742 and the Cornwall Company, a group of twelve Quaker businessmen led by Amos Garrett was granted a twenty-five year lease, producing stove plates (for Cornish-style ranges) as well as pig iron.

Grubb eventually got swept up in the events surrounding the American Revolution and the furnace was worked prolifically during the war. The conflict caused iron prices to nearly double. Revolutionary War cannonballs were manufactured at Cornwall Furnace. Eventually the Furnace passed into the hands of Robert Coleman – a shrewd Irish businessman who built an iron empire in the State, but it is good to know the place was founded by a Cornishman. Many of the miners at Cornwall Banks were Cornish.

Fred Conrad was an excellent guide who delivered his spin on the Forge at just the right pitch. We were joined on our tour by a couple from Michigan, who obviously had 'iron ore' interest, and it was interesting to watch Fred field questions from them and us.

Two parts of the Forge impressed me the most. The first was the Charging Floor. This was where the fillers, as directed by the founder, dumped their buggy loads of charcoal and iron ore, with limestone into the nineteen-inch mouth of the furnace, which resembled going down the opening of Empire Mine in Grass Valley. The second was the Casting Room itself. Twice a day the founder would tap the furnace, releasing the slag; then he would allow the red hot molton iron to flow out, guided by the gutterman through the 'sow' and into the 'pig' moulds made in the sand floor. Of course, this was the place were the Revolutionary War cannonballs were made. There was an irony there for me – a Cornish-founded foundry casting weaponry to be fired against the British regiments – many of whom had Cornishmen in their ranks. However, the 46th Foot Regiment, which became part of the Duke of Cornwall's Light Infantry, surprised a small American force at Paoli, Pennsylvania, during the night and pretty well wiped them out, killing and capturing four hundred, with a loss to themselves of only eight killed and wounded. As Salisbury-Trelawny shows in his history of the Duke of Cornwall's Light Infantry, the Americans vowed they would give no quarter to the British troops engaged so the units employed in the attack dyed their hat feathers red in order that they might be more easily distinguishable in the future.[3] This is the origin of the red backing on the cap badge today.

I can only describe Cornwall Forge to you as looking like something out of Gotham City, and if you are ever in eastern Pennsylvania, go and have a look at it. Its gothic revivalism needs to be used as a film location one day. The historian Carl Obinger who has studied the whole of the Cornwall area in Pennsylvania, calls it 'an Industrial Camelot'.[4] What an image.

Between Cornwall Forge and Harrisburg is the famous town of Hershey. Now to most people in Britain, that dun't mean a darn thing; but to every American, the name Hershey is symbolic of everything chocolate, rather like *Cadburys* or *Rowntrees* in Britain. The town of Hershey owes a lot to chocolate, and celebrates that fact all over town. There is a 'Hersheypark' – a kind of Disneyland with chocolate – and even the streetlamps are designed to look like Hershey's most famous creation – the silver paper wrapped chocolate kiss. Even though it was raining as we passed through, you could still smell something sweet in the air.

"Skunk!" went Dan.

No Dan. Chocolate.

I can't 'get on' (what a Cornish phrase that is!) with American chocolate on the whole. It always seems a little sour tasting compared to ours – something is either missing or added to make it taste different. I'll eat it, but it en't the same as a bar of *Dairy Milk*.

We passed through a lot of small Pennsylvanian towns on the way down, all of them filled with stores carrying punning names. It was as if modern, ironic advertising campaigns had never happened here. I'd stepped back in time to 1955 and 'Burma Shave' posters. My favourites had to be 'Puff n' Snuff: Discount Tobacco store' and the 'Flower Power' florists in somewhere like Bachmanville. I doubt if the hippies had even made it to Bachmanville. In reality, it is quite a long spin down to Gettysburg; I had to sympathise with the Union army. We revisited the spaghetti of Harrisburg, then took Route 15 south to some serious Civil War country. Civil War between the North and South ravaged the United States from 1861 to 1865. The South's economy depended on cotton plantations and farms worked by black slaves; the North on industry without slaves. They disputed whether slavery would be extended to new states being settled. The Southern General Robert E. Lee won the first battle at Bull Run in July 1861, but eventually the superior manpower of the North began to tell. A turning point came with the Union Victory at Gettysburg in 1863. Lee finally surrendered in April 1865, and despite efforts to rebuild the South's ruined economy ('Reconstruction') much bitterness between North and South remained.

You start to get the feel of the 'burg' of Gettysburg long before you arrive. Billboards on the side of the road announce various attractions and shopping experiences: 'all you can eat shrimp with cannons', and 'all-day diners with Confederate flags'. Most hotels offered the 'Civil War Experience' as well as 'Great Food and Lodging'. Various unofficial and offical guides were offering their personal services to tour McPherson Ridge. This summer was the 140th Gettysburg Re-enactment. These included 'The Great Battle Begins', 'Longstreet Attacks' and 'The Heroic Counterattack' and more. It all sounded like *Star Wars* with cavalry and muskets for weekend warriors. And all this was just getting to Gettysburg. You can't however, begin to imagine the sacred nature of the place or the sheer vastness of the battle until you get there. Gettysburg town was buzzing with tourists on the 5th of August. There were advertisements and experiences everywhere: 'Come and see the stuff Generals are made of: The Museum and White House of the Confederacy'. You are encouraged to 'Hear the Gunfire, See the Smoke, Smell the Powder' and 'March in History's Footsteps'. There were exhibitions such as 'Brother Against Brother', advertisments for Civil War experiences in other States (*Don't be the last to visit North Carolina – a civil place for a historic vacation* or *Whether Your Outlook is Blue or Gray . . . You'll find colorful History here*). In another magazine was an advert for the 'Sharpsburg Arsenal – Purveyors of Fine Civil War Memorabilia', while a leaflet for Civil War Trails offered the discerning visitor to 'Follow them to more than 400 Civil War sites'. The *History Channel* also had a large presence. I imagine they can probably do wall-to-wall Civil

War coverage every July, generating millions of viewers and revenue. It was like Manchester United v. Juventus – only with blues and grays. I could hear the presenter's voice – someone like James Earl Jones: "The American Civil War had far-reaching effects: by the many innovations and developments it stimulated, it became the forerunner of modern warfare . . ."

We swung into the town centre, viewing first the famous Lutheran Theological Seminary, where at the start, at least, the Union forces watched the surrounding battle from that building's cupola, and then headed out to the area known as the Railroad Cut. As Albert explained, and as we soon discovered, this was where elements of the two armies collided during the early morning hours of July 1st. The fighting escalated throughout the day as more and more Union and Confederate troops reached the field. By 4 p.m. the defending Federal troops had retreated through Gettysburg where many were captured. The remnants of the Union force rallied upon Cemetery and Culp's Ridge.

On the next day, the strength of both armies had arrived on the field. General Robert E. Lee launched an attack on the Union's left and right in an attempt to dislodge General Gordon Meade's army from its strong position. Lieutenant General James Longstreet's assault upon the Union left made good progress but was eventually checked by Federal reinforcements from the centre and right. On the Union's right, Lieutenant-General Richard S. Ewell's Confederate troops seized part of Culp's Hill; but elsewhere they were repulsed.

The third day is the stuff of legend. Lee turned his attention to the Union's centre. Following a two-hour artillary bombardment, he sent some 12,000 Confederate infantry to try and break the Union lines on Cemetery Ridge. Despite a courageous effort the attack (later dubbed 'Pickett's Charge') was repulsed with heavy losses. Eastwards, Lee's cavalry was also checked, and crippled by heavy loses. By the next day he began to retreat into Virginia.

You can take a tour of the various battlefields I've mentioned. The full experience can last a day. Some people spend a whole week there.

"If you thought Washington had lots of monuments, then be prepared – Gettysburg is like Washington on steroids . . ." remarked Albert.

He wudn' far wrong. After the first six monument to various cavalry and infantry regiments, I couldn't cope. It sounds crass, but it was even hard to sort out which side a particular monument recorded. We, like several other cars and sports utility vehicles, rounded the monuments as if at a Safari Park. It felt like at any moment, some of the statues would come to life and start ripping windscreen wipers off Albert's van, and expect to be fed peanuts. I had to laugh at the freebie tourist newspaper 'The Battlefield Journal'; one of the headlines ran 'A New Monument underway'. I was sobered though by the numbers of the dead: the total battle deaths for the North were some 110,100 lives; for the South 94,000.

After rounding the umpteenth statue we found a viewing platform, which the public could climb, to see for themselves the vast battleground. This, we duly did, and the panoramic diagrams give the visitor a better sense of place, and the whole enormity of the battle, those few days in July 1863. All the time I was thinking of Darryl Jones, Jim Wearne's friend. No doubt, he had visited the place on a few occasions; perhaps knowing as some people clearly do, every spot of ground. Well, it was the Confederate equivalent of the Cornish Blackheath.

We first entered the Visitor Centre and Gettysburg Museum of the Civil War. It houses the 'Electric Map', a vast bookstore carrying perhaps every single book every published about the conflict. Seemingly, any serious American historian had written their say on the Civil war and Gettysburg itself had been re-appraised from every single aspect possible: *Gettysburg: A Dormouse's Perspective on the Conflict* seemed something I might find, alongside *Pickett's Charge: A Re-assessment of the Sideburns of the Unionist Forces* next to *Confederate Moonshine Recipes: The Latest Evidence*. I joke – but it was hard to know where to begin. Everyone else seemed to be having the same problem. In one section, I looked for books on specific regiments of the conflict. Every State and County, colour and creed seemed to be available, but there was very little on any Cornish-related material, in particular the Miner's Regiment of southwest Wisconsin, and I ought to have found something on the Iron Brigade of the Upper Peninsula of Michigan too (I couldn't!). In the end I had to settle for a small, pathetic-looking pamphlet called *The Civil War Handbook* and a postcard of General Lee, looking perhaps a little over-confident. One word I did pick up in the bookshop, and liked a lot was 'Skidaddler'. This was the name of any soldier who decided that once his part was played in the war that he'd best skidaddle back home, out of the line of sight of any cannons. I dare say the Cornish skidaddled with the best of them.

Next to the bookshop is the museum itself, a fascinating display of objects found on the battlefield, but again, so extensive was the collection it was hard to take it all on board. Albert's main aim seemed to be to get us to the Cyclorama Centre, a building very close to the original 'high tide' of the Confederate forces. Such a high tide and the Confederacy is, of course, a concept very dear to my good friend, Tim Saunders, and I couldn't help but think of him here. Indeed, I even bought him a map and postcard – just writing 'high tide' on the message. His poem *The High Tide* is actually about the 54th Massachusetts Infantry at Fort Wagner, Charleston, South Carolina, 18th July 1863. Nevertheless, I could hear the poem's lines now, and they seemed to be reflective of the reach of the Confederates here, not to mention the entire Civil War:

Du ydh o tonnow'nn lanwez
a-hyz ann gworwel ha'y lez,
gwynn ann traeth kul ma y'ponsonz
a-dreus lestow feuz ha' chonz,
kann ann kribow durewynn
ma y'c'hwevre mîl vizeug ynn,
rudh ann pennlanw hoarnlomm,
mordrosow trenkvog ha' plomm.

[Black were the waves of the tide the length and breadth of the horizon, white the narrow beach where they ran over barriers of fate and chance, shining white the crests of steel foam where a thousand slender bayonets glistened, red the iron-bare high tide, billows of sour smoke and lead.][5]

We entered the Cyclorama's 1970s' style auditorium, and followed the spiral up to the 360 foot Gettysburg Cylcorama. It is a spectacular painting by Paul Philip-Poteaux of Pickett's Charge, which apparently was traipsed around America for a long time afterwards, so that people (pre- radio, cinema and television) could see what actually happened. The painting, now a Registered Historic Object, is displayed with a sound and light programme illustrating the progress of the Charge. Panels are illuminated so that the painting comes to life stage by stage. Sections of it form the cover-art for a thousand books back in the 'Electric Map'. I rather liked the fact, that even though the artist was not present at the battle, he painted himself in, doing a sketch of it all anyway. A sign clearly stated no flash photography on the wall, but Albert seemed *very* determined to take some pictures.

"I've switched the flash off," he said to us, as he lined up a section of the Cyclorama, but the flash phutted anyway.

"Naughty camera!" he said, giving it a hard slap. Security gave him a mean stare, but Albert had his picture, and went down the walkway smiling to himself. As we passed one of the countless pictures on the wall, a young couple, who looked like they might be on honeymoon, gazed at Albert. I could see why he looked so ethereal, as if from the time of Gettysburg, which was so enshrined in the very building we were in. They saw what I saw. Albert Jenkin looked like a Calvary commander on one side or the other. I'd better say *Unionist*, because that was the side most of the Cornish fought on. As we stepped out into the ferocious heat of the day, it was clear we needed a drink. Dan and I were gasping. The 'Reliance Mine Saloon', with its concrete rock and plastic mining cart, looked inviting, but it was closed, so we headed back into the centre of Gettysburg, and found a small bar that served cold Bass and Extra-Cold Guiness. We kicked back for a bit and relaxed, trying not to wind up an Irish-American at the end of the bar, who seemed a little dismissive of the Cornish presence in North America. Albert put him right.

"The Cornish fought right here in Gettysburg," he said.

Two English guys at the bar, who were out in Gettysburg running, of all things, a soccer school, also seemed amused at the Cornish presence.

"So were there many Cornish in America?" one of them asked, slightly disbelieving.

"Hundreds of thousands," I answered.

The English looked rather mazed and went back to their lager.

Gettysburg done, we gathered our souveniers and sanity, and in the late afternoon entered the baking interior of Albert's van. It would be a long trip back across the State. Coming back on Highway 23 East, we passed through Amish and Mennonite Country. Now, I'd seen the Amish back in Illinois before, but never quite in the way I was about to experience.

"Keep your eyes peeled," said Albert, as if he was prospecting for gold. "You normally see their buggies round here . . ."

Champi and Dan checked all horizons for any sign of the Amish. Albert's van was silent. We went on through places like Groffdale and New Holland. No-one spoke. Suddenly Dan leapt forward in the same way he normally did upon smelling skunk.

"There's one," he went, feverishly pointing up to a side track, where an elderly and respectable Amish man drove his buggie down to the road we were on. Suspiciously Albert turned down the track and we passed him by, then even more suspiciously we turned around and followed him out again. The Amish man knew we were tourists wanting to have a geek at 'un.

I have tried hard honest, but I don't quite 'get' the Amish. I mean, if you're going to stop at frivolity and decoration, then fine, but all this anti-technology thing? Come on – someone had to invent the wheel didn't they? And sometime someone must have an idea for a buggie? Weren't they technology? I mean, just where do you draw the line?

"With buggies . . ." said Albert, seemingly hearing my thoughts.

Champi meanwhile, was remembering that film with Harrison Ford in it.

Dan was Amish-watching still. The Puerto-Rican was fascinated by them.

Suddenly, at speed, an elderly Amish lady cycled past us.

"There's mother!" exclaimed Dan.

We drove on half a mile.

"*Witness*," said Dan. "Thas' it . . ."

"If we're lucky we might see an Amish girl in-line skating . . ." chipped up Albert.

Yeah right, we all thought. That just seemed an Amish too far. I mean buggies yes. And for Mennonites, it was even okay if all the chrome was taken off your standard black motor. But in-lines skates? Surely that was MTV and California beach fronts, not barn-building and funny little John Harris-style beards.

Then, just as we came round the next bend, there she was. Just as Albert had said. It was as if he'd set it up for us.

"What did I say?!" said Albert smugly!

The girl went rushing by us, all prim and proper in white bonnet and long black dress, then fluorescent roller skates . . . It looked a little incongruous.

"In-line-skates are okay," said Albert, as if to confirm that and everything else in the Amish universe.

At the next service station, we went in and bought postcards of Amish buggies and then quickly drank down some cans of *Coca-Cola*. For me, that felt a little incongruous too.

That evening I discovered another of Albert's secrets. Like my friend James in Las Vegas, Albert was a bit of a Trekkie.

"I have the pilot episode on video," he enthused.

"Thas' the one that's not got Kirk in it, and is partly in black and white, and colour," said Champi, who seemed to know a thing or two about Klingons too.

"It's called *The Cage*," said Albert. "Want to see it?"

Ever a Sci-Fi geek, I couldn't refuse. I had to admit I had never seen the episode before. Curiously enough, although Spock was there in stunning pointy-eared glory, there was no Captain Kirk. Instead, there was one Captain Christopher Pike, played by some square-jawed hunk named Jeffrey Hunter. Apparently, after the pilot episode Gene Roddenberry and the producers (probably more the producers than Gene) decided that a whole new range of characters needed to be introduced to make the series work. So enter William Shatner and exit Jeffrey Hunter. I had to wonder what happened to him – battling anonymity instead of battling androids.

Champi and Dan were ready to hit the sack, but I sat down a little longer with Albert. In this kind of heat I would need the air conditioning on full throttle to even begin to sleep, and Albert seemed keen to chat further. We covered a lot of ground, ranging from the Civil War to the state of the nation, and Albert's thoughts on Cornwall. He must have been feeling sentimental since he decided to put on a CD for me.

"Have you heard this?" he asked. "If I was a little younger, I could easily fall in love with this maid. Such a beautiful voice . . ."

He handed me the CD case. The singer was from Canada, but of Cornish extraction. Her name was Heather Dale and the album was called 'May Queen'. Many of the songs had a Cornish influence, one in particular based on the story of Tristan and Iseult. Albert was right. She had a beautiful voice in the atmospheric contemporary folk genre of Clannad or Enya, but with the resonance and range of Loreena McKennitt. So Albert and I sat there in the night heat, hearing Heather Dale's voice, and I suppose we were both transported to some far off mystical Celtic place – a bit like Columcille really. It seemed the perfect end to another perfect day.

We had to be leaving the next morning. In order to fit a schedule that meant we had to be in Mineral Point by the weekend, and Calumet by the following Monday, it was time to head west. We had to go north first though. For some time Champi had been playing that most Cornish of card games – euchre, on the internet with various people in the USA. The plan was to meet up with his pals in, of all places, Niagara Falls, and for him to prove himself – well, to be a real 'champ' at the game by beating the lot of them in a 'real' (i.e. not virtual) tournament. It was a case of Cornwall taking on America: the World Euchre Championships. We rose early once again, and following another one of Albert's fantastic breakfasts, loaded up the car with our bags as well as several pieces of slate. It was hard saying goodbye to Albert. I wasn't sure when I'd next see him – and I had a feeling he was going to miss our company. We were certainly going to miss his company and good humour. We pulled away from Carwinnion Cottage, feeling like we were leaving Cornwall. You can't say more than that. The collection of postcards we'd been collecting and writing had built up over the past few days, and before leaving Pottstown, these were duly dumped in a US mail box.

We swung past the First Methodist Church again, and followed part of the route we had taken earlier that week up to the Slate Belt, but then diverted off on a toll road heading north. Toll roads are popular in the mid-west and east of the USA, but you tend to see less of them further west. I suppose they are the kind of thing we can expect more of in the UK over the next few years. The road was fast though, which we were grateful for, because we had several hundred miles to go that day. It headed north to the left of the Slate Belt through the Lehigh Tunnel which ran under the Blue Mountains, then it was up to join Interstate 81 at Stranton. 81 runs across the Pennsylvania – New York State line meeting the sprawling town of Binghamton, and continues its journey north towards Lake Ontario. If we'd had the time, I suspect it might have been fun to call in on a town called Cornwall in Ontario, on the St Lawrence River, just at the New Jersey – Canada border, but it was probably another day's drive. Besides we knew two Cornwalls well enough by now.

The car was mutating and taking on a feel of being 'on-the-road'. A small mountain of fast-food debris was growing behind my driver's seat, and we flipped between the decent rock radio stations and Country and Western. This part of New York State seemed very flat, and the road runs alongside lakes which stretch like liquid snakes from north to south. They had names Cayuga and Seneca, which kept being signposted from 81. We might have headed across country in a more north-westerly direction to Niagara Falls, but the sensible choice really, was to once again take a toll-road across, straight beneath Lake Ontario. We picked up this at Syracuse, and then stopped off at a rest stop. Champi was beginning to panic slightly because although he knew where his friends were staying:

274

the 'Best Hotel', Niagara Falls, it wasn't clear whether this was on the US or Canadian side. He tried phoning with a phone-card he had now purchased, but had no luck getting through. By now it was early in the afternoon, and we still had a fair proportion of the State to cross. Apparently the tollway we were on was the New York State Tollway, and there seemed a lot of traffic heading west. Everyone was going to Niagara Falls. Well, it was summer . . . Niagara, Honeymoons, Viagra, romance . . . oh, and euchre.

Because initially we felt the hotel was on the American side, we stopped at the Whirlpool, and looked over the gorge at the river. A cable-car structure gave people rides across the centre of the Whirlpool. It wasn't something any of us really fancied. Then we stopped at the Falls proper, trailing around the Parks and viewing platforms. Below the American Falls we viewed the 'Maid of the Mist' boats and saw the masses of yellow machintoshed visitors awaiting to climb onboard the next available ride into the mist of the spectacular Horseshoe Falls. For such a powerful rush of water, there were surprisingly few safety precautions in place. It felt like several small children might be swept away each day and Superman might have to fly down and rescue them, like he did with Lois Lane in one of the films.

Beneath the American Falls, there was an attraction called 'The Cave of Winds' which was billed as something like a cross between *Indiana Jones* and Kevin Costner's *Waterworld*. Here you also got a distinctive mackintosh; this time coloured blue, as well as a pair of special shoes to walk through the cave, and just about be hit by the falling water. A set of very slippery looking wooden steps run in and out of the American Falls. I checked out a few facts about the Falls in one of the many souvenir shops. Did you know for instance, that twenty percent of the earth's fresh water flows over Niagara Falls? No – well consider this fact lovers: The Horseshoe Fall is 2600 feet across its brink and 167 feet high. Each second 600,000 gallons of water fall from its brink. Wow – you needed to know that didn't you? The Bridal Veil portion of the American Falls is so named due to its appearance and the reputation of Niagara Falls as the 'Honeymoon Capital' of America comes partly from this. To me, Niagara Falls looked about the last place in the world I'd want to take a honeymoon, but it takes all sorts. And did you know that The Niagara River isn't actually a river at all. It's actually a strait connecting Lake Erie with Lake Ontario. Had enough? I have. I call it 56 Inch Cylinder Syndrome with H_2O. Maybe I need to check into some therapy again.

We scoured the New York side of the Falls for the 'Best Hotel', but to little avail. Champi was ready to give up, and not play. I told him Cornwall's honour was at stake. We had the time to drive over to the Canadian side, so lined up our passports and like thousands of others, crossed to Rainbow Bridge. By the bi-lingual signs it was clear Canada was just ahead. After the border patrol guard had given our passports a very cursory look we swung down Niagara Falls Boulevard and took a look at them from the Canadian side. Everyone had said that we must do this, and they were right. Now you could see the waterfalls in their full glory. The euchre match however, was still the main goal. We made some enquiries but nobody seemed to know where the 'Best Hotel' was. I concluded that a) it was either so exclusive that no-one else stayed there at all, or b) that it was called that, because actually it might be the worst hotel in town – something like the Lazy L in Boulder, Colorado. I didn't say anything to Champi. He'd travelled a long way to meet these friends and to play for his country.

"We'd better go on," said a disappointed Champi. "I don't know where it is. I've tried phoning. We've looked for it on maps . . ."

"Let's give it one last try," I said.

We explored Stanley Avenue and Robinson, stopped at other motels and making enquiries. From one of them, Champi came out smiling and pointing across the road.

"It's this one," he said, "They've just re-named it."

I can't tell you what they re-named it, because I can't remember (I put that down to sleep deprivation, old age, alcohol and coffee), but it was certainly no longer called the 'Best Hotel'. I voted that it ought to be re-named the 'Most Difficult Hotel to Find'. We found Mark's friends soon enough though, and they came down to the lobby, apologising profusely about the name change. No wonder Champi's phone calls weren't getting through. As soon as they'd arrived, they had realised we might have a problem, but at least we'd got there. It's always fun to meet people you have only chatted to over the internet, so we had a blast. Blondie, who was the leader of the euchre-playing group was a real live wire: 65 going on 16, and a total gob on a stick. She ordered us a trayful of beer and food, and we sat on a balcony in the balmy heat of Niagara. In the distance we watched the Skylon viewing tower grow neon, and saw night-time Helicopter flights over the Falls. The illumination from the Falls themselves lit up the night and the Falls ricocheted with the sound of people having fun.

Around our euchre table, it felt a little like a Wednesday night at Probus Comrades Club, but with frosty glasses and pretzels. I don't understand euchre, even though my father won several trophies. I've tried, but now in my mid-thirties, I've pretty much come to terms with the fact that I'm no card player. Instead, I enjoyed watching the match. There were a couple from Iowa who were great fun (one of whom looked like Freddie Mercury during his biker years), and another woman from Indiana, whose son found the three Cornish fascinating and couldn't get over our accents. We bought him root beer, and he soaked up this new internationalism.

"So where's Cornwall?" he asked.

Champi played a blinder though. Cornwall won. World Euchre Champions. We lifted Champi above our shoulders and went running around the balcony. That night, after giving everyone and anyone lots of hugs, we got triumphantly into the car, and followed the streets back down Clifton Hill to Rainbow Bridge. The town was absolutely buzzing. It was hard picking a way through the thousands of pedestrians swarming the streets. Fairground rides threw people up into the air at immense speeds, while an enraged giant green promotional Hulk gazed down onto our car. There was noise everywhere, as if the Falls themselves were now the last thing on everybody's mind.

For a fleeting moment earlier on, we thought we might have stayed in Niagara Falls for the night, but now it was so late that it hardly seemed worth going to bed. I looked at the map, as we got the full interrogation coming back into the USA.

"Where have you been?" said the border guard.
"Over there . . ."
"What is your business in the USA?"
"On holiday . . . on a tour around . . ."
Behind and in front of me were thousands of others doing the same thing – going into Canada for the day. So there was Canada letting the tourists in with open arms and there was the US doing Area 51.

Once outside of the touristy part of Niagara, I pulled over and gave the Rand McNally road atlas a good, long, hard stare. In this light Chicago didn't look too far away. It was only down the shore of Lake Erie and across a bit . . .

"We'll drive through the night then," I said, but Champi and Dan were already asleep. I left them in the car and went into the 'Flying J' to buy a large coffee.

I suddenly came to the realisation that I'd been euchred into night-drive across three States. There were Bennys being placed down on the table too: two little cards you may have heard of – Ohio and Indiana.

Notes

1. James B. Stewart (2000) *Heart of a Soldier: A Story of Love, Heroism and September 11th*, New York: Simson and Schuster.
2. Rob Roy (1999) *Stone Circles: A Modern Builder's Guide to the Megalithic Revival*, White River Junction, Vermont: Chelsea Green Publishing Company.
3. P.M. Salisbury-Trelawny (n.d.) *The Duke of Cornwall's Light Infantry Regimental Museum*, Bodmin: Duke of Cornwall's Light Infantry Regimental Museum, p.4.
4. See Carl Oblinger (1984) *Cornwall: The People and Culture of an Industrial Camelot 1890-1980*, Harrisburg, Pennsylvania: Pennsylvania Historial and Museum Commission.
5. Tim Saunders (1999) *The High Tide: Collected Poems in Cornish 1974–1999*, London: Francis Boutle Publications, pp.24-5.

11

Welcome to Pardtown . . .

If I was in rock n' roll, I would have written a song about
that drive, and call it *Nightride to Indiana* or something like
that. Guns n' Roses might one day record it, if they
eventually get around to finishing the album they began ten
years ago. We were pushing west on Interstate 90, running
below the picturesque scenery of Lake Erie. You wouldn't
know it though. The road was pitch-black ninety percent of
the time, except for the occasional glaring lights of a scary
Peterbilt truck coming eastwards. Strong coffee was keeping
me wide awake. Dan had some front.

"Are you a'right t'drive?" he kept saying, then instantly
falling back to sleep.

Champi was still in euchre dream-land.

We stopped a couple of times to pee. All that Canadian
ale was now re-emerging out of the two of them. All I can
remember is a lot of groaning and staggering into places
that sold more velvet Elvis posters and resin wolves. I
bought more coffee – going easy on the milk and overdosing
on caffeine. We had to stop either side of Cleveland, though
managed to make it to Toledo in one fell swoop. The name
of this city reminded me of my first car – an ugly cream-
coloured Triumph Toledo, with wooden dashboard and a
rusty wing. I loved that car though. I learnt all Cornwall's
by-ways in it the summer I passed my driving test. And now
here I was putting pedal to the metal on the so-called James
W. Shocknessy Tollway.

Not too far to the north was Detroit. I'd considered a stopover there. Detroit, at one point, had been a very Cornish city, but I'd visited it before, and had already tried to trace any remnants of the Cornish with little success. The automobile industry had been very attractive to the Cornish – apparently large numbers of the Cornish used to gather at Cadillac Square on Saturday evenings, much to the anger of the mainly Irish police-force of the city. Detroit is much changed these days; the last time I was there, the quite run-down city centre undergoing massive urban renewal.

It was either late or early that we got into Indiana. I believe there was a bit of dawn light behind us. I like that time of day. It's very powerful somehow – a time not much of the world sees. By this hour, you aren't tired any more. You're past caring. The car is *you* and *you* are the car. The occasional skunk brought Dan's senses to life briefly – before he went back to sleep some more. We rested for a couple of hours in Indiana. We were right on the Michigan-Indiana border, a few miles east of Elkhart. Were we really in Pennsylvania the previous morning? It seemed a lifetime away. That was America for you. Distances made time expand. We wanted Albert, bagpipes and the *passing* of some *pass*-tee.

As the sun rose more fully, feeling slightly refreshed after a bit of doze, I began the second-stage of the 'Driving Benny' across the State to Illinois. Chicago really begins in the north-east of Indiana these days, with places like Gary (not a good place to stop we gathered from various people), and I had a feeling it would take a hefty chunk of the morning to get across to Chicago itself. Dan – the are-you-a'right-to-drive Puerto Rican co-pilot – found a good rock radio station and we danced up 294 listening to Van Halen, and funnily enough Chicago, all of us mouthing along like old croaners to 'If you leave me now, you'll take away the biggest part of me, ooh ooh . . .'. Simon Cowell of *Pop Idol* would undoubtedly be impressed/unimpressed (delete as appropriate).

The plan was to head up to where I'd stayed before around Woodridge and Downers Grove. I knew Jim wouldn't be around this summer, so I figured we'd find some cheap motel and stay there the night. In the morning we could head into Chicago for the day and Mark and Dan could have a taste of the 'Windy City'. They were giving me a bit of the 'we're country boys' ideology after Washington DC, but I thought they'd like Chicago. It was my kind of city at least. Downers Grove didn't have as good a range of motels as I'd expected. We found a beat-up one, pretty much only a quarter of a star at the most up from the one in Washington, but at least the bedrooms had showers and of course, beds: those large beds that you only ever seem to find in American hotels and motels. The shower was wonderful after the night drive. It felt like Niagara Falls was landing on me' head – all 600,000 gallons per second of it. We went and had a taco (the Mexican pasty) at 'Taco Bell', strolled around 'K-Mart', read and watched television. In the evening Dan and I ordered a pizza and found a liquor store. We bought some Miller Genuine Drafts and flopped in front of the motel room's television watching the Tom Hanks NASA-flick, *Apollo 13*. Sleep came easy that night.

There was some slight anxiety in the morning. Downers Grove is no place to park in. There were signs everywhere saying 'Parking for 2 hours only', 'Don't even think of parking here – especially any Cornish' and 'Stop here for one second and we crush your automobile'. We planned on being gone for most of the day. I asked a few local people and they pointed candidly to the Church car park, like it was an unspoken path to enlightenment. Champi and Dan didn't seem keen.

"You'll be clamped," they said, ever pessimistic.

"I'll pay the fine if we are . . ." I said. "Besides . . . look at the sign."

They looked at the sign. It read The Downers Grove United Methodist Church.

"If they clamp me, I'll tell them I was here researching our ancestors . . ." I joked. By the time we hit the Station I had Champi convinced he was still a Methodist.

"Was' the difference anyway, I mean, between Methodists and the other crowd . . . the Church of England . . . ?"

"How long have you got?"

I thought of a campaign that I knew was happening back home to try a found an independent Church of Cornwall, somewhat like the Church of Wales.

You know my routine for Chicago by now – so I showed Dan and Champi the sights. The only thing different I did was to use the city's free trolley-cars to get about instead of the yellow taxis. These trolley-cars are pretty similar to the ones you find in San Francisco, and so it seemed a good idea to take one of these out to Navy Pier. Navy Pier had been in Chicago for years, but of late, it has been 'done up' to become an adult playground. There are speed-boats, and clubs, and bars, and seagulls, and shops that sell gewgaws. On the Pier we watched America on holiday, dodging a teacher's conference (I have enough of that the rest of the time) and heading into a bar for some excellent, but expensive seafood.

Last year the weather had been scorching hot. My Chicago sunburn had lasted until Christmas. This time it was a little more overcast, with the low cloud making the skyline mysterious and mythical. The skyrise buildings looked like the standing stones at Columcille. Back in the city centre, we stanked around 'Fortnum and Masons' for a bit, feeling a bit like ducks out of water, after a further visit to the 'Shedd Aquarium'. Champi likes his fish (he is the Secretary of the Probus Fishing Club), so he took to that . . . well, like a duck in water. Soon though, it was time to head back, or rather head north-west again (that seemed to be the only direction on our compass). Getting out of Downers Grove was easy enough. Of course, it was Friday rush-hour by now, and everyone and his dog was trying to get out of Chicago alive for the weekend. I say alive because there was some mad driving going on around us. I just tried to stay calm and dreamt of life before being on the road.

"Was there a life before this car?" I asked myself.

It was getting on for half-past eight at night before we landed in Mineral Point. I knew the route now as well as the A30 out of Cornwall: the Northwest Tollway to Rockford, then pick up 90 north to Madison. Jim Jewell, Mineral Point postman and author came to meet us at a garage. Jim is aged fifty-four and of Cornish extraction. I had been corresponding with him for a few years now. His name, for me, is inextricably linked to the modern revival of Cornish identity in America, and he had done much work locally and nationally to raise the profile of Cousins Jacks and

Jennies and their impact on the American economy and its culture. Jim had been out of town last summer, and to be honest, there was not much time to chat at the previous year's Mineral Point Gathering, but he had then given me a copy of his excellent book *Cornish in America: Linden, Wisconsin*, which I'd taken home and read from cover to cover.[1] Since then, I'd wanted to speak to him further about south-west Wisconsin, specifically Linden and Dodgeville, the two Cornish towns that now seem to stand in the shadow of the more famous Mineral Point.

In the gathering darkness, we headed out to the west, on a winding road that headed out to Linden. Jim's address is Sunny Slope, Mineral Point, although in my view, it's nearer to Linden than the former town. There was just enough light to see us pass by a small airfield, and then we turned right into the Jewell's hereditary farmstead. Sunny Slope is an interesting house; it is one of those rather futuristic houses which is built into the hillside, so that earth and grass cover the roof of the property: something like you might expect to see at the Eden Project or the Gaia Centre, near Delabole. We were not staying there, however. Instead, the Jewell family owned a log cabin, which had been Amish-manufactured, and transported to the site of the former Jewell Mine.

We followed a dirt track down from the road by Sunny Slope and then turned into another track that looked less like a track and more like a vague crossing of the field. The moon was starting to come up by now and fireflies dotted the field. This was a magical prelude to what Jim had for us. The road twisted around to the right, then entered the old mine surrounds proper – it looked something like an old pioneer mining camp, but had, in actual fact been worked relatively recently. Across from the mine was our accommodation, looking like something out of *Little House on the Prairie*.

"It's my niece's really," went Jim. "She'd had fun doing it up . . ."

We entered the cabin via the mesh-covered door (to keep out the bugs, wasps and fireflies), which ran onto the enclosed porch. There were rugs and rocking-chairs, pictures of cockerels, Self-Help books and fly-fishing books,

283

antique furniture and kit that you might somehow need in a cabin: oil lamps, blankets, jugs and washing bowls (I was suddenly standing there in a deerskin jacket with an Albert-Jenkin-style handlebar moustache about to boil a pot of coffee and some beans). Champi grabbed the bedroom proper, and Dan decided on the sofa. I was up in the attic section on an inflatable mattress, reached by a set of retractable stairs. The place smelt of wood, varnish and nature, and everything good about America. After the busy urbanity of Chicago we'd now flipped the coin. This was complete isolation and it felt wonderful, as if we were pioneers. There was no telephone. Instead, Jim showed the air-horn, so that just in case anything happened, we might be heard a few miles away.

"I'll leave you to settle in then," said Jim, "and then I'll be down in the morning t'take y'to breakfast."

There was a lot to explore in the cabin. First off, there was the kitchen. It had no sink, so we had to improvise with the bowl. There was a fridge though, and Jim's wife Sarah had kindly prepared a few 'fixings' for us. Champi had found a copy of Mother Theresa's biography while I re-read parts of Cecil Todd and David James' edition of *Ever Westward the Land*, the story of Samuel James and his Cornish family on the trail to Oregon and the Pacific North-West in the years 1842-52.[2] It was like Samuel was sat right next to me in this cabin, and in some ways, it felt very similar to the cottages down in Pendarvis, a few miles away.

The attic was interesting too. From there you could look back to the mine and the Jewell estate, while on the other side Wisconsin went on forever. A few wasps had managed to circumnavigate the security systems, so they were dealt with – *ahem* – firmly. By now it was late. For a while, we all sat on the porch and watched the moon over the lake. Outside there were small mammals in the undergrowth, darting beneath the cabin and across to the old mine tailings. The beers we had left from Chicago were as warm as the night, but it didn't much matter. This was the small piece of Cornish-American heaven we'd been after . . .

In the morning Jim picked us up and we headed into Mineral Point for breakfast. I went for biscuits and gravy, while Dan and Champi had the *Special* – 'links' (which are sausages) with eggs and pancakes. All around us sat men with tractor-company base-ball caps and dungarees. It was obviously a place of some considerable quality. Now completely stuffed, Jim showed us the Cornish area known as Hoare's Hollow, not that far away from the Schmitz resident. Apparently a Cornishman named John Hoare had built a Cornish hedge down there to remind him of home. Not of slate, this one was of weathered sandstone, but nevertheless you could tell the influence, even today, with it re-built. From there we headed down to Pendarvis to take the tour – or rather Dan and Champi did. I actually wanted to head up to the Mineral Point library to do some research. We agreed to meet up for lunch. The Mineral Point library is tucked in behind the Opera House, and is a basement room crammed with the history of south-western Wisconsin. A Cornish language sign pointed to the way in; a nice touch. Jim introduced me to the librarian and I was given leave to search its contents. I found some articles on the Miner's Regiment in the Civil War, and a few poems and stories. I also made photocopies of the original menus and recipes of Pendarvis, when for a while, it was a restaurant. Then I came across a 1956 article titled *The Peoples of Wisconsin: Scripts of the Ethnic History Radio Series, Sounds of Heritage.* Here I found this:

Narrator: Tell me, my Cornish friend, when did you come from England?
Voice: I didn't come from Hengland. I came from Cornwell.[3]

I wudn from Hengland either.

Lunch was at the 'Lawinger's Red Rooster'. I was now a familiar customer there; the menu tickling me as before with its quote from the 1984 *Telegraph Herald* from Dubuque, Iowa – 'Cornish Pasty: rhymes with nasty but it's a tasty pastry'. Hell, in Dubuque, they were almost as good as puns and poetry as the shops in central Pennsylvania. We ordered up some pasties. When they arrived Dan and Champi wudn' too impressed.

"What the hell's that?" went Champi.

He had a point.

Since the last time I'd been in Mineral Point, the pasties had . . . *ahem* . . . altered a fair bit. Either that or proper crimping just hadn't been taught.

"It d'look more like a splat than a pasty," Champi continued, gaking at the mutant monstrosity before him.

It didn't taste bad, but visually at least, this did look more like a pie. It was hard because a group of very friendly people who had trailed around Pendarvis with Mark and Champi, had come specifically up to 'Lawingers' to taste this thing called a pasty. What they got wudn' the real article, we explained – slightly desperate for them to appreciate the true nature of a pasty. Then again, secretly, I was all up for adaptation and interpretation. Maybe this was just the natural direction of the twenty-first century pasty in Mineral Point: from pasty to splatsy.

That afternoon Dan and Champi wanted to get some rest (the pasty crime had upset them something chronic), but I knew this would be my only chance to chat to Jim properly and learn more about his own identity and background. He was taking me to his step-son's bar in Linden – the appropriately named 'Pardtown Pub'. Outside is a pub sign with two rampant griffins clutching a shield with a pick and shovel, a sheath of corn and a glass of foaming beer. It's only a couple of miles away from the cabin, and the cool fans of the bar were well-received after the heat of strolling around that morning. Linden is a town just west of Mineral Point; smaller, but nonetheless just as Cornish. Serious mining first started there in 1833, the Linden Mining Company working the area until the year 1853 producing some 40 million pounds of lead in twenty years. Linden was also the destination of the earlier mentioned Wearne family, who had travelled down from Quebec to Milwaukee, then made their way across southwestern Wisconsin in the fall, having to quickly erect shelter before the vicious winter set in. It must have been a lonely place to have ended up in 1848.

We actually began however with a little bit of abstinence, via a quick tour of the nearby Linden Methodist Episcopal Church, designed by one Thomas Blake, who was originally from London, but must have had some idea of what a Methodist Chapel in Cornwall might look like. It had a

286

beautiful dark wooden balcony and gently curved pews. A semi-circular window let in light from the road-side entrance, while dedicatory stained glass windows shed the sun onto the side seating. In one I found the name Thomas Hicks, in the green bordering glass of a window decorated with arches and ornate swirls. In the Sunday School, it smelt of Cornwall. Even the slight peeling of paint on the window sills and that pervasive air of damp that goes with every chapel I have known since childhood was present. On the wall was a map of Cornwall.

"Who put that there?" I asked.

"Guess who," replied Jim.

We strolled out of the church and looked up and down the main street in Linden. An African-American boy – aged around five – went by, wearing a Celtic T-shirt marked by a four-leafed clover. It was obviously a local basketball or baseball team. The Irish co-habited here with the Cornish. According to local knowledge, the area was once mined at Pedlar's Diggings or Pedlar's Creek, founded by an Irish peddler named Patrick O'Meara, but in 1834 began to be over-run with Cornish miners.[4] For a while, the people of the area submitted Pedlar's Creek to the US Post Office Department as its name, but this was rejected as unacceptable. The name Linden was chosen, submitted and accepted. Two local theories surround this. One suggests that the name was inspired by the Linden trees in the village, while another says that the name was chosen because there was not a single Linden tree there! Either way, for many years Linden was also known locally as 'Pard Town'. This was derived from the old Cornish method of tributing, when miners usually had a partner or 'Pard' who worked with them. No doubt, Pard Town was used to common Cornu-English expressions such as 'How be 'ee doin' Pard?' during this phase. I liked the thought of somewhere being called Pard Town, and wished Linden had adopted its nickname. Still, who was I to argue, a century or more later? Linden intrigued me because it also at one time, had a Linden Business men's baseball team, that was a source of pride for many Cornish-Americans.[5] As well as this, there was a hotel once owned by Hicks (perhaps the Hicks on the stained glass window) and several Cornish businesses owned by names like Tredinnick, Goldsworthy, Pollard, Vivian and Vial. There was also a Cornish miner fight song sung by cheerleaders at Linden High School:

> When you hear the roll of the Linden drum,
> Then you will know that the Cornish have Come,
> For the Cornish company is the best company
> That ever came from the old country.[6]

I liked the sentiment of this song, and it rolled around my head as I drove off from the cabin the next morning. We need more Cornish miner fight songs. Stop bleddy lamenting. Let's just have fight songs . . . I'm sure they would come in handy in places like Butte and . . . ah . . . Bodmin.

We ordered up a couple of dark lagers from the barman – himself a Rule of Cornish extraction – and in between gazing at the pickled pigs' trotters on offer – Jim began to tell me his story. He was born on October 5th 1948, back in Madison, and lived there briefly before his father took over the family farm near Linden. This was the Jewell Farm, although the original family farmstead had once been near the Laxey Cemetery. For the first eight years of his education he attended a one-room country school nearby, and then transferred to Dodgeville's High School, where succeeding in English, he left to join the School of Journalism at the University of Wisconsin in Madison, but then deciding on a change in direction, went off to Southwest Tech to major in Business Administration and Accounting. After five years completing this kind of work in the Post Office, he then quit the job to travel around the country – in particular southern Florida and Key West in 1975.

"It was the start of all the high rise motels down there – and we had some fun," Jim said. "After that, I went partying in New Orleans for a while . . ."

The mid-1970s excess was obviously a time of self-discovery for the growing Jewell.

The following year however, turned out to be an epiphany for Jim about his Cornishness. He'd always been aware of his identity from neighbours and surnames, but the real spark of his creativity and activism came in 1976, the bi-centenary of the founding of the United States. The BBC, who were making a television documentary, had come to Linden to speak to people about the roots of their culture. Although they did not then speak to Jim, there began the inspiration for his journey – when he was aged twenty-seven. Jim began to collect notes and materials for future books on the Cornish in the area, as well as over the rest of the United States. By 1978, he had gone back into journalism, to work firstly for the *Dodgeville Chronicle*, and then later for the *Democrat Tribune* in Mineral Point. This was the ideal position for Jim to be in – the stories and features which emerged in the course of his work gave him a wealth of material to draw upon. In 1980 he met his wife Sarah – of Scots-Irish ancestry from Tennessee – and they married shortly afterwards, one of his step-sons being Eric Griffith, the owner of the pub we sat in.

1982 was also a core year for Jim. It was the first time that he would go back to Cornwall. His parents travelled with him and he first visited Lanhydrock House, Tintagel, Boscastle and Trespareth, near Redruth – the latter the home of the Jewell family.

"I didn't know anyone really," said Jim, "except Harry Tregilgas, of St Austell . . . but somehow I've got to know a lot of people over there."

As we talked around five burly men entered the bar and ordered up a set of beers. They weren't the type of guys you'd want to upset. Nevertheless Jim introduced me to them, knowing much about each of their family history. Nearly all of them had some Cornish in there somewhere. They sat down and began appropriately enough, a noisy game of euchre. I was thinking of course, of the recent match in Niagara Falls and a poem I'd written a couple of years back while sat in Probus Comrades Club:

Shuffled lives come together.
Dealt hope reaches skywards,
as they square up like bottle o' piss . . .[7]

"I quit journalism again in 1985," Jim then continued. "I wanted more time to write what I wanted, so I went back to the post office again . . ."

Jim therefore had been Mineral Point's postman since then; another position which allowed him to get to know further all the histories of the properties and families of the area. Earlier that day, he had been talking about how the Athletic field in Mineral Point had been built on land leased by the Goldsworthys. All this was reminding me of people like the poets James Dryden Hosken (1861–1953) of Helston and Charles Taylor Stephens (1796–1863) of St Ives, who like Jim, had combined writing careers with postal deliveries.[8] Perhaps, I began to think there was a Cornish tradition here.

We went back to our beers again. They were empty. We ordered a couple more.

"Here's something you may not know about me," ventured Jim, smiling. "I was once the Vice President of the Linden Hard-Core Alcoholics – 1975–1980."

"What did that involve?" I asked.

"Well, it was basically a Cornish drinking group," Jim laughed. "I was the co-founder of the Easter Beer hunt. I'd hide beers in the park and then the guys would have to search them out. Then every few weeks we'd get a keg in and have what we'd call a 'chug off' . . . Couldn't do that anymore!"

It was good to hear Jim talk so candidly.

In 1995 Jim was back in Cornwall again; this time to be made a bard of the Cornish Gorseth.

"How did you find that?" I asked.

"It was a humbling experience," Jim replied. "My bardic name is *Yuthel Ystoryer an Howlsedhas* – Historian of the West."

I could think of no more fitting a title for Jim.

"I've got so much more to do," said Jim, "that I don't know if I'll be able to do it all. I'm fascinated with Mineral Point as the 'jumping off' point for America. And you're going to Butte aren't you? Well, there was always a strong connection between Mineral Point and Butte . . ."

Jim had hoped his step-son Eric might have been at the pub, but he was out of town. I regretted not meeting him, because only a few weeks later, when writing this chapter, I learnt that he had been killed. His car had hit a deer. Of course then, Jim and I knew nothing of this. Life sometimes throws you curved balls. I hope Jim and Sarah are able to get through this. After we'd chatted, Jim dropped me back at the cabin, not before showing me more of the old Jewell mine nearby. It somehow seemed very fitting that there was this zinc mine which happened to be on a Cornishman's land. As I mentioned earlier, it had actually been in operation relatively recently – from 1973–1975, with an incline of a quarter of a mile going down to some one hundred and twenty feet. Missouri's *Eagle-Picher* mining conglomerate had worked it for a while, and then in 1980 it was worked again by the *Inspiration Mining Company* of Canada.

"I don't suppose it'll ever be worked again?" I questioned.

Jim shook his head.

"They leased the mine for $100 a year but didn't re-open it, then dropped the lease a couple of years later."

Back in the cabin, everything was very relaxed. Champi and Dan were writing postcards, kicking back and enjoying life on the prairie. The evening saw a brief visit down to the 'Cruise', but we were all so tired that when sleep came, it was most welcome. The cicadas serenaded us into slumber.

On Sunday morning, Jim drove us up to Dodgeville for a proper look around. Now Dodgeville's rivalry with Mineral Point goes back years, since the towns are of similar size and age. Dodgeville's downtown does look a little more stately than Mineral Point, yet traces of its past are all over the place. There is for example, the now silent Dodgeville Furnace, worked, so Jim informed us, by several generations of Cornish. I went through my twelve-steps and managed to prevent myself from exploring it any further. That chimney stack must be at least 56 inches in diameter though . . .

Nearby is so-called Redruth Hollow, now hosting a new drive of the same name, where upwardly-mobile Dodgeville families have chosen to build grand new white-planked and prinked homes. I had to wonder how many knew it was named after a proud Cornish town – instead of some dodgy Dodgeville scarlet woman. We also viewed one of the earliest of Dodgeville's buildings – a Cornish mining cabin, the wood of which had been meticulously preserved by encasing it in a perspex covering. I peered inside the tiny windows, and imagined the conversations inside. The contemporary legacy of all of Dodgeville's past was the nearby 'Wal-Mart'. While Jim bought a new contemporary country and western album by a singer with the surname of Jewell, I looked for Cornish names on the employee's name badges, while dodging the guns and camouflage at the back. I saw a couple – Williams and Jago. Did they know what blood flowed in their veins as they checked out my dollar ninety-nine T-shirts? I had to tell myself to stop lamenting. Let's just have fight songs . . .

Someone who'd fought back at life, and was all the richer for it was Catherine Whitford, who owned a 'The Mineral Point Collection' Gift Shop with a Cornish section ('The Cornish Corner') in downtown Mineral Point. A widow three times, and now aged seventy-four, amazingly Catherine still worked five days a week as an accountant, and then spent her weekends at her store. Needless to say, Catherine was as Cornish as they come and a delight to talk to – and what a life she'd had!

"Did you know you were Cornish – or was this something more recent you discovered?" I asked, when I drove down there in the late morning.

"I've known it all my life," she replied. "My last name's Cornish now, but I was born a Hawke . . ."

Catherine was born in Linden. Most of her Cornishness had been passed down by her great uncle and aunt, John and Jennie Sleeman, who were born and raised in Lewannick. John had worked in china clay mining, and part-time as a farmer, often driving cattle all the way up to Plymouth market. All her childhood, her Cornishness was reinforced by stories, dialect and work around the home.

"I used to ask my Auntie and Uncle if they'd ever want to go back to Cornwall," she said, "but their response was always the same: 'Rocks are awful hard to eat'. I suppose that told me a lot about how hard it was in Cornwall back then . . ."

As a young woman, she married a gentleman named Richard F. Siedl, who was of Austrian-German extraction, in Madison, back in 1948, and they had a daughter, Mary Catherine, who was now aged fifty-three and lived in Phoenix, Arizona. I sensed she longed for Mary to live closer, and wondered about the distance, since it was effectively as far as I would be travelling on this tour.

Sadly, very soon after they were married Richard died, and Catherine was forced to bring up her daughter alone. Catherine's second husband was named Joseph W. Skidmore, who originated from nearby Hendon. A mason by trade, that marriage brought her back home to Linden. He died on January 15th 1978. Her third husband was Dale Whitford, who was half-Norwegian and half-Cornish. Dale died on September 7th 1988. At this, Catherine said to me, "The Good Lord puts on only those who can cope, an' I'm a tad bit like that . . . I've a very Cornish frame of mind, me . . . a survivor."

I remained intrigued at her tenacity and let her continue. The topic changed to the wider fate of the Cornish in America.

"Some of my people left here to go to the Californian gold-rush. But there were lots of letters coming back saying things like 'By no means should you leave Linden to come to California', so my family never went . . . so that's how we ended up here . . ."

It was a beautiful sunny Sunday morning as we sat talking and the light was streaming through the display at the front of the store. Beneath Catherine's desk was Tekler (Cornish: *precious* or *beautiful*) the Dog, a three-and-a-half year old Shih Tzu, who was very pleasant, perhaps because he was wearing a rather fetching black and white neckerchief. Catherine lived upstairs over the shop which had been opened a couple of years back. I asked her about her Celtic knotwork brooch by the St Justin jewellers.

"It symbolises my identity and eternal life," she commented so surely that it made me quietly admire this wonderful woman.

"Have y'eaten yet today?" she asked.

I explained I hadn't.

"Then go over to Lawinger's and get yourself a pasty. I'd come with you, but I need to keep the shop open . . ."

We parted with a hug and I headed over the road for another . . . um . . . splat.

That evening, I was due to give a reading down at the Brewery Creek Pub – marketed as a place with

293

'fresh-brewed beer and old-fashioned comfort food'. The venue was initially going to be at the Opera House, but this was viewed by Jim and the Southwest Wisconsin Cornish Association as a better venue. Champi and Dan agreed, and soon were tasting the various brews available. I wasn't sure how many people would show up, but in the end the place was packed. Marion Schmitz, Nancy Laity and Dorothy Beckwith arrived; Marion from Mineral Point, Nancy from the Quad Cities and Dorothy just down the road from Belmont. I was able to meet up with a number of old friends including Dick and Annette Baker, who had travelled across from their home near to Milwaukee, where they told me I should one day visit, for all the Cornish agricultural heritage there. Even the Mineral Point press showed up in the shape of a lady named Jeannie Lewis, who took a photograph of everyone outside the Brew pub. It was good to get such a reaction a couple of years on from my first reading at the Opera House. As we posed with a St Piran's flag, I realised that in many senses, I was feeling very much at home in this part of America. Time and distance seem to contract inside. A lot of Cornwalls rolled into one that day. Nancy Laity swapped a Celtic Highland games shirt for one of Champi's, and Dan and he showed me the Brewpub glasses they'd negotiated to buy off the owner. Marion and I had a lot of hugs and I began to wish we could stay longer.

"How d'y'think it went?" I asked Jim.

"Fantastic," he replied. "I think the owner was pleased too. He sold a lot of beer."

I looked at Dan and Mark. Much of it had surely gone their way.

But our time in south-western Wisconsin was swiftly drawing to a close. Our journey was due to continue the next day. Back in the cabin, I gazed with considered awe at the distance we had to go the next day. This was Sunday evening. By Monday evening, I had to be in Calumet, in the Upper Peninsula of Michigan, for another reading. We packed for an earlier start. By six a.m. we were running by Madison, this time heading as far north as I'd been so far in the United States. There was somebody I was looking for.

Notes

1. Jim Jewell (1990) *Cornish in America: Linden, Wisconsin*, Linden: Cornish Miner Press.
2. A.C. Todd and David James (eds.) (1986) *Ever Westward the Land, the story of Samuel James and his Cornish family on the trail to Oregon and the Pacific North-West in the years 1842–52*, Exeter: University of Exeter.
3. William J. Scherek (ed.) (1956) *The Peoples of Wisconsin: Scripts of the Ethnic History Radio Series, Sounds of Heritage*. Manuscript held in the Mineral Point Library.
4. Jewell, op.cit., pp.10-11.
5. Ibid., p.128.
6. Ibid., p.116.
7. Alan M. Kent (2002) *Love and Seaweed*, St Austell: Lyonesse Press, pp.58-59.
8. See Alan M. Kent (ed.) (2000) *Voices from West Barbary: An Anthology of Anglo-Cornish Poetry 1549–1928*, London: Francis Boutle, pp.04-98 and pp. 171-185.
9. Kent (2002) op.cit., pp.42-44.

12

In Search of Jack Foster . . .

"The voice is deep and sure and resonant. It commands attention. When he speaks, his skilful pace maximises the dramatic effect. Jack Foster tells jokes in the "Cousin Jack" (Cornish dialect) without wasted words. His tales conjure up historically important images and offer insight. This stuff comes from the heart. "I do it because I love it," says Jack. He is Calumet's master storyteller and a documentary filmmaker's dream . . ."

These words come from a promotional leaflet I have at home about Cousin Jack Foster; a legend who I have wanted to meet for several years. Setting out on the second leg of my travels in Cornish North America, I didn't know if I would find him or not. When Terry, a friend of mine, went to Calumet a few years ago, he was alive then, but aged eighty-four at least. It was Terry who'd given me the leaflet, and he'd met Jack Foster. It seemed to me that Jack was just the man I needed to talk to. Moreover he had everything I was looking for.

To find Jack Foster, that Monday morning, we headed north on Interstate 51 towards Plover and Steven's Point bang in the middle of Wisconsin, then at Merrill, when 51 stopped, we took Route 17 north-east passing Rhinelander and Sugar Camp. This was beautiful country with wide sweeping farmland, interspersed by clear-water rivers. I suppose by lunchtime, we'd made it as far as Land O' Lakes, which is on the Wisconsin-Michigan border, but it had been another hard drive. At least I knew I would make the reading in time. It was however, a bit of a slog through the remainder of the Upper Peninsula part of Michigan. The road cut down to two lanes only, and this slowed us down. Bruce Crossing was always some eternal distance away, like a mirage in the desert. We got there eventually, but not before we'd run out of things to say to each other and before we'd played all the compact discs a zillion times.

All that and we were still in the bottom half of the Peninsula. That's because the Keweenaw Peninsula is split into two halves. The lower half, comprised mainly of the Ottowa National Forest, is separated from the northwestern part of the Peninsula by Portage Lake, to the north of which is the Portage Ship Canal. On the Canal are located the twin towns of Houghton and Hancock, which are near an impressive road bridge. Houghton itself is now the main educational and economic centre for the region, though its past is always present. We found a bronze statue of a copper miner – complete with pasty pail and pick-axe – is featured on all of the tourist literature. High on a bluff above Hancock are the iconoclastic white buildings of the Quincy Mine, which operated from 1848 to 1945. Apparently the Quincy Mine is an engineering marvel. It holds the world's largest steam hoist at No. 2 shaft, which coincidentally is also the deepest in the Western hemisphere. A leaflet gave me loads of 56 Inch Cylinder Syndrome statistics. Weight: 1,765,000 pounds. Dimensions: 60 feet by 54 feet by 60 feet high. Engine: Cross-compound Corliss type, with two 32-inch diameter high pressure cylinders and two 60-inch diameter low pressure cylinders. 66 inch stroke. Was I impressed? Damn right.

Copper Art (est. 1976) was a shop located around one and half miles on from the Quincy Mine. As it was the first real taste of copper culture in the Keweenaw, we decided to pull in. There was beautiful work on display. I particularly liked a copper model of the Quincy Mine – complete with miners, trams and horses – but at a price tag of some three hundred dollars, it wasn't about to be travelling back to Cornwall with me.

I'd read up a bit on the Keweenaw before getting there. Some years ago, I'd obtained the classic work on the region:

Angus Murdoch's *Boom Copper: The Story of the First U.S. Mining Boom*, first published all the way back in 1943. It told me how the first really experienced miners to work the Keweenaw were the Cornish, who apparently were always astounded at the huge chunks of 'native' copper to be found there, since nothing like that could be seen back home. They arrived in the Keweenaw in the late 1840s and early 1850s; Central mine, according to Murdoch, was the main destination, with the Cornish heading for it "like homing pigeons".[1] Murdoch makes much of the Cousin Jack's Cornu-English "crake", so rich was it, that to other English speakers listening it sounded like a foreign language. He was right on the nail there, was boy Murdoch. Hymn-singing was important to the miners of Central, and one of the most famous singers of those early days was a Cornishman by the name Dick Buller. Dick Buller had a mighty bass voice and tales of his superhuman vocal achievements are legendary. As Murdoch notes:

> One Sunday morning when Dick was in especially fine vocal fettle he frightened the sinners at the Phoenix mine, eight miles away, out of their wits. The Phoenix preacher had just concluded a vigorous sermon on the certainty of eternal damnation for beer drinkers and backsliders when Dick commenced the bass solo in that stirring hymn 'Deliverance'. His voice carried the entire eight miles, gaining, if anything, in volume. "'Twas like a multitude singing as one man, coming out of the sky.' The sinners at Phoenix looked each other in the eye, and the superstitious amongst them fell to the floor like dead mean. Some said it must be the judgement day and the angel Gabriel be up on one of the shaft houses singing out a warning."[2]

With all this in mind, I was quite looking forward to seeing Central Mine's Methodist Church. Murdoch even puts Dick Buller's astounding singing down to the Cornish diet. Being so great a singer and talker, was dependent on the humble pasty. Murdoch concludes that 'the copper country owes many of its dividends to the men from the Duchy of Cornwall',[3] the 'Duchy of Cornwall' being the name for this area of the Keweenaw.

Although Murdoch established scholarship on the Keweenaw, his successor is Arthur W. Thurner. His 1994 book *Strangers and Sojourners: A History of Michigan's Keweenaw Peninsula* is the standard academic work on the region. Thurner has lots of interesting observations on the Cornish sojourn on the Peninsula. He begins his study with a look at one of the earliest developments – the Cliff Mine. The first bonanza in the Keweenaw started in the winter of 1845-6 and in 1847 around 120 miners were at work there. Around 70 of these were Cornish. A village grew up around Cliff which had periodic visits from a Clergyman 'to perform Divine services'.[4]

From the evidence, it seems that Cliff became the early jumping off point for the rest of the Cornish arriving in the region. One Cornish family in the region was named Jones and they worked on housekeeping duties for the richer John H. Pitezel. Pitezel was originally a mine labourer, but eventually became the local Methodist District Superintendent. He was said to be displeased with the sloppy housekeeping of the Jones family, as well as their neglect of religious duties. Jones and his family seem to be the exception however, since other Cornish miners were signing up in support of temperance causes.[5] According to Thurner, an observer who visited the mine in 1863 . . .

. . . watched miners placing drills and hammers in buckets, Cornish pasties in their pockets, fuse in other pockets, and descending quickly by ladders some twenty feet, then another descent until finally they reached bottom. They were "singing all the time". It sounded "fine" through the drifts.[6]

This of course, sounds very much like the Cornish. Elsewhere though, the Cornish were not seen as being "fine". In fact, one critical observer named Henry A. Hobart, arriving to work as a schoolmaster at the nearby village of Clifton sometime between 1863 and 1864, found the Cornish "coarse, dirty and rough" and "like hogs in every sense of the word".[7] Hobart's view of Cornish women wudn' much different either:

An old Cornish woman is as tight as the bark to a tree and the perfection of tyranny in her management always boasting about how smart she is and how her hired help and everyone else are good for nothing . . . The children of such a woman are self-conceited, tyrannical, foolish, silly things who are superior to everyone in their own minds.[8]

Ooh, hark at him!
An earlier observer, Wolcott Gibbs found the Cornish "at work, and all, as usual, very sanguine".[9] This sounds very much like Robert Louis Stevenson's view of us. The Cornish however, seem to have confronted Keweenaw with all their usual world-weary wit and dry humour. Apparently one time a group of Cornish miners, who insisted they wanted to only work underground, were walking to work and stopped to observe the place where a man engaged in building a fence on surface had been killed by a rolling log. One of the Cornish said, "Damme, I wouldn't work on the bloody surface. Man killed here building a fence."

Calumet was a great attraction for these miners who lived further up the Peninsula. From places like Clifton, Copper Harbor, Delaware and Copper Falls, Cornish miners would come there to spend their money. According to local history, Calumet was a place only for the young since a sixteen year old Welsh girl noted that "there were no gray heads in Calumet for the first few years".[10] However, the Cornish were perhaps responsible for ensuring well-being in old age since by 1870 it was they who suggested that a hospital should be set up for Calumet and nearby Hecla. We know too that Cornish musicians were present for the dedication of a bell to the patron of miners- Saint Barbara – at Saint Mary's church, .[11]

Here, as elsewhere in my travels throughout Cornish-American communities, the Irish and the Cornish didn't get on well. In the Keweenaw, it seems the Cornish found the Irish too volatile for their softer Celticism. Sometimes the Cornish would not allow the Irish to operate certain machinery. Other ethnic groups were very aware of the Cornish on the Keweenaw. The Finns labelled the *Daily Mining Gazette* as 'the Cousin Jack papers'[12] and the Cornish continued to dominate as management within the mines. It is said that of the seven members who made up the first class to graduate from the Michigan mining school, five were sons of Cornish mining captains.[13] Thurner is perceptive though when it comes to Cornish pride and confidence:

> Finns and other peoples at times bristled in mentioning the Cornish and used the term Cousin Jack derisively. The Cornish coined the term simply to describe the Cornish miner. The Cornish went their own way, nonplussed by what anyone thought. Their confidence is shown in such proverbs as "A miner has nothing to lose" and the miner is "never broke till his neck's broke." Several generations later, about 1937, a Calumet High School youth wrote to a Slovenian classmate, saying initially, "Let a good Cornishman set you, an Austrian, straight."[14]

Right on, Boy!
The Cornish were settin' themselves straight on Keweenaw much earlier though. In 1850, one Jinny Penhale, at the Northwest Mine, which lies between Eagle River and Eagle Harbor, wrote a Cornu-English dialect poem for relatives back home to explain to them how life was *out there*:

> We're livven at the North-West Mine
> And eer we found old Stephen Vine
> And Joey Blewett and lots more
> We war acquainted with before;
> And they were glad to see us too,
> And gov us hall a tastie stew;
> And cooked a oggon and a caake
> And put a pasty in to bake
> And gov us coffee and good tay
> And made us appy right away.[15]

The Cornish continued to celebrate their culture a good while after the main period of mining had finished. In 1934, an advertisement for the Cornish Picnic at Electric Park ran: 'Whether you are from St Austell, Camborne, Mevagissey or [are] a 'Devonshire dumplin' makes no difference, for we are all together on this big Cornish picnic'.[16] Cornish

301

wrasslin' continued to be popular on the Keweenaw for decades. As in Grass Valley, Cornish choirs also dominated. At the Quincy Mine, 1,150 children of the workers enjoyed ice cream, candy, Santa Claus, gifts and carols sung by a twenty-six member Cornish choir.[17] Interestingly, the local Calumet Cornish Club hosted the Rhondda Welsh Male Chorus on October 16th 1924 singing at both the Calumet Methodist Episcopal Church and the Hancock Methodist Church. There must have been some serious inter-Brythonic rivalry that night. Homecomings at Central Mine are still popular, and accompanied by a practice of planting flowers dear to the grandparents, an event initiated in 1907.[18] A joke that Champi, Dan and I liked is also told by Thurner:

> Two Cornish miners, asked by the superintendent not to be discouraged by difficult rock underground and told by him that what they needed was "pride and perseverance to help you," pondered the advice after the superintendent left. One miner asked. "Say Bill, who be they, Pride and Perseverance?" The other replied, "I don't know, Tom – guess they be the two Finns in the next stope."[19]

Two people who would appreciate that joke were Tom and Jean Ellis, a lovely couple who I had known since the 1997 *Keskerdh Kernow / Cornwall Marches On* 500th Anniversary of the 1497 Rebellion.[20] We were going to be staying with them. They'd been in the crowd with me at St Keverne, and we'd struck up a friendship. Tom and Jean are delightful people: genuine and kind, and very committed to their Cornishness. I'd been e-mailing them for a while.

"When are you going to make it up to Eagle Harbor?" their e-mails always ended.

A few weeks earlier I had e-mailed them back: "I'll be there in early August."

When we found their house in Eagle Harbor, for me it was like six years hadn't passed and we were still back on the Lizard watching the crowds at St Keverne. Champi and Dan were introduced and we soon sat down with cold sodas and cake. While Jean was busying herself with tonight's event, we chatted with Tom. The Ellis living room was crammed with Cornish memorabilia and images (To be frank, it was more Cornish than many back home).

Now aged seventy-two – but not looking a year of it – Tom was born in 1931 at Negaunee in the Upper Peninsula and grew up in the shipping port of Marquette; the harbour of Michigan's iron country. After being educated in grade and high school, he enlisted for service in the Korean War, which made me think back to the memorial in Washington DC. He completed a tour of duty as an instructor but didn't service in a combat area. He became a teacher in the methodology of detecting nuclear explosions and tested a good deal of weaponry in the Pacific. Upon being discharged in 1953 he went back to college to study at the Michigan Technological University at Houghton ("Our Camborne School of Mines," Tom quipped). As an undergraduate there he studied Chemical Engineering, then moved to Iowa State University at Ames where he completed a Doctor of Philosophy in Chemical and Nuclear Engineering. He'd completed his Doctorate by June 1965 and so moved back to the Upper Peninsula to lecture at the Technological University. He was by now married to his first wife – Marsha Ruth Gries, but she died when young, leaving him three children to look after in the family cottage at Eagle Harbor. Later he was to meet Jean one day down at the beach – and they soon married.

Tom has always been aware of his Cornishness. Indeed, he thinks it was the reason he went into the career he did. His father's family originated from 12 Foundry Hill, Hayle, and when he was about twenty-five he left Cornwall to work in America, ending up on the Keweenaw.

"My father had that brogue for storytelling," Tom recalled. "You'd have found him fascinating . . ."

His father had travelled over with his young wife – one Annie Gorden, whom he'd met in chapel. Annie's family roots were Scottish, but she was born in Wandsworth. She worked a while in London, but then after gaining the post of scullery maid, became Chief Cook at the *Harvey* Foundries.

"She used to tell me how they used to run their horses in the surf," said Tom.

Tom and Annie were married at St Erth and given a

303

wedding gift from her uncle – an artisan, who had helped to construct Trafalgar Square. The gift was two Second Class passages to America. They boarded ship at Southampton and disembarked in Montreal in Canada.

"The story runs like this," continued Tom. "They entered the USA along the St Lawrence river, going in through Detroit like thousands of others. Then they headed west and got to Chicago to meet a man named Henry Paull – my father's uncle, but Henry had moved up to the Iron Country, where he was working as a miner. So that's how the family ended up here. Helleva story, ain't it? So Uncle Henry went to work the Prince of Wales Mine, and father went to work there underground too."

That evening came my reading at the *Keweenaw Heritage Center*. This centre is found in the former church of St Anne's on the corner of Scott and Fifth Street. It is an excellent conversion of an imposing Gothic Revival church, built originally in 1900 to serve a growing French-Canadian Catholic population. A good-sized audience had turned out to hear me read my work. Such readings are very gratifying for me as a writer because people are so often genuinely moved. In particular the audience liked some of the Cornish language I read as well as the Cornu-English dialect.

Jean had prepared an excellent buffet for those attending. As well as this, I was able to catch up with some faces I'd met at previous Gatherings – among them Phil and Jan Medlyn – whom I'd be seeing again tomorrow. A lot of people there said how Jack Foster would loved to have met me. Although many of the people present were retired, it was gratifying to see some younger women become in-volved, such as thirty-two year old Antonia Burich of Houghton County. Antonia had an interesting heritage. Her father's mother was Slovenian, whereas her mother's father was Cornish. Educated to High School Diploma level, Antonia has four brothers, one sister and one foster sister. I asked her how she felt about her ethnicity in contemporary America.

"I have no feeling about it. I just accept who I am," she answered. "I don't know much about contemporary or historical Cornwall, but I just try to look at how times have been and how they are now, along with how they're changing . . ."

Antonia is the Treasurer of the Keweenaw Kerneweks. We talked about what it was like to live on the Keweenaw.

"I love living in the U.P. That's why I have never moved. I would not want to live anywhere else in the world that I know about . . . To me, this is Heaven – Home – no matter what heritage I am . . ."

This was a very thoughtful statement I felt; and perhaps reflective of not only here Cornish background, but her Slovenian one too. This Cornish-American thing is much more complicated than most people think. It was a delight to talk to Antonia. Her wish, like so many, is to one day make it over to actually see Cornwall. That sounds so obvious, but it is important to note.

As we chatted I viewed the interior of the Center. It had been beautifully restored with the repair of the stained glass windows and ceiling, as well as a revamped wooden floor and stunning stained glass artwork depicting the mining landscape of the region. On at that time, was an exhibition devoted to the construction of wooden-framed buildings which so dominated early Calumet.

A lot of this restoration and the development of such exhibitions had been completed through Jean's energy and commitment. She has a very interesting life. Jean was born in Laurium in Michigan in 1941, and attended Calumet High School and both Michigan State University and the University of Michigan, gaining a Bachelor of Arts in Secondary Education and later a Master of Arts degree in Classical Studies. Primarily a teacher and lecturer through most of her working life, she has taught Latin, French and English. Her parents were Ralph and Marion Medlyn. Ralph's father was one William Medlyn whose parents – John (born in Biscovey) and Elizabeth Hotten (born in Newlyn East) met in New Jersey. Her mother's parents were James and Elsie Davey who had origins in Liskeard and St Austell. Most of her family lived and died in the Calumet area and many are buried in the Lake View Cemetery. On the way back, Jean told me more her Cornish-American experience. I wanted to know more about her background. As you might expect, Jean is a lucid and consummate speaker:

"First, as a child, I loved to listen to my grandmothers talk about their roots. I grew up eating pasties, saffron, and when my dad would share it, scalded cream. My mother's mother sometimes shared Cousin Jack and Jenny stories as did my dad. In my high school days, many of my close friends were of Cornish descent. It's interesting to me that there seems for be some kind of subliminal recognition among those with Cornish roots."

"Why are your Cornish roots so important?" I asked her, as we passed an inn called 'Patrick's Pub and Pasty' – obviously one place where the Irish and the Cornish did get on.

"To a person who was intensely interested in the ancient Romans, it seems important that we know our past and honour it. I sincerely believe that George Santayana knew what he was talking about when he proclaimed that those who do not study the past are condemned to repeat its mistakes. Discovering Cornish roots has been an interesting process. I've learned a lot by doing so."

As we made the turning for Eagle Harbor, I reminded her about the 1997 March and Cornwall's on-going fight for political devolution. Unlike many Cornish-Americans, who are not very interested in this, Jean offered important insight as to why it is so important.

"As for devolution of Cornwall, it seems important to preserve and protect both the culture and all of its ramifications. Recognition of the Cornish language is important; so is protection of the dialect. Identity is a precious thing that is extremely fragile. We should do what we can to honour it and to respect our own as well as that of other ethnic groups. I'm convinced that even the Holocaust and the genocide of Native Americans would have been avoided had we recognised that no one should be regarded as primarily a representative of a group and that every person should be regarded as valuable."

Jean and Tom had two children – David and Keri – who were born in 1970 and 1973 respectively. David is now a sports broadcaster, employed by Michigan State University and Keri is an attorney.

"How do they feel about their Cornishness?" I asked.

"Well, David's not here . . . but you can ask Keri, because she's back in Eagle Harbor for the summer . . ."

306

Danny and Champi were staying in a small cabin round the back of Keri's house. The Ellis family often used it to house guests. I meanwhile was in the downstairs bedroom at Tom and Jean's house. Even though I had loved the cabin near Linden, this was more luxurious, with hot water showers and a very comfy bed. We headed out to the Eagle Harbor Inn for a beverage or two before hitting the sack. Very quickly, word went around that there were some strange-looking Cornishmen in town.

Eagle Harbor itself I can only describe as looking like a set from an Australian soap opera. The bay is perfection. On the north side of the harbour is an American picture book white and brown-painted lighthouse, which marks rock and the entrance to the harbour, then a wide sweep of child-friendly sand makes it way along the western side, meeting the ring road around the harbour. A small row of houses follow the road to the yachting facilities. The town itself only stretches a few blocks to the west, petering out in a park and basketball court. A community building which houses the council, fire station and meeting hall, lies about half-way between Keri's house, and the Eagle Harbor Inn. There had been promises made of some fishing and a ride on a Harley-Davidson, which Dan and Champi were keen to do, but Jean and Tom had organised a tour of the Copper Mining region for me, including a look at the massive Cornish township around the once huge Central Mine.

My guidance around it would be completed by Phil Medlyn. Phil was the same age as Tom. I'd known him since the Gathering in Mineral Point and enjoyed his company immensely. That day he looked very dapper in a yellow shirt and grey trousers. There was virtually nothing he didn't know about the Cornish and mining in the local vicinity. The great thing about Phil was that he wasn't all 56 Inch Cylinder Syndrome-ish. He was more interested in the people and the culture, rather than the size of the pumps and shafts. Phil lived only a few minutes walk away from Tom and Jean so we headed there first. In fact, Phil and Jan Medlyn lived in this summer house from May to October every year. The back of their property looked right over Lake Superior. It was the kind of dream cottage that one only normally tends to see in films. They showed me the back. You could virtually sit on the kitchen table and dangle your legs into the blue. Right now it looked heavenly, but other times of the years were not so idyllic – or so I gathered.

"It's too darn cold to be up here in the winter," offered Jan, pointing at Tom and Jean Ellis, "though these two are mad enough to stay through . . ."

Sometimes, ice from the Lake would literally attack the house.

Phil and Jan's house had fascinating things all over its walls: fishing equipment, nautical navigation maps, and photographs of Eagle Harbor from 1895.

Out we four went into the bright August sunshine. We were riding in a Chevrolet S10 four wheeler, which was effectively a small truck, but accommodated for comfort. It looked the perfect bit of kit to have 56 Inch Cylinder Syndrome in. The trailer part was just built for lugging around bits of metal. Tom swung Jean, Phil and me back around the tight corner, passing the yellow *Daily Mining Gazetter* delivery boxes, a forever-shut shop selling Agates and Gems, and drove along the road which followed the isthmus across the bay. We soon climbed into the mountains, passing the satellite station where television and most other communications were beamed to Eagle Harbor. You have to remember: this end of the Keweenaw is very remote.

We must have travelled five miles or so, before Tom pulled over the Chevy and pointed up to a track, that ran down from the top of the hill, through the third or fourth growth Aspen and Brich trees and headed down to the shore of Superior.

"That's Petherick Hill," he informed me, coming down from the copper mines. "Plenty of Cornishmen and women have walked up and down there."

No sign existed, but Jean and Phil concurred that everyone locally knew it as that. It was strange to see Cornish jiggling about amongst the other Native American names – such as Keweenaw itself. Nearby was Copper Falls, where once there had been located a Stamping Mill. The whole area was known as Brockway Mountain Drive – part of what was known locally as the Copper Falls Loop. Further down the valley was the Blight Fuse Factory – which produced all the fuses for Central Mine, but I'd be seeing that another day. All around Copper Falls were maple trees and patches of red thimbleberries. Down by the shore, rows of properties sold and made thimbleberry jam. It was a local delicacy. I'd tried some for breakfast that morning.

"Some people like the jam itself," commented Jean, "and others like the jelly . . ."

I had tried both – and found myself liking the jelly more. It was more smooth somehow, with no seeds to get stuck between your teeth. Jean and her daughter Keri had seemed to be making vats of it the day before and bottles of every size and description held red jam.

"It's easy to make," Jean continued. "One part sugar, one part berry."

I imagined the Cornish making good use of the berries – the Keweenaw not having quite the proliferation of black-berries as back home.

Between the thimbleberries and aspen trees, poked wild blueberries. These too, got made into jam. Up here, people really followed the course of the seasons; not surprising since all that jam needed to be made for the winter, and to quote, Newton G. Thomas, at least when 'the long winter ends'[21] there'd be more berries on the way. This seasonality I later learned, was very important to the Ellis family – something it seems to me, we've just about lost elsewhere on the planet. I was thinking about this as Tom and Jean discussed directions. She nudged me.

"See that . . . typical Cornish. I always say that about them . . . We're exactly like the St Piran's flag . . . never see any grey."

This statement of Jean's has stayed with me for a while, and the more I think about it, the more I think she's right. We need more fighting songs . . . oh, and a little more . . . um . . . grey.

The location of Central Mine was some 1300 feet above sea level. Primarily a fissure mine, it opened in 1855, and produced a record amount of copper in its first twelve months. Before it closed in 1898, it would produce some 51, 875, 507 pounds of copper and the company would pay $2,130,000 dividends on a capital investment of only $100,000.[22] That's some profit by anyone's standards.

Central in fact yielded 14 million pounds more than the Cliff Mine, which in itself had been very successful. Dotted around the Keweenaw are several pictures of Central Mine, and you can see what a vast urban centre it once was. There is a famous photograph of the area in the year 1896, with rows and rows of houses, stacks emitting steam and chemical emissions, piles of waste rock, thousands of miners returning from underground. Because Central was a fissure mine, the dip ran at 85 degrees, which meant that the stopes and raises were very steep. Coupled with this, the vein was only two foot deep, so this made all the stopes very narrow. Central was therefore famous for its winzes, I was told. Primarily they were put in for ventilation, but they were also dug for exploratory purposes and to come alongide masses of rock where large charges of powder were used to blow the mass from the stope.

I thought about this as we travelled into Central's reaches. Everything was very still, compared to the way it had once been. All that was left now were a collection of houses – preserved by the Keweenaw County Historical Society, but you could sense the ghost of the old town all around. We passed the mine doctor's house and the second captain's home, and looked briefly at a building that seemed on its very last legs – about to be renovated. Phil had a key and showed me the inside. The place still had what appeared to be nineteenth-century wallpaper on its walls. Still surviving was a wooden sink, and in the middle of the living room, stood an old stove. I heard the voices of hundreds of Cornishmen and women who'd walked through that front door.

Up the road one of the preserved houses had been converted into a visitor centre. On one wall was a panorama of Central Mine in its heyday. Outside now were endless trees, but back then it appeared to be a thriving metropolis.

"Over there is Boiler House No. 3 Incline Shaft . . . and that's the Stamp Mill," Phil spoke softly – as if in the presence of things of awesome significance. "That's No. 2 Shaft's rock shed. That one's something like a 3000 feet vertical . . ."

I peered at the incredible construction and investment

before me. No wonder so many Cornish wanted to end up here. Other arrows on the photograph pointed to the wing of the Drying Houses, the offices of the various Captains, blacksmith's shops, the Company Boarding House and the horse barns.

"How did the copper get here?" I asked, having a relapse into 56 Inch Cylinder Syndrome.

Phil obviously picked up on my need and began talking about the Canadian Shield, the Penokean Mountains and inclined Lava flows.

"You know he's a geologist, don't you?" winked Tom.

After I just about understood how the copper was made here, I viewed some of the items which helped to take it out. There were sticking tommies and clay thumbs for candles as well as sunshine lamps – burning either lard or hard oil. Then pictures of double-jacking and a beautiful photograph of Central School. Then there was the Central Silver Coronet Band, who looked like they'd just got back from Bugle. Besides them was a poster advertising the 'CALITHUMPIANS'. This apparently was the name of Central's games and sports day.

"They had wrasslin'" said Phil, "And the phrase 'He's a real stickler about that' survives round here . . ."

Tucked away in one corner I noted down a poem by one Laurie Leskinen, a former president of the Keweenaw County Historical Society who died in the mid-1980s. It was titled 'Old Central' and seemed very apt considering what had once been there:

Times past, these ruins grim and gray
Looked, too, on manhood, robust, gay,
Echoed to ringing teamsters cry,
Heard boots of miners hurry by
Now their bulk looms stranger and still
Silence envelopes deserted hill
The host has gone, these sentinels stay
In memoriam to a bygone day.[23]

Better than that though was a little poster advertising something called 'Ten Nights in a Bar-Room'. Now in many ways this sort of seemed appropriate for my travels

311

this summer, but actually it was marketed as a 'popular and reputable temperance drama' which in reality didn't sound up my street at all. Still I liked the narrative, which obviously appealed to the average Cornish-American in 1885. Indeed much of it sounded like the plot of a middle period Silas K. Hocking novel:

> T.S. Arthur's play tells the story of Joe Morgan, a likeable but weak-willed man who frequented a saloon run by the hard-hearted money-grabbing Simon Slade. Gradually Joe became addicted to alcohol and lost whatever will he once possessed. Devoid of all ambition he became increasingly irresponsible and spent all his time in the bar where his daughter Mary came to beg him to return home. One day poor Mary was struck in the head by a beer mug thrown at her father by Slade. Poor Mary died. Within a few days, Joe died as well, a victim of delirium tremens. Joe's wife was left a widow, childless and impoverished.

As you can see, a happy little tale, as were some of the poems written about mining disasters at Central. I've quite an interest in this genre of poetry, having collated a few in my *Voices from West Barbary* collection of Anglo-Cornish poetry a few years back. It was good to see that the 'Cornish disaster poem' had also began to express American events, with its rudimentary rhythm and rhyme still intact. One records 'the fearful (let me tell you, they are always fearful – a good word, that, – fearful) accident which occurred at the Central Mine, on Lake Superior, on the 22nd of April, 1872; by which ten miners lost their lives – eight from Cornwall and two from Devonshire':

> From Callington was Jacob Grey; –
> And William Barritt too;
> John Ivery from Camborne came they say,
> Edward Thomas from Marketjew.
>
> The names of those who were sav'd in the skip
> All three from Cornwall came.
> And one of them was a Gwinear chap,
> And Edward Trezise was his name.

John Pearce from Crowan known full well,
John Rowe from Camborne town.
And these were spar'd alive to tell
Of their comrades stricken down.

Four families at Lake Superior live,
With husbands and fathers gone;
Without some friends their wants relieve,
How sad in that land alone.[24]

The literary connections were still foremost in my mind, when after the Central Mine Visitor Centre, we turned back on ourselves and headed north to the grand old house of Duffy Liddicoat, aged seventy-seven. Duffy was sitting outside on the porch in a rocking chair, gently swaying in the August heat. Clad in a white top, she looked like an angel, but an angel drinking iced tea and enjoying a biscuit or two. The chair looked as venerable as she did. By the porch supports were collections of pebbles, and next to the iced teas sat a fern and some books. I was introduced to her and it felt like I'd known her all my life.

"My family was from Land's End . . ." she said clearly.

I couldn't help but think of the famous Cornish folktale of one Duffy and the Devil, recorded by that nineteenth-century hero of mine, William Bottrell.[25] Much of it was set at Castle Treen.

"Anywhere near Porthcurno?" I asked.

"Is that where the theatre is on the cliffs?" she asked.

"Yes," I said. "That's it . . ."

Duffy lived in the old Central Mine Post and Pay Office. In her hallway was a window, through which the miners received their wages. Duffy told me lots of stories about her time living at Central, and what the place used to be like. She and Phil swapped stories, but times were intermingling, and it was hard to pick out the when and where. Instead, I looked at the superb samples of float copper she kept before her grate. After we'd downed some more iced tea, Duffy entreated me to walk over to the Clerk's House. This house had barely been altered since the mine was in operation, and it really felt like stepping back in time. Obviously the Mine Clerk was a man of considerable means, and his property was richly furnished. Duffy told me the story of a famous elopement that once took place here.

"The Clerk's daughter was called Edith . . . and back in those days . . . well, you married your own. But she didn't. She fell in love with a miner – he was probably Cornish – and they ran off to Calumet on the back of a truck . . ."

We parted later that morning after she told me a few more tales about Central, which had I the time and space I'd tell you here.

"Make sure you send me that 'Duffy and the Devil' story," Duffy shouted after me.

"Don't worry. I will," I shouted back.

Our next stop was Central Mine Methodist Church, which now stands isolated and alone, but once was the centre point of the mine community here. The sun was high in the sky now, as I peered up at the wooden framed castellated tower, which I was told was built this way to remind the Cornish of their own churches back home. It was constructed in 1868 and became occupied the following year. The tower though, was perhaps the only thing unusual about it, since inside I could have been standing in any small Methodist Chapel from Bude to St Just-in-Penwith. Three rectangular windows on each side shed light onto plain benches. A carpet ran up the aisle to the end of the building to where the minister spoke. Huge chandelier lights hung down from the ceiling, which at some point must have been converted from oil to electricity. Everywhere was the serene smell of Methodism; the faint echo of Dick Buller's voice. It really was a wonderful testament to Cornish activity in America. According to R. Charles Stetter, the local historian of the church, it was built because the miners "needed a 'passionate gospel' to sustain them in their loneliness, and their need to adjust to life in a strange and different land".[26] I liked this idea of a 'passionate gospel'. It seemed to suit the Cornish so well.

Apparently, at Christmas, some local character would dress up and be lowered from the hatch in the ceiling into the congregation below. He would then distribute presents to the children on Christmas Day. A nice touch. Then there was the church bell, which originally summoned the faithful to worship for many years. After the mine closed in 1898, the bell was moved to the nearby church of Mohawk, I century later, local people and historians campaigned for it to be returned. However, this was not possible, so instead the former bell of the schoolhouse in Clifton was obtained and on the one hundreth anniversary of the building of the Central Church, it was installed into the original tower. Sunday school was an important social process at Central, encouraging literacy and reading and funding Christmas presents for the children. It was this culture which gave impetus for the now long-established 'homecoming' events which take place every year. Funny how back home, all the smaller chapels seem to be closing, while here, they'd managed to sustain longevity.

Phil, Jean and Tom wanted to take me high up on Brockway Mountain so I could see the whole peninsula. On the way up, Phil and Tom told some good Cousin Jack stories. Tom went first:

"This is a true story. There was a Cousin Jack who went by the name of Alfie Elliot. He was a handyman who rented out boats on Lake Mosquito. That's a real lake, mind – just over the way there. Jean's father used to rent boats off him – but only the beat-up unpainted ones. One day Mrs Elliot came down to the shore, and sat right on one of the freshly painted boats.

So Jean's father piped up, "Alfie, your wife is sittin' on one of the boats . . ."

"Er is," said Alfie.

"Alfie, you knaw the paint's wet dun't 'ee?"

"'Ess," said Alfie. "'Er'll knaw of it when she gets up . . ."

Phil followed this with:

"A Cousin Jack goin' down Petherick Hill met another one comin' up. The first Cousin Jack said to the second one, "Why are you walkin' s'fast? Where 'ee goin'?"

"I'm goin' over the doctor," said the second Cousin Jack.

"What fur?"

"'Tidn fur me. 'Tis fur me wife . . . I dun't like the look of 'er."

The first Cousin Jack stood thoughtfully for a while.

"I'll tell 'ee what. I'll join 'ee. I dun't like the look of mine either . . ."

Tom replied with another quickie:

"There were two Cousin Jacks goin' home from a shift, driving along in a car, when suddenly the car caught fire. Quickly they both got out, one out the front and one out the back.

"Here," said one of them to the other. "Let 'er blaze up a bit. I caan't see what I'm doin' . . ."

This was greeted by much groaning in the truck.

"Can you imagine those poor buggers when they arrived here in the middle of winter?" said Jean. "Back home they could grow palm trees in their gardens . . . and then they end up here."

I had already noted a massive snow-gauge on the way in to Eagle Harbor on Highway 41. It graphically depicts the record snowfall of 1978–9 which was 390.4 inches – thirty-two and a half feet. That's as high as most of the trees.

All the discussion about snow and winter in the Keweenaw got me thinking again about one of the finest Cornish-themed novels I know – Newton G. Thomas' *The Long Winter Ends*, which first emerged in 1941.[27] Thomas was born in Stoke Climsland, Cornwall, in 1878 and emigrated to the Upper Peninsula as a child. He came to know the ways of the Cousin Jacks intimately, and the novel tells the story of a year in the life a young emigrant miner, Jim Holman, who leaves Cornwall to work in the copper mines. He spends his first year living in a very typical boarding house with other Cornish miners. If you haven't read this novel, do so. What is amazing about it is Thomas's accuracy, not only in his depiction of Cornu-English speech patterns ("'Ow many years do a take t'do that – wash out a brogue, I mean?"), but also the first-hand knowledge of the ways of working underground ("That Corner hole was short. Us 'ave t'drill a pop in that nuck an' blaw un aout afore us can stand the leg."). The book isn't sentimental either: Jim Holman knows that his future lies in America. This novel was being unravelled before me on the Keweenaw. When I returned home, I read the novel with a renewed insight into Thomas's narrative. Of course, everyone connected with the Cornish in Upper Peninsula knows of it, and proudly claims its heritage. It was fun to talk to

Jean, Tom and Phil about the characters and how real they now seemed.

We ploughed on through tunnels of hardwoods to the Delaware Mine by late morning. Phil, Jean and Tom knew it well, so let me enter for a bit of a look around. Delaware's main period of production was between 1847 and 1887. Some eight million pounds of copper were removed from the five shafts that reached a depth of 1,400 feet with 10 levels. The site somehow reminded me again of the 'Poldark Mine' at Wendron, but was perhaps far more authentic, since when it closed, the mine was left untouched – virtually in mothballs. Outside you could see the pure veins of copper exposed in the walls of rock. Lots of visitors seemed to enjoy exploring the catacombs of passageways and excavations.

In the warm morning sun, Tom then pushed on all the way to the tip of the Peninsula and Copper Harbor itself. To me, this seemed a mythic place, always spoken of by the Cornish back home, and written about in history books. These days, it's something of a tourist hotspot, and that August day, was perhaps at the height of the season. Although there was not the time for a full tour, I had a quick nose at Fort Wilkins. This stockaded installation was constructed in 1844 to maintain the peace between the Native population and the incoming miners.

"You know actually," said Phil, "this was the only fort ever built to protect the Indian from the white man . . ."

In the grounds you can see log cabins, duplex-type dwellings occupied by married soldiers and square block ammunition buildings. Carriages and old canons litter the parade ground, though Phil told me that despite there being two companies of infantry present, no battles were ever actually fought there.

"This was important," noted Tom, "because in the early days of mining, the only land leases that were granted came from the war department."

We took lunch in a small restaurant named 'The Pines' wedged in between agate and fishing shops and talked over the landscape and people of the Peninsula. Winter was very much still the discussion point – how much of the population disappears. Either that or they hibernate. Tom and Jean were one of the few families these days who decided not to head south for the winter. I could see why most people did decide upon an annual migration.

After lunch, we took the beautiful but lonesome nine mile drive up to Brockway Mountain. Along this route, you catch spectacular views of Lake Superior and the surrounding panorama: forest upon forest upon forest. Already a few of the trees were starting to change colour – and I could imagine how incredible fall here must look. In the distance was Lake Bailey – shimmering in the afternoon sun. At the top of Brockway Mountain Drive was a small giftshop which we entered to buy more camera film. Then we walked around the edge of the mountain top, which in the west, fell to a steep chasm, but in the east sloped gently toward Superior. Phil came with me, pointing out small flakes of copper in the dirt track at the top.

In the late afternoon, Jean had planned for us all to have pasties from one of the shops in Calumet. The drive there and back would take an hour, so Tom suggested we went off to visit a tiny graveyard related to the Cliff Mine to be found deep in the forest. I was hoping that this graveyard might be the one that the Cornish poet and novelist D.M. Thomas mentions in his poem *A Cornish Graveyard at Keweenaw* (*"Harriet Uren*, 100, eighty years from Penzance, Died with the scent of saffron in the cloam"[28]) but I don't think so. It may well have been impossible to have found the exact site he had visited, because for one thing, there are so many Cornish cemeteries on the Keweenaw. The one we were going to see, however, was special, since according to Tom, it was very early, since several of the grave markers were wooden. Jean dropped us at the junction and we headed into the forest below a large cliff which sloped out towards Superior – hence Cliff Mine.

Picking our way through the forest, we eventually came to the site. Trees had long since grown through the white picket fence, but it was fascinating to see this Cornish spot. I took many photographs, though writing now, it is hard to pick out the names from the images. One was in memory of Elizabeth Jennings; another of the Thomas family – both obviously Cornish. Another, made of wood and so ancient that the white painted lettering had long worn away had been pushed to one side by a tree that had grown past it. Below and beneath were Cornish men and women whose fate it was to end up here. The combination of the still forest, the sticky heat and the knowledge that this tiny place had lasted all those years made it all overwhelming.

"I knew you'd like it here," said Tom smiling.

There was time before the evening meal to find out what Dan and Champi had been doing. They'd spent a lot of the day on the beach at Eagle Harbor, hanging out with Tom Ellis Jr and spending time in the Eagle Harbor Inn. Apparently Champi had been having fun. He'd been having a coffee in the beach cafe when a rather large American lady shrieked, "Oh my God – it's Robin Williams, the actor, isn't it?" She had flung herself at Champi exclaiming, "I loved you in *Mrs Doubtfire!*" Champi was quick to deny his new-found stardom but she insisted on it. So now we mused, we had Ricardo Tregaskis and Robin Williams on board.

One of the other characters they met, and to whom I was introduced, was Mike Braman, a friend of Tom Ellis Jr. Mike was aged forty-four and quite a local character. He ran the town dump and recycling centre and as well as being the town's sexton, he made money mowing lawns. Mike was a rocker (a member of the Kiss and Aerosmith fan clubs), and had long, straggly greying hair usually tied in a ponytail. He'd freely admitted he'd done just about every type of drug going, and was keen for us to see his Harley-Davidson Panhead built in 1963.

"Every year, I run this baby up to the strip clubs in Canada," he said proudly, wheeling the massive motorcycle out of his garage.

I noted three stickers on the bike. One read 'Grateful Dead', so my suspicions were confirmed: he was a definite 'Deadhead'. Another said 'POW Action' reminding me of our time at the Reflecting Pool in Washington DC. Finally on the rear pannier was his favourite: 'Dip me in honey, and feed me to the lesbians'. You cudn' help but laugh. After taking some snaps of all of us sat proudly on his limited edition Harley, he invited us into his house to see his collection of rock show ticket stubs – framed apparently for prosperity.

"Sorry about the mess guys," he said. "I don't get much time for cleaning . . ."

He was right. Bits of motorbike bobbed along with copies of the *Daily Mining Gazette*, next to Led Zeppelin albums and strange collections of minerals and Indian arrowheads. It was like the Royal Cornwall Museum, but better. You could tell that Mike was one of those who stayed in Eagle Harbor during the winter.

"Going south's for whimps," he said.

Later it transpired that Mike had lived an interesting life. He was brought up a Christian Scientist down in Indiana, and worked for much of his early life there in local factories. I tried to get a potted history of Christian Scientist living from Mike. I didn't know much about it, only that such people don't believe in using contemporary doctors or medicines. Cures – even for very serious illnesses – are sought through prayer.

"It was kinda tough," said Mike. "You know that's why I rejected it in the end . . ."

What was even more fascinating was that Mike's maternal grandfather was Cornish. He was a Bennetts, who had originally come from Cornwall and worked at Central Mine. I wondered if the Bennetts family were the same ones mentioned by Arthur W. Thurner. He tells a story how one Christmas at the Methodist Church at Central one R. Bennetts received a pocket knife, while he recalled that his father once rented a four-seater canopy-top wagon in order to drive to Fort Wilkins, where they slept on the floor of the deserted barracks after playing all day.[29] Another distant relative of Mike must have been John R. Bennetts, who recalled that his grandmother, left father, mother and six sisters back in Cornwall, knowing that she would never see them again.[30] Either way, somehow Eagle Harbor suited Mike and Mike suited Eagle Harbor. One day, I'll go back, share more beers with him, and hear more of his stories. Sometimes I see him at the Eagle Harbor Inn and wish I was there with him, talking about bikes and rock n' roll.

That evening, after the pasties and delicious blueberry pie, the three of us went 4x4ing in the forest above Eagle Harbor. I was still laughing at Jean's jokes over dinner: "Now you all know that the interaction of saffron and

320

testosterone leads to brain damage" and "I am convinced that to be Cornish and male is a handicapping condition". I'd never done 4x4ing before – certainly not in this kind of landscape, where the roads – well, were more like logging tracks than roads proper.

Our driver was Keri L. Ellis – Jean and Tom's daughter. She was born in 1973 and was currently working in the U.S. District Trial Court in Chicago, as a Law Clerk. What surprised and interested Keri, was that here were some younger Cornishmen whose identity was integral to who they were. Previously, she had thought most of the Cornish energy in her family had come via her parents – and that generally had been contact with elderly people – members of the Cornish Gorseth, and other Cornish associations across a America. As we spun around tree trunks and lumps of copper bearing rocks, she talked to me.

"I mean I remember when I was a kid being conscious of it. For my 4th of July costume – the theme was *It's a Small World*, and I dressed up as a Cornish bal-maiden . . . and then when I was six or seven, I did ice-skating. Before skating every girl dressed up in their ethnic colors – so I wore black and white, and carried a pasty . . . Can you believe that? Then there were these Cornish dance events in Milwaukee . . ."

Keri, I was to learn, was a very bright, witty and intelligent woman, clearly in charge of her life and destiny. Although now renting an apartment in downtown Chicago on East Wacker Drive (near the Wrigley Building), she came back home to Eagle Harbor every summer and for Christmas.

"I mean I knew I wasn't Finnish," she continued, "and that's important. Mum used to do all the Cornish food – making pasties, saffron bread."

"Do you consider yourself a Celt?" I asked.

"Yeah – definitely. I mean I even know a bit of Cornish: *Dydh da*. There y'go. That's Cornish isn't it?"

I nodded.

"When I was sixteen, I went to London, studying for a summer at Middlesex Polytechnic. I mean that was my first trip back to the 'old country' right? and I caught the train from Paddington, down to Hayle – because that's where my grandfather was from. So there I am wandering up and down Foundry Hill. I mean I went all that way without even knowing the number of the house or anything, but it was still good to actually be there. I went back the same day . . ."

Tom and Jean had told us that Keri had purchased an area of land near to Eagle Harbor so that the landscape would be preserved for nature.

"Yeah – it cost me a lot, but if I hadn't bought it, someone would have come in and developed it. This way it can just carry on being what it is . . ."

Clearly Keri was very proud of her Cornish heritage, as well as that of the Keweenaw. Even though she had a high pressure career in the city, it was still important for her to come home and make heaps of thimbleberry jam like generations of women had done on the Peninsula. I didn't know too many Cornish-American women like her. All this seemed to hammer home as the Jeep came to a halt and we walked out to the edge of the mountain. From there you could see much of the peninsula, and a long way out onto Lake Superior. The view was breath-taking, and as the sun eased its way down, it became certain how beautiful a place this was to live. Bats flittered overhead, while out on the lake, massive bulk tankers made their way up to Duluth.

On Wednesday 14th August we headed back down the Peninsula for a proper look around Calumet. Probably the best book going on the town is Arthur W. Thurner's *Calumet Copper and People: History of a Michigan Mining Community 1864–1970*, and I'd read this during our stay at Eagle Harbor. According to Thurner, it was once known as "Queen City of the North".[31] Calumet was founded during Michigan's copper boom sometime in the early 1860s, when the forest was felled and men mining locally first began to build cabins, shaft houses and homes. Apparently, these days, although it has the infra-structure for over eight thousand people, only two thousand live there. That's perhaps why it looks like a ghost town.

It was blistering hot by 10 a.m.. The town car park's tarmac seemed to be melting. We headed into a bank first off, because Dan was keen to change some Canadian dollars he'd had left over from Niagara Falls. He wudn' having much luck either. While he spent a while talking to the teller, Champi and I admired the various bits of old mining equipment on display inside the bank. We stayed there a bit longer than we might have, partly because the air-conditioning was so pleasant. The same went for one of Calumet's most famous shops: 'Copper World' on Fifth Street. 'Copper World' was like 'Copper Art', but miles better. Located in Calumet's oldest wood-framed building (c.1869) 'Copper World' is promoted by its owner Tony Bausano as 'Your Copper Store . . . with so much more!'.

They weren't wrong. We bought loads, including a Calumet Copper Kings baseball shirt. I found lots of interesting books; one by John R. Halsey – the State Archaeologist of Michigan on the role of copper in Prehistoric North America. The Native Americans of the region called it 'Miskwabik' [red metal]. Inside was a poem by Keatanang recorded around 1830. Though Native American, it seemed to me at least, to apply equally to generations of Cornishmen and women:

Thou asked much from me,
far more than if thou hadst
demanded one of my
daughters. The lump of copper
in the forest is great
treasure to me. It was so to
my father and grandfather.
It is our hope and our protection.
Through it I have caught
many beavers, killed
many bears. Through its magic
assistance I have been victorious
in all my battles, and with it
I have killed our foes. Through
it, too, I have always remained
healthy and reached that
great age in which thou now
findest me.[32]

Great isn't it? I suppose we Cornish don't get the opportunity to slay too many beavers or bears, but I expect you will get the point.

Everywhere I travel, I like to buy books about local dialects and non-standard Englishes. The Upper Peninsula of Michigan is no exception. Anyone who comes from the U.P. is described as a 'Yooper' whether your origins are Cornish, Finnish or German. In a way, perhaps the distinctive dialect of the U.P. (Yoopanese) has some of its origins in all of those countries. I bought *Da Yoopers' Glossary: A tourist's guide to a better understanding of the Yoopanese Language* for two bucks. Here are some of its finest examples:

DEREPADATED: Falling apart. "Benny drove me down to Shagago in his derapadated Ford."
PASTY: Yooper soul food.
PRE-NER: Somewhat close but not really exact. "We're pre-ner dat turn to Camp Cripple."
SKEETOES: A small native bird indigenous to da U.P. Dey come out by da towsands.
TOOL: To drive or cruise to pick up someone or something from somewhere.
"Why don't you tool over to Rudy's and swipe his big jack."
TREE: The number after one and two.[33]

You've probably got the picture. In just the three days I was there I found myself picking up these terms. Any longer and I'd be fluent in Yoopanese.

Guidebooks and leaflets talk a lot about Calumet's European air. I suppose by American standards, yes, there are parts of it with a vaguely European feel. The historic Calumet Theatre for example, looks like it has been plonked down from Paris. It originally opened on March 20th, 1900 and a quick glance inside told us how it was intended to reflect Italian Renaissance opulence. During its heyday, some of its shows included Douglas Fairbanks Sr., Lillian Russell, Sarah Bernhardt, and the gloriously named Madame Helena Modjeska. Seating around 700 people, it reminded me a lot of the Mineral Point Opera House. It's now on the National Register of Historic Places. What is it

324

about miners and high culture? I wouldn't have put the two together. Perhaps it was because the mining camp were always regarded at being rough and ready, that the civic authorities felt that adding a bit of high culture (Shakespeare, Opera and the like) would make them look slightly more sophisticated.

Much of the town though, reminded me of Camborne, which is perhaps fitting, seeing as how thousands of Cornishmen and women helped to shape it through the years. The road surfaces in central Calumet were being re-laid that August, so we paid little heed to the Green Cross Code and jaywalked across the streets. Calumet was filled with little reminders of Cornwall everywhere. There was 'Rowe's Furniture and Carpeting' store and 'Holman Block' (est. 1896) – a set of newly-refurbished apartments along Fifth Street. All the bakeries sold pasties, but we didn't buy any because Jean's fabulous breakfasts always left us full. On the sidewalk concrete were imprinted little signs saying "Do not spit on Walks" which seemed good advice; probably put in during the days of tuberculosis. I hate spitting at the best of times – and no-one seemed to be doing it. Apparently you could spend a night in jail if you were caught.

In 1995 the Cornish Gathering was held in Calumet, largely organised by Jean Ellis. She told me a fun story about one observer watching the Gorseth ceremony taking place that year.

"We'd never get away with this in North Carolina . . ." quipped the wit.

Of course, most Americans aren't used to people dressing up in strange blue robes and head-dresses, reminding them perhaps more of the Ku Klux Klan than Henry Jenner.

Dan and Champi had already got to know Tom Ellis Jr well, while I'd been gallivanting around with his father. Tom was aged forty-three and was a real live-wire in Eagle Harbor. Everyone knew him, but as well as being a pillar of the community (he served on the town council,) he was a total party animal.

"I couldn't believe it when Jean said you guys were coming. I mean, most of the Cornish we get over tend to be retired *wrinklies* you know . . . It's like don't they have any young people at these events . . . ?" questioned Tom.

Tom presently worked as an aircraft engineer for American Airlines down at Sawyer Marquette airport. He worked a lot of long night shifts, so seemed to stay down there for his working week, then drive back to Eagle Harbor for time off.

"My work's a lot of following standard practices – it's all R.A.I. You know what that means? Removed and Installed."

Tom Jr looked a bit like Tom Sr, and whilst we were there, was typically dressed in a white t-shirt and black shorts, sporting a thick moustache and sunglasses.

"I'm kinda weird you know," said Tom. "I'm a Union man, but I'm also a Republican. I mean, in the States, most union people are Democrats know what I'm saying?"

I did. Although, I told him that most Cornish were traditionally Republicans.

We carried on chatting. I learned that Tom was born in Ohio, his mother being Marsha Ruth Gries; Tom Sr's first wife.

"We lived for a while in Calumet, but every summer we'd come down here to Eagle Harbor. All of our family have grown up with it. I don't suppose I'll live anywhere else. I'm part of the furniture here . . ."

Tom had though. He had spent a number of years in the Army where he worked as air cabin crew. He was primarily an aerial scout, and worked with Cobra attack helicopters and close air support. Between 1978 and 1982 he'd served on Forward Air Control. It all sounded very top secret and exciting, like something out of a Playstation game. Tom told me all this as he played with his eight year old dog Habu, a Husky, was suffering a bit in the August heat, and most of his moulted fur had fallen onto the grass outside Tom's house, close to where Dan and Champi were sleeping.

We all got into Tom's Cherokee Sport and drove out along the coast road where jam-making seemed to be completed on an industrial scale. You couldn't help but notice Tom's rear licence plate: 'Michigan – Kernow – Great Lakes'. Very chic. It equalled the one on Tom and Jean's car that read 'Michigan – K[e]rnewek – Great Lakes Splendor'. I took photographs of the plate and a couple of houses sporting Saint Piran's flags. Tom was well-organised with a veritable fridge of cold beers and drinks in the back of the Cherokee Sport. We stopped off at tailing dumps, the Arnold Mine and a memorial stone dedicated to one Joseph Blight Senior, the founder of the Original Lake Superior Safety Fuse Company. Whenever safety fuses tend to be mentioned in a Cornish context, there's usually always a story about them being fairly unsafe, and I'm sure Tom told me one. Probably the factory burnt down.

The plan for the evening was a speedboat trip on Lake Superior. Champi was tired, but Dan and I were up for it.

"So let's get out there on *Gitche Gummee* . . ." said Tom, loading the regulation beers and cold drinks into the boat's fridge.

"*Gitche Gummee*?" Dan asked.

"That's the Native American name for Lake Superior," said Tom donning a rather fetching Sea Captain's hat.

We were joined by another Mike, – Mike Lantz – whose family in actual fact owned the boat. This Mike looked fit as a fiddle and none of his forty years. He lived and worked in New England making rifles, but every summer came to Eagle Harbor. The speedboat was, I suppose, as plush as anything you'd see down Restronguet Creek or Mylor, and was equipped with the kind of luxury that made Dan and I feel we were being treated like Kings. In fact, as we were guests, Mike insisted (like a lot of respectful Americans will) by calling us 'Sir'.

"You dun't have t'call me 'Sir'," Dan insisted, but it didn't seem to matter. It was like that weird kid in Schultz's *Peanuts* who calls Peppermint Patty 'Sir' too.

Dan and I settled back in our seats below a Stars and Stripes flag and started to enjoy several cold ones. Mike and Tom negotiated the boat through the small harbour entrance (avoiding rocks) and then we headed in an easterly direction towards Copper Harbor. Put simply, this boat-trip was stunning. We passed by tiny islands that looked like something you might find in *Swallows and Amazons*, expensive designer houses and beautiful creeks which looked untouched by modernity. In the west the sun began to set making the colours glorious. The boat's wake broke up the sun's reflection until the sun finally set, projecting a fragile pink over the western horizon.

While we were out on the boat, everything was so still and tranquil that I couldn't help but think about William Jack Foster. Jean had told me the day we arrived that Jack had died in April, only three months ago. The news of his demise made me feel saddened. My head was filled with a lot of "If onlys . . .": If only I had come here last year, I would have been able to see him. If only I'd come at Easter, I might have just caught him. Instead, I had to make do with Jean and Tom's memories of the man, as well as a video they had of him titled *Boom to Bust: Minetown USA*, which dealt with the general history of the region, and Calumet as a town in particular. The video box made much of the fact that the performance was filmed in the historic Calumet theatre and how the tale told would 'recall the hard life and times of miners and their families in the Copper Country of Michigan's Upper Peninsula'. On it, Jack was dressed up as a Cousin Jack miner with pasty pail and hard-hat. To look at, he reminded me of my old school mathematics teacher – Mr. Menday – with a thin, slightly sagging neck, but with a glint in his eyes. The delivery was not what I'd expected. There was barely a trace in my view, of any Cornish dialect in his voice, and his narration of *Boom to Bust* was somewhat stilted, as if he were taking too many pauses for dramatic effect.

"Cal – u – met was al – ways the cen – ter of the cop – per min – ing bus – i-ness," it began. Each of the above hyphens indicate a five second gap in the delivery.

There was one section where he narrated the story of a famous fire in Calumet, and tried to recreate the desperate cries of one of the children, who lost his mother in the fire.

"Mom! Where are you Mom? Are you there Mom?"

In our view it came across as a little over-the-top but there you go. Many at Monday night's reading spoke of Jack with high regard. Perhaps he'd had to compromise his ability to tell yarns on the video. Maybe the director was at fault. Jean summed it up with her line, "Well, that was Jack for you." So Jack, it seemed, was a bit of a contradiction; perhaps even a victim of his own success.

It became really dark by the time we got back to just outside Eagle Harbor. Tom stopped the engine and we just floated there for a while, watching the stars, and in the distance, the larger vessels heading back and forth out on the Lake. A few jokes were exchanged with another boat owner he knew, and then we ploughed back into the harbour. After completing a few spins in the shallows, we docked. I don't think there was ever a more relaxing time in all my travels in Cornish America. Some journeys you always remember – and this will be one of those.

It was really late when we got back to Tom's.

"Say, there is something I have that you should look at before you go tomorrow . . ."

My ears pricked up.

"It's some play . . . about Cornish miners . . ."

"Show me," I demanded.

Tom rooted around in various cupboards.

"My grandfather Walter Gries compiled it . . . It's called *Drill Core* . . ."

I must have been salivating at the mouth.

"He was featured in *National Geographic* – here, this one, March 1952 . . ."

Inside the faded magazine, sure enough, was a feature on the mining history of the Keweenaw, quoting his grandfather.

Tom went around the room talking to himself, trying to remember where he had put it. Eventually he reached into a cabinet and out came a box. Inside he pulled out a manuscript.[34] A quick glance told me it was no play, but rather the idea of a 'drama' of the Cornish heritage in Keweenaw, composed of an extensive collection of Cousin Jack stories, folklore and poems. Alongside it were Walter Gries's journals and scrapbooks, packed to the gills with songs and poems, stories and fragments.

"I must copy it," I said.

So Tom allowed me to do this. Late at night, he opened the nearby Civic Building to use their photocopier. All this in the last few hours of my time at Eagle Harbor. It was frantic – but what an incredible find.

So I never did get to meet Jack Foster. In fact, so it seemed to me, old Jack Foster was perhaps more myth than substance. The real stuff was here – undiscovered – right under my nose. The champion of the Cousin Jacks was of German extraction. I'd suddenly stumbled on what I'd came for. It had taken a lot of travelling but I'd found a lasting legacy of Cornish America.

Notes

1. Angus Murdoch (2001 [1943]) *Boom Copper: The Story of the First U.S. Mining Boom*, Hancock, Michigan: The Quincy Mine Hoist Association, p.202.
2. Ibid., p.204.
3. Ibid., p.206.
4. Arthur W. Thurner (1994) *Strangers and Sojourners: A History of Michigan's Keweenaw Peninsula*, Detroit: Wayne State University Press, p.44-5.
5. Ibid., p.58.
6. Ibid., p.66 .
7. Ibid., p.67.
8. Ibid., p.136.
9. Ibid., p.73.
10. Ibid., p.94 .
11. Ibid., p.148.
12. Ibid., p.138.
13. Ibid.
14. Ibid., p.137.
15. Ibid.
16. Ibid., p.138.
17. Ibid., p.224.
18. Ibid., p.257.
19. Ibid., p.313.
20. See Keskerdh Kernow/Cornwall Marches On (1997) *Keskerdh Kernow/Cornwall Marches On Souvenir Programme*, Truro: Keskerdh Kernow.
21. See Newton G. Thomas (1998 [1941]) *The Long Winter Ends*, Detroit: Wayne State University Press.
22. See Phil Medlyn 'Geology and Mining of Central' in The Keweenaw County Historical Society (eds.) (1998) *Central Mine: Years of Work – Lives of Pain and Hope*, Calumet: The Keweenaw County Historical Society, pp.4-16.
23. Also in ibid, p.44.
24. Ibid., pp.62-3.
25. See William Bottrell (ed.) (1873) *Traditions and Hearthside Stories of West Cornwall*, Penzance: Beare and Son, pp.1-26.
26. R. Charles Stetter (ed.) (1981) *The Central Mine M.E. Church: A Short History*, Central Mine: M.E. Church, p.4.
27. See Thomas, op.cit.

28. D.M. Thomas (1983) *Selected Poems*, Harmondsworth: Penguin, pp.60-61.
29. Thurner, op.cit., p.138.
30. Ibid., p.152.
31. Arthur W. Thurner (1974) *Calumet Copper and People: History of a Michigan Mining Community 1864–1970*, Hancock, Michigan: Arthur W. Thurner, p.i.
32. John R. Halsey (1992) *Miskwabik – Red Metal: The Roles Played by Michigan's Copper In Prehistoric North America*, Eagle Harbor: Keweenaw County Historical Society, p.i.
33. Anon (1998) *Da Yoopers' Glossary: A tourist's guide to a better understanding of the Yoopanese Language*, no publisher, pp.1-15.
34. Donald D. Kinsey (ed.) (n.d.) *Drill Core: Folklore of Michigan's Upper Peninsula from the Collection of Walter F. Gries MSS*.

13

Do not touch: Whiskey for Ernie and the Cousin Jacks . . .

"What do y'get when a piano falls down a mineshaft?" asked Dan as we pulled away from Eagle Harbor.

"Dun't knaw," said Champi and I together.

"A Flat Miner," dead panned Dan.

Groan.

"Alright . . . what do you get when a piano falls on an army base?" said Champi, picking up the bait.

"Dun't knaw!"

"A Flat Major . . ." Champi beamed.

Bruce Crossing was on the horizon again, and this was the level of humour we had descended to. This time though, we were definitely heading west – well, a bit more west than before at least. I double-checked to make sure the *Drillcore* manuscript was with me, when we pulled in for gas.

The Keweenaw was slipping away from us – like some polished piece of copper. It really was much like Cornwall – a tiny peninsula jutting into water. No wonder they'd ended up there, and continued to populate it. Our sojourn there however was over and we were now heading to Minnesota. Somehow that sounded very exotic. I mean you know loads of people who've been to Florida, but how many do you know who've been to . . . um . . . Minnesota? That said, Minnesota seems to be the butt of lots of jokes in America. First off, they are all supposed to speak funny there – something to do with the Scandinavian influence over time;

then there's the whole snow and isolation thing – about how cold it is there for nine months of the year, and how the only thing to do is drink beer and go lumberjacking.

To reach Minnesota, you have to go through Ironwood – just about the last place you can be in – in Michigan, then follow Route 2 across the northern edge of Wisconsin. Here, that State borders Lake Superior. North of the port town of Ashford are the Apostle Islands, which the huge bulk tankers dodge as they run up to Duluth, right on the eastern edge of Superior. You have to remember that this is the last port going before a whole lot of land; the reason why it is still such a major centre of commerce. The drive around Saxon and Odanah is particularly beautiful, with sweeping fields running down to the lakeside. Duluth itself has the feel of somewhere like Bristol, or more particularly Avonmouth. Lots of fly-overs run over the Lake, while oil and gas terminals dominate the port. As a whole though, much of the landscape in this area is remarkably similar to that of the Keweenaw. It's only when you push northwards into the territory above Duluth that you notice the scenery becoming more isolated, mountainous and forested. You could seriously get lost. It was looking more like Canada – or at least how I imagined Canada to be – as mile by mile we headed north.

In my mind, I was heading for Ely, because that's where I'd associated the Cornish presence in Minnesota. I mean, I knew that Tommi and Bob O' Hagan spent time in a cabin up there, and that one of the recent Cornish Gatherings took place there (though to be honest, you could say that about much of Cornish America). Ely was one of the lead towns of the Vermilion iron mining district, and on the map, this looked reasonably close. I had the idea too that Littlefork, where our hosts, Bruce and Violet Polkinghorne lived, was pretty close to Ely.

Well, I got that wrong.

Littlefork is certainly much further north, and it was late afternoon before we turned off Route 53 onto the Littlefork road. Route 53 is incredible to drive along. You rarely see any other traffic. The rest of America had not dared to come up this far. Surrounding the road is a wall of trees, so it's as if you're stuck in a tunnel of woodland – very beautiful but

333

somewhat eerie as well. You get an idea of what Littlefork is like where you read its tourist blurb: 'Littlefork, always home. Nestled between the evergreens and tucked into the logging and farmlands of Northern Minnesota is a folksy little town with the name of Littlefork. Now if you're looking for skyscrapers and honking traffic – better keep going. Come for the hunting and fishing, go four-wheeling or snowmobiling, experience canoeing and kayaking on the river or just enjoy the friendly flavor of the local shop-keepers and a meal like Mom used to make. And, while you're there, listen carefully and you might just hear the faint sound of water bubbling over the riverbed and the laughter of children playing in the park.' It all sounds very nice, and to be honest, Littlefork was an unexpected high-light of my travels. It is the kind of place you want to raise children in.

When we pulled up at Bruce and Violet's place, it was as if I'd been drinking with them in Mineral Point only last week. Both of them are as gregarious as they come and massive fun to hang out with. Now, in case you don't know, the name Polkinghorne is a very honourable old Cornish name, most readily associated with the sport of wrasslin' and one 'Gentleman Jim Polkinghorne'. Out they rushed to welcome us; Violet, looking none of her seventy-two years old, wearing a blue t-shirt and white trousers, while Bruce extended his hand to us all. He looked very dapper in blue jeans, and a chequered shirt. Bruce's hair was naturally blond but now had more than a few waves of grey; giving him a distinguished look. There was something very Cornish about him and his seventy-three years.

"Good to see you again, Alan," said Bruce. "It's a long way to come, but you'll like it up here . . ."

"How y'all doin'?" said Violet. "Now you'll want a cold one won't you?"

We didn't need asking twice. The hot day and drive made the beer delicious and we collapsed on their living room sofas, catching up on the news and gossip. After we'd been shown our accommodation, we slumped down in front of a Little League baseball game. Champi and I were still recovering from the fact that we were to have separate rooms. That meant none of Dan's by-now famous snoring events. Bruce meanwhile, delighted in the fact that there were three real, live, breathing Cornishmen in his house, re-capped his connection with the famous Polkinghorne name.

"It means something like 'Pool of the Iron Chief' in Cornish doesn't it?"

I nodded in agreement.

"I didn't know he was Cornish first off," interjected Violet. "I thought he was Welsh . . . There were a lot of Welsh up here . . ."

Bruce's family originated from St Columb Major, and originally his grandfather, George Polkinghorne and his wife Lena came across to Canada, running a general store in Limehouse, in Ontario. They then moved across to Minnesota. However, Bruce's family is very much connected to the famous wrassler James Polkinghorne – James being his great great grandfather. On the granite facade of the 'Red Lion Hotel' in St Columb Major is a marble tablet depicting two wrasslers in a hitch. The tablet was unveiled in 1926 by the late Colonel E. N. Willyams of Carnanton who was a great supporter of Cornish wrasslin' and placed there by the St Columb Wrestling Committee to mark the then centenary of one of the greatest and most hotly contested wrasslin' contests of all time – between this James Polkinhorne of St Columb – champion of Cornwall – and one Abraham Cann, the champion of Devon (for that, read the whole of England).

Now although James Polkinghorne came from West Cornwall (he was born in St Keverne) it was from St Columb that, accompanied by his brother from St Stephen, they set off to Tamar Green in Devonport to uphold the honour of the Cornish. The Cornish historian Ivan Rabey gives a good account of this bout in his book,[1] but it appears that there was much controversy over the match at the time. In debate were the two different styles Cann and Polkinghorne used: Cann favoured a kicking technique, whereas Polkinghorne used more traditional thrusts and hugs to floor his opponent. At the time, Cann was declared the winner on a technicality, but according to spectators Polkinghorne was the better wrassler. Reports in newspapers varied, but according to Rabey, this decision was eventually reversed and Polkinghorne declared the winner. This then, was Bruce's prestigious Cornish heritage.

In such ways, you get to learn a lot about people when you travel and how their family interactions alters and changes: though Violet had Swedish ancestry, she had readily engaged with Bruce's Cornish heritage and felt it important that their children knew their roots. They had four children – all of whom knew about their Cornish roots, scattered across Minnesota. They had two sons and two daughters: Jeff was a mortgage banker, while Susan had a Ph.D in animal behaviour and lectured at St Thomas College in St Paul, while Sally was a massage therapist and Donald a biology teacher. This was all a long way from double-jack drilling underground. These were the contemporary Cornish getting on with their lives.

"Come on," said Bruce, with all the conviction of his wrasslin' ancestor, "we'll head on up to *Sha Shas* . . ."

None of us had a clue what *Sha Shas* was. It sounded like one of the strip clubs in Canada that Mike Braman travelled to on his Harley Davidson. The area we were in had been labelled the 'Border Waters' by the local tourist organisations, though much of this energy surrounded the leisure facilities on Rainy Lake, a large lake through which runs the American-Canadian border. On the Canadian side, it stretches down from Fort Frances to the spectacular Devil's Cascade. The town most associated with Rainy Lake on the US side is International Falls. We went north, first through International Falls and then on to *Sha Shas*, past the wonderfully named "Woody's fairly reliable guide service", and some dubious-looking roadhouse bars. *Sha Shas* turned out to be a lakeside bar and restaurant. From its terraces and screened gazebos, you could watch bald eagles and osprey fish for food, and feed chipmunks. The local delicacy was a fish caught in Rainy Lake called 'Walleye'. Much of the menu had Walleye cooked in various ways – so it seemed the thing to have.

"How did you find out about your Cornishness?" I asked Bruce as we gazed out over Rainy Lake.

"I can tell you exactly," said Bruce. "I was in Duluth. It was August 1966, and I was in the men's room taking a leak . . . And this guy came up to me and said, "Hey Cousin Jack

. . . you're Cornish . . ." His name was Polkinghorne too . . . and from then on, well, I've discovered more and more . . . Then when the Gathering came to Ely, that's when a lot of things came together . . ."

After we'd eaten, we wandered down to the Lake shore and sat on some of the wooden piers. It was very still and quiet – I suppose – in complete contrast to the days of the Rainy Lake Gold Rush of the 1860s and 70s. Bruce told me that one of the most famous mines was on Little American Island, a well-known landmark near Black Bay Narrows. A miner called George W. Davis found a promising quartz vein and so began the boom years of what David E. Perry calls 'the El Dorado of the north'.[2] There were soon two headframes over vertical shafts on the island, and the ore was then floated to the stamp mill at Rainy Lake City; itself a town which was erected in a few weeks, rather than months, due to the influx of miners.

Although it is not much written about, several Cousin Jacks made the trip across from the Keweenaw and up from south-western Wisconsin for the lure of gold. Within the early years of the 1860s, Rainy Lake was over-run with people trying to mine for gold, but the environment made it difficult. For one thing, much of the gold was to be found on the numerous islands dotted around the lake; for another the winters were hard and unrelenting up here. So despite some initial success, the crude log headframes did not last long, and the miners (the Cornish amongst them) travelled elsewhere. The final death knell was the lure of the Klondike and other Canadian gold fields. Apparently the phrase the miners here used for gold held within a vein was 'locked up'; as in, "That gold's locked up in that thare vein . . ." Peering out over the Lake, it would seem that a good deal of it was still locked up, and perhaps the place was now best left as a wildlife reserve. There was certainly more to be said and written though about the presence of the Cornish in this region.

That evening we headed into the 'Veterans of Foreign Wars' Club in Littlefork (Post 9641). There are thousands of these little clubrooms dotted across America – much like our own British Legion. As you might expect, there is high dose of patriotic memorabilia enshrined on the walls of the

337

building. Across America, everyone calls such clubs the 'VFW' – the W pronounced the George Dubya Bush way. The moment we walked in, I soon realised it was not the kind of place where you completed an in-depth critique of American foreign policy or said you enjoyed Michael Moore's *Bowling for Columbine*. There were bald eagles and stars and stripes everywhere. The place opened out to a three-sided bar, around which were stools but with no discernible beer pumps in the way you see them in Cornwall. Across from the bar were some booths, which looked like a place you could eat; nearby them a couple of pool tables.

It was a classic moment. Everyone looked at us. To be honest, it was quite scary initially. It perhaps wasn't the kind of place where you walked in on your own, without knowing anybody. Fortunately Bruce and Violet had the kind of local presence and knowledge which made sure nobody messed with us; though having said that, initial impressions are often wrong. The first thing I noticed where two huge bear-like men at the end of the bar, with big grizzly style ZZ Top-like beards and arms like tree trunks. Bruce introduced us and soon Joe Reller and Steve Horne were buying us beers. It turned out they were lumberjacks. This indeed, was the main industry of these parts. So I initiated a conversation about wood, which I know nothing about, but learnt a lot.

Apparently, the original trailblazers up in these parts were called 'Jackpine Savages' and physically, they almost resembled Cousin Jack miners, though instead of carrying pickaxe and shovel, they were usually pictured carrying felling axes. The culture of the forest-dwelling 'Jackpine Savage' was still central in people's minds here. Even on the corner of Bruce's shop was a chainsaw-carved statue of one, and we were to see many others over the next few days. Joe Reller and Steve Horne were Jackpine Savages of the twenty-first century. And I suppose, I couldn't help but think of *Monty Python* and how very manly this kind of occupation was. There and then, I wanted to wield chainsaws, smell sawdust and shout "Timber!" at the top of my voice.

When the beers eventually arrived, it was something of a

338

surprise. First off, there were only two choices of beer: Light or Dark. I didn't get the name of the product at all. No-one even seemed to care. More interestingly though, at the bottom of my frosted beer glass was an olive. Dan and I 'laughed it up' and asked Bruce for an explanation. It was obviously a tradition in this part of Minnesota.

"You put an olive in there – and eat it when you've finished. It's salty see – and that makes you thirsty for your next beer . . ." said Bruce, helping us to understand its purpose.

We soon got into the traditional way of drinking. More olives: more drinking. All this time though, Champi had managed to start a conversation with another member of the VFW, who we would later meet, so we asked Debbie Ohlquist the barmaid to put several more olives in his glass of beer so we could see his reaction. Predictably his eyes nearly popped out of his head when he saw the olives, much to the amusement of everyone at the VFW. Another drinker Truman Lindvall told us that, instead of having olives, some people had their beer with a slice of pickle – for that, read gherkin. Now – gherkin and beer, well, that had to be tried too.

Most people in the VFW knew of Bruce and Violet's Cornish connections and we were soon onto the topic of where we'd been and where we were going. The reaction was much as usual – that we were slightly crazy. That said, I knew Bruce almost fancied getting in the car with us for the next stages. When we'd become a bit more relaxed, the topic of conversation turned to the second Gulf War. There was general praise for Tony Blair, but much criticism of the French and Germans. Talking of other Europeans, Champi had earlier started talking to Ernie Carlson – a retired schoolteacher, of joint Croatian and Swedish ancestry, who seemed to spend more time at the VFW than just about anyone else. He has to be one of the most interesting characters I have met on my journey through Cornish America. A large droopy moustache covered his mouth, while his voice still had resonant Eastern European traces. He took an instant like to Champi, Dan and myself, and us to him. Initially, he couldn't quite work out who we were, who and what the Cornish were. Ernie had been divorced twice and obviously enjoyed a drink or two. Aside from service in Vietnam, he'd spent most of his life teaching across in Ely.

"We're Cornish," Dan said again. "We're not English. We're mining stock."

Ernie suddenly stopped drinking.

"We're Cousin Jacks," I said.

A very bright light seemed to go inside Ernie's head.

"Cousin Jacks?" he inquired.

We nodded.

"Now I know who you are. I taught loads of Cousin Jacks over in Ely. Never called 'em Cornish though – always Cousin Jacks . . . That's who you are then . . ."

This was the spark he needed. I could see him thinking through all the Cousin Jack children who'd once sat in front of him.

"Ah – I taught many of them. All with names like Tre, Pen and Pol . . ."

In the morning we went to see the Polkinghorne family store in downtown Littlefork. I can't begin to explain how wonderful their shop is. If you ever find yourself in Littlefork, Minnesota, put it to the top of the places you must visit. Built in 1928 on 4th and Main, it is an old-fashioned style ironmongers – none of your 'B&Q' rubbish – and it is crammed to the gills with products that you actually want, and wish you could buy. Even though it had been taken over by the 'Hardware Hank' chain ("You have a lot more going for you with Hank!"), the place retains its individuality. It had wooden floors, and you can buy single nails (not huge bagfuls), and red *Radio Flyer* children's trolleys and toy pedal cars (like the ones you see in American Christmas movies), and sarsaparilla. Out back in the warehouse, it was even more incredible: row upon row of everything a Jackpine Savage could possibly want – including floral wallpaper. Surely there was nothing the 'Polkie' store (as it was known locally) didn't carry? Mike Polkinghorne – Bruce's nephew – now runs the store, but you can tell Bruce sometimes itches to get back behind the counter and sell a couple of screws or a length of timber. Laura Polkinghorne (Mike's wife) had married into all this Cornishry and seemed quite amazed as we entered the emporium. A local boy, Joel Ray Marty, aged ten, who happened to live across the road from Bruce and Violet came in to the store for a soda, and found us intriguing. He found our accents amazing. I suspect we sounded like aliens from another planet. We showed him where we were from and gave him a t-shirt from Cornwall. Apparently he would now do his school project on Cornwall.

We came away laden with t-shirts and gifts from the Polkinghorne legend in Littlefork; the most fascinating of all was a tiny 'Hardware Hank' raingauge, which I now have in my Probus garden, as well as the Polkinghorne's 'secret recipe' steak salt. Because we'd enjoyed chatting to the lumberjacks the night before, one of them, invited us over to his shop to swop t-shirts – as he ran a t-shirt emporium for the 'Border Waters' area. He was a massive man, who looked like he could throw grizzly bears all too easily. We picked out some items and loaded these into Bruce's car. The store was fascinating too. Instead of hardware, it sold real man's clothes and kits for lumberjacking – huge *Carhartt* overalls and dungarees for working in sub-zero conditions; reinforced gloves for working with chainsaws, and snow-shoes and boots. I could have bought the place out, but there was, upon reflection, little use for a pair of extra-thermal dungarees back home.

Bruce had a lot of interests in Littlefork. We stopped off briefly at the North Star Electric Co-operative to meet everyone there. It was then that I realised how far we were away from conventional power and electrical services. It was an independent community power company. They also dealt with anyone's satellite, cable and television needs. Somehow this was fitting to see this twenty-first century Cornishman co-ordinating such activity. We talked more about his experiences as a Cornishmen in twentieth and twenty-first century America. I learnt that he started flying lessons when aged only fifteen. He obtained his pilot license at the age of seventeen. Bruce graduated from high school in 1947 and the same year he enlisted in the USAF. Up until 1951 he worked in Air Force Training Command as an Instructor, training aircraft mechanics on C-54 Dakotas (which took part in the Berlin airlift) and B29 Super-fortresses (used in the Korean War). After the war he worked as a flight line mechanic for Northwest airlines, but then returned to Littlefork and joined the family hardware business. The family tradition continued when he sold the store to Mike and Laura in 1989 – the third generation of Polkinghornes. It had been Bruce's father Ernest, who had started the business all the way back in 1928. As we headed further north, we also learnt that Bruce has spent four years in the early 1990s cold-weather testing Land Rovers.

"That was great fun," recalled Bruce. "Well . . . they're a British company right?"

In International Falls we pulled in at Rainy River Community College, where there is an exhibition devoted to Bronislaw "Bronko" Nagurski (1908–1990), a 'moose of a man', who is perhaps one of America's greatest sporting heroes. 'Master of the Midway' Bronko was born in 1908 in Rainy River, Ontario, of Ukranian immigrants, but grew up in International Falls. He spent nine years playing for the Chicago Bears as a fullback and defensive tackler. Bronko, the exhibition told me, was a 'synonym for strength and power' and had 'Bunyanesque proportions'. What was intriguing was that after his illustrious football-playing days were over, he then became a professional wrestler – eventually earning the title of Heavyweight Champion of the World (Pity he wudn' a Cornishman). There's probably not a sports' fan in America who had not heard of Bronko, so it was illuminating to see his life so well celebrated in International Falls. That said, he was probably about the only famous person ever to emerge from there.

The rest of Friday was to be spent on a houseboat touring Rainy Lake, looking at some of the old islands where mining had taken place, but also generally relaxing. Now, a houseboat, in my fairly ignorant view, is rather like a caravan on water and is something of a bizarre sight. That said, there are numerous house boats that you can hire or spend an entire vacation in, on Rainy Lake. We were lucky enough to be travelling with some friends of Bruce – Dave Parmeter, a retired school principal, who in my view, resembled an older Ernest Hemingway (who coincidentally spent some time fishing at Rainy Lake), and his partner Phyllis Kuluvar. Now Phyllis had been in the house boat business from 1958 to 1978 so there wasn't much she couldn't tell me about them. We spent the whole afternoon running up and down the lake, talking about the timber barons of old, and sneakily crossing a couple of times into Canada. It was just as beautiful as the trip on Lake Superior.

"We're on the Laurentian divide," noted Bruce. "All rivers here flow north . . ."

As well as geology, Bruce and I were discussing a book he had at home by Charlie and Ann Cooper. The volume was called *Tuskegee's Heroes* and its subject-matter was the U.S. Air Army Corps, and their success at Pantelleria and Anzio, but more specifically African-American pilots and aircrew. The book had been written as a reaction against the racist statement that it was 'impossible for a black man to fly an aeroplane' and it recorded the crews and missions of aeroplanes like the Mustang and Warhawk. Intriguingly one of the African-American pilots was named James Polkinghorne, and Bruce had been puzzling over the connection and name. We could only conclude that perhaps it had been the name of his family's one time plantation owner, since in the days of slavery, slaves often took the names of their owners. It would, we concluded be quite possible for people of Cornish ancestry to run plantations. Even so, it was an intriguing Cornish-American connection.

The evening saw the VFW fish-fry event, so it was important to be back in good time; although we did stop to take pictures of some miniature horses. The fish fry was a all-hands-on-deck community kind of affair, where the men went out and caught the walleye and then brought home the fish for the women to fry up, serving it along with potato salad and corn-on-the-cob. We were guests of honour, and I have to say that I developed quite a taste for walleye. The Fish Fry was very much like the kind of ice cream social I have seen elsewhere in America – an event and occasion that will continue forever, such is its celebration of community and culture. I went home to bed stuffed, and despite the heavy heat of the evening, was soon asleep.

On Saturday Bruce and I set off for Ely. It's a two hour drive. Knowing that I would be spending much of my time reading and researching, Dan and Champi had elected to chill out in Littlefork, helping Violet with the day's chores and living it up at the VFW. We began our journey soon after breakfast, taking Bruce's impressive dark green 98 Buick Park Avenue Ultra out of the garage and gearing up for an air-conditioned morning ride across the State. Bruce pointed out lots of landmarks, and honked his horn ten miles down the road.

"He's one of our closest neighbours," he joked.

We crossed the Rat Root River and entered Kabetogama State Forest, retracing our route up the State. At Angora, we headed east over to Ely, through thick forest along to Tower and Soudan. These were both early mining locations, attracting the Cornish in large numbers. Local bakeries and shops sold pasties; the influence was still there. At Soudan we looked at the Mine. It was now an Underground State Park, and like at the Delaware on the Keweenaw, you could take a subterranean tour. According to the literature we picked up about it, the Soudan was opened in 1882, originally as an open-cast work, but ten years later, it had progressed to working completely underground. The mine's value was the special kind of ore it produced: it had a high oxygen content, and was primarily used to make high quality steel in open-hearth furnaces. Momentarily, I thought back to Cornwall Forge in Pennsylvania. To the south-west was the Mesabi Iron Range – also something of a Cornish area. Mesabi is a Native American word meaning 'red rock', and of course, it is the iron which makes the earth red. Much of the mining in this area we had seen on our way up from Duluth, and in the distance the quarries and spoil-tips reared up like prehistoric creatures – all wonderfully coloured.

As we passed them, Bruce spoke more about his family, "I have a half-brother – by the name of George Polkinghorne. He was born in 1917 and died earlier this year. He lived in LA. He worked for Spielburg on *Close Encounters of the Third Kind*. He built the space-ship that appears above Devil's Tower . . . Then he did *Bladerunner* . . . He invented something called monkey motion that they still use in films now . . ."

This was good – hearing the Cornish contribution to Hollywood. I suspect I'd like to have met George. It was interesting how both George and Bruce had ended up in the 'hardware' industry – there was something very Cornish about that. As we chatted we passed by Tower – an old mining town next to Lake Vermilion. Rock outcroppings shared the landscape with Finnish farmsteads; the latter sometimes erected around rock piles.

"The ore here is some of the richest in the world," said Bruce. "Years ago, they just creamed off the top, but now they're 're-cycling' it . . ."

Of course Bruce meant they had taken all the high grade ore years before and were now having to work the lower grades formerly discarded; the story of mining the world over.

Gradually the road ended at Ely, now named the 'Gateway to the Canoe Area'. Ely greenstone, which attracted miners from all over the world to the area, is perhaps one of the oldest rocks in the world, and why when they were younger, all of Bruce's children used to call one local – and very green – rock pile the Jolly Green Giant's Mountain after the figurehead of the canned produce. Geologists have apparently called the place the most extraordinary freak of nature on the continent, since some of the rock here contains 70% metallic iron. In effect, the rocks below Ely contain a solid wall of mineral. Our first stop was the Ely-Winton Historical Museum, which lies in the premises of the local high school: Vermilion Community College. Unlike a lot of museums I've visited, the Ely-Winton Historical Museum paid little attention to current museum interpretative trends and instead just piled lots of interesting old material together. Best of all, was a scale model of the Ely mines, which gave me considerable understanding of open-cast working methods here. Note was made of the importance of the Cornish as well, which Bruce was keen to point out to me. 56 Inch Cylinder Syndrome – which had been rather quiet for the past few days – suddenly welled up inside of me. It was a frightening moment. I had to go outside and look at the shop.

Among the most useful purchases I made at the museum was a compilation of re-prints from the local newspaper *The Ely Miner* since 1888.[3] It was titled 'Marriage, Mining, Mischief and More' and was crammed with lots of information; for example, we are told that on January 18th

345

1895, a pasty and mince pie social was held at the Presbyterian Church. The shops of Fenske and Lawrenz offered 'Miner's and Explorers' Supplies' while W.C. Hoskin sold 'Ginger ale, Pop, Birch Beer and Soda'. A Captain John Pengilly was nominated for Mayor on March 25th 1892, while in 1894 a Mr W.R. Opie took steps to found a library and literary society in Ely. A recitation meanwhile was offered by Mrs W.B. Davey at the Opera House, Ely on January 21st 1898, titled 'The Curfew must not ring tonight'. On the 4th July 1903, number one on the list of activities at the Fall Lake Celebration was a 'Wrestling Match' to take place in the rear of Thomas Kearney's ice house. In such ways, I could see the impact of the Cornish on life in Ely.

"The place is still running with us," commented Bruce. "Ely's as Cornish as it comes in Minnesota . . ."

Ely is into marketing itself as a winter resort these days. I'm told to 'make tracks to Ely, Minnesota for breathtaking adventure in a million acres of winter'. The city also says that it 'can show you how to dress warm and comfy, how to play, where to stay and where to eat. We've been enjoying winters forever and we're here to make sure you will too'. On this booklet, a wolf is scrambling over a snowscape on a bright winter morning. I checked to make sure there were no wolves heading down East Sheridan Street. Also handed to me was the Ely Snowmobile Route Map – something very handy in August. Still, there was fun stuff in Ely: the 'International Wolf Centre' ("Teaching the World about Wolves"), the 'Chainsaw Sisters Saloon', shops like 'Mostly Moose and More', as well as 'Walsh Septic Systems'. I noted a place called the 'Miner's Inn' on West Chapman Street which offered bed and breakfast 'retreat for all seasons'. It was probably a good deal more comfortable than some of the early boarding houses the first Cornish miners stayed in out here.

One of the most famous outlets in contemporary Ely is 'Steger Mukluks'. I wondered what on earth this was when Bruce first mentioned it, but I soon got the picture. A Mukluk is a Native American style of boot, which has been adopted as a trendy fashion accessory in early twentieth-century America, somewhat like the present trend for Celtic

Sheepskin-style boots in Britain. Will Steger and his colleague Paul Schurke completed a very successful expedition of the North Pole in 1986 – hence the endorsement of the elkhide shoes for winter wear. I picked up a catalogue. You can buy just about any kind of mukluk you want from Stegers: there are the tall and short expedition mukluks, the Yukon Jack Mukluks, and designs from the Navajo and Kodiak. I think you get something of an impression of Ely now. What is it about these old Cornish mining towns that now makes them so trendy? Ely – yes, it's like Boulder, but with mukluks and canoes. Oh – and pasties.

Bruce took me over to Ely's United Methodist Church on East Camp Street. The Pastor there, Dana Thompson obviously ran the place with an eye on the area's Cornish heritage. It was founded in 1892 and was as Cornish as the Church at Central Mine, back on the Keweenaw. There was a regular Pastie fellowship to raise funds, and memorial windows and brass plates on the altar rail to notable Cornish figures such as Charles Trezona, Emelie Trezona and Beatrice Nicholas. I saw references too, to Flora Jane Toms and Reuban Toms – Flora 'Tommi' O' Hagan's grandmother and grandfather. Her Cornish and Irish connections with Ely are long-standing since her mother and father also lived in Ely. Her mother Mary "May" Meenahan was born in St Paul, and her family moved to Michigan when she was young, then returned to the Mesabi iron range when she was around twelve years old. Her Irish father ran the rail engine, hauling ore in an open-cast quarry. When she was eighteen she went to live in Duluth to train as a nurse, then eventually came back to Ely to work around 1922. Tommi's grandfather Reuben started his mining career in the Upper Peninsula of Michigan, then married Flora Jane McLaughlin in Ishpeming. In 1895 they had moved to Minnesota and her father Edwin William Toms was born in that year. By January of 1898, the family had moved to Ely. Not only does this show the mobility of the Cornish in Tommi's family, but also a long-standing sense of place.

Many of the figures in the United Methodist Church connect to the best article I've read on the Cornish in Ely

347

and in the iron ranges of Minnesota. This is Carlton C. Qualey's 1991 text, titled 'The Cornish: A Mining Elite'.[4] Qualey does a first-rate job in explaining their history, and I recommend it. According to Qualey, the first Cornish to arrive in this area of Minnesota were originally recruited for work in the Vermilion range, but it was one Elisha J. Morcom – a Cornish captain in the Menominee Range of the Upper Peninsula of Michigan who really kickstarted the Cornish operation in Ely. From there, Qualey found 350 men, woman and children and they all travelled to Vermilion to begin mining in 1884. He comments on how frustrating it was to research the Cornish in the area, since as at Grass Valley, on the 1900 census schedules many of the Cornish were labelled 'English' even though they weren't. The townships of Breitung and Stuntz were centres for the Cornish. Fewer, so it is said, worked in the Mesabi, because the Cornish were snobby about the unskilled "ditch diggers" there.[5] Names such as Thomas, Pascoe, James, Williams, Caddy and Tregillis dominate the local mining history. The Cornish weren't just miners here. They became very prominent citizens and industrial leaders here and in the rest of Minnesota and America. W. Hugo Trevanion, born at Boconnoc, came first to Kingston, Ontario, passed through Ely, and later became a consulting engineer and mayor of Duluth. Samuel Richard, born in Camborne in 1881 became the Cap'n of the Mohawk Mine, while Martin Trewhella, born in Cornwall in 1861 became Cap'n of several mines in the Mesabi region.

One of the most famous familes was the Trezona family. Richard Trezona served as superintendent and cap'n at the Fayal Mine at Eveleth, while Charles Trezona, born in Cornwall in 1856 had an illustrious career; perhaps accounting for his memorial window at the United Methodist Church. He emigrated to the United States in 1885, worked in Michigan mines until 1895, did mining exploration around Ely 1890–1891, served as shift boss in the Franklin Mine at Virginia, as cap'n of the Pioneer Mine, and became general superintendent for the Oliver Mining Company of the Vermilion Range 1902–1931 and served as mayor of Ely in 1913 and again in 1930–31.[8]

After the Methodist Church, Bruce drove me down to

Trezona House, which is where the family lived in Ely. Apparently up until very recently Trezona had been a guest house; Bruce stayed there for the Ely Gathering. When our view of Trezona was complete, Bruce turned north and headed down Miner's Drive. This is now a business development park next to the area known as Miner's Lake – the flooded iron quarries. You know the kind of thing: there are lots of them in Camborne and Redruth – all nicely designed sheds for technological industries of the future. The Pioneer Mine still stands here though lying opposite Ely's Grand Masonic Lodge. It seemed to challenge development agencies to knock it down, though it appeared to me that the Lodge stands guard over it – not wishing it ever to be re-developed.

Knowing my need to investigate Cornish-American literature, as well as the history of mines like Pioneer, Bruce suggested a visit to Ely's library might be helpful. There, the librarian Rachel Heinrich directed me to some interesting sources. Ruth King was a former librarian at Ely, who was born in 1923, and included an optimistic poem about mining in the area for her 1942 volume of reflections and folklore, titled *Yes, Really it's Ely*:

In winter and summer miners grind
Beneath the surface where the iron lies,
With tiny shining lamps to help them find
The ore. While up and down the shaft there flies
A busy skip that totes rich loads of ore
From pockets down below, to fat stock piles.
Enormous hills are formed that shrink before
The huge machines that load the miles and miles
Of ore cars rolling down long endless tracks.
They lead out into cities far and near
For vital industries. A miner lacks
Privation, miseries and any fear
Of insecurity, for now the times
Are pressing needs, and ore is in our mines.[7]

Most of the mines had unfortunately closed by the time this was written. A closer look through the records however, supplied me with this more depressing depiction of

Cornish-America. With the closing of one of Ely's last mines, the following poem titled 'The Sheave Wheels have stopped Turning' was composed by Leonard Koponen in 1922. I suppose, in its way, it reflects not only much twentieth-century experience for familes, in Ely, but also those back in Cornwall. When I found these lines in the library that Saturday, I could only think of places like Geevor and South Crofty:

The sheave wheels have stopped turning
On the headframe of the mine
No longer does the whistle blow
To signal quitting time.

The dryhouse is now empty
Of clothes hung up high
No laughing, joking miners
Changing in the dry.

The water seeping in the drifts
Is filling up the sump
No longer can you hear
The rhythm of the pump.

The ore chutes all are rotten
The rails thin lines of rust
There's just a ghostly silence
Spider webs and lots of dust

The sheave wheels have been turning
On the head frame of the mine
As long as I remember
And long before my time.

I often hurried to the mine
When I was just a lad
And watched the sheave wheels turning
While bringing lunch to Dad.

Twenty years I labored there
Some miners twenty more

The sheave wheels kept on turning
Bringing up the ore.

There's empty houses on the street
Where children once did play
Fellows I once worked with
Have packed and gone away.

Yes, this is my story
Of a changing time
The sheave wheels have stopped turning
On the headframe of the mine.[8]

After the library Bruce and I took lunch, then visited a few of Ely's bookshops. There were some general books with titles like *Pioneer Life in Ely*; but comparatively little on mining. In *Chapman Street Books* though I did come across a volume I'd been after for a few years: Samuel Eliot Morison's *The European Discovery of America*.[9] First published in 1971, this is a gem of a work, which looks at how Europeans first made it across to the continent. It is crammed full of apocryphal stories and legends, not to mention vague theories on how they set sail from Europe. For someone like me, it was a real treasure trove which would deprive me of sleep for several nights. There's a load of material on Celtic America, and St Brendan, on mysterious islands called 'Surlenge' between Land's End and America, on Lundy, John Cabot, obscure references to Cornish fishermen off Newfoundland in the early 1500s and the fascinating tale of St Ursula, the Cornish princess, and her eleven thousand sea going virgins. Apparently the latter story was so prevalent during the Middle Ages that it explains why so many islands are named the Virgin Islands around the world. In addition Morison tells the story of how a French ship tried to sail across to America and near died of starvation were it not for them eating their dead colleagues, ending by returning to Europe and making a landfall at St Ives, Cornwall in October 1536. Not only that, but Morison has lots of stories about Richard Grenville in Puerto Rico. Put simply, I was made up.

We passed lots of pasty shops along the way (ZUP'S

351

supermarket also do a nice line in frozen ones!) but didn't stop since I knew Violet, Dan and Champi would be firing up the barbecue at our return. We did however, stop at the Bois Forte Heritage Center belonging to the local group of Ojibwe Native Americans. The Heritage Center lies in the middle of the Ojibwe's reservation and is crammed with artifacts and interpretation from that group. We are asked by the Center to 'respect tradition'; the center's logo being a turtle which represents the earth. I read the interpretation: "The four claws of the turtle represent four directions. Meanwhile the red circle is the red road on which we travel and the footprints go from east to west, the same way we dance at a pow-wow, signifying how far we have come and how far we have to go in the never ending circle of life. There are twelve small flowers that signify the twelve moons. The central flower shows that we are a woodland people and is turned to the west to honor those who have gone before us. The colors red, white, yellow and black are for the four races while the green and blue are the earth and sky." Phew. This all sounded like *The Lion King* meets Carlos Castaneda for me – but I suppose they have a point. I found it a little ironic though, considering just up the hill was a massive hotel and casino run by the Ojibwe. Maybe these days you have to mix symbolic turtles and circles of life with gambling chips and one-armed bandits.

More interesting though was the part of the exhibition which talked about how disrespectful the miners (many of them Cornish, and many of the photographs showing bowler-hatted clad Cornish Cap'ns) were to the Bois Forte Band of the Ojibwe, taking land and ethnically cleansing districts when the Europeans wanted to mine them. I know we moan about Athelstan, but we're just as guilty. It reminded me of my cruise around Alcatraz where Native Americans had claimed the island as Indian land. Now feeling like some kind of offspring of a holocaust-wielding culture, Bruce and I felt we should stop in at the Casino just to see what it was like. I tried on an Ojibwe cologne, peered into the gambling hall and 'respected tradition'. I felt the Cornish and Ojibwe were now at peace.

Violet had organised a huge barbecue for us. Chicken and

corn-on-cob were on the menu. In the hot early evening light, the food tasted wonderful.

"What have you been doing?" I asked Champi and Dan.

Apparently Truman Lindvall had asked them if they wanted to go bear-baiting,

"Bear-baiting?" I asked dumbfounded.

"Yeah – honest," went Dan. "He wanted us to go with him . . ."

I was amazed. I hadn't even thought of hunting bears, but somehow this far north it somehow seemed appropriate. I'm no hunter, but the prospect of this seemed to be like something out of a nineteenth-century adventure story. Here you could become a real Jackpine Savage.

"We chickened out," said Dan, "and just went down the VFW and helped Violet hoover round the house . . ."

This was our last night in town. Tonight, we were all in the mood to party hard. The beers, olives and pickles were flowing freely at the VFW. Put simply, we were quite an event at the VFW. Initially perhaps sceptical of these mad Cornishmen who had shown up out of nowhere, I know now that this is one place I could just stroll in for a beer, and be welcomed as if I'd never left. Like the 'Cruise' in Mineral Point, 'Pardtown Pub' in Linden, the 'Holbrooke' in Grass Valley and the 'Eagle Harbor Inn', I felt completely at home there. The usual crowd were in. Mike Polkinghorne too, who had already taken on Danny at pool – and inevitably lost (Dan's a mean pool player). The round red VFW drink tokens were flipping back and forth across the bar, and somehow it felt like we could have stayed there forever, discussing lumberjacking, Cousin Jacks, mining and bear-baiting. This was a man's world, and we loved it. Ernie too, was in fine fettle – already half-cut by early evening and reminiscing about his days teaching the Cornish in Ely.

"Yous going in the morning?" he asked us.

We had to be moving on.

"Thass a pity. Yous all welcome here anytime . . ."

There was an emergency: Ernie's drink stocks were getting low. You see, they have this odd system in Littlefork – something I think to do with local licensing laws, that you must bring your own liquor to the VFW. Then you label it up and pay a sort of corkage or pouring fee. There is only a very limited range of spirits to buy otherwise, although just about everyone in town seems to have their own favourite tipple behind the bar. More frequent customers kept their drinks in an ice-bucket at the front end, for easy access.

Champi and I stanked over to the Off-License and bought Ernie a bottle of his favourite cheap whiskey. He almost cried when we presented it to him. Summoning over the barmaid, she gave him a pen and some sticky labels that everyone used to mark their drink in the VFW. Carefully, I watched him label up the bottle. He looked up and spoke.

"Read that!" he said to the three of us.

I looked down at the bottle: "Do not touch," it read, "Whiskey for Ernie and the Cousin Jacks."

It was quite an emotional evening for all of us. We gave Ernie some presents and he cried. We almost cried when he presented us with his Veteran of Foreign Wars hat, which proved his service in Vietnam.

"Take this back with yous," he said. "I really want you to have this . . ."

It humbled the three of us. Clearly, this was a gift of some measure. We tried not to take it, but he insisted. There and then, we agreed that Ernie's hat would have a special place back in the Comrades Club of Probus. I asked him to write a short message to everyone which we could mount alongside the hat.

"If all you Cousin Jacks are as fine as these three," he wrote carefully and slowly, "then you have a fine country . . ."

We set off that morning – all very saddened to be leaving Violet and Bruce, and Littlefork: champion little town of all little town competitions forever. Champi summed it all up by saying that it was like he'd found a new mother and father. We were on early – but Violet was up too – making us eggs and bacon for breakfast and strong coffee to keep us awake. They really did not want us to go, and we didn't really want to go either. Littlefork will always be a home from home for all of us.

"Woncha' consider staying another day?" asked Violet.

We explained we couldn't. We still had an enormous journey in front of us; perhaps the most challenging yet –

and then there was the schedule to be met. We needed to be in Phoenix by August 23rd.

"Well, you all come back again for Christmas," said Violet, still optimistic of our quick return.

"Will you host us – and your children?"

"Sure – if you don't mind sleeping in the cellar!"

Getting out of Littlefork was something of a disaster. Dan was navigating. I must not have been fully awake.

"Turn left here," he said. "Trust me on this one Al!"

I turned left there. It was a dead end. I turned the car around.

"Turn right here," he said. "Trust me . . ."

I turned right there. It was a dead end. I turned the car around. How could we be this lost, in a town with a total population of 836? There were only two main roads. Well, in all fairness to Dan, the road we wanted wasn't remarkably well labelled. It was important that we got on the right one too; otherwise we'd have ended up in deepest Canada. We wanted Route 71 south, but only signs for north seem to be appearing.

"Just go anywhere – but not in the direction of International Falls," said Champi in the back.

In the end, that's what we did. Come to see, on the map itself, there weren't too many other options – just a lot of white space, which we had come to learn in America, usually meant lots and lots of forest. Bear, deer and beavers. Despite the possibility of such wildlife, we were subdued that morning. Violet and Bruce's kindness to us had been humbling, as had Ernie's presentation. The mood wasn't enhanced by the fact that seemingly the whole of America was staring us in the face – hard and mean. The country seemed to be shaking its fist and saying to me, "Come and drive me – if you think you're hard enough."

"Yeah, I'm hard enough," I said to it. "Remember, I've done Iowa an' Nebraska . . ."

"You Cornish think you can cross me, do you?" it said.

"Yeah, we do actually," I replied.

"Well then, first y'gotta cross North Dakota . . ." the country said, its evil laughter resounding from behind every signpost along the way.

It was Sunday morning and a light mist ran along the

355

side of the road. We spotted deer testing the fresh grass, scampering away as we came close to them. A few wasted skunks made Dan wake up. Grand Falls, Big Falls, Not so Big Falls, Itsy-Bitsy Teenie-Weenie Falls all passed by in a bit of a blur. We had a pee break at the suitably named Mizpan then reached the East Indian-sounding Bimidji by mid-morning. In the winter, much like Ely, this was skiing country. There were more lakes and roads which looked like they'd been featured in the 1996 film *Fargo*. We passed policewomen by the side of the road who looked like they had been in *Fargo* too.[10]

The signs kept on mentioning North Dakota, but really we weren't that near to it. We still had to cross the eastern side of the State, cutting around the White Earth Indian Reservation to a place called Detroit Lakes. Usually those kind of places were named by some bunch of Detroit madmen who'd stanked out here in 1872 and came up with that highly original place-name. There, you picked up 10 to head across to Interstate 94. Now I thought 10 merited some 'serious' driving but once into North Dakota, you find out how much you can take.

Back in the suburbs of Chicago, we'd met up with some guy who'd got out of a van, unshaven, moaning and who looked slightly frazzled. We'd asked where he'd been.

"Went over to Washington for my vacation. Drove back through the Dakotas . . ."

"What are they like?" I'd asked, thinking we'd be there fairly soon.

"It's a whole lotta' nothun' . . ." he said, "a whole lotta' nothun' . . ."

The van driver looked like he needed psychological care, after the agony of the Dakotas. An ambulance soon showed up to take him away.

It sometimes seemed like Americans needed 'something' rather than 'nothing' to make sense of the world. I was prepared for 'nothing' though.

"Brace! Brace! Brace!" I shouted as we crossed the State line into North Dakota. Dan and Champi put their heads in their hands and assumed the position. Then when it wasn't scary any more, they sat up and drank some more raspberry *Gatorade*. You look at North Dakota on the map

356

and it seems an innocuous little thing. I mean, in the Rand McNally, it fits in on one page. It's huge though, and when you're inside it, you suddenly realise how far north you are. Places like Wisconsin seem to be somewhere in the south, just next to Florida – it's that disorientating. Interstate 94 goes straight through the bottom third of the State and it hardly bends at all – just up and down and on and on. We noticed a strange smell as we progressed on.

"It's wet dog," said Dan.

"Na," said Champi, "it's something else . . ."

We all sniffed again, the fragrance mystifying us.

It was present all the time though, as we went through landscape that reminded me of the section of the A30 near Temple Moors. Then Champi had a revelation.

"It's cattle idn't it?" he went.

He was right. I will forever associate the smell of cattle with North Dakota; a strange wet-haired, manure-like odour.

"Bleddy stinks dun't ut?" Champi continued.

I mean this was summer. What was it like in winter, when there was rain and all that cow-ness became damp? I suppose in places like Buffalo and Wheatland you get used to it. You know it too, even in the sophisticated towns of North Dakota, like Bismarck and Jamestown. You came out of the Opera House to the smell of cow.

"It says here that North Dakota is known as the 'Peace Garden State'" said Dan, reading from the Rand McNally road atlas.

"More like the Dung Heap State," offered Champi. They need to hire Champi in any new campaign to promote North Dakota's tourism.

In all the reading I'd ever done on Cornish America, I'd never found any Cornish connection to North Dakota. The only thing I could think of was a place called Dakota farm on the moors near to Mên-an-tol in Penwith. Perhaps someone had come back from America, and decided to set up shop there. Perhaps they'd got all the way to North Dakota and said to themselves, "This place ent any different than Polcrebo Moors. We'll head us back home again!"

"Perhaps it smelt the same," said Champi.

Driving these kind of distances, as I've said before, is not only a physical challenge; they are a mental one too. How truck drivers do this kind of thing in America on a daily basis I don't know. I suppose, like everywhere else, distances shrink if you do them every day or every week – only in Dakota, it looked like it might take you a whole day to pop over to your neighbours and borrow a cup of sugar. Who knows what it would be like doing the weekly shop. Maybe you had to go across to Minnesota. I mean, mystical places like Saskatchewan (bound to be 'Bigfoot' country) were looking close. The challenge came when we started to head south – obviously enough into South Dakota. We came off just after Dickinson and headed down 85 past Tracy Mountain, the Burning Coal Vein and Cave Hills. Warning: <u>Never ever</u> in a million years drive this route. It is the most boring road on the earth. I would venture even to go as so far to say that it is even more boring than the stretch home from Exeter to Launceston – and that's saying something.

South Dakota's deceiving on the map too. Again, they only give it a page, just to make it look little.

"You want to be heading towards Spearfish?" Bruce had said to us.

"What kind of name is that?" asked Dan. "I mean how many fish are there in the middle of South Dakota . . . The sea's miles away . . ."

"Maybe the Indians were catching fish there," said Champi, now, like the rest of us, out of our tiny minds with boredom on the length of Route 85.

Things got quite scary as we approached Spearfish. In the south-east (the direction we were headed) a massive thunder-storm had started. The Black Hills mountains were attracting barrages of forked lighting which looked as if Victor Frankenstein were pulling down the lever on re-animating his monster somewhere near Mount Rushmore. There wudn' much we could do, except push on. Rain hammered down and for around fifty miles, the driving got very difficult. With my wipers on top speed, the visibility decreased and we all wondered if we were even going to make it to Mount Rushmore by nightfall. It was going to be very tight indeed.

Spearfish doesn't lie that far from the Wyoming border, but in order to reach Mount Rushmore, we had to head east on Interstate 90 down towards Rapid City and Keystone. There was no time to stop – and even if we did I doubt I might have found anything out – at Deadwood. I'd half-wanted to visit the place because it was the supposed home of the legendary Cornish gunslinger Deadwood Dick. Not too many people back home now know the significance of Deadwood Dick, but he was a legendary figure of the Wild West, so much so, that later impostors took his name and he even became transmuted into a character of a famous set of 'dime' pulp cowboy novels.[11]

In case you didn' knaw, Deadwood Dick's real name was Richard Bullock, a Cornishman who was born at Ruthvoes (that's *Ruthers*) near St Columb on August 20th 1847. His father, John Bullock had worked as a Cap'n over Retew clayworks, and his five sons worked with him there. As a boy and young man, Richard had worshipped at Indian Queens' United Methodist Free Church and had been a member of the choir. Apparently, in their spare time they particularly enjoyed pigeon shooting – and by the time he was in his late teens, Richard had established himself a reputation as a crackshot. A friend of Richard's, one Ned Hocking of nearby Fraddon, tells the story of how at a shooting match at St Stephen-in-Brannel Feast Week, Richard boasted to a man they met on the way that he would return with the top prizes and he did just that. Supposedly, on another day, Richard's dog flushed out four partridges in local woods; two of which flew to the left, and two to the right. He shot two with one barrel and the other pair with the second barrel.

How Dick came to end up in South Dakota is interesting. Although he'd married a local girl by the name of Susie Poad, and having a young son, he realised that he would never make his fortune mining china clay (tell that to the Martyn family or *Imerys*), so resolved to emigrate. He began as a gold miner, but became increasingly fed up with the quantity of gold-carrying stage coaches and wagons which were held up and robbed for their load. First off, Richard volunteered to become a bullion guard for the Homestake Mine, the gold of which was carried by the so-called Deadwood Stage Coach. The Stage ran along the dangerous route from Cheyenne to Deadwood via Laramie, Buffalo Gap, Lame Johnny Creek, Red Canyon and Squaw Gaps – all sites of frequent raids and robberies from bandits and Indians alike.

In 1882, Dick had started to ride shotgun and most famously the Stage was once held up by Lame Johnny who stepped into the middle of the road, with two pistols in his hands. Very calmly, Dick Bullock shot him dead and this earned him the name 'Deadwood Dick'. Other areas then hired Dick to sort out 'Wild West' crime and this is how his transformation occurred: the writer Edward L. Wheeler made Deadwood Dick a hero of a novel, and there followed many stories following his adventures.[12] Dick ended up retiring in Glendale in California, where he died at the age of seventy-three in 1921 – a very long way away from Indian Queens – yet his reputation as the china clay cowboy has just about survived.

One day, I resolved – as we passed the exit for Deadwood – to write a book about Richard Bullock, but at least I'd passed through some of the landscape he had known. Now that landscape seemed to be dominated with casinos and mock-Western motels. There was even one casino named after Deadwood Dick himself. I'm sure that would have gone down well with the United Methodist Free Churches. What is amazing is that the more you research Deadwood Dick over the years, the more you discover that many other characters and people have claimed the name of Deadwood Dick – including the famous African-American cowboy Dick Brown, and another man named Richard Clarke, but none of these were the originals. That title belonged to a Cornishman.

Light was starting to fade and we still weren't seeing any signs for that American icon – Mount Rushmore. Surely there would be an exit coming up soon? Why were we visiting Mount Rushmore? I mean, unlike Deadwood, there was no Cornish connection. Well, I suppose I'd wanted to see it 'in the flesh – er – stone' since I was a child. There aren't many more American symbols than Mount Rushmore are there? The Statue of Liberty? Tick. Done that. The Empire State Building? Tick. Done that. The Golden Gate

Bridge? Tick. Done that – last summer. Niagara Falls? Tick. Done that – last week.

But then something had inspired me a long, long time ago at Foxhole Methodist Chapel's Friday Night Youth Club. While the organisers had hoped that we might follow the word of God, and colour in pictures of donkeys, we were upstairs behind the organ listening to the diabolic sounds of Iron Maiden and Black Sabbath on an old mono record-player. Then one day, one of the more enlightened organisers gave me a tape dating from 1970, which until this very day, continues to be one of my favourite albums. It's Deep Purple's *In Rock* and instead of Presidents George Washington, Thomas Jefferson, Abraham Lincoln and Theodore Roosevelt, carved on the cover of that tape is a mock Mount Rushmore made up of Ian Gillan, Ritchie Blackmore, Jon Lord, Roger Glover and Ian Paice.[13] Ever since that time when I first heard songs like 'Speed King', 'Blood Sucker' and 'Child in Time', I've wanted to see the real thing and hold up that tape in front of it. So that's what I did.

We got to Rapid City and started climbing into the Black Hills. They did look black – very black. Originally of course, the Cornish had stanked here, looking for gold. But then when there wasn't much to be found, they'd went off again to California.

Lightning was still striking in the distance. We drove onward and upwards into Keystone, the nearest town to Rushmore. Keystone is like England's northern seaside resort Blackpool, but with presidents. In short, it is horrible. It has every tacky pun going on Mount Rushmore; for example – "Even Presidents Get Stoned at Mount Rushmore" – and every tacky sweatshirt, t-shirt and piece of merchandise you ever wanted bearing the presidential images. In the shops you see countless statues to place on mom's mantelpiece home in Oregon. There are neon signs everywhere depicting the Mount and most of middle America seems to be visiting it.

At the end of Keystone, you start to climb a canyon and it is at the top of this canyon it your first view of Mount Rushmore. At last we were before America's "Shrine of Democracy". Its sculptor, one Gutzon Borglum and his crew removed some 450,000 tons of rock at a cost of nearly one million dollars from 1927–1941. Here's what the National Park Service has to say on its website, in typical National Park Service style:

> The four figures carved in stone on Mount Rushmore represent the first 150 years of American history. The birth of our nation was guided by the vision and courage of George Washington. Thomas Jefferson always had dreams of something bigger, first in the words of the Declaration of Independence and later in the expansion of our nation through the Louisiana Purchase. Preservation of the union was paramount to Abraham Lincoln but a nation where all men were free and equal was destined to be. At the turn of the Twentieth Century Theodore Roosevelt saw that in our nation was the possibility for greatness. Our nation was changing from a rural republic to a world power. The ideals of these presidents laid a foundation for our nation as solid as the rock from which their figures are carved.

Very nice – and so too – is the live webcam, but have you ever seen a mountain move? In short however, despite being talked up by the National Park Service and every single shop in Keystone, it's a complete and utter disappointment. You expect it to be vast – at least not small, but from this angle at least, it looks well, rather puny really. You can't stop anywhere. Signs along the winding road prevent you from doing this, so instead you drive into a large visitor complex below the carvings that reminded me of the architecture of the Tate Gallery in St Ives. There you can stay, visit the museum about its creation, and get closer to the presidents. We were underwhelmed, so decided not to stop, instead hopping out just beyond the parking area, and taking all the pictures we wanted, thus avoiding the ten dollar parking fee. All that driving for a lump of rock. We might as well have gone up Bal Pit. Still I had my picture – holding *In Rock* next to Mount Rushmore. I suppose that had been worth the cattle fragrance of North Dakota on its own.

Darkness was falling rapidly. On reflection, as we came off Mount Rushmore, there was some satisfaction. I mean not everyone even gets there. It's so far away from everything else in America, and yes, it was another icon to tick. We stopped in Keystone for some fuel, then after some food at an *Applebees'* restaurant, made our way back to a motel we'd noticed had vacancies on the way in. We struck a deal, and crashed. We'd had a vague mad idea to visit the creation of another mountain statue – the so-called *Crazy Horse* Memorial begun by the Boston-born sculptor Korczak Ziolkowski (what is it with these sculptors and their names?). The project was to carve in stone a vast testament to the impact of Native American civilisation, to rival Mount Rushmore, but that was another couple of hour's drive south. Besides, we'd seen a model of its projected finished state at Jean Ellis' place. I mean that would have been nice, *Bury my heart at Wounded Knee* n' all, but when you're Cornish, you tend to know rocks all too well. We'd give Crazy Horse a miss. Sorry Geronimo. My head was spinning slightly. I think it was because I'd stopped driving. It felt like I'd lived in American forever. Had we really been in Minnesota that morning? It seemed like we'd driven across the world in one go. Where were you, Ernie? I needed some of that whiskey.

Notes

1. A. Ivan Rabey (1976) *1826: Polkinghorne v. Cann*, St Columb: Penmellyn.
2. David E. Perry (1993) *Gold Town to Ghost Town: Boom and Bust on Rainy Lake*, International Falls, Minnesota: Lakes Interpretative Association, p.2.
3. The Ely Shopper, Inc. (1988) *Marriage, Mining, Mischief and More: Authentic Reprints of Articles and Photos from Ely's Newspapers Since 1888*, Ely: The Ely Shopper, Inc.
4. Carlton C. Qualey 'The Cornish: A Mining Elite' in Michael G. Kami (ed.) (1991) *Entrepreneurs and Immigrants: Life on the Industrial Frontier of Northwestern Minnesota*, Chisholm, Minnesota: Iron Range Research Center, p.74.
5. Ibid., p.77.
6. Ibid., p.78.
7. Ruth King (1942) *Yes, Really it's Ely*, Minneapolis: The Lund Press, p.88.
8. Cited in John W. Somrock (1976) *A History of Incredible Ely*, Ely: Cyko-Art Print Crafts, pp.77-78.

9. Samuel Eliot Morison (1971) *The European Discovery of America*, New York: Oxford University Press.
10. In this film, directed by Joel and Ethan Coen, and set in Minnesota, Jerry Lundegaard's inept crime falls apart due to his and his henchmen's bungling and the persistent police work of pregnant Marge Gunderson.
11. See Warren Wilkins (2003) 'The days of Deadwood Dick' in *Newquay Voice*, 20th August, p.16; E. S. Turner (1948) *Boys will be Boys*, London: Michael Joseph, p.240-6.
12. See Mildred Fielder (1984 [1974])*Deadwood Dick and the Dime Novels*, Deadwood: Centennial Distributors.
13. See Deep Purple (1970) *In Rock*, London: Harvest.

14

Kick my Butte . . .

Apparently, I'm not the first one to make that joke – but I am absolutely certain I won't be the last. Butte, as I was to learn, has been the – *ahem* – 'butt' of quite a few jokes over the years, but because of its success in mining, it also has rightly been labelled 'the richest hill on earth'. I knew I had to go there. I knew too, that getting there would be a drag. Butte lies in south-western Montana, the so-called 'Treasure State', and it genuinely feels about as far away from anywhere else in the USA as you can get. The fact that the Cornish even made it there fills me with awe. But I'm ahead of myself. We weren't quite in Butte yet. There was most of Montana to push through – seemingly the whole 145,558 square miles of it.

The reason I had wanted to go to Mount Rushmore was of course Deep Purple-related. So it turned out, the *In Rock* album cover was actually more spectacular than the mountainside carvings themselves. It won't surprise you then to hear that one of my favourite *double-entendre* lyrics of all time was written by Deep Purple's singer Ian Gillan in the song 'Puget Sound' off 1979's *Mr Universe* album. The song's all about touring America and in particular the northwest. At one point, Montana is mentioned in a fine piece of nudge-nudge, wink-wink lyricism:

Moving over your knee was new territory
We were passing through Billings Montana

As we slipped through Spokane you said something profane
And I shifted up into Nirvana.[1]

I cudn' 'zactly shift up into Nirvana. For one thing, the
car was an automatic. For another, I knew what he meant.
Montana had a lot of land. I mean, earlier on there had
been Iowa and Nebraska – they both had land, then there
had been the Dakotas, they had land – but it was just more
flat land; here it was LAND – huge, massive chunks of land
that looked like they could just eat you up. Somehow it was
all very prehistoric and ancient – like the State had been
untouched for millions of years. Dan moved the map back
over his knee – we'd moved about a millimetre from the last
time we looked. Especially on maps of these larger States,
you don't move much. It took a long time to get from the
Wyoming-Montana border, up through the Crow Indian
reservation to Billings. Billings is not Montana's capital city
– that honour goes to Helena further north – but it is the
State's largest city.

The Gillan lyric was still in my mind as we approached
Billings, but all that was visible from the Interstate was a lot
of cement works and dust. They seemed to be big on dust in
Billings. Consequently, we didn't stop for any length of
time, except to buy the regular sodas and road-food. Civilisation seemed to end "though" the moment we parted
company with that town. The mountains got wilder and
more menacing and the road seemed to place more land
before us. It was unnerving and unreal. There were lots of
signs warning drivers of deer, and creatures with huge
antlers.

Even though we'd set out early from our lodgings back in
Keystone, South Dakota, it took most of the morning to
cross Montana. I knew our time there was going to be
limited, and then there was still the final part of the journey
to do – down to Arizona. The pressure was on. I drove on,
high into the northern Rocky Mountains and into a small
Alpine-style basin drained by Silver Bow Creek. We were a
mile above sea level now. There was a huge ninety foot
statue high on the mountain-side that we later found out
was called 'Our Lady of the Rockies'. Yes – it's a statue
of Mary, mother of Jesus, begun in 1979 and completed

366

in 1985; probably a modern manifestation of the Irish Catholic influence in the State.

"That would have gone down well with the Methodists," quipped Dan.

As we approached Butte, the landscape gradually changed. You know those old black and white photographs you've seen of Camborne and Redruth in their industrial heyday? Well, in Butte it still looked like that. You could literally taste mining in the air. It was a taste many Cornishmen before us had experienced. For example, I'd always been fascinated by the story of Jack Clemo's father – Reggie Clemo – going to work and live in Butte. This was another reason to visit Montana.

Clemo describes all this in his 1949 autobiography *Confession of a Rebel*. In 1908 Reggie Clemo left for America when he was eighteen years old, according to Jack, in search of 'liberation'.[2] Instead, while working at one of the biggest mines – the Anaconda – he found 'the grosser roots of materialism [and] . . . the tawdry degradation of Butte saloons'.[3] Somehow that phrase has always appealed to me. It was this very sort of 'tawdry degradation' which had been part of the Cousin Jack experience in Montana. Of course, Jack, and his mother Eveline greatly disapproved of Reggie's behaviour abroad – but for me, and having lived just a mile away from Reggie and Eveline's home – I had to see with my own eyes, – *ahem* – Reggie's Butte.

"It looks 'zactly like Camborne," said Champi, as I pulled off the Interstate and headed up into Butte's climbing central streets.

Champi was right. Parts of it did look like Camborne, but in all honesty, Butte looked more like the most rip-roaring, rootin' tootin' western town I'd encountered in the whole of Cornish America. It was even more rip-roarin' than Grass Valley on a Friday night – an' thas' sayin' somethun'. I was completely certain that any second a rickety saloon door on the left-hand side of the street might burst open and out would stagger fifty stocky Cornishmen, fists up, ready to fight with fifty Irishmen from another saloon on the right-hand side. It looked that kind of place where bar-room brawls were still common. Apparently, as I was soon to learn, Butte had a history of brawls – among them Irish and

367

Cornish ones – that put just about every other 'row' – either in America or back home into some kind of perspective. 'Es – 'twas rough as rats – exactly as I'd wanted. It was even good to see that 'tawdry degradation' still apparent. Like Clemo, A. L. Rowse might not have approved, but he does mention how ". . . the goings-on in Butte, Montana, were more familiar to us than those in London."[4] That shows just how Cornish, Butte City was, *and* still is.

You can't help but learn quickly about places such as Butte. It is a remarkable place; perhaps the most remarkable of all my travels and experiences in Cornish America. The mineral riches of the area lured thousands and thousands of people here, and millions of dollars profit were made. You may wonder how the town got its name. It is called Butte because at the nothern end of the valley – on which the town clings is a furrowed hill which was once known as 'Big Butte'. Locally, people still call it 'the Perch of the Devil'. Like other Cornish centres in the west of America, its origins lie with gold mining. In the year 1864, at Silver Bow Creek, some fifteen years after the Californian Gold Rush had ended, there was another rush which brought about a sudden influx of people into the area. The rush was over, however, by 1870, although earlier on in 1856 an early mining pioneer called Caleb E. Irvine, had noted that the local Crow and Shoshoni Indians seemed to have mined 'placer' copper using elk antlers as picks.

But all this is simply the precursor for the great age of Butte in the later quarter of the nineteenth century. As Michael P. Malone has lovingly detailed in his book *The Battle for Butte, Mining and Politics on the Nothern Frontier 1864–1906*, much of Butte's initial history in the late nineteenth century was dependent on the rivalry between two 'copper kings': the banker-merchant William Andrews Clark (1839–1925), who focused his attention to Butte's vein mining in 1872, and the mine developer Marcus Daly (1841–1900).[5] Any Cornishman working in Butte in the last quarter of the nineteenth century would have known of these two men, and any working after that time too, such was their influence and power, not only in Butte but in the national politics of the USA as well. Clark and Daly represent, according to Malone, two stereotypes of the

American past. Clark has the Protestant work ethic, while Daly arrived from Ballyjamesduff in Ireland progressing from rags to riches. It was the development of smelting facilities which cemented their hold over Montana, since it meant that the copper did not have to be transported east – or even back across the Atlantic to Wales – to be refined.

Put simply, whether it was land rights, smelting, internal family feuds, or even running for the Senate, Clark and Daly were rivals from day one, and played many dirty tricks to try and win favour with the voting public. However, it is perhaps their rivalry which not only put Butte on the map for the American public, but also had a lasting influence on the development of the town. Daly had interest in one of the area's most famous mines – *The Anaconda*, but Clark initially had more influence in Butte itself, and expanded his empire into lots of other industries. Effectively both operated as barons, manipulating public opinion with newspaper propaganda and bribes.

Butte, as you might expect, is full of stories about the Cornish, who had been some of the earliest to come and mine there. By the late 1800s Butte was dominating world production and corporations such as the Boston-based Bigelow copper family and the Lewisohn brothers of New York were expanding their hold by forming the *Boston and Montana Consolidated Copper and Silver Mining Company*. This company apparently worked in close collaboration with one Cap'n Thomas Couch, who was its superintendent for many years. According to Malone, Couch was 'the epitome of the expert Cornish miner . . . capable, imperious, conservative and opinionated. He supervised every detail of the "B. & M." operation meticulously and prided himself as a Protestant and Republican pillar of the community'.[6] This fits with all I knew about the Cornish in America during this phase.

As we wondered the streets of the town that day, I found lots of descriptions of past Butte, but there were ghosts everywhere I went of this past. Apparently newspapers in the east of America once presented Butte as a nasty place to be. One described the town as 'simply an outpost of hell . . . the women and children there looked with indifference upon crime of every kind.' Had I suddenly found myself at the bottom of Dante's Inferno? Another newspaper noted that, 'Every business man in Butte and every miner is a walking arsenal. He carries a brace of pistols in his belt and a bowie knife in his right boot'.[7] Was this worse than a Foxhole boy walking down through Nanpean late at night?

The noted journalist and historian Ray Stannard Baker, visited Butte in 1903, only five years before the young Reggie Clemo arrived. Baker described it as 'the most Western of American cities . . . It gives one the impression of an overgrown mining-camp awakening suddenly to the consciousness that it is a city, putting on the airs and proprieties of the city, and yet often relapsing into the old, fascinating, reckless life of the frontier camp . . . A nearer view gives one an impression of tremendous disorder, of colossal energies in play.'[8]

I agree with this observation. Colossal energies were still in play. To the east of Butte itself was the huge Anaconda Hill, which the American novelist Gertrude Atherton once described it as a 'tangled mass of smokestacks, gallow-frames, shabby grey buildings, trestles . . . [looking] like a giant shipwreck'.[9] In all honesty, things hadn't changed that much. Even though Butte had plenty of twenty-first-century civic pride, the shabbiness from a century ago was still there haunting the present. It was an incredible sight – as shocking as when one first looks at somewhere like Blackpool clay-pit. Meaderville, further to the east than Anaconda itself, I was told was once the home of several Welsh and Cornish smeltermen and their families, but these days, following an influx of Italians and Slavs, the place is now known as 'Little Italy'. One of the most interesting, if somewhat condescending, depictions of the town comes from Mary Maclane, perhaps Butte's most famous native author, who describes a typical street scene composed of the Irish and Cornish at the turn of the twentieth-century:

> There are Irishmen – Kelleys, Caseys, Calahans, staggering under the weight of much whiskey, shouting out their green-isle maxims; there is the festive Cornishman, ogling and leering, greeting his fellow-countrymen with alcoholic heartiness, and gazing after every feminine creature with lustful eyes; there are Irish women swearing genially at other in shrill peasantry, and

370

five or six loudly vociferous children for each; there are round-faced Cornish women likewise, each with her train of children . . .[10]

So that's us is it? Oglers and leerers? Alcoholic heartiness? Well, I suppose not much has changed. The Keweenaw peninsula's Henry A. Hobert would have loved it here.

The Cornish and the Irish in Butte had what we might term an 'interesting' relationship. The problem was that though the Cornish never came close to the Irish in terms of sheer numbers or political power, the Cornish were the hard-rock mining elite, and when Butte rose in copper production, Cousin Jacks had poured in. According to Malone, the Cornish were more 'taciturn and conservative', and 'typically held the Shanty Irish in contempt both as miners and human beings'. The Cornish were remarkably clannish too:

> At the Mountain View Mine, whose work force was so Cornish that it was called the "Saffron Bun," the foreman airily dismissed Irish job seekers with the famous line: "Thee are in the wrong line, my boy!" Each group had its own churches, its own bars, and its own sports. The Irish preferred Celtic football and boxing, while the Cornish loved greyhound racing and their own special brand of wrestling, in which the opponents wore heavy vests with straps on them by which each tried to throw the other. Each had its own brotherhoods: the Irish Ancient Order of Hibernians, and the Cornish Sons of St George. Admittedly, the two groups eventually learned to get along. They finally came to intermarry freely. On occasion, they even exchanged celebration of their favourite holidays, St Patrick's Day and St George's Day.[11]

All this perhaps sounds remarkably strange in our more nationalistic era, where to celebrate St George's Day is somehow a denial of one's own ethnicity, with St Piran now once again in favour.[12] However, as you may know, there is actually a strong linkage to the St George motif in Cornish folklore – for instance the lyrics of Helston's Hal-an-Tow song mention him, as do many of the traditional and revived / invented Mummer's Plays of Cornwall.[13] In my

371

view, this St George motif is part of our difference – perhaps due to our early accommodation within the English nation state, but I daresay there will be those who aren't keen on 'un.

There was then no pan-Celtic Hugh MacDiarmid-style 'Celtic Union of Socialist Soviet Republics' then either. Supposedly many mine owners in Butte took advantage of this ethnic tension by breaking up the solidarity of the labour, causing internal quarrels amongst the unions. No doubt, because both of the groups liked to drink, many fights resulted from Cornish-Irish tension; the most famous of which was the notorious "A.P.A." riot of 1894. A.P.A. stands for the American Protective Association, a nation-wide, anti-Catholic and anti-Immigrant organization, probably fairly well supported in the Cornish quarter, and when two saloons in Butte displayed the A.P.A. shield in their windows, the usual fisticuffs expanded into a full-blown riot in which one policeman was killed. No doubt just as many Cornish were throwing paving stones as the Irish.

Actually, the first place we headed to in Butte was the so-called 'World Museum of Mining'. To get there we headed up Montana Street and then turned left on Park towards Montana Tech. You pass a statue of Marcus Daly and turn into the old site of the 'Orphan Girl Mine'. Now, I'd already been to the 'National Museum of Mining' back in California, so I had high hopes. I had seen the 'World Museum of Mining' on the map for some time, and because it was not just Butte, or Montana's Museum of Mining – but the 'World' Museum of Mining, I expected great things: you know, hi-tech interactive displays, handles you turned, computers and head-sets with different languages. It wudn' 'zactly like that. The 'World Museum of Mining' was much more localised than its somewhat over-ambitious title suggests.

What you do see is an accurate depiction of mining life in Montana during the past one hundred and fifty years. Yet, if anywhere deserves the title of 56-Inch Cylinder Syndrome nirvana, then this is it. In terms of industrial and mining debris, this place perhaps even surpassed the mines at Grass Valley. I have never seen so many kibbles. The cages of the

'Orphan Girl Mine' looked as if they'd stopped working just yesterday. Everything else more or less looked as though it hadn't been arranged. It was more a case of where it was last dumped – well, that's where it was going to stay. It was hot that afternoon, and we were glad of the shade under the head-frame. In the distance, and all across the city were around twenty-five others, still proudly standing, despite much of the mining having now swapped to open-cast.

A white picket fence had been erected around the site, which seemed somewhat incongruous, given that mine and mining debris, merged with other mines and mining debris nearby, and that to distinguish different sites must have been tricky at the best of times. There weren't many other people visiting the Museum that afternoon, even though it must have been peak season. I suppose there weren't really that many people visiting Montana, so maybe their visitor book reached a peak that day. No doubt we three Cornish-men will contribute greatly to their next application for State funding.

To get out of the heat we went into the drying shed which had been converted into an exhibition. Every variety of 'Danger' signs saying 'No smoking, matches or naked lights' were on display, as were explanations like 'What Mining means to Americans' (To summarise: they think it's important!). Then there were lumps of heavy metal (I have no idea what for) manufactured by Fraser and Chalmers Engineering of Chicago, Illinois. In a preserved poster one 'Dr Pierce offers $5 reward for women who cannot be cured of female weakness' (whatever that is). I read a short poem called *Vagrant Voices* with lines in it about 'ancient heaps of rubble' and how in the 'pine trees, those voices never die'. I could hear Cousin Jack Foster's voice mouthing it back in Michigan.

High above all the paraphrenalia, was a vast Robert Lenkowicz-style mural filled with characters from Butte's mining past. Tramps and vagrants merged with Cousin Jack-looking miners who'd entered one of Butte's bars for what was known as a 'growler' – or a jug of beer. Apparently, there were other varieties of liquid refreshment available too – the 'Coming off Shift Special', the 'Morning

After Special', the 'All Day Special' and the 'Good Night Special'. I needed the 56 Inch Cylinder Syndrome Special. The whole exhibit had the feel of some old-timer saying, 'Butte's a town where they never allowed the dust to settle'. Another poem by an unknown writer from 1904 seemed to sum up the harsh life and fatalism of anyone working here:

Wasn't it a pity I came to Butte City,
To receive my death warrant,
On the nineteenth of May.
Lay me away, and place the sod o'er me,
Because I am a mucker,
And know I done wrong,
Six jolly miners to carry my coffin,
Six more to bear me along,
Play the death march as you carry me along,
And beat the drum slowly
For I am a mucker from the Big Mountain Con.

Right next to the exhibition part of the musuem is the reconstruction of an 1890s' mining town that has been named 'Hell Roarin' Gulch'. Here, we were encouraged to 'stroll along the brick-lined street and marvel at over 750 exhibits carefully arranged from that era'. We were also told to 'be amazed at the unique displays'. Well, we tried to marvel and be amazed but it wasn't easy. Like most exhibits of this type, it needed a bit of love and attention. There was the 'Nugget Café' and 'Jos. Richards, Undertaker'. We wondered if he was Cornish, and perhaps they'd serve saffron cake at the café like they once did back at Pendarvis.

Only though when Champi noticed a display saying 'Hard Rock Mining Exhibit' did my senses prick up. There had to be Cornish stuff in there surely? Well, there was. On the walls, around the endless displays of hard-rock drills and bits, signs which read 'Bad Air, Keep Out' and gear like the 'Ingersoll Rand Butterfly Type Jackhammer' were lots of beautifully-drawn cartoons of Cousin Jack miners, like early versions of the ones by Oswald Pryor and Ian Glanville. Only here did the impact of Cornwall's contribution truly come across. It was such a pity it didn't say *Cornish* as much as other displays seemed to mention the Irish.

I felt obliged to mention this to the poor woman behind the counter of the shop. To my utter surprise, she responded with, "I'm glad you think that. They should make more of the Cornish . . . I'm part-Cornish you know . . ."

"Really?" I said introducing myself, Champi and Dan.

"Yeah – I'm Marie Kraus. Or rather that's my married name. My maiden name is Pollard. That's Cornish isn't it?"

There were lots of Pollards back home in Probus. We had a long chat with Marie about the museum. She ran a good shop. There was every kind of book one would ever need on the history of mining in Butte and Montana, as well as a range of fun mining gear for children: plastic drills and helmets. Cool. At least there was somebody fighting for the Cornish there.

"You know why they were called Cousin Jacks, don't you?" enquired Marie.

Well, I thought I did. I mean, I'd heard a hundred reasons by now, but Marie was to give me a slightly different spin on it.

"It's because so many of the Cornishmen were named Jack, and so many sent passage money to their cousins of the same name, that it wasn't long until any Cornishmen, no matter what their names were called Cousin Jacks . . ."

"That's a neat explanation," I said. Indeed, I hadn't heard it put so succinctly in all my travels.

One of the most interesting books recommended to me by Marie was originally assembled and published in 1943. It was called *Copper Camp: The Lusty Story of Butte, Montana, The Richest Hill on Earth* and is an oral history of the town led by one William A. Burke and assisted by Workers of the Writers' Program of the Work Projects Administration in the State of Montana. It's one of those works which had to be done there and then or much of the material would have been completely lost. During the 1940s, Burke and his co-writers basically listened to the stories of many older residents of Butte, who could re-call its most famous period and characters. In here, there several memories of Cornish-American Butte.

Apparently elections caused much controversy in the town. The Irish of Butte were one hundred percent Democrat, while the Cornish, of course, were Republicans.

Burke interestingly questions 'whether the Irish out-
numbered the "Cousin Jacks", were more adept at winning
converts to their cause, or carried some secret vote-getting
power cannot be explained; but the fact remains that the
Democrats were winners far more frequently than their
rivals'.[14] Apparently, one eccentric Cornish miner named
Tabey Daley had his own explanation:

> "Thee robbing Irish," he would say, "they not honly 'ave two
> votes heach on Helection day, but thee buggers vote seven years
> hafter they 'ave been dead and buried."[15]

Also recorded is the story of a Cornish character by the
name of Eddie Mitchell. Now Eddie, apparently, after
working his shift at the Belmont Mine, used to go round the
three hospitals of the town helping people to convalesce. It
is said that he had a smiling face and always gave the cheery
greeting, "How is everyone is this room tonight? . . . That's
fine, just splendid. Is there anything I can do for anyone?
Any letters to be mailed; any messages to be sent out; need
any cigarettes, tobacco, reading material?"[16] Many in Butte
used to think he was a minister, and perhaps there is
something of that in him. I am certain you will recognise
the Cornish type though. I have seen twenty-first century
versions of him strolling the corridors of Treliske Hospital.

Another moment in the life of Cornish-American Butte is
a good deal more tragic. On October 19th, 1915, sixteen
men were grouped around the shaft of the Granite
Mountain mine awaiting the 12:30 whistles to announce
the time for the lowering of the mine cage to take them to
work. From a cause that has never been determined, twelve
boxes of powder exploded with a roar that could be heard
for miles. The sixteen men standing around the shafter
were blown to smithereens. Apparently fingers with rings
attached to them were found half a mile from the scene of
the explosion. What they found was sealed in one casket
and a combined public funeral was held. One wag is said to
have commented with morbid fascination:

> "Hm-m-m. Puttin' 'em all together in one basket – Corkmen,
> Far-downs, Cousin Jacks, Democrats, Republicans, Masons,

and Knights of Columbus. There's goin' to be a helleva mix-up on Resurrection Day!"[17]

There was less mix-up over the name of mines in Butte. *The Orphan Girl* was named so, because the original prospector became rather sentimental over the initial remoteness of the claim. Meanwhile, it is said that *The Nipper* was named by a Cornishman for a neighbourhood small boy or 'nipper' who spent the greater part of time around the workings. William A. Burke seems to feel 'nipper' is Cornu-English dialect but I'm not so certain.[18] To me it's more of a Cockney phrase, but no matter. The mine still has a Cornish origin.

No doubt the Irish and Cornish came into competition in the regularly-held drilling contests as well. Contests were held all over Montana, from Spokane to Helena, but Butte held the largest contests and when an event was on, the whole town stopped work. Usually by the time the contestants appeared 'on the rock', most observers had a stake in the result. There were usually two types of competition: double hand and single hand. Double-handed drilling requires two men: one to strike the drill steel and the other to hold it in the hole and turn it after each blow. In single-hand drilling one man both strikes and turns the drill steel. Among the most famous double-jackers were two Cornishmen – Henry Rodda and Mike Davey – both blind, and former Butte miners who had lost their sight as a result of an explosion in the mines. According to the memories of Butte citizens, to see them drill was an incredible experience. Their timing was perfect and their striking a work of art. They took part on many competitions all over America and finally turned their talents to exhibition drilling, including an appearance at Madison Square Gardens, in New York City.[19]

Although much has been made over time of Cornishman's propensity for rugby, wasslin' and hurlin'; very little of late has been discussed over that other favourite nineteenth-century sport of the Cornish: coursing. Perhaps, because we live in more politically-correct and anti-bloodsport times, this has become less fashionable to document. Even so, the reality was that coursing was very much a natural economic activity back home. Times were hard in nineteenth-century Cornwall and any meal was a welcome one. According to Butte memory, the Cousin Jacks came to the United States of America, because it was a place where "a man could get 'imself a meal and 'is dog a bloomin' bone". It is said that many a Cornishman would "send 'ome for 'is Cousin and tell 'im, 'Be sure to bring along the racin' dog.'"[20] So it is said, the first coursing track was built in Butte in 1898 – and named the West Side Coursing Track. During its heyday, some five to six thousand people watched events there – many of them Cornishmen and women. Two dogs were usually matched in a race, to chase the rabbit – but there were times in Butte when events were cancelled – due to a lack of rabbits. The general view of the Cousin Jacks though, was that the sport deteriorated after the invention of the electric rabbit in 1918. As one old boy was heard to comment in the finest Cornu-English, "You give the 'are 'is 'ole and you give thee 'ound hay treat 'ee hunerstands. Both the blighters get a chance, my son, in coursin'."[21] The Cornish were probably involved in dog and cock-fighting as well, but these were activities that took place in many mining camps across America at one stage.

Wrasslin' however, had a special place in Butte history. One old Cousin Jack was supposed to have said that, "The bloody ways of the fahncy blokes cahnt compare to the 'eel and helbow gents indulgin' in a bout of Cornish-style man throwin'!"[22] Among the famous Cornish wrasslers of the early days were Nick Crewell, Tony Harris, Tim Harrington, the Chapman trio, Charley Vellenweth and Bill Andrews. Thousand dollar side bets were common wagers and many more thousands of dollars would change hands upon a contest. The scene of most of the matches in Butte was the so-called Arena on Talbot Avenue in the rear of the Union Hall, a swing-door emporium that helped ease the thirst of many a Cornish wrasslin' fan. In 1900, Tony Harris was the most popular champion of the camp, and was said by every Cornishman upon the Hill to be 'the best man to ever wear a jacket'.[23] So confident of Harris were all the Cousin Jacks, that in an incredible ethnic challenge, they once invited an English wrestling champion named Pierce to come out to Butte and take on the Cornishman. We should not be surprised to learn that the Englishman did not make his way to Montana.

Pasty-lore was all over Butte, but there was also mention of a foodstuff called 'Boxty' – supposedly popular with all the Celts of the Camp – the Cornish, Irish and Welsh.[24] Boxty was made from the first milk taken from a cow immediately after calving. This timing was supposedly very important, and this milk, a thick, yoghurt-like substance was strained thoroughly and mixed with eggs (my stomach was already turning) and cornstarch or flour and steamed into a kind of pudding. Most Cornish families owned a cow, so boxty was an annual treat. Apparently the eating of it is supposed to give virility to the males and fecundity to females. No wonder it was popular.

In the late afternoon we wandered around some of Butte's streets half-looking for a bit of boxty, but instead noting the Butte Copper Company ("You're in Copper Country!" ran its slogan), the Uptown Cafe ("Civilised dining in the wild, wild West") and Lucky Lil's Casino ("Butte's Most Liberal Casino"). How *liberal* was *liberal*? Then we had a quick yap with the busy shopkeeper of 'Joe's Pasty Shop' which promised Butte's Famous Pasties'.

"The beef must be top quality – Montana beef is best," she said. "You must dice it to the size of the third joint of a Cornish woman's little finger . . ."

"I never heard it put like that before," I said, "though it's what my mother does . . ."

I explained that I'd heard that pasties were called Cousin Jack's mouth-organs in America and explained how they were first eaten.

"I never heard that," the lady said, "but here in Butte we called them 'letters from home'".

I liked that: the Butte pasty had its own name. Splats, letters from home, mouth-organs. I'd had the lot. Very good, there were, too. We sat on a bench, eating and surveyed the whole of the town. I'd better not give them a rating. The Butte pasty lady might send me a letter.

The bottom end of town is still known as 'the Flats', as it was a century ago. All around and above are still dotted the stark, dark headframes of mines such as Kelley, Steward, the Original, Belmont, Granite Mountain, Bell Diamond,

Badger State, Travona, Lexington, Mountain Con and the Anselmo. All those mines and all those 'letters from home' consumed in their depths. If we'd had the time we could have taken the Old No.1 Trolley tour, but after the pasty-break we had a brief look at the Charles Clark Mansion – Home for the Arts in Butte. Built in 1898 as a home for Charles Clark – the son of Copper King, William Andrews Clark, this has now been redeveloped as an Arts Centre. On 219 West Granite, we also drove past the senior Clark's mansion, lush with nineteenth-century opulence. Then we headed briefly out along Continental Drive to Berkeley Pit, a huge and now flooded open-cast quarry which was begun in 1955 and closed in 1982. It looked exactly like some-where on Hensbarrow Down, with its eerie mineral-green water. There was so much more we could have seen – the Lexington Stamp Mill, the Granite Mountain Memorial (dedicated to the 168 men who in 1917 lost their lives in a fire disaster) – or even the Dumas Brothel Museum (with its mantra of "First came the miners to work on in the mine, then came the ladies who lived on the line"). But there was no time for such delights. We had to be making tracks south. Maybe my pal Michel from Grass Valley could find work up here.

On the way out of Butte, I suppose I felt slightly saddened that beyond the pasty and perhaps that hard-rock mining exhibit, the Cornish presence there had been slightly brushed under the carpet. There were still, for instance, shops like *Cavanaugh's County Celtic and Beyond*, shop full of Leprechaun green Emerald Isle merchandise. I particularly liked the Butte, Montana skater-boy hoodies complete with green Celtic lettering. Then there was the *Minings Chinese Restaurant*, offering the 'city on the hill' buffet special. Perhaps, I wondered, that the Cornish really didn't need to stamp their identity on the town anymore. Perhaps all those head-gears frames and all those dumps stood much larger testament to our presence here.

Before we left, we pulled into a rest-stop and bought some postcards. I had to laugh. The one I bought of Butte was not exactly the most picturesque view of the town. In fact, it looked like every pollutant possible was being released into the earth's atmosphere. On the back it read,

'Butte, Montana at sub-zero temperatures, where steam from present-day heating systems is a vague reminder of the the heyday of the copper mining and smelting industries of the 1800s'. Mmm – *pleasant* imaginings of sulphur-fumed past. I wrote a few out.

"Wish you were here," I said, "in Sulphurville, Montana."

At the Museum shop, me being me, I'd also picked up a bizarre collection of verse by the Sullivan sisters (Margaret Kathryn, Mae Jean and Margaret M.) titled *Sunset in the Rockies and 20 Mule Teams on Old Butte Hill*.[25] It had sentimental and melodramatic pioneer-style poems in it like 'The Hanging of Diamond L. Slim' and 'The Lights of Butte' – perhaps written in an age when the romance of the west was still there. It made interesting reading. If we'd arrived slightly earlier on in the day, then we might also have witnessed one of the Orphan Girl Theatre's Butte Melodramas. Dan had picked up a leaflet about it. These were promenade plays performed in and around the World Mining Museum over the summer. Titles included 'Come Butte or High Water', 'A Ghost in the Vault' and 'Luck o' the Chinese'.

But the melodrama of Butte was over for the Cornish – and for we three, so into the night we went, the State of Idaho like entering an American mine for the first time – just a whole load of blackness. The radio was on, playing formulaic country rock – some song with lyrics like "Bubba was just a man from Texas, Bubba was dealing with the sexes".

I thought back to the conversation I'd had with Marie Pollard over her Cornishness earlier that day, in the *World Museum of Mining* shop. It was just as we were leaving that I spied it. There, between the so-called 'sharp-eyed drawings of mining' by J. C. O'Donnell and the Anaconda Mining Company safety posters, sat the very item I'd somehow been spiritually or intuitively seeking all this time. Not a pasty mind. No 'letter from home'. Not that kind of mouth-organ this time; instead, a neatly-boxed *Victory Harmonica*, priced three dollars. It looked the very kind of thing Eric Clapton might play on some unplugged album sometime. Somehow that little instrument had come along just at the right moment. I handed Marie three dollars and pocketed the mouth-organ.

"I expect a lot of Cornish songs got played on those in Butte years ago," said Marie smiling.

"Yes," I said. "I'm sure they did . . ."

And I thought of Reggie Clemo, Cap'n Couch, Tabey Daley n' Eddie Mitchell and all those other assassins of grammar who ended up at 'the richest hill on earth', coursin', wrasslin' and minin'. All that travelling. All that endless road. All that 'tawdry degradation'. All those endless pasties. And back in Butte, I'd found it – a mouth-organ. Still driving, I reached into a sidepocket of my trousers and pulled out the harmonica, and gave it a lonesome bluesy throaty toot, like some Canadian-Pacific train reaching its final destination, briefly shaking Dan and Champi from their slumber. It was an unforgettable moment. Colossal energies were in play. Finally, I'd found me a mouth-organ. All I had to do now was learn how to play it.

Notes

1. Gillan (1979) *Mr Universe*, London: Acrobat Records.
2. Jack Clemo (1975 [1949]) *Confession of a Rebel*, London: Chatto and Windus, p.3.
3. Ibid., p.7 and p.21.
4. A. L. Rowse (1991 [1969]) *The Cornish in America*, Redruth: Dyllansow Truran, p.22.
5. Michael P. Malone (1995 [1981]) *The Battle for Butte: Mining and Politics on the Northern Frontier 1864–1906*, Helena, Montana: Montana Historical Society Press, pp. 11-33 and pp. 80-132.
6. Ibid., p.48.
7. These are quoted in *Anaconda Standard*, 24th August 1919.
8. Ray Stannard Baker 'Butte City: Greatest of Copper Camps' in *The Century*, April 1903, pp.870-75.
9. Cited in Malone, p.61.
10. Ibid., p.63.
11. Ibid., pp.65-6.
12. See general iconography in Bernard Deacon, Dick Cole and Garry Tregidga (2003) *Mebyon Kernow and Cornish Nationalism*, Cardiff: Welsh Academic Press.
13. See numerous examples in Tony Deane and Tony Shaw (2003) *The Folklore of Cornwall*, Stroud: Tempus.
14. Writers Project of America (1970 [1943]) *Copper Camp: The*

Lusty Story of Butte, Montana, The Richest Hill on Earth, Helena, Montana: Riverbend Publishing, p.50.

15. Ibid.
16. Ibid., p.79.
17. Ibid., p.173.
18. Ibid., p.207.
19. Ibid. See pp.231-3.
20. Ibid., p.233.
21. Ibid. See pp.233-4.
22. Ibid., p.234.
23. Ibid., p.235.
24. Ibid., p.254.
25. See Margaret Kathryn Sullivan, Mae Jean Sullivan and Margaret M. Sullivan (1978) *Sunset in the Rockies and 20 Mule Teams on Old Butte Hill*, Hollywood: Sullivan Publications.

15

Chilli, Cousin Jacky and the Whiskerinos . . .

Considering the overdose of 56 Inch Cylinder Syndrome I'd had at the 'World Museum of Mining' in Butte, as I drove through Idaho, it felt somewhat ironic listening to a set of Country and Western 'returning from rehab' songs that seemed to litter the radio waves that night. I had to admit it to myself: I'd fallen off the wagon again. I'd not cured anything. The Syndrome was as much a part of me, as I was of it. We were symbiotic. We lived off each other like those little birds who clean the jaws of hippopotomuses.

Another genre of Country and Western music that evening was that of the new generation of Shania Twain 'attitude' women who sang songs that 'went out to all the girls about forty-two'. You won't believe how addictive some of those songs are. In the next few days, I was to find myself casually scanning the 'country and western' section at 'Wal-Mart'. Thankfully Danny eventually came over and steered me into the 'Rock' section once again. Thank goodness for true friends or right now, I'd be listening to Garth Brookes 24-7.

I'm afraid I can tell you very little about Idaho. From Butte, we headed down Interstate 15 passing the Beaver-head National Forest and the Pioneer mountains. I think we stopped in Dillon for fuel, then pushed on to the conurbation of Idaho Falls and Pocatella. Aside from Boise in the east of the State, these places seemed to be just about the only real civilization going; the rest of the State's pan-handle being dominated by mountains and forests and Bigfoots. No doubt, it looked very pretty in the daylight. I knew the Boise Basin had some Cornish connections; there was lots of alluvial gold-mining activity during the early years of the western Gold Rush. I knew too that several of the Jewell family had headed out here from Wisconsin, having some success in mining and eventually moving into agriculture. Idaho itself however, seemed rather an oasis from mining activity – a place where the Cornish moved to once they'd made a bit.

Interstate 15 led down into Brigham City and Ogden, now more or less the northern end of Salt Lake City. To the west was the Great Salt Lake itself, then the Desert of the same name. By now I was almost back on last year's route – the Bingham Copper Mine and Interstate 70 coming in from Colorado. By the time I'd touched Provo, we must have hit the half-past three a.m. mark. I still felt awake enough to drive, so we ploughed in a south-easterly direction at Provo, running on old Route 6. This was ancient mountain mining country. By the time dawn began to break, we were running through Wellington, east of the Roan Cliffs. Great copper coloured open-cast mines opened before us in the eastern sunrise. It was utterly magical, and combined with all the mining buildings, stacks, and mills, looked very much like a sequence out of a science-fiction film set on Mars. It would have been nice to have stopped longer here, but we were on a mission to see some rocks . . . some very unusual-looking rocks.

South of 70 was the Arches National Park, and further to the south, Monument Valley. We did the Canyonland first though. It does what it says on the label. What you get is hundreds and hundreds of canyons in varying shapes and sizes and colour schemes. *Selecto-Canyon* was it. I was 'pitying the fools' – Mr T-style – who decided to get to California this way. It felt like Roadrunner might appear at any moment, and Wiley Cayote might manoeuvre a huge boulder to fall down upon us. The Arches National Park was incredible though. First, one had to climb to a plateau and up there are rock-weathered arches seemingly straight out of early dinosaur films. Here, it felt like a fur-clad Raquel Welch might step out from behind one of the strangely formed pillars to be roared at by some Ray Harryhausen dinosaur. Imagine Mên-an-tol, and times it by one thousand. We did it all though – walking around with the necessary jaw-drop action. Some of the caves and arches were vast, so large apparently you could fly aeroplanes through them. I was reminded of what Kristen's father had told me last year in Las Vegas.

Monument Valley snuck up on us unexpectedly. We had already been driving through incredible scenery. There were places like Looking Glass Rock, Wilson Arch, Mexican Hat, Navajo Twin Rocks, Alhambra Rock – in short, every kind of weird-looking stone formation you could imagine – so much so it looked like the course of the pod-racing circuit in *Star Wars Episode 1: The Phantom Menace*. For a few minutes I was Anakin, burning up Sebulba. I took loads of photographs of them, but after a day of driving through such natual wonders, once you've seen one amazing marvel, well, you've pretty much seen them all. In my view, over the years, the Valley itself has been much enhanced by clever photography. Those perfect mesas and buttes which seem to predominate album and video covers (witness the Led Zeppelin DVD), postcards and movies, not to mention Marlboro cigarette advertising, aren't quite in the formations I've always imagined them to be. Neither is the road running through. I'd thought the road ran through two sets, twisting and winding, so that at any point, I could be observed with a mesa and butte behind me. Believe me – it isn't quite like that. However, when you do look back and see the landscape below a bright blue American sky, there is still something wonderful about it. I'm glad to have driven through there. I may never get there again.

Our next planned stop was a motel somewhere south of Grand Canyon, named the 'Anasazi Inn' (I was in Room 184, with a dodgy sink and toilet). I'd been to the said Canyon a few years back, but for Dan and Champi, the vast chasm was going to be one of their trip highlights. On the way down, we put into a very lonely looking garage to top up on gas. Little did I know but we were about to have another moment. Dan, or should I say, his alter-ego of 'Ricardo Tregaskis', had since Idaho, or perhaps earlier, become somewhat fascinated with Indian culture during our travels. I'd whacked on some Navajo radio for him to listen to. At the garage, a young girl, obviously Native American, served him his *Gatorade* and some strange new variety of road food. Champi and I watched carefully. Here's how the conversation went:

Ricardo Tregaskis: Thank you very much. What tribe are you, Maid?
Native American girl: *(with dignity)* I am Navajo.
Ricardo Tregaskis: *(with no dignity)* Really? Me – I'm Cornish . . .
Native American girl: I don't know that tribe . . .

Champi and I hit the floor as a dozen customers sent tomahawks in our general direction. Carefully, crawling on our bellies besides the Circus Peanut sweet stand, we managed to make it outside. The door closed – a hail of arrows failing to harm us. Not really, but I think you know how embarrassed Champi and I felt. It had been a narrow escape from being scalped.

"What?" said Dan munching his new road food. "I just wanted to talk to her thaas' all . . ."

"Sure Dan . . ." Champi and I both said on cue.

That evening a storm came in. It was a massive one that we later learnt had almost washed away parts of Las Vegas, but was now directly passing over Black Mesa and the villages of the Painted Desert. We'd tried heading up to Grand Canyon that evening, but when lightning started landing close to the Navajo jewellery stalls and the canyons of the Little Colarado, well, it was time to head back to our motel, or be frazzled. Given that I'd been on the road for almost forty-eight hours non-stop, it seemed like the perfect time for some serious sleep.

The morning's television news brought us pictures of a washed-out Las Vegas. Casino chips were floating along in rivers of mud. The newscasters were full of reports on how there had been the worst flooding in the city for over a half a century. I supposed they didn't get much rain in Vegas. Maybe they were exaggerating. Still, it was worrying because we were due to spend a couple of nights there back in the home of Kristen and James.

First though, came Grand Canyon. What can I say. My thoughts of it haven't changed much since I wrote a poem called 'Canyons' about it back in the late 1990s:

We meet you in the Arizona dawn
and face a grand red chasm at sunrise,
where the blue Colorado carved a yawn.
Its sheet vastness can't fail to suprise.

Why it startles I can't begin to guess.
It's not like I grew up without holes;
Gothers, Melbur, Blackpool and Littlejohns' mess.
I knew intimately their humbling souls.

At the Southern Rim, backpackers set out,
while in gift shops Santa Fe dreamcatchers spin.
Back home, there were no souvenirs about;
only sparkling rock with mica in.

One sees such layers, the time inside.
These are the canyons that open us wide.
The world about somehow seemed larger that day
and I smaller, like a footing had worn away.[1]

Like me, Dan and Champi were suitably awestruck with the vastness of the place. It is literally impossible to take in the scale of the Canyon, and so we trundled along the southern rim, stopping every so often to look down into the hole and take yet more photographs. Eventually the road steered south to Tusayan and we followed it down to rejoin Interstate 40. We were heading west towards Kingman. It was here that we realised how far we were across the country. A little further and I'd be back in California again. This time though, we were going towards the northwest and took Route 93 to Vegas. On the way I couldn't resist stopping at one of those strange highway zoos you only seem to get in the west of America. You know the score – lions and rattlesnakes, run by men and women who might just use you as food for their menagerie. I did buy Dan a cuddly toy skunk however, just to remind him of his American road-trip.

388

"Skunk," he said, out of habit, but fortunately it had no smell.

Dan seemed a little disappointed.

We mounted the skunk between the front windscreen and the mirror.

In so many ways, arriving at Vegas was like coming home. I'd had such a blast there last summer, and wanted Dan and Champi to share in its tacky wonder. I did it all again. This time, 'Excaliburs' had a 'Haunted Mine Ride' (located on the 'fantasy faire' level), and this time we cruised the 'Barbary Coast' and 'Caesar's Palace' casinos, the latter of which we walked out of on top. On the sidewalks, we were handed many promotional prostitution sheets giving a 'special two-for-one offer' one evening. Of course, this was Nevada . . . where anything went. It definitely had the 'tawdry degradation' factor.

"Two for one," went Champi. "This is better than Redruth . . ."

This was perhaps one reason why things had changed for our hosts. Kristen I learnt, was pregnant again, and James was back to full fitness. They were about to move though – all the way across to North Carolina, to James' family farm.

"Vegas is no place to bring up a couple of kids. I have these clients and there kids are involved in all sorts – you know, drugs, and gangs and prostitution and so on," James told me. "You'll have t'come an' see us there . . ."

Dan, Champi and James all turned out to be fans of the movie *Roadhouse* starring Patrick Swayze. I'd never seen it.

"That's *such* a guy film," said a dismayed Kristen.

"Yeah," we all said, staring avidly at the film with cold beers in our hands, enjoying the now classic fight scenes that strangely now reminded me of past times in Butte. Basically *Roadhouse* has a plot based around as many bar-room brawls as it is possible to have in one film. That, and nude chicks.

The torrential rain had affected their property we later learnt. A small tree in their front garden had been washed out and had fallen over. It was agreed that as a thank you for hosting us, the three Cornishmen would re-erect the tree, despite the fact that Kristen and James would be shortly moving.

Dan was sweating and talking to James in time with his shovelling.

"You know – what they say – wherever – there's a hole in the ground – you'll always find – a Cornishman – in it . . ."

"Really?" said James.

"We're the masters of hard-rock mining . . ." said Champi taking over, like he'd just come down to Vegas from a rock-drilling competition at Butte.

The new hole for the tree wudn' gettin' very far at all.

The problem with Las Vegas is that beneath the layers of coloured garden stone and concrete, is just desert. Every time the hole was dug, the sand poured back in and filled it again.

We had a 'we won't be beaten attitude though'. Hell: if we've dug all over this country, we can dig this little hole here.

Eventually the tree was forced back into the hole and stamped in good and proper. Then like true miners of old, we staked it solid. Any cave in, flood or earthquake wudn' goin' t' move that tree every again. I think we all liked that – that maybe we could go back in fifty years time, and that tree would still be standing in some Las Vegas suburb.

The next morning we began the final phase of the trip down to Globe. In some respects my own Cornish American journey had come to completion back in Butte. I wouldn't find a more perfect symbol to end my travels than that little harmonica. However, we still had a good few miles to go. There was Champi's relative 'Jacky Champion' or rather Jacky Champion's grave to be found somewhere in the middle of Arizona – no doubt surrounded by vultures, cowboy-film cacti with right angle 'stems', and lots of desert. Glancing at the map in the early morning light, that still seemed a long way away. We had to follow 93 back down to the Interstate. Just to the south of Vegas of course, is the Hoover Dam. We'd crossed it on the way up, but that morning, there was enough time to take a wander across it, and sit on the edge. Post-September 11th there was heavy security presence around the dam, and the traffic was busy, perhaps why the authorities were building a by-pass around the attraction.

I don't know why the Hoover Dam fascinates me.

Perhaps its those oddly positioned pylons which cling to the sides of the canyon where it is located, or it could be the James Bond-set feel of the location. You imminently expect warning sirens to go off and men in orange boiler suits holding submachine-guns to emerge out of nowhere, all shooting at Bond, but inevitably missing him. Obviously it was this place's hydro-electric power that kept Vegas twinkling.

The spin down to Phoenix went quickly. This was Cactus country for certain. You know – the type of classic cactus that children draw. Some of them beside the road on Route 93 looked – rather like the 'World Museum of Mining' – as if they'd needed a bit of love and attention. Some drooped at curious angles, while others were secured in place by stakes. Apparently they'd hired a team of three Cousin Jacks from Vegas to do the work. Interestingly, the road even split in places where it needed to go around protected species of cactus. You won't be surprised that we stopped every so often and took photographs of ever more spectacular types of cacti. Alongside the cacti, the only other thing that seemed to increase were the numbers of rusting cars in garages along the road. Arizona was definitely the place for dying cars to come to rest. As well as this, wandering vagrants appeared by the side of the road thumbing lifts south – perhaps to Phoenix, perhaps further south.

There was no surprise then when gated communities began to appear on the nothern edge of Phoenix, all expanding out into the desert with a kind of alarming futuristic terra-formation, and interspersed with golf courses kept green by a huge network of irrigation and sprinklers. We turned onto Interstate 10 and went around the top of the city – admiring the central business district skyscrapers and viewing planes landing at the airport. We headed east to Apache Junction (what a great name!) on the southern edge of Mazatzal mountains. We wound through the mountainous roads around Florence Junction and Superior then dipped as we went down to the twin towns of Miami-Globe.

Miami-Globe's beginnings are related to a find of silver at the Silver King Mine in 1874, and initially it produced gold and silver, but very soon it was discovered how rich the rock in the area was with copper. It was at this point that the so-called Old Dominion Smelter was built and by the end of the 1880s there were six smelters at work. According to A.L. Rowse it was after this that Cornish miners travelled into the district, apparently having three main settlements on three hills – Noftgers, Pascoe and School. Pascoe Hill is actually now known as 'Pasty Hill'.[2] This part of Arizona was once Apache territory so it was dangerous to get in and out, but by the end of the nineteenth century the Old Dominion Mine was one of the greatest copper mines in the world, rivalling even those up in Butte.

The Gila County museum was just across the Parking Lot from Globe Chamber of Commerce building. We wandered in and immediately ignited the curiosity of its curator, the seventy-five year old Jim Davies, born in Texas, but a long-term resident of Globe. Admittedly, the Gila County museum looked the kind of place which did not have, say, the visitor numbers of the Eden Project, so he was more than glad to show us around, directing Champi to a catalogue of the graves in the churchyard and me to all kinds of Cousin Jacks sources and literature. Jim was of Scotch-Welsh background, and knew plenty about the Cornish who worked primarily at Old Dominion Mine. Importantly this was where Champi's Cousin Jacky had worked.

"BHP Copper Incorporated is now reclaiming that old place," said Jim. "You should go up and have a look at it . . ."

We did later on in the day.

Curiously on the wall were two sepia-tinged photographs of two eminent citizens of Globe – Charles F. Pascoe (1862–1942) and Clara Bell Pascoe (1870–1953). I made the connection that these two were probably connected with the two famous Pascoe brothers – Benjamin and Thomas. Benjamin was the town's nightwatchman guarding against Apache attack, while Thomas, though born in Galena, Illinois grew up in California and after years of mining, eventually became Gila County's sheriff.

The Gila County museum was stuffed with lots of mining tools as well as a very interesting mine rescue station. In the Old Dominion Library portion of the building, several posters made much of the so-called 'whiskerinos': these were people of Arizona with particularly spectacular beards and moustaches. There were lots of Cornish names on the poster. Dan, Champi and I all at this phase having goatees, there and then resolved to join this honoured throng. As we'd not shaved for a few days, this somehow seemed entirely appropriate. Of course, all of us thought of Albert Jenkin back in Pennsylvania, with his wonderful handlebar moustache.

Jim did not want us to go. He wanted us to stay all day and talk about Cousin Jacks and whiskerinos. We had things to do though. Flora 'Tommi' O'Hagan had recommended that I contact the local Cornish representative in Globe: Linda Carnahan. Due to work commitments however, she explained that it would be hard for her to meet up with us, but she was helpful in giving us a few pointers to the Cornish elements of Globe. In particular she suggested where we might find Champi's relative.

Before heading up to the graveyard, we elected for a drive and a stroll around Globe itself. Globe didn't look too different than any other small American town in the south-west, all quiet shops with air-conditioning; the occasional truck honking its way through. We found an arty style shop that sold copper-work and postcards. I snapped up a postcard made of copper that depicted an open-cast quarry (a 'Kopper Kard') and a particularly grim-looking view of the Miami-Globe industrial landscape that would put Nanpean – and even Butte – to shame. I bet I was the only person to buy that card in the last ten years.

The lady who owned the shop sensed our Cornishness right away. It was as if we'd got saffron cake and clotted cream tied round our necks. She pointed out where Noftgers, Pascoe and School were and then told me I needed to speak to Jack and Mildred Sowton.

"They're Cornish . . . and they make the most delicious pasties . . . Gotta feeling they're outta town today though . . . They'd love to have met you guys . . ."

She handed me the Southern Arizona telephone directory.

"Take a look through here," she said. "Maybe you'll spot a few Cornish names . . . Here, even better, take this one with you – it's last years . . . It hasn't changed much . . ."

Now was this an A.L. Rowse moment or what? Casually, I opened the directory at the letter T. I scanned the pages. Yes, Treloar, Trevillyan, Trevizo . . .

To the uninitiated, Globe Cemetery looked vast. Much of it was high on a small hillock to the south of the town, while over the years, as more space for the dead was needed, it had gradually spread to the valley below, and there had neatly kept graves bordered by poplar trees. Linda had suggested looking at the older section of cemetery high on the hill. As we climbed the tight bends, the weather started to turn. The rising heat of the late afternoon was turning into a thunderstorm, and the sky cracked above us. The whole scene suddenly turned very gothic, and once the car was parked, it was with a strange foreboding that we twisted between the labels of the graves to find our own Champion. Champi had a photocopy of a faded colour photograph of the grave taken some years back. All we knew was that the gravestone was rectangular, made of a brownish-coloured rock, and that behind it stood a small tree. There were lots of brownish-coloured gravestones though and lots of small trees – all seeming very attractive to the bolts of lightning that were connecting to the ground around us. The numbering system of the graves seemed somewhat illogical too. A run of them would suddenly stop, and it was hard to discern where they picked up again.

As Dan and Champi negotiated the section on the top of the hill, it was agreed that I would go back and pick up the car, and swing on the anti-clockwise route towards them. I drove slowly along this route. Right next to me was around a fifty-foot drop to the valley bottom. I stopped because I noticed a tree. It wasn't any old tree. It somehow had the feel of Champi's photocopy. I tried to orientate myself so that the perspective of the original photograph would suddenly appear. I scanned rows of flat, concrete graves, packed in so tight that it was impossible to walk between them, then traversed towards the left. I saw the base first. It had the rough-hewn qualities that Champi had shown me one night back home in Probus Comrades Club. Then it became obvious; the top two thirds of the grave, had in the meantime, fallen over. I gave Champi and Dan a shout, and they came running down from the top of the hill. The block was too heavy to lift on my own, so I had to wait until they arrived. There was a hesitancy on all our behalfs to put our fingers under the block.

"I bleddy well 'ope there idn naw snakes under here," said Champi.

Somehow that made the final revelation more magical. We three levered up the gravestone and swung it forwards, Danny and I reaching for smaller stones to prop its weight. Under perhaps years of mud, we saw the name carved: Jacky Champion. I dun't knaw how long we were silent. We'd found our Cousin Jack. There were more than a few tears in our eyes. It was as if the whole of my journeying across this vast country immediately rolled up and slapped me in the face. Here, in this bit of Arizona desert was precisely how far pards got to roam.

A few minutes later, we'd fetched some water from the car and washed the front of the stone. At the same time a light rain fell from the thunderclouds.

"'Ee cudn' have a better name cud a?" remarked Dan, "I mean – for a Cornishman in America . . ."

We took some chalk and highlighted the lettering so that it would stand out in a new photograph. The next word was 'Native'. Then came 'Peace'.

"Thaas near Redruth ennit?"

'Cornwall' came next. We proudly chalked those eight letters.

"We'll leave the England bit out shallus?"

So we did.

Last of all came his dates: '1853–1917'.

So now Cousin Jacky's grave is standing tall once again. And for me, like the mouth-organ I'd found in Butte, it was another tiny metaphor for all of Cornish America. It's perhaps unlikely I'll ever visit Globe, Arizona again, but I'm glad there's a piece of my past there. The stone gads we 'eaved under that gravestone, should mean it'll be standing for the next thousand years – a menhir to Cornish industry, mining and emigration. A proper job.

The next morning, after a good night's sleep at the Globe 'Travelodge' on Highway 60, we drove back to Phoenix. We went past a vast sign near on the outer limits of Globe's sister-mining town – Miami. It read, 'We remember the miners and farmers who founded this community'. This was nice to know. There was a burning temptation in me to try to head south towards the US-Mexican border. Down there was Tucson, which seemed a Rolling-Stones-kind-of-a-place to visit, as well as the Cornish-cowboy town of Tombstone. Tombstone, I knew had many Cornish connections, not least in the form of former BBC Radio Cornwall's sports producer, the late Jerry Clarke, who had been given earlier that year the status of honorary citizen of the town for renewing historic links between Cornwall and Tombstone. In particular he had been very interested in the early St Day-born pioneer, one Frank Garland, whose American home is now a museum. Jerry had suffered a stroke while over there and sadly had died just before we'd left.[3] I first knew him when I was on school work experience at *The Packet* newspaper office in Falmouth. He was perhaps best known though, for his reportage of 1991's incredible rugby final between Cornwall and Yorkshire at Twickenham; the year the victorious Cornwall team celebrated the territory's first championship in eighty-three years.[4]

But Tombstone was too far away, and I'd done enough driving for the past three weeks. We'd covered almost four thousand miles. Instead we returned our car to the hire company, and found our pockets filled with odd bits of American coinage which we were determined to spend. Phoenix Sky Harbor International Airport is very trendy. It reminds me a lot of Santa Fe. You expect Shania Twain to check in, followed by Georgia O'Keeffe. It was full of people saying, "How are ya?" and "Hellooow. Yoooou loook goood". Rich guys with ponytails joked about heading to Mexico to play golf for a "week without the wife". All of us meanwhile ogled the goddess-like tanned female models who strutted across the concourse.

"They've gotta be in porn," noted Champi, Dan rolling back his tongue into his mouth, and picking up Champi's eyeballs. "Maybe I can get a two for one deal . . ."

We had our final taste of Cornish America at 'Margarita's Bar' at Sky Harbor. There, our bartender, the fifty-three year old Virginia, explained where our Cornish-American odyssey had ended up.

"This far south honey, we're more Mexican than American . . ."

She was right. A look around the airport saw a heavier Hispanic influence than anywhere else on my travels.

"Dun't get any bright ideas," said Dan to me sharply. "Travels with Speedy Gonzales or anything . . ."

I was one step ahead. I was already thinking of Cecil Todd's work on the Cornish searching for silver in Mexico.[4] Then there were other journeys – other mouth-organs – in Australia, New Zealand, Southern Africa, South America . . . the list was endless.

"Virginia," said Champi very earnestly, "have you ever heard of such a thing as a pasty?"

"Oh sure," she said. "My father – Ignacio Jimenez, he worked in the mines for fifty years. I was born in Sonora in Mexico, but my father worked all over the place for the Magma Copper Company . . . He worked with the Cornish up in San Jose in California. Oh yes, he had his Cornish lunchbox . . . and in there was his pasty. All the Mexican pasties had chillis in them . . . you know, that don't you?"

We didn't, but now we did. I told Virginia we had chocolate and banana ones back home. Then there were the curried chicken ones . . .

She shook her head.

"You ain't tried nothin' til you've had a pasty with chilli in . . ."

Virginia and I talked about San Jose. She'd never been there. I explained that she ought to go – just to climb that hill like I'd done last summer.

We tipped her well and left for our flight.

"It's been so neat to meet you guys. I'm so proud of that link . . ."

I could have kissed her. There could have been no more fitting an end to my travels. I was desperately trying to imagine what a chilli pasty might taste like.

The tanoys around bounced out messages of 'overload situations' where air cabin crew appealed for people to relinquish their seats, and receive free accomodation and two hundred dollars towards their next flight.

"Could anyone interested in relieving us of this situation,

397

please come and see us at B23 . . ." the tanoy announcement continued.

Suddenly we knew what all those Cousin Jacks of the Silas and Joseph Hocking novels felt like,[6] when they mined, logged, gambled, drunk, and wrassled bears all the way across America. You got to the other side and you were thinking of that place back home in the old country that began with Tre-, Pol- or Pen- or in our case – *ahem* – Probus. And my 56 Inch Cylinder Syndrome? Hey – once a 56 Incher, always a 56 Incher.

The night-flight passed quickly. I watched two films – Disney-Pixar's *Finding Nemo* with its surfing turtles, who spoke like everyone at the Bowgie over Holywell Bay, and another film called *Holes* – about American boys at borstal-style desert camp digging for lost treasure. There were never two films more appropriate: holes and surfing – old and new Cornwall rolled into one. Heathrow became Bristol and Bristol became Exeter. We headed into the old country over the Tamar, like miners who'd made a mint, past Lanson castle, past Bodmin Moor, heading for gloriously strange-sounding and romantic places – like Bugle, Foxhole, Nanpean – and Probus. In the distance I could see clay tips and minestacks. Into sight came Probus Church and the Comrades Club. It was time for a celebratory pint of *Skinners*.

"We've dun un by gar," said Champi.

"'Es," me an' Dan went.

I wudn' sad t'all.

In me pocket was Cousin Jack's mouth-organ.

Notes

1. Alan M. Kent (2002) *The Hensbarrow Homilies*, Penzance: The Patten Press, p.22.
2. A. L. Rowse (1991 [1969]) *The Cornish in America*, Redruth: Dyllansow Truran, p.386.
3. See *West Briton*, July 31, 2003, p.27.
4. See Jerry Clarke and Terry Harry (1991) *Tales of Twickenham*, Redruth: Harry and Clarke.
5. See A.C. Todd (2000 [1977]) *The Search for Silver: Cornish*

Miners in Mexico 1824-1947, St Austell: Cornish Hillside Publications.
6. See Alan M. Kent (2002) *Pulp Methodism: The Lives and Literature of Silas, Joseph and Salome Hocking; Three Cornish Novelists*, St Austell: Cornish Hillside Publications.